TWENTY-FOUR
ONE-ACT PLAYS

SELECTED BY
JOHN HAMPDEN

7/07

INTRODUCTION

It is the custom nowadays for the anthologist to begin with an apology, and rightly. He must stand and deliver some justification of his presumption, for the making of books has become a minor industry to an extent which adds new bitterness to the ancient lament. The collector of plays is not yet perhaps so suspect as the collector of poems, but since Mr J. W. Marriott took the amateur dramatic world by storm in 1924 with the first English anthology of one-act plays many editors have followed suit.

Hitherto, however, all anthologies have had severe, self-imposed limitations. Many have been intended mainly for schools, some for casts of women only, some for children. Others have been made from a limited period or exclusively from unpublished work. The present volume, with an editor conscious of his temerity, is the first attempt to make an anthology of one-act plays, English, Welsh, Scottish, and Irish, chosen simply for their quality and variety to represent as fully as possible the work of this century.

The hope of being completely representative was disappointed at once by insurmountable difficulties of copyright, and it might be argued that this volume should begin with blank pages reserved for Barrie and Galsworthy, Mr W. B. Yeats, Mr Bernard Shaw, and one or two others. Yet even with notable absentees and a necessary limit to the number of invitations issued, here is a gathering of one-act plays more distinguished than any previous period of our dramatic literature could provide.

It is not that the one-act play is a new thing. The anonymous authors of the mystery plays and of *Everyman*, *The Interlude of Youth*, and *The World and the Child*, demonstrated long ago the heights which it can reach. Wandering players have found it indispensable for centuries, and folk-drama has always had a place for it: the mummers of Chipping Campden still go the rounds with a one-act comedy which derives, in changeful but unbroken oral tradition, from the fertility rites and human sacrifices of a dim prehistoric past. But English drama became wholly professional during the sixteenth century, to its great gain in many ways, and in the professional

v

theatre the one-act play has never been at home. The seventeenth century banished it from the stage, and although the eighteenth century recalled it in a flood of farces and burlesques, these degenerated in value until the nineteenth century came to admit the one-act play only for ignominious performance as a 'curtain-raiser,' while late arrivals stumbled into the stalls. As an artistic form it seemed fated to extinction when the repertory theatre movement, part of a great dramatic renaissance, gave it new life.

This is easily understood. Partly because the 'triple bill' asks more of the audience it has much less appeal to the general public than the full-length play (like the volume of short stories in the circulating library) and the commercial theatre will therefore have none of it, but the case is different for enthusiasts whose main concern is not with the box-office. The artistic limitations of the one-act play are those of the short story as compared with the novel, the sonnet with the ode, and in none of these categories can brevity be regarded as an invalidation. That the artistic possibilities are very great this volume alone would show, and the technical difficulties are not less than in the full-length play, although they may appear so. The one-act play is too short to recover, as a full-length play will sometimes recover, from clumsy exposition, redundant dialogue, or partial uncertainty of aim. Dealing with a single episode or situation and having no space to show the development of character in action, it is necessarily much more climactic in structure and demands therefore great skill in exposition of circumstance and personality and the utmost economy throughout. At the same time a group of one-act plays is easier to rehearse, usually easier and cheaper to stage, and offers much more variety for a given effort than a full-length play, so the shorter form has obvious attractions for playwrights, players, and producers with limited resources who are trying their strength and consciously experimenting with new methods. Such experiment was vital to the 'New Drama' of the eighteen-nineties, which brought our stage again into contact with contemporary life and culture after its long degeneration, and the repertory theatres called into being by that renaissance provided just the conditions in which the one-act play could flourish.

The first repertory theatre in the English-speaking world was the Abbey Theatre, Dublin, established in 1904, when

Miss A. E. F. Horniman gave it to the amateur Irish Literary Theatre which Mr Yeats, Lady Gregory, and others had founded in 1899. While J. T. Grein and Mr Granville-Barker, William Archer, Mr Shaw, and John Galsworthy established the 'drama of ideas' in London, the Abbey Theatre established folk-drama in Dublin. Its leaders had the supreme advantage of working among a peasant people who, unlike Monsieur Jourdain, had spoken poetry all their lives without knowing it—an advantage fully acknowledged in J. M. Synge's pregnant foreword to *The Playboy of the Western World*. Hence the richness of idiom, the strong idiosyncrasy of character, and the sincere emotional power of *The Rising of the Moon* and *Riders to the Sea*. Both are 'good theatre.' Both are quintessentially Irish. And *Riders to the Sea*, at least, has the universality of all great art. It is one of the masterpieces of our dramatic literature.

Two other Irish dramatists are represented in this volume, but neither belongs to the Abbey, although Lord Dunsany's first plays were staged there and Mr St John Ervine (an Ulsterman) managed it for a short period. Since the War the full-length play has predominated in Irish drama, probably because the Abbey Theatre now finds that its stage stretches from Broadway to Shaftesbury Avenue.

Manchester Repertory Theatre was founded, also by 'Queen' Horniman, in 1907 and this too gathered a distinguished company of dramatists and players. The Liverpool Playhouse was opened in 1911. In Lancashire the typical English 'repertory play' was born—by *A Doll's House* out of *The Workhouse Ward*—the play of ideas with a lower middle-class or working-class setting. Lancashire speech and character fertilized its drama with a richness second only to that of Ireland, and it is significant that its finest achievements are Lancashire plays, with an interest far more than local. The one-act play found high favour here, developing as in Dublin an artistic value, a hold upon reality, which it had not had since Tudor times.

Hindle Wakes (1912) was the first English repertory play to reach a world-wide audience, but Stanley Houghton, like J. M. Synge, died far too young. He appears at his best in a one-act comedy and tragedy, *The Dear Departed* and *The Master of the House*, both of them derived from shrewd observation of Lancashire life. Mr Harold Brighouse showed from the first an attachment to the one-act play and great versatility in choice of subject and setting. He has never surpassed *Lonesome-like* and *The Price of Coal*, but *Followers*, included here for the virtue of contrast, shows that mastery of the form which has given him his enduring popularity. He is the doyen of one-act playwrights, with an enormous audience.

As further repertory theatres were established the one-act play found new settings and inspirations. John Drinkwater's shorter plays were written when the munificence of Sir Barry Jackson transformed the amateur Pilgrim Players into the Birmingham Repertory Theatre. Harold Chapin, who set his best comedy in a Glasgow tenement, was a member of the Glasgow Repertory Company. His varied stage experience fostered his instinctive genius for the one-act play, but he had no time to develop it fully; he was killed at Loos in 1915. *It's the Poor that 'elps the Poor* is typical of his best work in its merciless yet sympathetic observation of character, its trenchant economy of dialogue, and its structural skill. It is not only one of the best Cockney plays ever written but a small masterpiece of irony.

There are still in England many repertory theatres serving local needs, but much of the glory has departed. In its first decade 'repertory' was so provincial in the best sense that it made itself more truly national than English drama had been at any time since the death of Shakespeare. The War, however, weakened 'repertory' as it did all drama, and other factors helped. The one-act play might well have followed many more important things into oblivion but for the amateur movement.

What determined the tremendous revival of amateur drama which began in 1918 it must be left to the future historian to decide. No doubt the emotional and nervous strain of the War, the mechanization of work and entertainment, and the urbanization of life all played their part, with results which are artistically and psychologically among the significant phenomena of the past twenty years. Some landmarks are obvious. The Village Drama Society was founded by Miss Mary Kelly at Kelly, North Devon, in 1918, the British Drama League by Mr Geoffrey Whitworth in London in 1919, and the two organizations, amalgamated in 1931, now have a membership of four thousand three hundred. A Welsh Drama League, Scottish Community Drama Association, and Northern

[Irish] Drama League are also in being, besides a Religious Drama Society, and other organizations are doing very valuable work. Great influence has been exercised by the festivals, particularly the B.D.L.'s National Festival, which began with six entries in 1926 and had six hundred and forty-eight in 1937; they have firmly established the one-act play and their public adjudications have raised the whole level of acting and production. All these regimentations from above could have accomplished nothing in themselves, however. The vital thing is that several hundred thousand people, in towns and villages all over Great Britain, feel the need to find expression in drama, and find it.

During the nineteen-twenties the amateurs lived largely by pre-War one-act plays and by new plays written, often with the amateur stage in mind, by the older dramatists. In the thirties, as a desire to experiment has grown, far more new, untried plays have been performed, many of them by young playwrights who are graduates of the amateur theatre.

Lord Dunsany is one of the older writers, but his work belongs almost entirely to the amateurs. A romantic and a satirist, in revolt against the growing ugliness of our times, he has ploughed a rather lonely furrow with his fantastic fables of three hemispheres. *A Night at an Inn*, as effective as it is macabre, shows him at his best. Its air of careless efficiency is typical, and its theme a favourite one with the author: the intervention of a supernatural power at the moment when human evil is about to triumph.

As both dramatist and critic Mr St John Ervine belongs to the professional theatre, but like Mr Shaw and others he has written a few one-act plays which amateurs have seized upon with delight. *Progress* poses in the simplest and most poignant human terms a problem increasingly urgent, and reveals once more the potency of drama as propaganda. In this volume it represents not only its distinguished author, but the host of anti-war plays which amateurs have performed in the last few years.

Village drama has its own distinctive needs, which no town-bred patronage can rightly meet, and it is fortunate to have found such a leader as Miss Mary Kelly, whose work has been informed always by vision and humour and a real understanding of country folk; she has made the greatest single contribution ever made to village drama. *The Spell* shows what she might have done with time for writing, for it is the quintessence of tragedy and in many villages still has an uncomfortable ring of truth. *Mr Sampson*, equally close to village life, has that rich humour touched with poetry and pathos which make Mr Lee's west country stories so delightful. Written in 1911, it remained unknown until its very successful production in 1927 by the Welwyn Garden City Theatre Society. Since then it has been produced all over England—though there is now no paucity of local drama. Every county and dialect has its own playwrights, so diverse as Sheila Kaye-Smith, Ida Gandy, Bernard Gilbert, Austin Hyde, and Constance Holme.

In Scotland the new movement began later than in England, which perhaps explains why the Scottish Community Drama Association did not secede from the British Drama League, to secure the benefits of home rule, until 1933. Once started, however, the enthusiasm spread with even greater rapidity than in England. The Scots began with a few one-act plays peculiarly their own, notably Mr John Ferguson's tragedy, *Campbell of Kilmohr*; the number was soon increased by Mr 'John Brandane,' J. J. Bell, Mr Neil Grant, and others, and more recently 'James Bridie' (Dr O. H. Mavor) has also contributed. In *The Pardoner's Tale* he has made a medieval fable into a powerful play as completely Scottish as 'John Brandane's' version of *Maître Patelin*. Mr Carswell, adding pity to terror without falling to pathos, strikes a deeper tragic note with *Count Albany*, which is far more moving in its realism than any sentimental - romantic picture of Bonnie Prince Charlie; here is history treated as the modern one-act play should treat it. Mr Joe Corrie's vein and style are very different. Self-taught in drama and writing always of life as he himself has lived it, he is perhaps more completely a graduate of the amateur movement than any other playwright in this book. His plays need no artifice to give them poignancy and conviction.

In evangelical Wales the swift conquest made by amateur drama has been even more surprising than in Calvinistic Scotland. Its playwrights, in Welsh and English, now multiply rapidly, but none is more representative than Mr J. O. Francis. *Birds of a Feather* has moreover an open-air freshness all too rare in the amateur theatre.

Mr Sladen Smith stands as much alone as Lord Dunsany. He has served the amateur movement with distinction as playwright, producer, adjudicator, lecturer, reviewer, and not least as a director of the well-known Unnamed Society of Manchester. Nearly all his plays are in one act. Few of them have so much passion as *The Man who wouldn't go to Heaven*; most of them have even more whimsicality of style, and an oblique, fantastic wilfulness of imagination which he makes curiously effective.

Though much amateur work has followed conventional lines, explorations and experiments have not been lacking, and one of the most interesting, in choric drama, has been led by Dr Gordon Bottomley and Miss Marjorie Gullan. Miss Gullan began the modern revival of choric speech when she founded the Glasgow Verse-Speaking Choir in 1923 and the London Verse-Speaking Choir two years later. A great artist as well as a great teacher, she has trained her choirs to increasing mastery, and fully justified as their work has been by its own beauty it has had the additional value of interacting with Dr Bottomley's by providing speakers with whom he could experiment. In such plays as *Culbin Sands* he has given us not only poetry which is also drama, austere, remote, yet real and beautiful, but something new besides; a form of drama in which for the first time the choruses are the protagonists. This invention no one has yet borrowed, but choric speech was adopted by Mr T. S. Eliot and Miss Elsie Fogerty for *Murder in the Cathedral*; others have followed, and still more will do so.

In the same period there has been another revival of an ancient art, that of mime, led by Miss Irene Mawer and others. Pure mime can find no place in this anthology, but Miss Vallance's delightful blending of mime with choric speech is play as well as mime. *Pandora's Box*, a beautiful thing to see and hear, opens a new vista in drama.

Even more valuable perhaps than these revivals is the return of English drama to its birthplace, the English church— a return signalized by the Canterbury Festivals. No play-wright has done so much to secure the wide acceptance of religious drama as Mr Laurence Housman, who has captured the amateur theatre with his *Little Plays of St Francis*. There has been nothing like them and their popularity since the Middle Ages. They have set the early Franciscans on the stage in their habit and humour as they lived, and none is more successful than *Brother Sun*.

Yet another new development, but this very much less desirable, is the growing demand in Women's Institutes, clubs, and girls' schools for 'plays for women only.' So many such plays are feeble, crippled by the playwrights' obvious determination to keep the men in the wings at all costs. *Unnatural Scene* is a splendid exception. It has no falsifications because its problem is wholly and genuinely feminine, yet it has the clash of character and idea which makes drama, presented with remarkable truth and skill.

Mr Noel Coward represents no one and nothing but himself, unless it be the law that genius makes its own laws. The professional theatre abhors a 'triple bill'; Mr Coward made it enjoy one. *Hands across the Sea* was the funniest thing in *To-night at 8.30*, and it is all the more welcome because first-rate one-act farces are so extremely rare.

The present anthology, being an attempt to survey work done in the one-act play during the past thirty-eight years, is necessarily somewhat conservative. Moreover, although it is evident that once more a new yeast is working, the younger poets have hitherto passed over the one-act play, aiming at the professional theatre and the radio. So there is nothing here of the newest drama.

Mrs Ratcliff, one of the most versatile and promising of the 'amateur' playwrights, stands between the new and the old. In *We got Rhythm* she has, with a fierce irony, twisted the cacophonies of the dance-band to serve her purpose and used deliberate discords to attack the makers of discordance. The play is menace rather than promise if it means that the clash of 'ideologies' which threatens all contemporary life is to obsess the arts also. But it is a very effective one-act play and, for good or evil, the herald of something new.

1938   JOHN HAMPDEN.

The reissue of this volume, in the new format of Everyman's Library, has given me a welcome opportunity to add four plays and to make good one of the omissions for which I expressed regret in 1938. W. B. Yeats is now represented, not by his uncharacteristic masterpiece in drama, *Purgatory*, nor by one of his earlier, better-known plays, which are too long, but by the *Dreaming of the Bones*. It is not only very Irish, it is representative of its author in its theme and technique, its dramatic weaknesses, its haunting charm, and most of all in its distinctive poetic quality; no one but Yeats could have written it.

Mr Sean O'Casey is Irish with a considerable difference, for he has not limited himself to Irish subjects; and while Yeats found his raw material in folk-lore and myth, Mr O'Casey has drawn largely on the harsh realities of town life in our own times. *A Pound on Demand* is entertainment between comedy and farce, but it has distant echoes of the savage satirical ironies of *Juno and the Paycock* and others of his major plays. As a revelation of abysses of fatuity it makes an interesting contrast with *Sweeney Agonistes*.

Jewish drama is represented, for the first time in this collection, by *The Bespoke Overcoat*, which is doubly valuable on that account, although Britain, unlike some other countries, has never had a Jewish theatre flourishing as an independent entity. Mr Wolf Mankowitz is the youngest author in this book—he was born in Bethnal Green in 1924, the son of Jewish-Russian immigrants—but he began young, for while still 'reading' English literature as an exhibitioner at Downing College, Cambridge, he won a publisher's prize for 'a writer of exceptional promise' and he has already made two reputations: as an expert in Wedgwood ware and as a novelist of life in the East End of London, for his second novel, *A Kid for Two Farthings* (1953), attracted a great deal of attention and secured a large public. *The Bespoke Overcoat* is his second play. It calls for no comment here beyond that which he has himself provided in his shrewd and modest Author's Note; enterprising drama groups will be quick to realize the opportunities it offers.

Mr T. S. Eliot's power and influence as poet, critic, and dramatist demand his representation here, although he has written no one-act plays and it has been necessary to go back to his first essay in drama, *Sweeney Agonistes*, which was written in 1926. For the first production, in U.S.A. in 1933, Mr Eliot wrote a concluding scene, but he appears to have discarded it promptly and later productions, professional and amateur, have used only the 'fragments' which were first published in 1932 and are included here. They are 'melodrama' in both senses of the term, since they are interspersed with songs and the element of sensational violence is introduced by Sweeney's account of the man who 'once did a girl in.' The two scenes have been described as 'a rather sterile appendix to *The Waste Land*,' but this sterility, like their incompleteness, is of the essence of their effect. All the persons except Sweeney inhabit a waste land of futility in which superstition is substituted for religion, thought is lost in empty clichés and sensational, meaningless news, and 'a good time' takes the place of love. The realities of 'birth, and copulation, and death' can produce no reactions except boredom and fear. There can be no completion, no final shaping, of existence as it is seen here; it can only break off into vacuity at the ninefold knock of doom. Sweeney, although he realizes that he's 'gotta use words' if any sense of realities is to be brought home to his companions, uses them in vain. But Mr Eliot has rarely used words more effectively. Their nerveless repetitive rhythms, as harshly insistent as inferior jazz, generate the peculiar haunting power of this play.

JOHN HAMPDEN.

1954.

NOTE

The following is the approximate chronological order of composition of the plays:

	PAGE		PAGE
The Rising of the Moon	1	Progress	155
Riders to the Sea	13	The Man who wouldn't go	
The Dear Departed	25	to Heaven	173
The Dreaming of the Bones	333	Culbin Sands	197
Mr Sampson	41	A Pound on Demand	357
It's the Poor that 'elps the		Unnatural Scene	219
Poor	59	Pandora's Box	243
Followers	75	Brother Sun	253
A Night at an Inn	91	The Pardoner's Tale	265
Birds of a Feather	105	Hands across the Sea	275
Sweeney Agonistes	345	Hewers of Coal	295
The Spell	125	We got Rhythm	315
Count Albany	131	The Bespoke Overcoat	373

CONTENTS

		PAGE
INTRODUCTION	*John Hampden*	V
THE RISING OF THE MOON . .	*Lady Gregory*	1
RIDERS TO THE SEA . . .	*J. M. Synge*	13
THE DEAR DEPARTED . .	*Stanley Houghton*	25
MR SAMPSON	*Charles Lee*	41
IT'S THE POOR THAT 'ELPS THE POOR .	*Harold Chapin*	59
FOLLOWERS	*Harold Brighouse*	75
A NIGHT AT AN INN . . .	*Lord Dunsany*	91
BIRDS OF A FEATHER . . .	*J. O. Francis*	105
THE SPELL	*Mary Kelly*	125
COUNT ALBANY . . .	*Donald Carswell*	131
PROGRESS	*St John Ervine*	155
THE MAN WHO WOULDN'T GO TO HEAVEN	*F. Sladen-Smith*	173
CULBIN SANDS	*Gordon Bottomley*	197
UNNATURAL SCENE . . .	*Kathleen Davey*	219
PANDORA'S BOX . . .	*Rosalind Vallance*	243
BROTHER SUN	*Laurence Housman*	253
THE PARDONER'S TALE . . .	*James Bridie*	265
HANDS ACROSS THE SEA . . .	*Noel Coward*	275
HEWERS OF COAL	*Joe Corrie*	295
WE GOT RHYTHM	*Nora Ratcliff*	315
THE DREAMING OF THE BONES .	*W. B. Yeats*	333
SWEENEY AGONISTES . . .	*T. S. Eliot*	345
A POUND ON DEMAND . . .	*Sean O'Casey*	357
THE BESPOKE OVERCOAT . .	*Wolf Mankowitz*	373

ACKNOWLEDGMENTS

For permission to use the plays in this volume thanks are due to:

Gordon Bottomley and Constable & Co. Ltd for *Culbin Sands*; James Bridie and Constable & Co. Ltd for *The Pardoner's Tale*; Harold Brighouse for *Followers*; George Allen & Unwin Ltd and the executors of the late J. M. Synge for *Riders to the Sea*; Donald Carswell and H. F. W. Deane & Sons, The Year Book Press Ltd, for *Count Albany*; Joe Corrie for *Hewers of Coal*; Noel Coward and William Heinemann Ltd for *Hands across the Sea* from *To-night at 8.30*; Kathleen Davey for *Unnatural Scene*; Lord Dunsany for *A Night at an Inn* from *Plays of Gods and Men* (Putnam); St John Ervine and George Allen & Unwin Ltd for *Progress*; J. O. Francis and the Welsh Outlook Press for *Birds of a Feather*; Laurence Housman and Sidgwick & Jackson Ltd for *Brother Sun* from *Little Plays of St Francis*; Mary Kelly for *The Spell*; Charles Lee for *Mr Sampson*; Nora Ratcliff and Thomas Nelson & Sons Ltd for *We got Rhythm* from *Eastward in Eden*; F. Sladen-Smith for *The Man who wouldn't go to Heaven*; and Rosalind Vallance and Thomas Nelson & Sons Ltd for *Pandora's Box* from *Plays in Verse and Mime*, Samuel French Ltd for *The Dear Departed* by Stanley Houghton and *It's the Poor that 'elps the Poor* by Harold Chapin; Putnam & Co. Ltd for *The Rising of the Moon* from *Seven Short Plays* by Lady Gregory; Mrs W. B. Yeats and Macmillan & Co. Ltd for *The Dreaming of the Bones* from *The Collected Plays of W. B. Yeats*; T. S. Eliot and Faber & Faber Ltd for *Sweeney Agonistes*; Sean O'Casey for *A Pound on Demand*; and Wolf Mankowitz and Evans Bros. Ltd for *The Bespoke Overcoat*.

The editor is indebted to the Library of the British Drama League, and to Miss Dorothy Coates and Miss H. M. Garnham, for invaluable help in the compilation of this anthology.

J. H.

FOR

R. AND J.

THE RISING OF THE MOON

Lady Gregory

This play was first performed in the Molesworth Hall, Dublin, on 25th February 1904, with the following cast:

MAURYA, an old woman . . .	*Honor Lavelle*
BARTLEY, her son	*W. G. Fay*
CATHLEEN, her daughter . . .	*Sara Allgood*
NORA, a younger daughter . .	*Emma Vernon*

MEN AND WOMEN

SCENE. *An island off the West of Ireland*

Applications for permission to perform this play must be made to Samuel French Ltd, 26 Southampton Street, Strand, London, W.C.2, or to their authorized agents. The fee for each and every representation of the play by amateurs is one guinea. Upon payment of this fee a licence will be issued for the performance to take place. No performance may be given unless this licence has first been obtained.

THE RISING OF THE MOON

SCENE. *Side of a quay in a seaport town. Some posts and chains. A large barrel. Enter three policemen. Moonlight.*

Sergeant, who is older than the others, crosses the stage to right and looks down steps. The others put down a pastepot and unroll a bundle of placards.

POLICEMAN B. I think this would be a good place to put up a notice.   [*He points to barrel.*

POLICEMAN X. Better ask him. [*Calls to Sergeant.*] Will this be a good place for a placard?   [*No answer.*

POLICEMAN B. Will we put up a notice here on the barrel?
                                         [*No answer.*

SERGEANT. There's a flight of steps here that leads to the water. This is a place that should be minded well. If he got down here, his friends might have a boat to meet him; they might send it in here from outside.

POLICEMAN B. Would the barrel be a good place to put a notice up?

SERGEANT. It might; you can put it there.
                                    [*They paste the notice up.*

SERGEANT. [*Reading it.*] Dark hair—dark eyes, smooth face, height five feet five—there's not much to take hold of in that—it's a pity I had no chance of seeing him before he broke out of jail. They say he's a wonder, that it's he makes all the plans for the whole organization. There isn't another man in Ireland would have broken jail the way he did. He must have some friends among the jailers.

POLICEMAN B. A hundred pounds is little enough for the Government to offer for him. You may be sure any man in the force that takes him will get promotion.

SERGEANT. I'll mind this place myself. I wouldn't wonder at all if he came this way. He might come slipping along there [*points to side of quay*], and his friends might be waiting for him there [*points down steps*], and once he got away it's little chance we'd have of finding him; it's maybe under a load of kelp he'd be in a fishing boat, and not one to help a married man that wants it to the reward.

POLICEMAN X. And if we get him itself, nothing but abuse on our heads for it from the people, and maybe from our own relations.

SERGEANT. Well, we have to do our duty in the force. Haven't we the whole country depending on us to keep law and order? It's those that are down would be up and those that are up would be down, if it wasn't for us. Well, hurry on, you have plenty of other places to placard yet, and come back here then to me. You can take the lantern. Don't be too long now. It's very lonesome here with nothing but the moon.

POLICEMAN B. It's a pity we can't stop with you. The Government should have brought more police into the town, with *him* in jail, and at assize time too. Well, good luck to your watch.   [*They go out.*

SERGEANT. [*Walks up and down once or twice and looks at placard.*] A hundred pounds and promotion sure. There must be a great deal of spending in a hundred pounds. It's a pity some honest man not to be the better of that.

    [*A ragged man appears at left and tries to slip past. Sergeant suddenly turns.*

SERGEANT. Where are you going?

MAN. I'm a poor ballad-singer, your honour. I thought to sell some of these [*holds out bundle of ballads*] to the sailors.
                                    [*He goes on.*

SERGEANT. Stop! Didn't I tell you to stop? You can't go on there.

MAN. Oh, very well. It's a hard thing to be poor. All the world's against the poor!

SERGEANT. Who are you?

MAN. You'd be as wise as myself if I told you, but I don't mind. I'm one Jimmy Walsh, a ballad-singer.

SERGEANT. Jimmy Walsh? I don't know that name.

MAN. Ah, sure, they know it well enough in Ennis. Were you ever in Ennis, Sergeant?

SERGEANT. What brought you here?

MAN. Sure, it's to the assizes I came, thinking I might make a few shillings here or there. It's in the one train with the judges I came.

SERGEANT. Well, if you came so far, you may as well go farther, for you'll walk out of this.

MAN. I will, I will; I'll just go on where I was going.
                                    [*Goes towards steps.*

SERGEANT. Come back from those steps; no one has leave to pass down them to-night.

MAN. I'll just sit on the top of the steps till I see will some sailor buy a ballad off me that would give me my supper. They do be late going back to the ship. It's often I saw them in Cork carried down the quay in a hand-cart.

SERGEANT. Move on, I tell you. I won't have any one lingering about the quay to-night.

MAN. Well, I'll go. It's the poor have the hard life! Maybe yourself might like one, Sergeant. Here's a good sheet now. [*Turns one over.*] *Content and a Pipe*—that's not much. *The Peeler and the Goat*—you wouldn't like that. *Johnny Hart*—that's a lovely song.

SERGEANT. Move on.

MAN. Ah, wait till you hear it. [*Sings*]:
'There was a rich farmer's daughter lived near the town of Ross;
She courted a Highland soldier, his name was Johnny Hart;
Says the mother to her daughter, "I'll go distracted mad
If you marry that Highland soldier dressed up in Highland plaid."'

SERGEANT. Stop that noise.

[*Man wraps up his ballads and shuffles towards the steps.*

SERGEANT. Where are you going?

MAN. Sure, you told me to be going, and I am going.

SERGEANT. Don't be a fool. I didn't tell you to go that way; I told you to go back to the town.

MAN. Back to the town, is it?

SERGEANT. [*Taking him by the shoulder and shoving him before him.*] Here, I'll show you the way. Be off with you. What are you stopping for?

MAN. [*Who has been keeping his eye on the notice, points to it.*] I think I know what you're waiting for, Sergeant.

SERGEANT. What's that to you?

MAN. And I know well the man you're waiting for—I know him well—I'll be going.   [*He shuffles on.*

SERGEANT. You know him? Come back here. What sort is he?

MAN. Come back is it, Sergeant? Do you want to have me killed?

SERGEANT. Why do you say that?

MAN. Never mind. I'm going. I wouldn't be in your shoes if the reward was ten times as much.   [*Goes off stage to left.*] Not if it was ten times as much.

SERGEANT. [*Rushing after him.*] Come back here, come back. [*Drags him back.*] What sort is he? Where did you see him?

MAN. I saw him in my own place, in the County Clare. I tell you you wouldn't like to be looking at him. You'd be afraid to be in the one place with him. There isn't a weapon he doesn't know the use of, and as to strength, his muscles are as hard as that board.   [*Slaps barrel.*

SERGEANT. Is he as bad as that?

MAN. He is then.

SERGEANT. Do you tell me so?

MAN. There was a poor man in our place, a sergeant from Ballyvaughan.—It was with a lump of stone he did it.

SERGEANT. I never heard of that.

MAN. And you wouldn't, Sergeant. It's not everything that happens gets into the papers. And there was a policeman in plain clothes, too. . . . It is in Limerick he was. . . . It was after the time of the attack on the police barrack at Kilmallock. . . . Moonlight . . . just like this . . . waterside. Nothing was known for certain.

SERGEANT. Do you say so? It's a terrible country to belong to.

MAN. That's so, indeed! You might be standing there, looking out that way, thinking you saw him coming up this side of the quay [*points*] and he might be coming up this other side [*points*] and he'd be on you before you knew where you were.

SERGEANT. It's a whole troop of police they ought to put here to stop a man like that.

MAN. But if you'd like me to stop with you, I could be looking down this side. I could be sitting up here on this barrel.

SERGEANT. And you know him well, too?

MAN. I'd know him a mile off, Sergeant.

SERGEANT. But you wouldn't want to share the reward?

MAN. Is it a poor man like me, that has to be going the roads and singing in fairs, to have the name on him that he took a reward? But you don't want me. I'll be safer in the town.

SERGEANT. Well, you can stop.

MAN. [*Getting up on barrel.*] All right, Sergeant. I wonder, now, you're not tired out, Sergeant, walking up and down the way you are.

SERGEANT. If I'm tired I'm used to it.

MAN. You might have hard work before you to-night yet. Take it easy while you can. There's plenty of room up here on the barrel, and you see farther when you're higher up.

SERGEANT. Maybe so. [*Gets up beside him on barrel, facing right. They sit back to back, looking different ways.*] You made me feel a bit queer with the way you talked.

MAN. Give me a match, Sergeant. [*He gives it and Man lights pipe.*] Take a draw yourself? It 'll quiet you. Wait now till I give you a light, but you needn't turn round. Don't take your eye off the quay for the life of you.

SERGEANT. Never fear, I won't. [*Lights pipe. They both smoke.*] Indeed it 's a hard thing to be in the force, out at night and no thanks for it, for all the danger we 're in. And it 's little we get but abuse from the people, and no choice but to obey our orders, and never asked when a man is sent into danger, if you are a married man with a family.

MAN. [*Sings*]:
'As through the hills I walked to view the hills and shamrock plain,
I stood awhile where nature smiles to view the rocks and streams,
On a matron fair I fixed my eyes beneath a fertile vale,
As she sang her song it was on the wrong of poor old Granuaile.'

SERGEANT. Stop that; that 's no song to be singing in these times.

MAN. Ah, Sergeant, I was only singing to keep my heart up. It sinks when I think of him. To think of us two sitting here, and he creeping up the quay, maybe, to get to us.

SERGEANT. Are you keeping a good look-out?

MAN. I am; and for no reward too. Amn't I the foolish man? But when I saw a man in trouble, I never could help trying to get him out of it. What 's that? Did something hit me?
[*Rubs his heart.*

SERGEANT. [*Patting him on the shoulder.*] You will get your reward in heaven.

MAN. I know that, I know that, Sergeant, but life is precious.

SERGEANT. Well, you can sing if it gives you more courage.

MAN. [*Sings*]:
'Her head was bare, her hands and feet with iron bands were bound,
Her pensive strain and plaintive wail mingled with the evening gale,
And the song she sang with mournful air, I am old Granuaile.
Her lips so sweet that monarchs kissed. . . .'

SERGEANT. That 's not it. . . . 'Her gown she wore was stained with gore.' . . . That 's it—you missed that.

MAN. You 're right, Sergeant, so it is; I missed it. [*Repeats line.*]
But to think of a man like you knowing a song like that.

SERGEANT. There 's many a thing a man might know and might
not have any wish for.

MAN. Now, I dare say, Sergeant, in your youth, you used to
be sitting up on a wall, the way you are sitting up on this
barrel now, and the other lads beside you, and you singing
Granuaile? . . .

SERGEANT. I did then.

MAN. And the *Shan Bhean Bhocht*? . . .

SERGEANT. I did then.

MAN. And the *Green on the Cape*?

SERGEANT. That was one of them.

MAN. And maybe the man you are watching for to-night used
to be sitting on the wall, when he was young, and singing
those same songs. . . . It 's a queer world. . . .

SERGEANT. Whisht! . . . I think I see something coming. . .
It 's only a dog.

MAN. And isn't it a queer world? . . . Maybe it 's one of the
boys you used to be singing with that time you will be ar-
resting to-day or to-morrow, and sending into the dock. . . .

SERGEANT. That 's true indeed.

MAN. And maybe one night, after you had been singing, if the
other boys had told you some plan they had, some plan to
free the country, you might have joined with them . . . and
maybe it is you might be in trouble now.

SERGEANT. Well, who knows but I might? I had a great spirit
in those days.

MAN. It 's a queer world, Sergeant, and it 's little any mother
knows when she sees her child creeping on the floor what
might happen to it before it has gone through its life, or who
will be who in the end.

SERGEANT. That 's a queer thought now, and a true thought.
Wait now till I think it out. . . . If it wasn't for the sense I
have, and for my wife and family, and for me joining the
force the time I did, it might be myself now would be after
breaking jail and hiding in the dark, and it might be him
that 's hiding in the dark and that got out of jail would be
sitting up where I am on this barrel. . . . And it might be
myself would be creeping up trying to make my escape from
himself, and it might be himself would be keeping the law, and
myself would be breaking it, and myself would be trying maybe to put a bullet in his head, or to take up a lump of a stone

the way you said he did . . . no, that myself did. . . . Oh! [*Gasps. After a pause.*] What's that? [*Grasps Man's arm.*

MAN. [*Jumps off barrel and listens, looking out over water.*] It's nothing, Sergeant.

SERGEANT. I thought it might be a boat. I had a notion there might be friends of his coming about the quays with a boat.

MAN. Sergeant, I am thinking it was with the people you were, and not with the law you were, when you were a young man.

SERGEANT. Well, if I was foolish then, that time's gone.

MAN. Maybe, Sergeant, it comes into your head sometimes, in spite of your belt and your tunic, that it might have been as well for you to have followed Granuaile.

SERGEANT. It's no business of yours what I think.

MAN. Maybe, Sergeant, you'll be on the side of the country yet.

SERGEANT. [*Gets off barrel.*] Don't talk to me like that. I have my duties and I know them. [*Looks round.*] That was a boat; I hear the oars.

[*Goes to the steps and looks down.*

MAN. [*Sings*]:
  'O, then, tell me, Shawn O'Farrell,
    Where the gathering is to be.
  In the old spot by the river
    Right well known to you and me!'

SERGEANT. Stop that! Stop that, I tell you!

MAN. [*Sings louder*]:
  'One word more, for signal token,
    Whistle up the marching tune,
  With your pike upon your shoulder,
    At the Rising of the Moon.'

SERGEANT. If you don't stop that, I'll arrest you.

[*A whistle from below answers, repeating the air.*

SERGEANT. That's a signal. [*Stands between him and steps.*] You must not pass this way. . . . Step farther back. . . Who are you? You are no ballad-singer.

MAN. You needn't ask who I am; that placard will tell you. [*Points to placard.*

SERGEANT. You are the man I am looking for.

MAN. [*Takes off hat and wig. Sergeant seizes them.*] I am. There's a hundred pounds on my head. There is a friend of mine below in a boat. He knows a safe place to bring me to.

SERGEANT. [*Looking still at hat and wig.*] It's a pity! It's a pity. You deceived me. You deceived me well.

MAN. I am a friend of Granuaile. There is a hundred pounds on my head.

SERGEANT. It's a pity, it's a pity!

MAN. Will you let me pass, or must I make you let me?

SERGEANT. I am in the force. I will not let you pass.

MAN. I thought to do it with my tongue. [*Puts hand in breast.*] What is that?

[*Voice of Policeman X outside.*] Here, this is where we left him.

SERGEANT. It's my comrades coming.

MAN. You won't betray me . . . the friend of Granuaile.

[*Slips behind barrel.*

[*Voice of Policeman B.*] That was the last of the placards.

POLICEMAN X. [*As they come in.*] If he makes his escape, it won't be unknown he'll make it.

[*Sergeant puts hat and wig behind his back.*

POLICEMAN B. Did any one come this way?

SERGEANT. [*After a pause.*] No one.

POLICEMAN B. No one at all?

SERGEANT. No one at all.

POLICEMAN B. We had no orders to go back to the station; we can stop along with you.

SERGEANT. I don't want you. There is nothing for you to do here.

POLICEMAN B. You bade us to come back here and keep watch with you.

SERGEANT. I'd sooner be alone. Would any man come this way and you making all that talk? It is better the place to be quiet.

POLICEMAN B. Well, we'll leave you the lantern anyhow.

[*Hands it to him.*

SERGEANT. I don't want it. Bring it with you.

POLICEMAN B. You might want it. There are clouds coming up and you have the darkness of the night before you yet. I'll leave it over here on the barrel. [*Goes to barrel.*

SERGEANT. Bring it with you, I tell you. No more talk.

POLICEMAN B. Well, I thought it might be a comfort to you. I often think when I have it in my hand and can be flashing it about into every dark corner [*doing so*] that it's the same as being beside the fire at home, and the bits of bogwood blazing up now and again.

[*Flashes it about, now on the barrel, now on Sergeant.*

SERGEANT. [*Furious.*] Be off, the two of you, yourselves and
your lantern!
> [*They go out. Man comes from behind barrel. He and
> Sergeant stand looking at one another.*

SERGEANT. What are you waiting for?

MAN. For my hat, of course, and my wig. You wouldn't wish
me to get my death of cold?   [*Sergeant gives them.*

MAN. [*Going towards steps.*] Well, good night, comrade, and
thank you. You did me a good turn to-night, and I 'm
obliged to you. Maybe I 'll be able to do as much for you
when the small rise up and the big fall down . . . when we
all change places at the Rising [*waves his hand and disappears*]
of the Moon.

SERGEANT. [*Turning his back to audience and reading placard.*] A
hundred pounds reward! A hundred pounds! [*Turns towards
audience*] I wonder, now, am I as great a fool as I think I am?

CURTAIN

RIDERS TO THE SEA

J. M. Synge

CHARACTERS

Sergeant
Policeman X
Policeman B
A Ragged Man

This play was first produced at the Abbey Theatre, Dublin, on 9th March 1907.

RIDERS TO THE SEA

Cottage kitchen, with nets, oilskins, spinning-wheel, some new boards standing by the wall, etc. Cathleen, a girl of about twenty, finishes kneading cake, and puts it down in the pot-oven by the fire; then wipes her hands, and begins to spin at the wheel. Nora, a young girl, puts her head in at the door.

NORA. [*In a low voice.*] Where is she?

CATHLEEN. She 's lying down, God help her, and maybe sleeping, if she 's able.

[*Nora comes in softly and takes a bundle from under her shawl.*

CATHLEEN. [*Spinning the wheel rapidly.*] What is it you have?

NORA. The young priest is after bringing them. It 's a shirt and a plain stocking were got off a drowned man in Donegal. [*Cathleen stops her wheel with a sudden movement, and leans out to listen.*] We 're to find out if it 's Michael's they are, sometime herself will be down looking by the sea.

CATHLEEN. How would they be Michael's, Nora? How would he go the length of that way to the far north?

NORA. The young priest says he 's known the like of it. 'If it 's Michael's they are,' says he, 'you can tell herself he 's got a clean burial, by the grace of God; and if they 're not his, let no one say a word about them, for she 'll be getting her death,' says he, 'with crying and lamenting.'

[*The door which Nora half closed is blown open by a gust of wind.*

CATHLEEN. [*Looking out anxiously.*] Did you ask him would he stop Bartley going this day with the horses to the Galway fair?

NORA. 'I won't stop him,' says he; 'but let you not be afraid. Herself does be saying prayers half through the night, and the Almighty God won't leave her destitute,' says he, 'with no son living.'

CATHLEEN. Is the sea bad by the white rocks, Nora?

NORA. Middling bad, God help us. There 's a great roaring in the west, and it 's worse it 'll be getting when the tide 's turned to the wind. [*She goes over to the table with the bundle.*] Shall I open it now?

B 947

CATHLEEN. Maybe she'd wake up on us, and come in before
we'd done. [*Coming to the table.*] It's a long time we'll be,
and the two of us crying.

NORA. [*Goes to the inner door and listens.*] She's moving about
on the bed. She'll be coming in a minute.

CATHLEEN. Give me the ladder, and I'll put them up in the turf-
loft, the way she won't know of them at all, and maybe when
the tide turns she'll be going down to see would he be floating
from the east.

[*They put the ladder against the gable of the chimney; Cathleen
goes up a few steps and hides the bundle in the turf-loft.
Maurya comes from the inner room.*]

MAURYA. [*Looking up at Cathleen and speaking querulously.*]
Isn't it turf enough you have for this day and evening?

CATHLEEN. There's a cake baking at the fire for a short space
[*throwing down the turf*], and Bartley will want it when the
tide turns if he goes to Connemara.

[*Nora picks up the turf and puts it round the pot-oven.*]

MAURYA. [*Sitting down on a stool at the fire.*] He won't go this
day with the wind rising from the south and west. He won't
go this day, for the young priest will stop him surely.

NORA. He'll not stop him, mother; and I heard Eamon Simon
and Stephen Pheety and Colum Shawn saying he would go.

MAURYA. Where is he itself?

NORA. He went down to see would there be another boat
sailing in the week, and I'm thinking it won't be long till
he's here now, for the tide's turning at the green head, and
the hooker's tacking from the east.

CATHLEEN. I hear someone passing the big stones.

NORA. [*Looking out.*] He's coming now, and he in a hurry.

BARTLEY. [*Comes in and looks round the room ; speaking sadly
and quietly.*] Where is the bit of new rope, Cathleen, was
bought in Connemara?

CATHLEEN. [*Coming down.*] Give it to him, Nora; it's on a nail
by the white boards. I hung it up this morning, for the pig
with the black feet was eating it.

NORA. [*Giving him a rope.*] Is that it, Bartley?

MAURYA. You'd do right to leave that rope, Bartley, hanging
by the boards. [*Bartley takes the rope.*] It will be wanting in
this place, I'm telling you, if Michael is washed up to-morrow
morning, or the next morning, or any morning in the week;
for it's a deep grave we'll make him, by the grace of God.

BARTLEY. [*Beginning to work with the rope.*] I've no halter the

way I can ride down on the mare, and I must go now quickly.
This is the one boat going for two weeks or beyond it, and the
fair will be a good fair for horses, I heard them saying
below.

MAURYA. It 's a hard thing they 'll be saying below if the body
is washed up and there 's no man in it to make the coffin, and
I after giving a big price for the finest white boards you 'd find
in Connemara. [*She looks round at the boards.*

BARTLEY. How would it be washed up, and we after looking
each day for nine days, and a strong wind blowing a while
back from the west and south?

MAURYA. If it isn't found itself, that wind is raising the sea,
and there was a star up against the moon, and it rising in the
night. If it was a hundred horses, or a thousand horses, you
had itself, what is the price of a thousand horses against a son
where there is one son only.

BARTLEY. [*Working at the halter, to Cathleen.*] Let you go down
each day, and see the sheep aren't jumping in on the rye, and
if the jobber comes you can sell the pig with the black feet if
there is a good price going.

MAURYA. How would the like of her get a good price for a pig?

BARTLEY. [*To Cathleen.*] If the west wind holds with the last
bit of the moon let you and Nora get up weed enough for
another cock for the kelp. It 's hard set we 'll be from this
day with no one in it but one man to work.

MAURYA. It 's hard set we 'll be surely the day you 're drowned
with the rest. What way will I live and the girls with me,
and I an old woman looking for the grave?

[*Bartley lays down the halter, takes off his old coat, and puts
on a newer one of the same flannel.*

BARTLEY. [*To Nora.*] Is she coming to the pier?

NORA. [*Looking out.*] She 's passing the green head and letting
fall her sails.

BARTLEY. [*Getting his purse and tobacco.*] I 'll have half an hour
to go down, and you 'll see me coming again in two days, or in
three days, or maybe in four days if the wind is bad.

MAURYA. [*Turning round to the fire and putting the shawl over her
head.*] Isn't it a hard and cruel man won't hear a word from an
old woman, and she holding him from the sea?

CATHLEEN. It 's the life of a young man to be going on the sea,
and who would listen to an old woman with one thing and she
saying it over?

BARTLEY. [*Taking the halter.*] I must go now quickly. I 'll

ride down on the red mare, and the grey pony 'll run behind
me. . . . The blessing of God on you.   [*He goes out.*

MAURYA. [*Crying out as he is in the door.*] He 's gone now, God
spare us, and we 'll not see him again.   He 's gone now, and
when the black night is falling I 'll have no son left me in the
world.

CATHLEEN. Why wouldn't you give him your blessing and he
looking round in the door?   Isn't it sorrow enough is on every
one in this house without your sending him out with an unlucky word behind him, and a hard word in his ear?

> *Maurya takes up the tongs and begins raking the fire aim-
> lessly without looking round.*

NORA. [*Turning towards her.*] You 're taking away the turf from
the cake.

CATHLEEN. [*Crying out.*] The Son of God forgive us, Nora,
we 're after forgetting his bit of bread.

> [*She comes over to the fire.*

NORA. And it 's destroyed he 'll be going till dark night, and he
after eating nothing since the sun went up.

CATHLEEN. [*Turning the cake out of the oven.*] It 's destroyed
he 'll be, surely.   There 's no sense left on any person in a
house where an old woman will be talking for ever.

> [*Maurya sways herself on her stool.*

CATHLEEN. [*Cutting off some of the bread and rolling it in a cloth ;
to Maurya.*] Let you go down now to the spring well and give
him this and he passing.   You 'll see him then and the
dark word will be broken, and you can say 'God speed you,'
the way he 'll be easy in his mind.

MAURYA. [*Taking the bread.*] Will I be in it as soon as himself?

CATHLEEN. If you go now quickly.

MAURYA. [*Standing up unsteadily.*] It 's hard set I am to walk.

CATHLEEN. [*Looking at her anxiously.*] Give her the stick, Nora,
or maybe she 'll slip on the big stones.

NORA. What stick?

CATHLEEN. The stick Michael brought from Connemara.

MAURYA. [*Taking a stick Nora gives her.*] In the big world the
old people do be leaving things after them for their sons and
children, but in this place it is the young men do be leaving
things behind for them that do be old.

> [*She goes out slowly.   Nora goes over to the ladder.*

CATHLEEN. Wait, Nora, maybe she 'd turn back quickly. She 's
that sorry, God help her, you wouldn't know the thing she 'd do.

NORA. Is she gone round by the bush?

CATHLEEN. [*Looking out.*] She 's gone now. Throw it down quickly, for the Lord knows when she 'll be out of it again.

NORA. [*Getting the bundle from the loft.*] The young priest said he 'd be passing to-morrow, and we might go down and speak to him below if it 's Michael's they are surely.

CATHLEEN. [*Taking the bundle.*] Did he say what way they were found?

NORA. [*Coming down.*] 'There were two men,' says he, 'and they rowing round with poteen before the cocks crowed, and the oar of one of them caught the body, and they passing the black cliffs of the north.'

CATHLEEN. [*Trying to open the bundle.*] Give me a knife, Nora; the string 's perished with the salt water, and there 's a black knot on it you wouldn't loosen in a week.

NORA. [*Giving her a knife.*] I 've heard tell it was a long way to Donegal.

CATHLEEN. [*Cutting the string.*] It is surely. There was a man in here a while ago—the man sold us that knife—and he said if you set off walking from the rocks beyond, it would be in seven days you 'd be in Donegal.

NORA. And what time would a man take, and he floating?

[*Cathleen opens the bundle and takes out a bit of a shirt and a stocking. They look at them eagerly.*]

CATHLEEN. [*In a low voice.*] The Lord spare us, Nora! Isn't it a queer hard thing to say if it 's his they are surely?

NORA. I 'll get his shirt off the hook the way we can put the one flannel on the other. [*She looks through some clothes hanging in the corner.*] It 's not with them, Cathleen, and where will it be?

CATHLEEN. I 'm thinking Bartley put it on him in the morning, for his own shirt was heavy with the salt in it. [*Pointing to the corner.*] There 's a bit of a sleeve was of the same stuff. Give me that and it will do. [*Nora brings it to her and they compare the flannel.*] It 's the same stuff, Nora; but if it is itself aren't there great rolls of it in the shops of Galway, and isn't it many another man may have a shirt of it as well as Michael himself?

NORA. [*Who has taken up the stocking and counted the stitches, crying out.*] It 's Michael, Cathleen, it 's Michael; God spare his soul, and what will herself say when she hears this story, and Bartley on the sea?

CATHLEEN. [*Taking the stocking.*] It 's a plain stocking.

NORA. It 's the second one of the third pair I knitted, and I put up three-score stitches, and I dropped four of them.

CATHLEEN. [*Counts the stitches.*] It's that number is in it. [*Crying out.*] Ah, Nora, isn't it a bitter thing to think of him floating that way to the far north, and no one to keen him but the black hags that do be flying on the sea?

NORA. [*Swinging herself half round, and throwing out her arms on the clothes.*] And isn't it a pitiful thing when there is nothing left of a man who was a great rower and fisher but a bit of an old shirt and a plain stocking?

CATHLEEN. [*After an instant.*] Tell me is herself coming, Nora? I hear a little sound on the path.

NORA. [*Looking out.*] She is, Cathleen. She's coming up to the door.

CATHLEEN. Put these things away before she'll come in. Maybe it's easier she'll be after giving her blessing to Bartley, and we won't let on we've heard anything the time he's on the sea.

NORA. [*Helping Cathleen to close the bundle.*] We'll put them here in the corner.

[*They put them into a hole in the chimney-corner. Cathleen goes back to the spinning-wheel.*

NORA. Will she see it was crying I was?

CATHLEEN. Keep your back to the door the way the light'll not be on you.

[*Nora sits down at the chimney-corner, with her back to the door. Maurya comes in very slowly, without looking at the girls, and goes over to her stool at the other side of the fire. The cloth with the bread is still in her hand. The girls look at each other, and Nora points to the bundle of bread.*

CATHLEEN. [*After spinning for a moment.*] You didn't give him his bit of bread?

[*Maurya begins to keen softly, without turning round.*

CATHLEEN. Did you see him riding down?

[*Maurya goes on keening.*

CATHLEEN. [*A little impatiently.*] God forgive you; isn't it a better thing to raise your voice and tell what you seen, than to be making lamentation for a thing that's done? Did you see Bartley, I'm saying to you?

MAURYA. [*With a weak voice.*] My heart's broken from this day.

CATHLEEN. [*As before.*] Did you see Bartley?

MAURYA. I seen the fearfullest thing.

CATHLEEN. [*Leaves her wheel and looks out.*] God forgive you; he's riding the mare now over the green head, and the grey pony behind him.

MAURYA. [*Starts, so that her shawl falls back from her head and shows her white tossed hair. With a frightened voice.*] The grey pony behind him. . . .

CATHLEEN. [*Coming to the fire.*] What is it ails you at all?

MAURYA. [*Speaking very slowly.*] I've see the fearfullest thing any person has seen since the day Bride Dara seen the dead man with the child in his arms.

CATHLEEN and NORA. Uah.

[*They crouch down in front of the old woman at the fire.*

NORA. Tell us what it is you seen.

MAURYA. I went down to the spring well, and I stood there saying a prayer to myself. Then Bartley came along, and he riding on the red mare with the grey pony behind him. [*She puts up her hands as if to hide something from her eyes.*] The Son of God spare us, Nora!

CATHLEEN. What is it you seen?

MAURYA. I seen Michael himself.

CATHLEEN. [*Speaking softly.*] You did not, mother. It wasn't Michael you see, for his body is after being found in the far north, and he's got a clean burial, by the grace of God.

MAURYA. [*A little defiantly.*] I'm after seeing him this day, and he riding and galloping. Bartley came first on the red mare, and I tried to say 'God speed you,' but something choked the words in my throat. He went by quickly; and 'The blessing of God on you,' says he, and I could say nothing. I looked up then, and I crying, at the grey pony, and there was Michael upon it—with fine clothes on him, and new shoes on his feet.

CATHLEEN. [*Begins to keen.*] It's destroyed we are from this day. It's destroyed, surely.

NORA. Didn't the young priest say the Almighty God won't leave her destitute with no son living?

MAURYA. [*In a low voice, but clearly.*] It's little the like of him knows of the sea. . . . Bartley will be lost now, and let you call in Eamon and make me a good coffin out of the white boards, for I won't live after them. I've had a husband, and a husband's father, and six sons in this house—six fine men, though it was a hard birth I had with every one of them and they coming to the world—and some of them were found and some of them were not found, but they're gone now the lot of them. . . . There were Stephen and Shawn were lost in the great wind, and found after in the Bay of Gregory of the

Golden Mouth, and carried up the two of them on one plank, and in by that door.

[*She pauses for a moment, the girls start as if they heard something through the door that is half open behind them.*

NORA. [*In a whisper.*] Did you hear that, Cathleen? Did you hear a noise in the north-east?

CATHLEEN. [*In a whisper.*] There's someone after crying out by the seashore.

MAURYA. [*Continues without hearing anything.*] There was Sheamus and his father, and his own father again, were lost in a dark night, and not a stick or sign was seen of them when the sun went up. There was Patch after was drowned out of a curragh that was turned over. I was sitting here with Bartley, and he a baby lying on my two knees, and I seen two women, and three women, and four women coming in, and they crossing themselves and not saying a word. I looked out then, and there were men coming after them, and they holding a thing in the half of a red sail, and water dripping out of it—it was a dry day, Nora—and leaving a track to the door.

[*She pauses again with her hand stretched out towards the door. It opens softly and old women begin to come in, crossing themselves on the threshold, and kneeling down in front of the stage with red petticoats over their heads.*

MAURYA. [*Half in a dream, to Cathleen.*] Is it Patch, or Michael, or what is it at all?

CATHLEEN. Michael is after being found in the far north, and when he is found there how could he be here in this place?

MAURYA. There does be a power of young men floating round in the sea, and what way would they know if it was Michael they had, or another man like him, for when a man is nine days in the sea, and the wind blowing, it's hard set his own mother would be to say what man was in it.

CATHLEEN. It's Michael, God spare him, for they're after sending us a bit of his clothes from the far north.

[*She reaches out and hands Maurya the clothes that belonged to Michael. Maurya stands up slowly and takes them in her hands. Nora looks out.*

NORA. They're carrying a thing among them, and there's water dripping out of it and leaving a track by the big stones.

CATHLEEN. [*In a whisper to the women who have come in.*] Is it Bartley it is?

ONE OF THE WOMEN. It is surely, God rest his soul.

[*Two younger women come in and pull out the table. Then*

men carry in the body of Bartley, laid on a plank, with a bit of sail over it, and lay it on the table.

CATHLEEN. [*To the women as they are doing so.*] What way was he drowned?

ONE OF THE WOMEN. The grey pony knocked him over into the sea, and he was washed out where there is a great surf on the white rocks.

[*Maurya has gone over and knelt down at the head of the table. The women are keening softly and swaying themselves with a slow movement. Cathleen and Nora kneel at the other end of the table. The men kneel near the door.*

MAURYA. [*Raising her head and speaking as if she did not see the people around her.*] They 're all gone now, and there isn't anything more the sea can do to me. . . . I 'll have no call now to be up crying and praying when the wind breaks from the south, and you can hear the surf is in the east, and the surf is in the west, making a great stir with the two noises, and they hitting one on the other. I 'll have no call now to be going down and getting Holy Water in the dark nights after Samhain, and I won't care what way the sea is when the other women will be keening. [*To Nora.*] Give me the Holy Water, Nora; there 's a small sup still on the dresser.

[*Nora gives it to her.*

MAURYA. [*Drops Michael's clothes across Bartley's feet, and sprinkles the Holy Water over him.*] It isn't that I haven't prayed for you, Bartley, to the Almighty God. It isn't that I haven't said prayers in the dark night till you wouldn't know what I 'd be saying; but it 's a great rest I 'll have now, and it 's time, surely. It 's a great rest I 'll have now, and great sleeping in the long nights after Samhain, if it 's only a bit of wet flour we do have to eat, and maybe a fish that would be stinking.

[*She kneels down again, crossing herself, and saying prayers under her breath.*

CATHLEEN. [*To an old man.*] Maybe yourself and Eamon would make a coffin when the sun rises. We have fine white boards herself bought, God help her, thinking Michael would be found, and I have a new cake you can eat while you 'll be working.

THE OLD MAN. [*Looking at the boards.*] Are there nails with them?

CATHLEEN. There are not, Colum; we didn't think of the nails.

ANOTHER MAN. It 's a great wonder she wouldn't think of the nails, and all the coffins she 's seen made already.

*B 947

CATHLEEN. It 's getting old she is, and broken.

[*Maurya stands up again very slowly, and spreads out the pieces of Michael's clothes beside the body, sprinkling them with the last of the Holy Water.*

NORA. [*In a whisper to Cathleen.*] She 's quiet now and easy; but the day Michael was drowned you could hear her crying out from this to the spring well. It 's fonder she was of Michael, and would any one have thought that?

CATHLEEN. [*Slowly and clearly.*] An old woman will be soon tired with anything she will do, and isn't it nine days herself is after crying and keening, and making great sorrow in the house?

MAURYA. [*Puts the empty cup mouth downwards on the table, and lays her hands together on Bartley's feet.*] They 're all together this time, and the end is come. May the Almighty God have mercy on Bartley's soul, and on Michael's soul, and on the souls of Sheamus and Patch, and Stephen and Shawn [*bending her head*]; and may He have mercy on my soul, Nora, and on the soul of every one is left living in the world.

[*She pauses, and the keen rises a little more loudly from the women, then sinks away.*

MAURYA. [*Continuing.*] Michael has a clean burial in the far north, by the grace of the Almighty God. Bartley will have a fine coffin out of the white boards, and a deep grave surely. What more can we want than that? No man at all can be living for ever, and we must be satisfied.

[*She kneels down again, and the curtain falls slowly.*

THE DEAR DEPARTED

Stanley Houghton

This play was first produced at the Gaiety Theatre, Manchester, by Miss Horniman's company on 2nd November 1908, with the following cast:

MRS SLATER	*Ada King*
VICTORIA SLATER, her daughter, aged ten .	*Enid Meek*
HENRY SLATER, her husband . .	*Henry Austin*
MRS JORDAN, her sister . . .	*Louise Holbrook*
BEN JORDAN, Mrs Jordan's husband .	*Joseph A. Keogh*
ABEL MERRYWEATHER, her father . .	*Edward Landor*

The action takes place in a provincial town on a Saturday afternoon.

Applications for permission to perform this play must be made to Samuel French Ltd, 26 Southampton Street, Strand, London, W.C.2, or to their authorized agents. The fee for each and every representation of the play by amateurs is one guinea. Upon payment of this fee a licence will be issued for the performance to take place. No performance may be given unless this licence has first been obtained.

THE DEAR DEPARTED

The scene is the sitting-room of a small house in a lower middle-class district of a provincial town. On the spectator's left is the window, with the blinds down. A sofa is in front of it. On his right is a fireplace with an armchair by it. In the middle of the wall facing the spectator is the door into the passage. To the left of the door a cheap, shabby chest of drawers, to the right a side-board. In the middle of the room is the table, with chairs round it. Ornaments and a cheap American clock are on the mantel-piece, in the hearth a kettle. By the sideboard a pair of gaudy new carpet slippers. The table is partly laid for tea, and the necessaries for the meal are on the sideboard, as also are copies of an evening paper and of 'Tit-Bits' and 'Pearson's Weekly.' Turning to the left through the door takes you to the front door; to the right, upstairs. In the passage a hat-stand is visible.

When the curtain rises Mrs Slater is seen laying the table. She is a vigorous, plump, red-faced, vulgar woman, prepared to do any amount of straight talking to get her own way. She is in black, but not in complete mourning. She listens a moment and then goes to the window, opens it and calls into the street.

MRS SLATER. [*Sharply.*] Victoria, Victoria! D' ye hear? Come in, will you?
    [*Mrs Slater closes window and puts the blind straight and then returns to her work at the table. Victoria, a precocious girl of ten, dressed in colours, enters.*
MRS SLATER. I 'm amazed at you, Victoria; I really am. How you can be gallivanting about in the street with your grand-father lying dead and cold upstairs I don't know. Be off now, and change your dress before your Aunt Elizabeth and your Uncle Ben come. It would never do for them to find you in colours.
VICTORIA. What are they coming for? They haven't been here for ages.
MRS SLATER. They 're coming to talk over poor grandpa's affairs. Your father sent them a telegram as soon as we found he was dead. [*A noise is heard.*] Good gracious, that 's

27

never them. [*Mrs Slater hurries to the door and opens it.*] No,
thank goodness! it 's only your father.
  [*Henry Slater, a stooping, heavy man with a drooping mou-
  stache, enters. He is wearing a black tail coat, grey
  trousers, a black tie, and a bowler hat. He carries a little
  paper parcel.*
HENRY. Not come yet, eh?
MRS SLATER. You can see they haven't, can't you? Now,
Victoria, be off upstairs and that quick. Put your white
frock on with a black sash.   [*Victoria goes out.*
MRS SLATER. [*To Henry.*] I 'm not satisfied, but it 's the best
we can do till our new black 's ready, and Ben and Elizabeth
will never have thought about mourning yet, so we 'll out-
shine them there. [*Henry sits in the armchair by the fire.*] Get
your boots off, Henry; Elizabeth 's that prying she notices the
least speck of dirt.
HENRY. I 'm wondering if they 'll come at all. When you and
Elizabeth quarrelled she said she 'd never set foot in your
house again.
MRS SLATER. She 'll come fast enough after her share of what
grandfather 's left. You know how hard she can be when
she likes. Where she gets it from I can't tell.
  [*Mrs Slater unwraps the parcel Henry has brought. It contains sliced tongue, which she puts on a dish on the
  table.*
HENRY. I suppose it 's in the family.
MRS SLATER. What do you mean by that, Henry Slater?
HENRY. I was referring to your father, not to you. Where are
my slippers?
MRS SLATER. In the kitchen; but you want a new pair, those
old ones are nearly worn out. [*Nearly breaking down.*] You
don't seem to realize what it 's costing me to bear up like I am
doing. My heart 's fit to break when I see the little trifles
that belonged to grandfather lying around, and think he 'll
never use them again. [*Briskly.*] Here! you 'd better wear
these slippers of grandfather's now. It 's lucky he 'd just
got a new pair.
HENRY. They 'll be very small for me, my dear.
MRS SLATER. They 'll stretch, won't they? I 'm not going to
have them wasted. [*She has finished laying the table.*] Henry,
I 've been thinking about that bureau of grandfather's that 's
in his bedroom. You know I always wanted to have it after
he died.

HENRY. You must arrange with Elizabeth when you 're dividing things up.

MRS SLATER. Elizabeth 's that sharp she 'll see I 'm after it, and she 'll drive a hard bargain over it.   Eh, what it is to have a low money-grubbing spirit!

HENRY. Perhaps she 's got her eye on the bureau as well.

MRS SLATER. She 's never been here since grandfather bought it.   If it was only down here instead of in his room, she 'd never guess it wasn't our own.

HENRY. [Startled.] Amelia! [He rises.]

MRS SLATER. Henry, why shouldn't we bring that bureau down here now?   We could do it before they come.

HENRY. [Stupefied.] I wouldn't care to.

MRS SLATER. Don't look so daft.   Why not?

HENRY. It doesn't seem delicate, somehow.

MRS SLATER. We could put that shabby old chest of drawers upstairs where the bureau is now.   Elizabeth could have that and welcome.   I 've always wanted to get rid of it.

[She points to the drawers.

HENRY. Suppose they come when we 're doing it.

MRS SLATER. I 'll fasten the front door.   Get your coat off, Henry; we 'll change it.

[Mrs Slater goes out to fasten the front door.   Henry takes his coat off.   Mrs Slater reappears.

MRS SLATER. I 'll run up and move the chairs out of the way.

[Victoria appears, dressed according to her mother's instructions.

VICTORIA. Will you fasten my frock up the back, mother?

MRS SLATER. I 'm busy; get your father to do it.

[Mrs Slater hurries upstairs, and Henry fastens the frock.

VICTORIA. What have you got your coat off for, father?

HENRY. Mother and me is going to bring grandfather's bureau down here.

VICTORIA. [After a moment's thought.] Are we pinching it before Aunt Elizabeth comes?

HENRY. [Shocked.] No, my child.   Grandpa gave it your mother before he died.

VICTORIA. This morning?

HENRY. Yes.

VICTORIA. Ah!   He was drunk this morning.

HENRY. Hush; you mustn't ever say he was drunk, now.

[Henry has fastened the frock, and Mrs Slater appears carrying a handsome clock under her arm.

Mrs Slater. I thought I 'd fetch this down as well. [*She puts it on the mantelpiece.*] Our clock 's worth nothing and this always appealed to me.

Victoria. That 's grandpa's clock.

Mrs Slater. Chut! Be quiet! It 's ours now. Come, Henry, lift your end. Victoria, don't breathe a word to your aunt about the clock and the bureau.

[*They carry the chest of drawers through the doorway.*

Victoria. [*To herself.*] I *thought* we 'd pinched them.

[*After a short pause there is a sharp knock at the front door.*

Mrs Slater. [*From upstairs.*] Victoria, if that 's your aunt and uncle you 're not to open the door.

[*Victoria peeps through the window.*

Victoria. Mother, it 's them!

Mrs Slater. You 're not to open the door till I come down. [*Knocking repeated.*] Let them knock away. [*There is a heavy bumping noise.*] Mind the wall, Henry.

[*Henry and Mrs Slater, very hot and flushed, stagger in with a pretty old-fashioned bureau containing a locked desk. They put it where the chest of drawers was, and straighten the ornaments, etc. The knocking is repeated.* .

Mrs Slater. That was a near thing. Open the door, Victoria. Now, Henry, get your coat on. [*She helps him.*

Henry. Did we knock much plaster off the wall?

Mrs Slater. Never mind the plaster. Do I look all right? [*Straightening her hair in the glass.*] Just watch Elizabeth's face when she sees we 're all in half mourning [*Throwing him 'Tit-Bits.'*] Take this and sit down. Try and look as if we 'd been waiting for them.

[*Henry sits in the armchair and Mrs Slater left of table. They read ostentatiously. Victoria ushers in Ben and Mrs Jordan. The latter is a stout, complacent woman with an impassive face and an irritating air of being always right. She is wearing a complete and deadly outfit of new mourning crowned by a great black hat with plumes. Ben is also in complete new mourning, with black gloves and a band round his hat. He is rather a jolly little man, accustomed to be humorous, but at present trying to adapt himself to the regrettable occasion. He has a bright, chirpy little voice. Mrs Jordan sails into the room and solemnly goes straight to Mrs Slater and kisses her. The men shake hands. Mrs Jordan kisses Henry. Ben*

kisses Mrs Slater. Not a word is spoken. Mrs Slater
furtively inspects the new mourning.

MRS JORDAN. Well, Amelia, and so he 's gone at last.

MRS SLATER. Yes, he 's gone. He was seventy-two a fortnight
last Sunday.

[She sniffs back a tear. Mrs Jordan sits on the left of the
table. Mrs Slater on the right. Henry in the armchair.
Ben on the sofa with Victoria near him.

BEN. *[Chirpily.]* Now, Amelia, you mustn't give way. We 've
all got to die some time or other. It might have been worse.

MRS SLATER. I don't see how.

BEN. It might have been one of us.

HENRY. It 's taken you a long time to get here, Elizabeth.

MRS JORDAN. Oh, I couldn't do it. I really couldn't do it.

MRS SLATER. *[Suspiciously.]* Couldn't do what?

MRS JORDAN. I couldn't start without getting the mourning.
[Glancing at her sister.

MRS SLATER. We 've ordered ours, you may be sure. *[Acidly.]*
I never could fancy buying ready-made things.

MRS JORDAN. No? For myself it 's such a relief to get into the
black. And now perhaps you 'll tell us all about it. What
did the doctor say?

MRS SLATER. Oh, he 's not been near yet.

MRS. JORDAN. Not been near?

BEN. *[In the same breath.]* Didn't you send for him at once?

MRS SLATER. Of course I did. Do you take me for a fool? I
sent Henry at once for Dr Pringle, but he was out.

BEN. You should have gone for another. Eh, Eliza?

MRS JORDAN. Oh, yes. It 's a fatal mistake.

MRS SLATER. Pringle attended him when he was alive and
Pringle shall attend him when he 's dead. That 's professional etiquette.

BEN. Well, you know your own business best, but——

MRS JORDAN. Yes—it 's a fatal mistake.

MRS SLATER. Don't talk so silly, Elizabeth. What good could
a doctor have done?

MRS JORDAN. Look at the many cases of persons being restored
to life hours after they were thought to be 'gone.'

HENRY. That 's when they 've been drowned. Your father
wasn't drowned, Elizabeth.

BEN. *[Humorously.]* There wasn't much fear of that. If there
was one thing he couldn't bear it was water.
[He laughs, but no one else does.

Mrs Jordan. [*Pained.*] Ben!   [*Ben is crushed at once.*

Mrs Slater. [*Piqued.*] I 'm sure he washed regular enough.

Mrs Jordan. If he did take a drop too much at times, we 'll not dwell on that, now.

Mrs Slater. Father had been 'merry' this morning. He went out soon after breakfast to pay his insurance.

Ben. My word, it 's a good thing he did.

Mrs Jordan. He always was thoughtful in that way. He was too honourable to have 'gone' without paying his premium.

Mrs Slater. Well, he must have gone round to the 'Ring-o'-Bells' afterwards, for he came in as merry as a sandboy. I says, 'We 're only waiting Henry to start dinner.' 'Dinner,' he says, 'I don't want no dinner, I 'm going to bed!'

Ben. [*Shaking his head.*] Ah! Dear, dear.

Henry. And when I came in I found him undressed sure enough and snug in bed.   [*He rises and stands on the hearthrug.*

Mrs Jordan. [*Definitely.*] Yes, he 'd had a 'warning.' I 'm sure of that. Did he know you?

Henry. Yes. He spoke to me.

Mrs Jordan. Did he say he 'd had a 'warning'?

Henry. No. He said, 'Henry, would you mind taking my boots off; I forgot before I got into bed.'

Mrs Jordan. He must have been wandering.

Henry. No, he 'd got 'em on all right.

Mrs Slater. And when we 'd finished dinner I thought I 'd take up a bit of something on a tray. He was lying there for all the world as if he was asleep, so I put the tray down on the bureau—[*correcting herself*] on the chest of drawers—and went to waken him. [*A pause.*] He was quite cold.

Henry. Then I heard Amelia calling for me, and I ran upstairs.

Mrs Slater. Of course we could do nothing.

Mrs Jordan. He was 'gone'?

Henry. There wasn't any doubt.

Mrs Jordan. I always knew he 'd go sudden in the end.

[*A pause. They wipe their eyes and sniff back tears.*

Mrs Slater. [*Rising briskly at length; in a businesslike tone.*] Well, will you go up and look at him now, or shall we have tea?

Mrs Jordan. What do you say, Ben?

Ben. I 'm not particular.

Mrs Jordan. [*Surveying the table.*] Well, then, if the kettle 's ready we may as well have tea first.

[*Mrs Slater puts the kettle on the fire and gets tea ready.*

HENRY. One thing we may as well decide now; the announcement in the papers.

MRS JORDAN. I was thinking of that. What would you put?

MRS SLATER. At the residence of his daughter, 235 Upper Cornbank Street, etc.

HENRY. You wouldn't care for a bit of poetry?

MRS JORDAN. I like 'Never Forgotten.' It's refined.

HENRY. Yes, but it's rather soon for that.

BEN. You couldn't very well have forgot him the day after.

MRS SLATER. I always fancy 'A loving husband, a kind father, and a faithful friend.'

BEN. [*Doubtfully.*] Do you think that's right?

HENRY. I don't think it matters whether it's right or not.

MRS JORDAN. No, it's more for the look of the thing.

HENRY. I saw a verse in the *Evening News* yesterday. Proper poetry it was. It rhymed. [*He gets the paper and reads.*
'Despised and forgotten by some you may be
But the spot that contains you is sacred to we.'

MRS JORDAN. That'll never do. You don't say 'Sacred to we.'

HENRY. It's in the paper.

MRS SLATER. You wouldn't say it if you were speaking properly, but it's different in poetry.

HENRY. Poetic licence, you know.

MRS JORDAN. No, that'll never do. We want a verse that says how much we loved him and refers to all his good qualities and says what a heavy loss we've had.

MRS SLATER. You want a whole poem. That'll cost a good lot.

MRS JORDAN. Well, we'll think about it after tea, and then we'll look through his bits of things and make a list of them. There's all the furniture in his room.

HENRY. There's no jewellery or valuables of that sort.

MRS JORDAN. Except his gold watch. He promised that to our Jimmy.

MRS SLATER. Promised your Jimmy! I never heard of that.

MRS JORDAN. Oh, but he did, Amelia, when he was living with us. He was very fond of Jimmy.

MRS SLATER. Well. [*Amazed.*] I don't know!

BEN. Anyhow, there's his insurance money. Have you got the receipt for the premium he paid this morning?

MRS SLATER. I've not seen it.

[*Victoria jumps up from the sofa and comes behind the table.*

VICTORIA. Mother, I don't think grandpa went to pay his insurance this morning.

MRS SLATER. He went out.

VICTORIA. Yes, but he didn't go into the town. He met old Mr Tattersall down the street, and they went off past St Philips's Church.

MRS SLATER. To the 'Ring-o'-Bells,' I 'll be bound.

BEN. The 'Ring-o'-Bells'?

MRS SLATER. That public-house that John Shorrocks 's widow keeps. He is always hanging about there. Oh, if he hasn't paid it——

BEN. Do you think he hasn't paid it? Was it overdue?

MRS SLATER. I should think it was overdue.

MRS JORDAN. Something tells me he 's not paid it. I 've a 'warning,' I know it; he 's not paid it.

BEN. The drunken old beggar.

MRS JORDAN. He 's done it on purpose, just to annoy us.

MRS SLATER. After all I 've done for him, having to put up with him in the house these three years. It 's nothing short of swindling.

MRS JORDAN. I had to put up with him for five years.

MRS SLATER. And you were trying to turn him over to us all the time.

HENRY. But we don't know for certain that he 's not paid the premium.

MRS JORDAN. I do. It 's come over me all at once that he hasn't.

MRS SLATER. Victoria, run upstairs and fetch that bunch of keys that 's on your grandpa's dressing table.

VICTORIA. [Timidly.] In grandpa's room?

MRS SLATER. Yes.

VICTORIA. I—I don't like to.

MRS SLATER. Don't talk so silly. There 's no one can hurt you. [Victoria goes out reluctantly.] We 'll see if he 's locked the receipt up in the bureau.

BEN. In where? In this thing? [He rises and examines it.

MRS JORDAN. [Also rising.] Where did you pick that up, Amelia? It 's new since last I was here.

[They examine it closely.

MRS SLATER. Oh—Henry picked it up one day.

MRS JORDAN. I like it. It 's artistic. Did you buy it at an auction?

HENRY. Eh! Where did I buy it, Amelia?

MRS JORDAN. Yes, at an auction.

BEN. [Disparagingly.] Oh, second-hand.

MRS JORDAN. Don't show your ignorance, Ben. All artistic things are second-hand. Look at those old masters.

[*Victoria returns, very scared. She closes the door after her.*

VICTORIA. Mother! Mother!

MRS SLATER. What is it, child?

VICTORIA. Grandpa's getting up.

BEN. What?

MRS SLATER. What do you say?

VICTORIA. Grandpa's getting up.

MRS JORDAN. The child's crazy.

MRS SLATER. Don't talk so silly. Don't you know your grandpa's dead?

VICTORIA. No, no; he's getting up. I saw him.

[*They are transfixed with amazement; Ben and Mrs Jordan left of table; Victoria clings to Mrs Slater, right of table; Henry near fireplace.*

MRS JORDAN. You'd better go up and see for yourself, Amelia.

MRS SLATER. Here—come with me, Henry.

[*Henry draws back terrified.*

BEN. [*Suddenly.*] Hist! Listen.

[*They look at the door. A slight chuckling is heard outside. The door opens, revealing an old man clad in a faded but gay dressing-gown. He is in his stockinged feet. Although over seventy he is vigorous and well coloured; his bright, malicious eyes twinkle under his heavy, reddish-grey eyebrows. He is obviously either Grandfather Abel Merryweather or else his ghost.*

ABEL. What's the matter with little Vicky? [*He sees Ben and Mrs Jordan.*] Hello! What brings you here? How's yourself, Ben?

[*Abel thrusts his hand at Ben, who skips back smartly and retreats with Mrs Jordan to a safe distance below the sofa.*

MRS SLATER. [*Approaching Abel gingerly.*] Grandfather, is that you? [*She pokes him with her hand to see if he is solid.*

ABEL. Of course it's me. Don't do that, 'Melia. What the devil do you mean by this tomfoolery?

MRS SLATER. [*To the others.*] He's not dead.

BEN. Doesn't seem like it.

ABEL. [*Irritated by the whispering.*] You've kept away long enough, Lizzie; and now you've come you don't seem over-pleased to see me.

MRS JORDAN. You took us by surprise, father. Are you keeping quite well?

ABEL. [*Trying to catch the words.*] Eh? What?

MRS JORDAN. Are you quite well?

ABEL. Ay, I'm right enough but for a bit of a headache. I wouldn't mind betting that I'm not the first in this house to be carried to the cemetery. I always think Henry there looks none too healthy.

MRS JORDAN. Well, I never!

[*Abel crosses to the armchair and Henry gets out of his way to the front of the table.*

ABEL. 'Melia, what the dickens did I do with my new slippers?

MRS SLATER. [*Confused.*] Aren't they by the hearth, grandfather?

ABEL. I don't see them. [*Observing Henry trying to remove the slippers.*] Why, you've got 'em on, Henry.

MRS SLATER. [*Promptly.*] I told him to put them on to stretch them, they were that new and hard. Now, Henry.

[*Mrs Slater snatches the slippers from Henry and gives them to Abel, who puts them on and sits in armchair.*

MRS JORDAN. [*To Ben.*] Well, I don't call that delicate, stepping into a dead man's shoes in such haste.

[*Henry goes up to the window and pulls up the blind. Victoria runs across to Abel and sits on the floor at his feet.*

VICTORIA. Oh, grandpa, I'm so glad you're not dead.

MRS SLATER. [*In a vindictive whisper.*] Hold your tongue, Victoria.

ABEL. Eh? What's that? Who's gone dead?

MRS SLATER. [*Loudly.*] Victoria says she's sorry about your head.

ABEL. Ah, thank you, Vicky, but I'm feeling better.

MRS SLATER. [*To Mrs Jordan.*] He's so fond of Victoria.

MRS JORDAN. [*To Mrs Slater.*] Yes; he's fond of our Jimmy, too.

MRS SLATER. You'd better ask him if he promised your Jimmy his gold watch.

MRS JORDAN. [*Disconcerted.*] I couldn't just now. I don't feel equal to it.

ABEL. Why, Ben, you're in mourning! And Lizzie too. And 'Melia, and Henry, and little Vicky! Who's gone dead? It's someone in the family. [*He chuckles.*

MRS SLATER. No one you know, father. A relation of Ben's.

ABEL. And what relation of Ben's?

MRS SLATER. His brother.

BEN. [*To Mrs Slater.*] Dang it, I never had one.

ABEL. Dear, dear. And what was his name, Ben?
BEN. [*At a loss.*] Er—er—   [*He crosses to front of table.*
MRS SLATER. [*Right of table, prompting.*] Frederick.
MRS JORDAN. [*Left of table, prompting.*] Albert.
BEN. Er—Fred—Alb—Isaac.
ABEL. Isaac? And where did your brother Isaac die?
BEN. In—er—in Australia.
ABEL. Dear, dear. He 'd be older than you, eh?
BEN. Yes, five years.
ABEL. Ay, ay. Are you going to the funeral?
BEN. Oh, yes.
MRS SLATER and MRS JORDAN. No, no.
BEN. No, of course not.   [*He retires to left.*
ABEL. [*Rising.*] Well, I suppose you 've only been waiting for
  me to begin tea. I 'm feeling hungry.
MRS SLATER. [*Taking up the kettle.*] I 'll make tea.
ABEL. Come along, now; sit you down and let 's be jolly.
  [*Abel sits at the head of the table, facing spectators. Ben and
    Mrs Jordan on the left. Victoria brings a chair and sits
    by Abel. Mrs Slater and Henry sit on the right. Both
    the women are next to Abel.*
MRS SLATER. Henry, give grandpa some tongue.
ABEL. Thank you. I 'll make a start.
        [*He helps himself to bread and butter.*
  [*Henry serves the tongue and Mrs Slater pours out tea. Only
    Abel eats with any heartiness.*
BEN. Glad to see you 've got an appetite, Mr Merryweather,
  although you 've not been so well.
ABEL. Nothing serious. I 've been lying down for a bit.
MRS SLATER. Been to sleep, grandfather?
ABEL. No, I 've not been to sleep.
MRS SLATER and HENRY. Oh!
ABEL. [*Eating and drinking.*] I can't exactly call everything to
  mind, but I remember I was a bit dazed, like. I couldn't
  move an inch, hand or foot.
BEN. And could you see and hear, Mr Merryweather?
ABEL. Yes, but I don't remember seeing anything particular.
  Mustard, Ben.   [*Ben passes the mustard.*
MRS SLATER. Of course not, grandfather. It was all your fancy.
  You must have been asleep.
ABEL. [*Snappishly.*] I tell you I wasn't asleep, 'Melia. Damn
  it, I ought to know.
MRS JORDAN. Didn't you see Henry or Amelia come into the room?

ABEL. [*Scratching his head.*] Now let me think——

MRS SLATER. I wouldn't press him, Elizabeth. Don't press him.

HENRY. No. I wouldn't worry him.

ABEL. [*Suddenly recollecting.*] Ay, begad! 'Melia and Henry, what the devil did you mean by shifting my bureau out of my bedroom? [*Henry and Mrs Slater are speechless.*] D'you hear me? Henry! 'Melia!

MRS JORDAN. What bureau was that, father?

ABEL. Why, my bureau, the one I bought——

MRS JORDAN. [*Pointing to the bureau.*] Was it that one, father?

ABEL. Ah, that's it. What's it doing here? Eh? [*A pause. The clock on the mantelpiece strikes six. Every one looks at it.*] Drat me if that isn't my clock, too. What the devil's been going on in this house? [*A slight pause.*

BEN. Well, I'll be hanged.

MRS JORDAN. [*Rising.*] I'll tell you what's been going on in this house, father. Nothing short of robbery.

MRS. SLATER. Be quiet, Elizabeth.

MRS JORDAN. I'll not be quiet. Oh, I call it double-faced.

HENRY. Now, now, Elizabeth.

MRS JORDAN. And you, too. Are you such a poor creature that you must do every dirty thing she tells you?

MRS SLATER. [*Rising.*] Remember where you are, Elizabeth.

HENRY. [*Rising.*] Come, come. No quarrelling.

BEN. [*Rising.*] My wife's every right to speak her own mind.

MRS SLATER. Then she can speak it outside, not here.

ABEL. [*Rising ; thumping the table.*] Damn it all, will someone tell me what's been going on?

MRS JORDAN. Yes, I will. I'll not see you robbed.

ABEL. Who's been robbing me?

MRS JORDAN. Amelia and Henry. They've stolen your clock and bureau. [*Working herself up.*] They sneaked into your room like a thief in the night and stole them after you were dead.

HENRY and MRS SLATER. Hush! Quiet, Elizabeth!

MRS JORDAN. I'll not be stopped. After you were dead, I say.

ABEL. After who was dead?

MRS JORDAN. You.

ABEL. But I'm not dead.

MRS JORDAN. No, but they thought you were.

[*A pause. Abel gazes round at them.*

ABEL. Oho! So that's why you're all in black to-day. You thought I was dead. [*He chuckles.*] That was a big mistake.
[*He sits and resumes his tea.*

MRS SLATER. [*Sobbing.*] Grandfather.

ABEL. It didn't take you long to start dividing my things between you.

MRS JORDAN. No, father; you mustn't think that. Amelia was simply getting hold of them on her own account.

ABEL. You always were a keen one, Amelia. I suppose you thought the will wasn't fair.

HENRY. Did you make a will?

ABEL. Yes, it was locked up in the bureau.

MRS JORDAN. And what was in it, father?

ABEL. That doesn't matter now. I'm thinking of destroying it and making another.

MRS SLATER. [*Sobbing.*] Grandfather, you'll not be hard on me.

ABEL. I'll trouble you for another cup of tea, 'Melia; two lumps and plenty of milk.

MRS SLATER. With pleasure, grandfather.
[*She pours out the tea.*

ABEL. I don't want to be hard on any one. I'll tell you what I'm going to do. Since your mother died, I've lived part of the time with you, 'Melia, and part with you, Lizzie. Well, I shall make a new will, leaving all my bits of things to whoever I'm living with when I die. How does that strike you?

HENRY. It's a bit of a lottery, like.

MRS JORDAN. And who do you intend to live with from now?

ABEL. [*Drinking his tea.*] I'm just coming to that.

MRS JORDAN. You know, father, it's quite time you came to live with us again. We'd make you very comfortable.

MRS SLATER. No, he's not been with us as long as he was with you.

MRS JORDAN. I may be wrong, but I don't think father will fancy living on with you after what's happened to-day.

ABEL. So you'd like to have me again, Lizzie?

MRS JORDAN. You know we're ready for you to make your home with us for as long as you please.

ABEL. What do you say to that, 'Melia?

MRS SLATER. All I can say is that Elizabeth's changed her mind in the last two years. [*Rising.*] Grandfather, do you know what the quarrel between us was about?

MRS JORDAN. Amelia, don't be a fool; sit down.

MRS SLATER. No, if I 'm not to have him, you shan't either. We quarrelled because Elizabeth said she wouldn't take you off our hands at any price. She said she 'd had enough of you to last a lifetime, and we 'd got to keep you.

ABEL. It seems to me that neither of you has any cause to feel proud about the way you 've treated me.

MRS SLATER. If I 've done anything wrong, I 'm sure I 'm sorry for it.

MRS JORDAN. And I can't say more than that, too.

ABEL. It 's a bit late to say it, now. You neither of you cared to put up with me.

MRS SLATER and MRS JORDAN. No, no, grandfather.

ABEL. Ay, you both say that because of what I 've told you about leaving my money. Well, since you don't want me I 'll go to someone that does.

BEN. Come, Mr Merryweather, you 've got to live with one of your daughters.

ABEL. I 'll tell you what I 've got to do. On Monday next I 've got to do three things. I 've got to go to the lawyer's and alter my will; and I 've got to go to the insurance office and pay my premium; and I 've got to go to St Philips's Church and get married.

BEN and HENRY. What!

MRS JORDAN. Get married!

MRS SLATER. He 's out of his senses.   [*General consternation.*

ABEL. I say I 'm going to get married.

MRS SLATER. Who to?

ABEL. To Mrs John Shorrocks who keeps the 'Ring-o'-Bells.' We 've had it fixed up a good while now, but I was keeping it for a pleasant surprise. [*He rises.*] I felt I was a bit of a burden to you, so I found someone who 'd think it a pleasure to look after me. We shall be very glad to see you at the ceremony. [*He gets to the door.*] Till Monday, then. Twelve o'clock at St Philips's Church. [*Opening the door.*] It 's a good thing you brought that bureau downstairs, 'Melia. It 'll be handier to carry across to the 'Ring-o'-Bells' on Monday.

[*He goes out.*

CURTAIN

MR SAMPSON

CHARLES LEE

'*Mr Sampson*' *was performed by The Welwyn Garden City Theatre Society on 21st February* 1927, *at the New Theatre, London, with the following cast:*

Catherine Stevens ⎫ Two maiden sisters ⎰ *Joyce Raby*
Caroline Stevens ⎭   ⎱ *Elsie Colson*
Mr Sampson, their tenant next door .   . *Ernest Shelley*

Scene. *The kitchen of a cottage on a moorland road in the west country*

The Play produced by C. B. Purdom

This production was awarded the Lord Howard de Walden Cup in the British Drama League's Festival of Community Drama and the David Belasco Cup in the New York 'Little Theatre' Tournament.

The first public performance of the play was given by the Letchworth Dramatic Society in 1911.

MR SAMPSON

*The scene represents the kitchen of a west country cottage. At the
back of the stage, in the centre, is a latticed window, with
geraniums in pots on the inner sill. To the right of the window
(from the spectator's point of view) is a door communicating with
the front garden; to the left, a tall grandfather clock; beyond that
again, a cupboard. On the right side of the stage, a dresser, well
garnished with crockery; a small pile of books on one of the
shelves. Beyond the dresser, another door. On the left side, a
kitchen range, in which a fire is burning.*

*Beside a table in the middle of the room Caroline Stevens, a gentle,
timid, plump, soft-spoken woman of forty or so, sits darning a
sock. As the curtain rises, the clock strikes four. Caroline
glances momentarily towards the clock and begins to talk to it, as
people who are much alone are in the habit of talking to a cat or a
canary. There are pauses when her work requires special
attention; and now and again she repeats a phrase dreamily, as
her thoughts wander.*

CAROLINE. Four o'clock, grandf'er? Sister's late, an't she?
She don't use to be so late, market day—you know that so
well as I do. 'Tisn' often you put *she* to shame. . . . Wish I
could say so much for myself. Four o'clock Saturday arternoon, and the baking not begun, and Mr Sampson's socks not
finished mending—aw, scand'lous! I'm ashamed to look 'e
in the face, grandf'er, that I am—ashamed—to look 'e—in the
face. . . . What's keeping of her, I wonder? She haven'
been so late from market, not these fifteen year. And Mr
Sampson coming in any minute now to pay his rent, and
looking for a bit of a chat, and me never knowing for the life
of me what to say to 'm. Aisy enough talking to *you*, grand-
f'er; but a rale live man, that do ask questions and look to be
answered back — that's different, and I haven' got used
to him yet. . . . He's another of your reg'lar ones,
grandf'er — slow and sure, like it might be yourself.
And I often think he favour you about the face — round
and solemn, like. And he growl in his throat when he's

43

going to say something, just like you before you strike up.
. . . But you 're an old friend, grandf'er—oldest friend we
got, and we 'd never set eyes on *he* three months ago; so you
needn' be jalous—no—grandf'er needn' be jalous. [*With a
sigh she gets up, goes to the fire and tends it, and then wanders to
the window and looks out for a moment, still talking.*] Yes, if
you 'll mind, it 's just three month come Tuesday since he
come to live next door; and considering of it one way it might
be three year, and considering of it another way 'tis more like
three weeks. But that 's the way with Time, grandf'er, and
always will be, for all your stiddy tick-tocking. Ayther 'tis
crawling around like a worm, or else . . . or else 'tis wal-
loping along like a butcher's cart. . . . Aw me! . . . [*By this
time she is seated again.*] Sister 's late, grandf'er! Never
knowed her to be so late before. If something should have
happened!

> [*She starts at the sound of a tap at the garden door. It opens,
> and Mr Sampson appears on the threshold. He is an
> oldish man, stiff in his movements, very deliberate of
> speech; a fringe of grey whiskers encircles his round red
> face. A shy confusion comes over Caroline.*

MR SAMPSON. [*After profoundly clearing a throat unaccustomed
to much vocal exercise.*] Arternoon, marm!

CAROLINE. Mr Sampson?

MR SAMPSON. [*Peering round.*] Sister in?

CAROLINE. No, Mr Sampson, not yet. I 'm getting a bit anxious.
She don't use to be later than four, and 'tis past that.

MR SAMPSON. Then you 're all alone?

CAROLINE. [*Acutely conscious of the fact.*] All alone. [*With an
obvious effort.*] Won't 'e step inside, Mr Sampson?

MR Sampson. [*After thinking it over.*] No, thank 'e. Can do
very well where I be. Got a mossel o' bacca in my cheek, you
see. More convaynient for spitting out here. [*He illustrates
the convenience from behind a respectful hand.*] Thought I heard
talking as I come up the path. Judged 'twas sister come
home.

CAROLINE. Talking? Aw, 'twas only me, chattering away to
myself. Leastways [*with a bashful titter*] I was conversing a
bit with grandf'er here.

MR SAMPSON. [*Craning his neck into the room.*] Grandf'er? Oh,
ay, the clock! Conversing with grandf'er, eh? [*With a short
laugh.*] Well, now, there 's a sarcumstance for 'e!

CAROLINE. [*Nervously echoing his laugh.*] 'Tis foolishness, I

allow. But I often chat a bit with grandf'er when I 'm alone.
[*Gathering a little confidence.*] He 's capital company—'most
like a Christian. Sister do often say he 's as good as a man
in the house. You see, Mr Sampson, 'tis he that do rule our
comings and our goings, telling us to do this and do that all
the while; now 'tis to get up and light the fire, and then 'tis to
bustle and get dinner, and then agin 'tis to rake out the ashes
and go to bed. Yes, grandf'er 's master here, I believe. So
'tis natural for two lonely females to look up to him and think
a brave lot of him, when they haven' nobody else to be dependent on. And there an't a stiddier clock, nor a handsomer,
in all the country.
MR SAMPSON. A stately old chap, sure enough. [*A pause: he
shifts his feet; she looks down and makes a few stitches.*] Those
my socks?
CAROLINE. Yes, Mr Sampson. They 're 'most done. [*Another
pause.*] Hope you found the pasty to your satisfaction.
MR SAMPSON. Capital pasty, to be sure. [*He advances a step into
the room.*] You take a lot of trouble about me, marm, you and
your sister.
CAROLINE. No trouble at all, Mr Sampson. We couldn't do
other, and you all alone next door with nobody to do for 'e,
and no more notion how to do for yourself than a new-born
baby.
MR SAMPSON. I 'm a terrible poor hand at the cookery, that 's
sartain. [*He advances another step.*] Frying-pan, I don't say;
but a man can't live by frying-pan alone. And as for darning
a sock—well, I 've tried. 'Twas like a fishing-net; the more
I mended, the more the holes came. Well, I reckon I 'm
pretty and comfor'ble now. Never was so comfor'ble in my life.
CAROLINE. [*Earnestly.*] Glad to hear 'e say so. Anything we
can do for 'e, you know you 've only to say the word.
MR SAMPSON. Thank 'e, marm; you 're very kind. [*He makes a
further advance, and assumes a confidential air. Her timidity
immediately returns in a flood.*] There *is* something I wanted
to say—something particular I got to tell 'e—came in for the
purpose. But seeing as how it do consarn both of 'e, I reckon
I 'll wait till sister comes back.
      [*He makes deliberate preparations for settling himself in a
      chair.*
CAROLINE. [*In an agony of nervous apprehension at the prospect of
a* tête-à-tête.] Can't think what 's keeping of her all this while.
Never before have she been so late. Mr Sampson——

MR SAMPSON. Marm?

CAROLINE. Would 'e mind—if 'tisn' asking too much of 'e—
would 'e mind going up the road a step or two, to see if you
can catch a glimp' of her?

MR SAMPSON. [*Rising without alacrity.*] Sartainly, marm, if you
do wish. No occasion for 'e to worry, though. She can take
care of herself very well. Howsomever, if 'twill aise your
mind, I 'll go so fur as the cross-roads and take a observation.
[*Going.*] Don't you fret; she 'll turn up all right. [*He goes.*

CAROLINE. [*Going to the window and watching him out of sight.*]
He 's walking awful stiff, grandf'er. A shame to turn him
out agin just when he was settling himself down comfor'ble.
But I couldn' do no otherwise. 'Tis all right when sister 's
here too; but to set down alone in a room with a man—no! I
couldn' bring myself to it, even if 'twas a proper thing for a
maiden to do. [*She turns away from the window and begins
clearing the table, continuing meanwhile her colloquy with
grandf'er.*] Something partic'lar to tell us? I wonder, now——
[*In some agitation.*] Can't be going to give notice! Aw,
nonsense! Don't be telling such foolishness, grandf'er! *He*
an't one of your changeable ones: you know better 'n that.
'Never so comfor'ble in my life'—those were his words; you
heard him yourself. . . . Wonder what 'a can be, though.
[*A sudden amazing thought strikes her.*] Aw, if it should be——!
Aw, ridic'lous! He 've never given no sign of *that*, by word
or look. Besides, if 'twas *that*, grandf'er, don't 'e see he wouldn'
wish to tell but one of us, whichever 'twas; and he said
partic'lar 'twas *both* of us he wanted to say it to. . . Aw, well,
us 'll know presently. [*She goes up to the clock.*] Aw, grandf'er!
Ten past four! Something 's happened; I know it have!
[*She sinks into a chair and begins to whimper.*] Aw, Cath'rine!
Aw, deary dear! . . . [*She turns reproachfully on the clock.*]
Tick-tock, tick-tock! *You* don't care! If 'twas Judgment
Day, you 'd go on with your tick-tock till the fire catched 'e.
If the truth was known, you 're nothing but a cage of wheels
arter all, and no more heart to 'e than a Waterbury watch.
[*Remorsefully.*] There! I didn' mane to spake sharp to 'e;
but you know how 'tis when things go wrong. [*Almost in tears.*]
You—you struck seventeen yourself when we moved 'e last
spring cleaning. . . . Ah! [*Hearing a sound outside, she runs
to the window.*] 'Tis all right, grandf'er; here she is at last,
thanks be!

[*The door is flung open; Catherine comes in hurriedly and sinks exhausted on a chair. She is older by several years than Caroline, and far more vivacious. Her movements are quick and abrupt, like a bird's, and she gesticulates freely when speaking. On her arm is a basket, containing the week's supply of provisions.*

CAROLINE. [*In an ecstasy of apprehension.*] Cath'rine, what is it? Aw, sister, what's the matter?

CATHERINE. [*In a faint voice, panting heavily.*] Aw, my dear nerves! Aw, that I should live to see the day! [*She sets the basket down.*] Never shall we hold up our heads again! . . . Sister, we're disgraced for ever!

CAROLINE. Sister!

[*She drops into her chair and begins to weep.*

CATHERINE. [*Recovering her self-possession with an effort.*] Stop crying, Caroline, till I give 'e something to cry about. I can do that, I promise 'e. [*She begins her tale with a kind of melancholy gusto, and with immense volubility.*] I fancied whether something was up last week, when I see some of 'em putting their heads together and nodding and grinning upon me—Mrs Parkyn, the old venom, she was one, and Grace Budley was another, and when they two put their heads together, they ben't concocting no testimonials, you may be sure. But I didn' take no notice; I'd scorn to take notice of the looks of such as they. Well, to-day I sold the chickens—chickens are down to one-and-nine, and lucky to get that—I sold the chickens, and I bought the flour and the sugar and the meat— nice bit of fat pork and sixpenn'orth of gravy beef—and everything but the butter—[*Getting up and taking off her hat, etc.*] butter's terrible scarce this week, gone up twopence, and everybody sold out, all but Mrs Parkyn—she's always the last to get rid of hers, and good reason why—well, I was bound to get *some* butter, if 'twas only her dirty old muck, so I went and bought a pound of her, and I won't say but what I might have sniffed to it a bit when I took it up; but she didn' say nothing, not till I'd paid her and she'd got the money safe in her gown-pocket—trust her for seeing to that first—and then she said: 'Very good butter, Miss Stevens,' says she, daring of me, like, to say '*twasn*' very good butter, but I wasn' going to tell no lies to plaise the likes of she, you may be sure, so I said: 'Us'll have to make it do, Mrs Parkyn, seeing there an't no better to be had,' says I; so then she up and say: 'You didn' use to be so partic'lar,' says she. 'Reckon your fancy man must have a terrible delicate stomick,' says she.

48   MR SAMPSON
CAROLINE. [*In horrified bewilderment.*] Fancy man! Sister! Who ever——?

CATHERINE. [*Grimly.*] Only one man just hereabouts that I know by.

CAROLINE. [*Gasping.*] Mr Sampson!

CATHERINE. [*With stony self-possession.*] That's the chap: our fancy man—yourn and mine; and when she said the word you might have knocked me down with a feather—couldn' find a word to answer back, and I could feel myself going black-red all over. So Grace Budley—she was standing by waiting her chance, I don't doubt, the old cat—so she up and say: 'Well may you blush, Cath'rine Stevens,' says she. 'If you'll take a friendly word from me,' says she, 'you'll hurry up, you and that half-baked sister of yourn, and make the best of a poor job,' says she, 'and get your old Sampson to make a h-honest woman of one or the other of 'e so soon as may be,' says she. [*Caroline screams and buries her face in her apron. Catherine shows signs of breaking down, but controls herself and continues.*] Shameful, so 'tis! We've always kept ourselves to ourselves and never spoke a hard word nor a scand'lous word agin nobody. How can't they leave us alone? [*She goes to the fire and pokes it.*] Something's got to be done, and done to once, too. [*After a moment's cogitation.*] Where is he?

CAROLINE. [*In broken phrases, muffled by her apron and shaken with spasms.*] 'A was here just now. . . . Got something partic'lar to say to us. . . . Wouldn' say it, not till you come home. . . . Went out to look for 'e up the road.

CATHERINE. I came round by the path over the downs; that's what made me so late. I wasn' anxious to be meeting people by the road, as you may guess. [*She sits down.*] H'm! Got something partic'lar to say to us, have 'um? Well, p'raps we'll have something partic'lar to say to he!

CAROLINE. [*Dropping her apron.*] Sister! You'll never tell him! I'll die of shame if you tell him!

CATHERINE. [*Irresolutely.*] I don't know. Something's got to be done, if only I can think what. My poor old head!—'tis all of a maze.

CAROLINE. [*Starting up.*] Sister! The gate! I heard the latch! Somebody's coming!

CATHERINE. [*Darting to the window.*] It's him! He shan't come in, though! Never agin shall he set foot in this house. [*She rushes to the door and bolts it.*] There!
[*With eyes fixed on the door, they await the event in breathless*

silence. The door is tapped gently. After an interval the latch is lifted and rattled. Another pause, and Mr Sampson's voice is heard.

MR SAMPSON. Anybody home?

CATHERINE. [*Going to the door and speaking through it.*] Grieved to say it, Mr Sampson, but you can't come in.

MR SAMPSON. How? What's up with 'e?

CATHERINE. I can't tell 'e, but you mustn't come in. Will 'e plaise to go away, Mr Sampson?

MR SAMPSON. [*After a pause for consideration.*] No, I reckon. Not till I know what's the matter.

CATHERINE. [*In despair.*] Aw, dear! I beg of 'e—go!

MR SAMPSON. [*With slow emphasis.*] Not till I know what's up. If you'll open door, you can tell me comfor'able. I won't come in if you don't wish, but I'm bound to know what's up.

CATHERINE. [*To Caroline, in a horrified whisper.*] He won't go! What's to be done? [*Caroline shakes her head miserably.*] If I should tell him——! [*Caroline throws up her hands in terror.*] He won't go if I don't tell him something. I'll wrap it up so well as I can. He'll be off quick enough when he know what it is. He shan't look us in the face—I'll take care of that. [*Nerving herself to the desperate act, she withdraws the bolt, opens the door an inch or so, and sets her shoulder against it.*] Keep outside, if you plaise. We can't look 'e in the face. If we must tell 'e, we must, but we can never look 'e in the face agin.

MR SAMPSON. So bad as that?

CATHERINE. Worse! Worse than anything you could think for. [*With a tremendous effort.*] Mr Sampson, they're talking about us.

MR SAMPSON. 'Us'?

CATHERINE. You and we. 'Tis all over the country—scand'lous talk. Aw, that I should live to see the day!

MR SAMPSON. [*Patiently.*] If you'll kindly give me the partic'lars, marm.

CATHERINE. [*On the verge of tears.*] We never thought no harm. 'Twas only neighbourly to offer to do for 'e, and you all alone and so helpless. 'Tis a sin and a shame to say such things.

MR SAMPSON. [*Inexhaustibly patient.*] Say what things?

CATHERINE. Say—[*with a rush*]—say that 'tis high time you took and married one of us!

[*In trembling expectation they await the result. It comes: first a long low whistle; then, to their amazement, an unmistakable chuckle. Catherine shrinks back from the door; it swings open, and Mr Sampson is revealed, broadly smiling.*

MR SAMPSON. That's a stale old yarn. Heard 'un weeks ago. Don't mind telling 'e, I mightn' have thought of it else.

CATHERINE. [*Bewildered.*] Thought of what?

MR SAMPSON. [*Placidly.*] Why, courting of 'e, to be sure.

CATHERINE. [*Gasping.*] You don't mane to say you——?

MR SAMPSON. Yes, I be, though. This fortnit come Sunday, if you'll kindly take it so, and no offence. [*To Caroline.*] The very thing I was coming in to talk about. Cur'ous how things do turn out!

CATHERINE. But—we never noticed nothing.

MR SAMPSON. No—'tisn' to be supposed you would. 'Tis like the cooking, you see; I 'm a terrible poor hand at it. Now 'tis out. Ben't vexed, I hope?

CATHERINE. Aw, no! But, Mr Sampson——

MR SAMPSON. There, think it over, will 'e? There's the saving to consider of, money and trouble both. And I 've put by a pound or two. Not so young as I was, but we 're none of us that. And not so dreadful old, nuther. Wouldn' think of parting you; reckon we could be pretty and comfor'ble together, the three of us, though of course I can't marry but one of 'e. So talk it over, will 'e? I 'll be round agin this evening.

[*He disappears. Caroline sits down, overwhelmed. Catherine, after a moment of blank bewilderment, goes to the door and calls out.*

CATHERINE. Mr Sampson! . . . Will 'e plaise come back for a minute!

MR SAMPSON. [*Returning.*] Well, marm?

CATHERINE. [*Greatly embarrassed.*] Ascuse my asking, but— would 'e mind telling *which* one you were thinking of—of courting?

MR SAMPSON. Now you'll be laughing upon me. Which one? Well, I don't know which one, and that's the truth. [*Cheerfully.*] But it don't make no odds. Settle it between yourselves; I ben't noways partic'lar.

CATHERINE. [*With an involuntary giggle.*] La, Mr Sampson! Who ever heard tell of such a thing? [*She sits down.*

MR SAMPSON. [*Chuckling quietly.*] That's right. Laugh so much as you 've a mind to. Sister laughing too? [*He peers at Caroline, who titters nervously.*] Now we 're comfor'ble. Reckon I can step inside now, and no scandal. [*He shuts the door, takes a chair, spreads his hands on his knees, and surveys the sisters with a broad-beaming countenance.*] Yes, I 'm like the cat in the bonfire—don't know which course to steer. I 've turned it over this way, and I 've rolled it over that way, and I can't come to no conclusion. Always seeing of 'e together, you see, I can't part 'e nohow, no more than milk from water. But it don't matter, as I said. If you 'll be so kind as to settle it up between yourselves——

CATHERINE. [*Emphatically.*] We couldn' do that.

MR SAMPSON. [*With an inquiring glance at Caroline.*] Couldn' 'e, now?

CAROLINE. [*Shaking her head.*] 'Twouldn' be proper.

MR SAMPSON. [*Resignedly.*] Well, you know best. Only I don't azackly see—— H'm!

> [*With his eyes on the ground, he ponders over the problem. The sisters, tensely still, stare straight before them. He lifts his head and looks in Caroline's direction.*

CAROLINE. [*Hurriedly, without meeting his eye.*] Cath'rine's the best to manage things. [*He looks hopefully at Catherine.*

CATHERINE. [*In haste.*] Caroline's the best cook by far.

MR SAMPSON. [*Thumping his knee.*] That 's where 'tis! The pair of 'e rolled up together 'ud make a complete masterpiece; a man couldn't look for a better wife than what the two of 'e 'ud make. That 's where 'tis; nor I can't see no way out of it—not in a Christian country. [*Meditatively.*] Ah! These heathen Turks—they know a thing or two after all, don't they?

CATHERINE. [*Greatly shocked.*] Mr Sampson, I wonder at 'e!

MR SAMPSON. 'Tisn' to be thought of, I know that. But I can't think upon no other way. [*A bright idea strikes him.*] Without we should spin up a ha'penny and bide by the fall of 'un.

CATHERINE. [*More shocked than ever.*] Never in this house!

MR SAMPSON. Don't see how we shouldn'. 'Tis just the same as casting lots, and that 's a good Scripture observance. The reg'lar way with these old patriarchs, so I 'm given to understand—only 'twas shekels with them, I reckon. But shekels or ha'pennies, 'tis all one.

CATHERINE. [*Dubiously.*] 'Tis uncommon like pitch-and-toss, and I can't fancy Abraham and Isaac a-doing of it. But if you 're sure 'tis Scriptural——

MR SAMPSON. Sound Bible doctrine, my word for it! [*To Caroline.*] An't that so, marm?

CAROLINE. [*Shyly.*] I mind a text in Proverbs which do say: 'The lot causeth contentions to cease.'

MR SAMPSON. [*Triumphantly.*] See there, now! 'The lot causeth contentions to cease'! Aimed straight at our case! Out of Proverbs, too! Old Solomon's the chap for we! See how he settled that argyment about the baby! And there was two ladies in that! Well, then? [*He looks inquiringly at Catherine, who shakes her head dubiously, but offers no further opposition. He feels in his pocket, produces a handful of coins, chooses one, and holds it up.*] Now, if 'a should turn up the old queen, then 'tis Cath'rine; but if 'tis the young lady with the pitchfork, then Caroline's the one. And up she goes. [*He spins the coin, but blunders in his attempt to catch it. It falls in a corner. He goes down on his hands and knees to recover it, while the sisters sit valiantly struggling to retain their composure.*] Well, I'm darned! [*He rises to his feet, holding out the halfpenny.*] If it had been a lime-ash floor, now!

CATHERINE. [*Faintly.*] What's wrong?

MR SAMPSON. Fell in a crack in the floor, my dear. Sticking there edge up, and no head to 'un, nor yet no tail. Old Solomon himself couldn' make nothing by 'un. But how come you to have a timber floor to your kitchen when mine's lime-ash?

CAROLINE. 'Twas father's doing when the houses were built. He always liked to take his boots off of a evening, and lime-ash is that cold-natured, 'tis apt to give 'e chilblains through your stockings.

MR SAMPSON. [*Sitting down.*] Well, to see how things do turn out!

CAROLINE. [*Solemnly.*] 'Twas ordained.

CATHERINE. [*With equal solemnity.*] A token, sure enough. And father's eyes upon us this very minute, I shouldn't wonder. Mr Sampson, I doubt 'tis all foolishness, and we'd best say no more about it.

MR SAMPSON. I don't see that. If your father didn' choose to wear slippers, that an't no lawful reason why I shouldn' get married if I want to. Must try some other way, that's all.
[*He ponders.*

CAROLINE. [*Timidly.*] If we should wait a bit, Mr Sampson keeping away from us meanwhile, p'raps his heart would speak.

MR SAMPSON. [*Dubiously.*] So 'a might; and then, agin, 'a mightn'. A mazy old organ, 'a b'lieve.

CATHERINE. Absence makes the heart grow fonder, so they say.

MR SAMPSON. That's very well; but how if 'a should make it

grow fonder of both of 'e? Where 'd us be then? But we 'll try if you like, though I fear 'tisn' much use. [*Rising.*] Queer state of things, to be sure! Like one of these mixed-up old yarns in the story-books. Some capital yarns in these story-books, though I 'm given to understand they 're mostly lies; and by what I can see——

CATHERINE. [*Stamping her foot.*] I 've no patience with 'e, drolling along with your story-books, when you ought to be down on your hands and knees, asking our pardon for bringing us to such a pass! A man of your age, and don't know how to make up his own mind! I 've no patience with 'e!

MR SAMPSON. [*Gazing at her admiringly.*] Ah! Some spirit there! You make me feel as if I was home again, living with my sister. She 's just such another. Many 's the time she 've lerruped me across the head with the rolling-pin when I wasn' quick enough about something to plaise her. And nobody ever made a better wife than she—twice over, too. I wonder now—— [*He continues to stare reflectively at Catherine, until, on Caroline making an involuntary movement, he transfers his gaze to her.*] Well, I don't know. Like to like, they say, and I 'm a quiet one myself. And so fur as looks do go . . . [*He looks from one to the other, scratching his head.*] Aw, I don't know. [*To Caroline.*] Well, marm, there an't nothing else for it that I can see, so we 'll try your plan. [*He goes to the door and pauses there.*] All the same, I can't help wishing I 'd been born a heathen Turk.

[*He goes out. The sisters remain sitting in silence. For the first time in their lives a veil of reserve is drawn between them, and each is obviously constrained and uncomfortable in the other's presence. Catherine is the first to stir.*

CATHERINE. [*Rising and speaking stiffly.*] Getting on for half-past four. Time to pitch baking.

CAROLINE. [*Rising and going on with her preparations.*] I 'll make a heavy cake, I reckon.

CATHERINE. [*Sniffing contemptuously.*] You can if you 've a mind to. I 've no opinion of your heavy cake, nor never had; you know that. But plaise yourself.

CAROLINE. [*Frightened, but holding her own.*] I 'll make one, a' b'lieve. [*She goes to the cupboard.*] Where 's the flour?

CATHERINE. In the basket, of course! Where else should 'a be? [*She picks up the basket, sets it on the table with a bang, and distributes the various parcels, some on the table, some in the*

cupboard.] There! Paddle away with your old heavy cake!
I'm going to see to the chickens.

[*She goes out by the side door.*

CAROLINE. [*Letting her hands fall suddenly in the midst of her preparations, and miserably appealing to the clock.*] Aw, grandf'er! What's up with sister, that she should spake so sharp to me? And what's up with me? I nearly answered her back! . . . Aw me! [*She continues her work listlessly.*] 'Twon't be much of a cake, I fear, grandf'er. I don't hardly know what I'm doing. . . . There! If I hadn' nearly forgot the eggs!

[*She goes out by the side door and returns immediately with a basket of eggs, one of which she breaks into a cup. As she is doing so, Catherine returns, casts a rapid glance at the table, and hardens into stone at the sight of the egg-basket.*

CATHERINE. [*In a tense whisper, pointing at the basket.*] You've been taking those Wyandotte eggs!

CAROLINE. [*After a horrified pause, faintly.*] S'posing I have!

CATHERINE. [*Raising her voice.*] You know very well I was going to set Toppy on those eggs to-day!

CAROLINE. [*Trembling, and clutching the table for support.*] S'posing I did!

CATHERINE. [*In a still higher key.*] Then how come you to take those eggs?

CAROLINE. I—I shall take what eggs I've a m-mind to—so there!

CATHERINE. [*On her top note, without any stops.*] A mean trick so 'tis to take my eggs what I'd been saving up for Toppy and she in her box this very minute as you do very well know wearing her heart and feathers out over the chaney nest-egg the poor fond little beauty! Of all the mean tricks, to take my eggs——

CAROLINE. [*With a wretchedly poor attempt at sarcasm.*] Aw, you and your bistly old eggs! [*She bursts into tears.*

CATHERINE. [*Running to her.*] Sister! Sister, dear! [*They embrace and mingle their tears.*] . . . To think of it! All these years with never a cross word, and now—— Aw, drat the man!

CAROLINE. [*Shocked.*] Sister!

CATHERINE. [*Revelling in her profanity.*] Drat the man, I say! I wish we'd never set eyes upon 'un. Sarve him right if we sent him about his business.

CAROLINE. Sister! When we've both as good as promised to

him! [*She sits down.*] Besides, he wouldn't go. He 's awful obstinate, for all his quiet ways.

CATHERINE. [*Viciously.*] A week's notice 'll settle him quick enough.

CAROLINE. Cath'rine, we couldn'! Good man—to be slighted by two in one day, and be turned out of house and home beside! We couldn'!

CATHERINE. [*Relenting.*] It do seem hard. But we can't go on like this, that 's plain.

CAROLINE. P'raps he 'll make up his mind after all.

CATHERINE. That 'ud be worse and worse. He can't choose but one of us; and then where 'll the other be? Tell me that.

CAROLINE. [*Drawing a long breath.*] Sister dear—I—I ben't in no partic'lar violence to get married.

CATHERINE. [*Sternly.*] Caroline Stevens, there 's the Bible 'pon the shelf. Lay your hand to 'un and say that agin if you can.

CAROLINE. [*Hiding her face in her hands.*] I—can't!

CATHERINE. No; and the same for me. And here we be the two of us careering around arter one man. At our age, too—'tis shameful! Two silly old women—that 's what *we* are!

CAROLINE. [*Shuddering.*] Aw, don't, sister!

CATHERINE. [*Relentlessly.*] Two—silly—old—women! But it shan't be so! Thanks be, I 've got some sense left in my brain, though my heart 's a caudle of foolishness. It shan't be so. The longer he stay, the worse 'twill be. How couldn' he make up his mind before he spoke? 'Twouldn' have happened so then.

CAROLINE. 'Twas forced upon him to speak.

CATHERINE. So 'twas. I mustn' be hard upon him. 'Twas Doom, I reckon; and better if Doom should keep to his battles and murders and sudden deaths, 'stead of coming and plaguing quiet dacent folk like we. Well, Doom shan't have it all his own way, nuther. There shan't be no jalous wife nor no sinful-thoughted sister-in-law in this locality.

CAROLINE. Sister! Such dreadful talk!

CATHERINE. 'Tis my duty to spake plain. There 's bound to be suffering come out of it, but anyhow we can choose to suffer respectable. Go he shall!

CAROLINE. [*At the window.*] Cath'rine! He 's coming back! And, aw, if I do live, he 've got gloves on!

CATHERINE. Gloves! Then he 've made up his mind already! But it 's too late now, and he shan't name no name, not if I can stop him. 'Twill be harder still if we know. [*Rapidly, in a low voice.*] Now, Caroline, you 're too soft for this job

*C 947

You leave him to me; don't say a word, and whatever you do, don't start crying. We've got to be hard, or we'll never get rid of him. Hoosh!

[*They brace themselves for the ordeal. The door opens, and Mr Sampson appears. His hands are encased in enormous black kid gloves; a substantial cabbage rose adorns the lapel of his coat; his face is one consistent solid smile.*

CATHERINE. [*With a rush.*] Mr Sampson, you'll kindly take a week's notice from to-day.

[*His smile slowly crumbles, and is as slowly replaced by an expression of ineffable astonishment. His eyes search the room for symptoms of universal disintegration. Caroline begins to whimper.*

MR SAMPSON. [*Feebly.*] I'm a dazy old bufflehead, I know; and I don't azackly seem to get to the rights o' this.

CATHERINE. [*Wildly.*] There an't no rights to it! (*Will* 'e stop snooling, sister!) 'Tis all as wrong as can be, and time to put an end to it. Nor you mustn' ask why, for we never can tell 'e. We're grieved to put 'e out in any way, and we're grieved to part with 'e; but go you must, and no questions asked.

MR SAMPSON. [*Collecting himself, and speaking with quiet dignity.*] If I ben't mistook, marm, there was words passed between us consarning matrimony.

CATHERINE. Foolish words. Foolisher words never were spoke. They've got to be took back.

MR SAMPSON. [*Continuing stolidly.*] If I ben't mistook, I was told to go away and make up my mind—or my heart, as you may say—if so be I could.

CATHERINE. It's too late. Say no more about it, and we'll be thankful to 'e all our lives.

MR SAMPSON. [*Glancing for corroboration first at his button-hole, then at his gloves.*] If I ben't mistook, I've now returned to say I've come to a conformable conclusion at last. I've come to say—with doo respect to the other lady, who's good enough for anybody—I've come to say I've pitched my ch'ice on the lady I should wish to commit matrimony with. And the name of that lady——

CATHERINE. [*Interrupting him, with her hands shielding her ears.*] Don't! You mustn'! You shan't! 'Tis hard enough already; don't go to make it harder. Whichever 'tis, her answer have got to be 'No.' An't that so, Caroline? [*Caroline assents speechlessly. Catherine continues in a softer tone.*] With best thanks all the same, and hoping you won't think too hardly of us, and never shall we think other than kindly of you, and proud we 'd have been, ayther one of us, if it hadn' been ordained otherwise, as you 'll mind we said to once when the ha'penny stood on edge, and—— Aw, *will* 'e go, and not stand staring there like a stuck pig!

MR SAMPSON. [*Stiffening his back.*] Very well, marm. [*He begins peeling off his gloves.*] I ben't one to force myself on nobody. [*Intent on the gloves.*] Nor I ben't going to state no grievances . . . nor ask no questions . . . nor mention no names. [*He rolls the gloves up in a ball.*

CATHERINE. [*Sniffing.*] You 'll spile 'em. Give 'em here.

[*She takes the gloves from him, smooths them out, lays them together, turns one neatly inside out over the other, and gives them back to him.*

MR SAMPSON. Thank 'e. Bought 'em for a funeral I didn' go to; never put 'em on till to-day. [*Putting them in his pocket.*] Queer how things do turn out. . . . Well, if I got to go, then the sooner the better. [*Taking the flower from his coat and laying it on the table.*] Meant for the lady of my ch'ice, not to mention no names. . . . The sooner the better; so I reckon I 'll be off now. [*Fumbling in his pocket.*] I can get a bed at the inn down yonder—capital beds at the inn, so I 'm told—and I 'll send up for my bits of things later on. [*Counting out some silver on the table.*] Three shillings—rent for this week and next, according to the law of the land.

CATHERINE. [*Quite overcome.*] Mr Sampson, we couldn't think of taking——

MR SAMPSON. [*Raising an implacable hand.*] *If* you plaise, marm, according to the law of the land, and not wishing to be beholden to nobody. And that 's about all, I think. [*At the door.*] Good-bye.

CATHERINE. Won't 'e shake hands before you go?

MR SAMPSON. No, I don't think so. 'Tis the Christian thing to do, I know; but there an't no mistake about it—I ought to have been born a heathen Turk.

[*He goes out. A miserable silence, broken at last by Caroline's wailing voice.*

CAROLINE. He 'll scorn us all his life!

CATHERINE. [*Valiantly defying her own misery.*] We 've done what 's right, so it don't matter what he think of us. *I* don't care, for one.

[*The discarded flower catches her eye. She takes it up and lifts it to her face.*

CAROLINE. [*Putting out her hand.*] Give it to me. I 'll take care of it.

CATHERINE. [*Whipping it behind her back.*] Meant for the lady of his ch'ice.　Maybe you think——

CAROLINE. I 've so much right as you to think——

> [*They confront each other with hostile looks. The crisis passes, with Caroline in a renewed fit of sobbing, with Catherine in resolute action.*

CATHERINE. It shan't be so! [*She goes to the fire and drops the flower in.*] And there 's a end to it all, and a proper end, too—dust and ashes.　And now, sister, crying won't help us, but work will, or so they say else.　Time to get on with the baking.　Come, bustle!

> [*The curtain falls as they silently set to work.*

IT'S THE POOR THAT 'ELPS THE POOR

HAROLD CHAPIN

This play was first produced at the Court Theatre, London, on 19th March 1913, with the following cast of characters:

MRS HARRIS	. . .	*Blanche Stanley*
MR HARRIS .	. . .	*Walter Hubert*
CHARLES KING	. . .	*. Allan Jeayes*
MRS PIPE .	. . .	*Armine Grace*
EMILY PIPE .	. . .	*Kathleen Russell*
WILLIE PIPE	. . .	*. R. Grassdorff*
MR PICKARD	. . .	*Sebastian Smith*
MRS MANLY .	. . .	*. Florence Harcourt*
KEITY	. . . .	*. Lisa Stecker*
ALFRED WRIGHT .	. .	*Vivian Gilbert*
WALTER WRIGHT .	. .	*. Sibley Hicks*
MRS HERBERTS	. . .	*Calypso Valetta*
TED .	. . . .	*Perceval Clark*

The fee for each and every representation of this play by amateurs is one guinea, payable in advance to Samuel French Ltd, 26 Southampton Street, Strand, London, W.C.2, or to their authorized agents. Upon payment of this fee a licence will be issued for the performance to take place. No performance may be given unless this licence has first been obtained.

IT'S THE POOR THAT 'ELPS THE POOR

SCENE. *A living-sleeping room off King Street, Camden Town. The furniture, of the 'Why-don't-you-marry-the-girl' hire-purchase variety, is comparatively new. The walls, covered with cheap but cheerful paper, harmonize with the flowered linoleum, which is only beginning to lose its decorated surface in the more trodden places. The door is left of centre. The fireplace with a small gas-stove standing out from it, down right. Against the wall opposite the fireplace is a rough—probably home-made—dresser. Against the back wall is a double bed, covered from end to end with a piece of green art serge. A small deal kitchen-table with a red-and-black cloth on it is left of centre. A cheap painted chest of drawers against wall between door and bed.*

An arm-chair of early Victorian pattern, and in second-hand condition, is above fire, rather far out into room to avoid the gas-stove. Below the stove is another chair—a kitchen elbow-chair of varnished wood. Two Windsor chairs stand one above the table and one at its left end with its back to the dresser. An assortment of cheap cups, saucers, etc., are on the dresser. A few pots and pans upon the gas-stove and in the hearth.

The curtain rises on an empty stage, but the heavy footsteps of a small procession are heard on the stairs. They hesitate outside, and a voice—a deep male voice—with the gruffness of a street-vendor, says, as the door remains a foot open :

THE VOICE (PICKARD). [*Off.*] You go in first, Kitty.

    [*Kitty enters. She is generally known as Mrs Harris. She is a fat matron of fifty-five with a red face and large neck. She is dressed heavily in black, with nodding plumes in her bonnet and twinkling jet (imitation) on her cape. She is followed by her husband, Harris, the eel-vendor. In weight he is her equal, but not in depth of mourning. He wears a dark 27s. 6d. suit, a black ready-made tie ; he carries a very hard bowler hat, the red imprint of which is indelibly marked upon his brow. Mr Pickard, who addressed Mrs Harris as 'Kitty,' stands back while they enter, and remains as door-holder for the rest of the procession, who are slowly climbing the stairs. Mr Harris follows his panting wife across to the hearth, and as she sits in the smaller arm-chair he sinks with a sigh of gratification into the larger one, and places his hat between his feet. Mrs Harris leans across and remonstrates with great solemnity.*

MRS HARRIS. I shouldn't take that chair if I was you, father.

MR HARRIS. [*Surprised.*] W'y not? [*Testing the strength of the spring by several sitting jumps.*] It 's all right.

MRS HARRIS. [*With reproach.*] It would be only decent to leave it for Mrs 'Erberts, pore sole!

MR HARRIS. [*Abashed.*] I wasn't thinkin'!

[*Lifts his hat and retreats to bed, where he sits.*

MRS HARRIS. [*More in sorrow than in anger.*] No, you never do.

[*The procession has continued, and an awkward young man, wearing large yellow boots, which contrast glaringly with the sombre garments of all the rest of the cortège, has entered. He is a typical coster: thirty years of age, slightly tanned and hardened, grey-eyed, with close-cropped fair hair and a curled fringe almost down to his eyes. He wears a cheap dark suit and a black tie over a dicky and turned-down collar, and a dark cap, which he forbears to take off. He is followed by Mrs Pipe, of the coal-shed, a little, puffing woman in black, who no sooner gets into the room than she collapses in a flood of tears into the chair above the table. A large, well-developed girl, entering behind her, looks at her impatiently.*

THE GIRL. Oh, chuck it, muvver! Wot 's the good of startin' again?

HER MOTHER. I can't 'elp it. Straight, I can't. It brings things into me 'ed. I 've lost five, an' I knows wot it means.

[*A boy of fifteen enters. He addresses the big girl with the air of one discussing a distant phenomenon.*

THE BOY. Muvver started again?

THE GIRL. [*Expressively.*] Not 'arf!

MRS HARRIS. [*Kindly but firmly, from her elbow-chair.*] If you can't control yourself, Mrs Pipe, it would be better if you went 'ome. You 'll only upset pore dear Mrs 'Erberts, pore sole!

THE GIRL. [*Shrugging hopelessly and regarding her weeping mother.*] That 's wot I tell 'er, Mrs 'Arris, but she 's such a one! There ain't no checking 'er.

HER MOTHER. [*Between sobs.*] It—brings—so much—back to me. [*Loudly.*] I 've buried five, Mrs 'Arris.

THE GIRL. [*Exasperated.*] Lor' love a duck! You 've got eight left!

> [*Mr Pickard has meanwhile tired of acting as door-keeper and entered the room. He now observes the empty arm-chair, and crosses to it. He sits in it as the mother's sobs cease. Mrs Harris leans forward and whispers. He says 'Eh?' She raises her voice.*

MRS HARRIS. It would be only decent to leave it for pore dear Mrs 'Erberts, pore sole.

> [*Mr Pickard rises and goes to the bed, where he sits next to Mr Harris.*

> [*There are now seven people in the room : Mrs Harris in the elbow-chair below fire ; Mr Harris on the bed ; on his left Mr Pickard, grizzly bearded and dressed in a shabby double-breasted blue serge suit, carrying a bowler, and sporting the inevitable black tie. He is a potato salesman. Mr King stands in front of the chest of drawers. The Pipe family are above the table. Emily, the big daughter, in her large black feathered hat and purple velveteen blouse, standing on the right of her diminutive mother, and Willy, the son, on her left. They have the unintentional air of threatening her. Eighth and ninth come Mrs Manley and her daughter aged eight, the widow and orphan of a deceased coster volunteer, who gave his life for his country and left his wife to live by doing half-days' charing for the wives of less patriotic mates. They are in magnificent and experienced mourning, especially the child, though hers is very small and short in the skirt for her. Mrs Manly escorts her down left of table, sits, and takes her on her knees.*

MRS MANLY. You 've got to be very good, Keity, and never not so much as open your mouth. [*Keity nods, big-eyed. Mrs Manly looks around, anxious to express herself.*] P'r'aps I 'adn't ought to 'a' brought 'er, but it would 'a' been crool 'ard to leave 'er be'ind.

MRS HARRIS. Of course.

MRS MANLY. [*Encouraged.*] You see, she 'asn't never been to a funeral, properly speaking. 'Er farver 'aving lost 'is life in Souf Africa an' 'er gran'farver 'aving been blown up an' pos'-mortemmed.

HARRIS. Benny 'Erberts 'ad a pos'-mortem on 'im, if it comes to that. It don't make no difference to the funeral.

MRS MANLY. [*With pride.*] Ah, but dad—'e was pos'-mortemmed proper.

[*Alfred and Walter Wright, brother costers of twenty-five or thereabouts, wearing the ubiquitous mourning garb, enter. Mrs Harris addresses them, rising.*

MRS HARRIS. Is she comin' up?

WALTER. [*Nodding.*] She asked us not to wait, but to come on up.

[*He moves to left corner above dresser, standing between Willy Pipe and the Manlys.*

MRS HARRIS. You drove slow.   [*Crosses to door slowly.*

ALFRED. [*Moving towards the large chair.*] There wasn't no 'urry. 'N' we 'ad to stop somewhere to break the luck.

PICKARD. [*Surprised.*] Wot luck?

MRS HARRIS. [*Severely.*] No one never goes straight 'ome after a funeral, 'Arry. Surely you knows that much?

PICKARD. [*Abashed.*] Of course, Kitty. I wasn't thinking.

EMILY PIPE. Take that cap o' yours off, Charlie King. Show some respeck for the living, if you can't show none for the dead with them brown boots o' yours.

KING. [*Guiltily.*] I 'adn't got no others.

EMILY. Couldn't you 'a' borrowed some?

KING. [*Mournfully.*] Not to wear.

[*Mrs Herberts appears outside the door. Mrs Harris bustles out to her and leads her in and across to the large arm-chair just as Alfred Wright has seated himself therein. He starts out of it guiltily, and finds refuge from Mrs Harris's glare on the bed to the right of the others.*

MRS HARRIS. [*Placing the chief mourner in the sacred chair.*] There, dearie. Now don't you worry about nothing. 'Ow pale you look! 'Ow do you feel?

MRS HERBERTS. Not ill. I——

[*She staves off approaching tears by wisely ceasing to speak, and leans back wearily. She is a fairly pretty girl of the coster type, not more than twenty-one or -two years of age, wearing a black blouse and skirt and a black hat with black feathers. Mrs Harris removes this and takes it to table.*

MRS HARRIS. [*In a businesslike tone.*] Willy, do you mind running out for a drop of something?

WILLY PIPE. [*Neither enthusiastically nor unwillingly.*] No.

MRS HARRIS. That 's a good boy! [*To Walter Wright.*] Reach me them jugs, will you, Walter? [*Walter obeys.*] 'Ere. [*She *gives Willy the smaller.*] A pint an'n'arf of stout. [*Gives the other.*] A quart of four-ale, and [*here she mysteriously produces a clean flask from her cash pocket under her dress and hands it over*] 'ere, a quartern of special Scotch. Now, can you manage?

WILLY. [*Pocketing the flask.*] Yes.

MRS HARRIS. That 's a good boy. 'Ere. [*Gives him money.*] Now look sharp.

[*Willy departs on his errand. Mrs Manly rises from her chair and proffers it.*

MRS MANLY. Sit 'ere, Mrs 'Arris.

MRS HARRIS. [*Complying.*] Thank you, Mrs Manly. [*To Mrs Pipe.*] You don't mind me sendin' Willy, I 'm sure, Mrs Pipe. 'E 's a good boy.

MRS PIPE. I only wishes as every mother 'ad as good a son. Some say girls is more haffectionate, but I 'm sure I ain't found them so, an' wot with eight living an' five I 've buried——

[*The completion of the sentence is deferred by a sharp blow in the ribs from Emily's elbow. Every one looks anxiously at Mrs Herberts, who seems not to have heard the remark.*

EMILY. [*Fiercely under her breath.*] Muvver!

MRS PIPE. [*Peevishly.*] Wot is it?

EMILY. Can't you be more tactful?

[*She indicates her meaning by a directive glance.*

MRS PIPE. [*Realizing her iniquity and accordingly offended with her daughter.*] You put your elbow right into me corsets, Emily; I believe you 've broke that bone I was a-tellin' you about only last night.

EMILY. Oh, shut up, muvver!

[*Mrs Herberts has taken out a handkerchief. The others watch her in silent apprehension. She merely blows her nose, however, and returns it to her bosom, when the silence in the room makes her look up to find all the others watching her. She smiles a little weakly, and speaks.*

MRS HERBERTS. You 're very good to see me 'ome. Ted 'll be most grateful to you all for looking after me so kind.

MRS HARRIS. [*With some pride.*] That 's nothing, dearie. We 'd 'a' done the same for any one.

ALFRED. [*From the bed.*] It 's the poor wot 'elps the poor.

MRS MANLY. [*Enthusiastically.*] That 's a true word. Ah, you 've got a lot to be thankful for, Mrs 'Erberts, dear! I only wish my poor Will could come 'ome and 'ear 'ow good every one 's been to me, same as your Ted can.

Mrs Herberts. Gawd knows 'ow I 'm going to tell 'im! 'E was that fond of the nipper; 'e fair idolized 'im!

Harris. 'E 'll get your letter——

Charles King. [*Quickly and with some heat.*] Not till 'is sentence is up, they don't——

Harris. [*Angrily.*] I know that, don't I? I 'm saying 'e 'll get it as soon as ever 'e comes aht.

Pickard. That 'll be a week from yesterday.

Walter. Do they let 'em out prompt?

King. [*With increased warmth.*] They jolly well 'ave to. Nice fing if they kept you after your time was up!

Emily. [*Scornfully, as she goes to chair below fire and sits.*] They could if they wanted to.

King. *They—could—not !* Fourteen days is fourteen days.

Mrs Manly. All for leavin' 'is barrer by the kerb w'ile 'e 'ad a drink with a friend!

Alfred. 'E shouldn't 'ave 'it the p'liceman.

Charles King. 'E did not 'it the p'liceman. 'E only pushed parst 'im, see? 'E 'd 'a' been summonsed for leavin' 'is barrer, anyway.

Mrs Pipe. There 's one law for the rich and another for the poor, that 's a fact.

Emily. Oh, shut up, muvver!

Walter. 'E oughtn't to 'a' got fourteen days just for shovin' a p'liceman.

Mrs Herberts. [*Simply.*] It was the same p'liceman wot 'e 'd 'ad trouble with before.

Pickard. [*From the bed.*] T't! Wot luck!

King. Ah! 'E 'ad a down on Ted; I saw 'im—'e was simply askin' 'im to 'it 'im. Fourteen days!

Harris. 'E 'ad the option.

King. [*Furiously.*] Wot 's the good o' the option to Ted? W'ere 's a pore bloke wot 's just bought a barrer-load o' plums to find forty bob an' costs?

Emily. Shut up, Ginger!

Mrs Harris. [*Oil on troubled waters.*] Don't get arguing *to-day*, Charlie, there 's a good boy.

> [*The door opens and Willy Pipe returns, a jug in each hand. He deposits them on the table, standing in Emily's old place, right of Mrs Pipe. He then produces the flask from his pocket, lays it beside them, then the change beside the flask. The company evince interest, but no enthusiasm. Mrs Harris rises and begins transplanting*

the stock of glasses and cups from the dresser to the table.

MRS HARRIS. That 's a good boy. T't! 'Ave I 'ad your chair all this time, Mrs Manly?

MRS MANLY. [*Regaining it.*] It don't——

WALTER WRIGHT. There 's some chairs just across the landing in Tom Adams's room.

MRS HARRIS. I 'm sure——   [*He wouldn't mind us, etc.*

WILLY PIPE. [*With a burst of goodness.*] I 'll fetch 'em. [*Goes out.*

MRS HARRIS. *Wot* a good boy 'e is!

MRS PIPE. They ses boys is more trouble, but if I was to 'ave fifty——

EMILY PIPE. Muvver!

MRS HARRIS. [*Presiding.*] Now. [*To Mrs Herberts.*] What do you fancy, my dear? A drop o' stout?

[*Mrs Herberts, taken off her guard, breaks into pitiful sobs and attempts to cover her face with her hands. Mrs Harris, officious but kindly, hurries round the table to her.*

MRS HARRIS. There, there, dearie! Don't give way like that. Wot ever is it?

[*It is some seconds before Mrs Herberts can control herself sufficiently to explain.*

MRS HERBERTS. Baby was that fond o' the smell o' a drop o' stout! Many 's the time me an' Ted 's let 'im 'ave a sniff at a glass—an' 'e used to laugh that pretty when the froth got up 'is nose. It used to make Ted laugh too, an' now—— Ow, Gawd!

[*And she leans against the edge of the chair-back and weeps unrestrainedly. The men look on in awkward sympathy. Mrs Pipe weeps silently. Mrs Manly sniffs, and the child looks on wide-eyed. Only Charlie King keeps his more human feelings in check by a glow of prejudice.*

CHARLES KING. I 'ope you never gave 'im none.

MRS HERBERTS. Ted wouldn't let me; 'e was that faddy about baby.

CHARLES KING. [*Warmly approving.*] Quite right. Why, it might 'ave started the taste in 'im!

MRS HERBERTS. [*Hopelessly.*] Wot does it matter wot it might 'ave done? 'E 's dead wiv all our faddin'.

CHARLES KING. [*Lacking the sense to stop, though realizing his blunder.*] Yes, but—you wouldn't like to fink——

EMILY PIPE. [*Rising and picking up Mrs Herbert's dropped*

handkerchief, and thereby interposing between her and King, who is roughly centre.] Shut up, Charlie King—arguing!
[*The return of Willy Pipe laden with two chairs breaks up the situation.*

MRS HARRIS. [*Who has returned to her task of pouring out at the table.*] There's a good boy. Now we can all sit down. Charlie——   [*Indicates the two jugs.*
CHARLES KING. 'Arf-an'-'arf, fanx.
        [*Takes glass and goes with it to foot of bed, where he sits.*
    [*Walter remains unseated, lounging against the dresser above table, left of Mrs Pipe. Mrs Manly, who has resumed her chair, takes her orphan daughter on her lap. Willy places one chair centre—that is, to right of table—and the other above table right of his mother. On this chair he himself sits, and produces from his pocket a bottle of ginger-beer.*
MRS HARRIS. [*Handing him a glass.*] Still Band of 'Ope, Willy?
        [*Willy does not deign to reply.*
MRS HARRIS. [*Knowing tastes, she only offers what will be accepted.*] Walter!
WALTER WRIGHT. Fanx.   [*Receives his drink.*
MRS HARRIS. [*Uncorking the flask.*] You'll take whisky, I know, 'Arry.   [*Pickard nods.*
MRS HARRIS. [*Pouring out some and adding water from dresser.*] Take Mr Pickard that, will you, Willy? [*To Harris.*] Farver?
MRS HERBERTS. Let me help.
    [*She rises and meets Willy, centre, where she takes his glass on to Mr Pickard, and returns to table for Harris's.*
MRS HARRIS. [*Protesting.*] No, no, dearie. You set still.
MRS HERBERTS. I'd rather be doing something.
        [*Takes Harris his glass.*
HARRIS. [*Raising it as he receives it.*] Thank you, my dear. Good luck!   [*The company is horrified.*
MRS HARRIS. Farver, I'm surprised at you!'
HARRIS. [*Surprised.*] I only said, 'Good luck!'
MRS HARRIS. [*Severely.*] I'd 'a' thought you'd 'a' 'ad more feeling!
HARRIS. [*Abashed, but defending himself.*] I meant—better luck next time.
MRS HARRIS. [*More in sorrow than in anger.*] I suppose it's no use, farver, for me to ask you to mind wot you're saying of.
MRS HERBERTS. [*Who has moved through this, quite unheeding it, and is now lifting a glass at the table.*] Is this for Alf?

MRS HARRIS. Yes; an' this 'ere is yours, dearie—you really ought to take a drop o' something.

MRS HERBERTS. All right.

[*She takes the two glasses, carries one to Alfred Wright on the far end of the bed, and goes with the other to below fire, where she sits. The large arm-chair is empty, and Emily Pipe is standing up, centre.*

MRS HERBERTS. [*Touching the arm-chair.*] Sit 'ere, Emily.

EMILY. It 's your chair.

MRS HERBERTS. I 'm quite comf'table w'ere I am. Do 'ave it.
[*Emily obeys.*

CHARLES KING. [*Rising from the foot of the bed with an inspiration.*] I know a toast is rarver out of place, but 'ere 's one as no one can't take exception to. [*With feeling.*] Absent friends!

[*The company is favourably impressed, and the glasses raised to a discreet chorus of muttered "Ear, 'ears!' and repetitions of the toast, Mrs Pipe trying to add something about 'An' may they soon——' but giving it up as the glass reaches her lips.*

MRS HERBERTS. [*After the others.*] Thank you, Charlie.

MRS HARRIS. [*Across the room.*] Finished your drop o' whisky, farver?
[*Harris nods.*

MRS HARRIS. [*Suggestively.*] Then don't you think——?

HARRIS. [*Suddenly understanding.*] Oh, ah! [*Rises and makes for the door, where he pauses.*] You was coming with me, Pickard, wasn't you?
[*Pickard rises.*

MRS HERBERTS. You 're not going, Mr 'Arris?

MRS HARRIS. 'E 's just got somefing 'e 's got to see to. 'E 'll come back, won't you, farver?

HARRIS. [*With surprising emphasis.*] Not 'arf! [*Goes out, followed by Pickard, who closes the door cautiously behind him.*
[*The orphan Manly suddenly tunes up.*

KEITY. Wot 's Mr 'Arris gone for, mummy?

MRS MANLY. 'Ush, Keity! I told you as 'ow——

KEITY. [*Still more loudly.*] 'E winked——

MRS MANLY. [*Shaking her severely.*] I told you to 'ush, miss!
[*The child is subdued.*

MRS PIPE. [*Making conversation in the pause that follows.*] It 's been a lovely day for it.

MRS HARRIS. I never see such weather! Not a drop o' rain since last Tuesday week—an' wot a Bank 'Oliday!

ALFRED. I could 'a' done wiv a drop o' rain, it lays the dust.

MRS HARRIS. [*To Mrs Herberts.*] We missed you, my dear. It was only just about four o'clock when I ses to farver, 'I wonder 'ow Ted 'Erberts's spending '*is* Bank 'Oliday, pore feller!'

MRS MANLY. Four o'clock?

MRS HARRIS. Yes, an'——

MRS MANLY. [*Greatly impressed.*] W'y, that was just w'en Benny died, wasn't it—four o'clock?

MRS HERBERTS. No.

MRS MANLY. [*Checked.*] I fought you said——

MRS HERBERTS. 'E was breaving when I went round to try an' find the doctor. That was nigh on five.

MRS MANLY. Well, 'e must 'a'——

[*There is a quick clatter of feet outside, and a young coster enters. He is well into the room before he realizes that there are many people round him. Then he stops, vaguely thrown out of his bearings by their presence. Mrs Herberts rises in surprise, as do the others without exception.*

MRS HERBERTS. Ted!

TED. [*Staring round.*] Wot——?

CHARLES KING. [*Recovering first from the general surprise.*] Ted, ol' man, wot O! Aht before yer time?

[*He attempts to seize Ted's hand.*

TED. Wot are you all doing 'ere?

MRS HARRIS. We 're a-keepin' of 'er company after the funeral.

TED. [*Understanding.*] He 's buried, then? [*A universal nod.*

TED. [*More impressed than grief-stricken.*] Buried, Gawd's truth! An' las' week 'e was as 'ealthy——

MRS HARRIS. [*Consolingly.*] 'E 'ad a cough, Ted.

TED. [*Furiously.*] 'Ad a cough? 'E died 'ungry! It was in the papers. The bloomin' 'Ome Sekeratery 'ad me let out bekos of it. They came an' told me in me cell—died o' negleck an' starvation! Coroner's verdick, 'lack o' nourishment.' Couldn't you do nothing for 'im, Lil?

MRS HERBERTS. Ted, I did all I could.

TED. 'N' 'e died 'ungry! Couldn't you feed 'im?

MRS HERBERTS. Ted, I 'adn't got nothin' in the place.

TED. Couldn't you get nothin'? Wouldn't nobody give you nothin'?

MRS HERBERTS. They was all away. It was Bank 'Oliday, Ted. I ran short.

TED. Ran short! Fine, ain't it? An' 'e died o' negleck!

MRS HARRIS. [*With some asperity.*] No, 'e didn't, Ted Herberts.
Death *haxcellerated* by negleck was the——
TED. 'Cellerated be damned! [*To his wife.*] Do you mean to say
as you 'adn't nothin'—nothin'? W'y—'adn't you bought
nothin' in?
MRS HERBERTS. 'Ow could I buy anything in, Ted? I 'adn't got
no money. I 'd pawned me bes' blouse 'n'——
TED. Wouldn't nobody lend you nothing?
MRS HERBERTS. [*With sweet reasonableness.*] They couldn't be
expected to keep on, Ted.
TED. Moi Gawd! [*To others fiercely.*] You let Benny die, you——
MRS HERBERTS. It was all through it being Bank 'Oliday, Ted,
an' every one that busy on Saturday. 'E 'ad 'is cough, Ted.
I didn't know w'ich way to turn, straight I didn't! Charlie
King, 'e lent me 'arf a crahn, but I got Benny's med'cin' 'n'
advice wi' that. I counted on Mrs 'Arris, an' she couldn't
oblige me.
TED. [*Turning on Mrs Harris.*] You——
MRS HERBERTS. Oh, but she 'ad before, Ted, straight she 'ad;
'n' she 's been that good ever since. So 's everybody. I 'm
sure the funeral must 'a' cost poun's an' poun's, an' Mr 'Arris
an' Mr Pickard an' Walter an' Alfred 'ave paid for it, every
penny.
TED. Paid for it! That 's good! Paid for 'is funeral! You
couldn't 'ave lent me the money to keep me out an' workin'
for 'im, could you? You couldn't lend Lil 'ere the money to
feed 'im while I was in prison? Call yourself pals! I don't.
MRS HARRIS. Thank you.
TED. Ah! 'Thank you!' When I come to your 'usband to
arsk 'im to lend me a thick 'un t'wards me fine, 'e laughed fit
to kill 'isself. Yus! An' ol' Pickard sed as 'ow fines didn't
ought to be paid.
CHARLES KING. I lent you ten bob.
TED. So you did, ol' pal, an' I 'ad it put away for me in prison
w'ile—— Oh, Gawd! if you 'd sent to the governor, Lil.
MRS HERBERTS. I didn't know w'ich way to turn, Ted, straight
I didn't. The plums wot you 'd bought went bad wiv keepin'
an'—— It took me all of a sudden——
MRS HARRIS. [*With some feeling.*] You ain't doin' no good
roundin' on the pore young thing like that, Ted 'Erberts.
You ought to be a-comfortin' of 'er, not——
TED. You mind your own business.
FEMININE CHORUS. Well!

TED. [*Generally.*] Yus! 'Well!' An' get outside my room, the 'ole blooming lot o' you!

MRS HARRIS. [*Rather finely.*] I 'm sure I 've no wish——

MRS PIPE. [*Rising.*] Thank you for your gratitude, Ted 'Erberts!

EMILY. Shut up, muvver!

CHARLES KING. [*Coming down left of Ted.*] Look 'ere, ol' Ted. [*His tone is one of brotherly remonstrance.*] I don't think as you ought to rahnd on them as 'as done all they could for you, an' spent good money on 'avin' the little chap buried, an' all.

TED. I know you 've done your best, ol' pal.

MRS PIPE. An' *we* 'aven't? Thank you!

CHARLES KING. [*Kindly.*] No one can't blame you for being upset.

> [*The scene is once more interrupted, this time by the entrance of Harris and Pickard, bearing between them a picture-frame of a couple of feet square, or thereabouts, wrapped in flimsy paper.*

HARRIS. [*Seeing the master of the house.*] Wot, Ted!

PICKARD. [*With similar cordiality.*] Out before your time?

TED. [*Not responding.*] Looks like it. Wot do you want?

HARRIS. We 've got something 'ere for you an' Mrs 'Erberts, Ted. We was going to—— [*He plucks off the paper, revealing a cheap enlargement of a photograph of an anaemic-looking infant some six to eight months old.*] There! Ain't it like 'im?
> [*His pride is great.*

> [*Mrs Herberts regards the photograph with intense admiration, of which an exclamation of 'Ow!' is the culminating point. Ted is only mystified by its sudden appearance.*

TED. W'ere d'you get it?

HARRIS. [*Proudly.*] We 'ad it done as a little surprise for you. We passed the 'at round among——

TED. [*Calmly and slowly.*] Moi Gawd! If this ain't the limit! You—— [*His rising passion suddenly finds vent in a whirl of the arm, with which he snatches the picture and flings it against the door.*] Take the bloody thing away!
> [*His wife gives a genuine cry of pain and reproach.*

MRS HERBERTS. Oh, Ted! Benny's photorarf! An' w'en they 've all been so kind to us!

> [*The reproach in her voice pulls him up strangely. He stares wildly about him. On every face is the expression of genuine commiseration—though not of appreciation of this outburst. They are all still and uncomfortable. He*

looks last at his wife; a sob chokes him; he puts out a hand to recover the picture, then changes his mind and flings himself on his knees with his face in his wife's lap, sobbing.   There is a chorus of pitying approval from the others, Mrs Harris being loud in expressing the general opinion that :

Any one might be'ave a bit queer wot 's been through all wot 'e 'as.

[*Which not only proves that it 's the poor who help the poor, but that they understand and can make allowances for each other's occasional bursts of ingratitude.*

CURTAIN

FOLLOWERS

A 'CRANFORD' SKETCH

HAROLD BRIGHOUSE

Mrs. Gaskell is an excellent author to steal from, but, though her novels are equally a possession of us all, a dramatic common or open space where every dramatist has rights, *Cranford* offers perhaps the least promising field for stage adaptation. The theatre is a terribly downright place, and the subtleties of the stage are the platitudes of life. It was, therefore, purely in an experimental spirit that I set out to see whether the fragile delicacy of *Cranford* could be translated with any measure of success into terms of the stage. I began by taking a story which very well might have been, and almost was, in *Cranford*, and I pretended that my little town was not Mrs Gaskell's 'Cranford,' but a neighbouring place rather like it. People read the result and said: 'But this is "Cranford"'—which was precisely what I dared to hope they might say. It seemed to hint success. But there remained the stage, the only test for any play. Books are their authors', but, in the making of a play, author, producer, actors, and audience must all collaborate, and it is wise, in addition, to engage a good fairy to watch over the birth of one's play. *Followers* happened to be lucky. Miss Irene Rooke is an actress of genius; that has been said before, but truth does not stale with repetition. Her performance in *Followers* was a thing of wistful beauty, and it is first to Miss Rooke's acting, and second to Mr Milton Rosmer's skilled producing, that I owe the success which this little play achieved on the stage.

H. B.

TO

IRENE ROOKE

Produced by Mr Milton Rosmer's Repertory Company, at the Princes' Theatre, Manchester, on Monday, 12th April 1915, with the following cast:

LUCINDA BAINES .	.	*Miss Irene Rooke*
HELEN MASTERS .	.	*Miss Dorothy Ripley*
SUSAN CROWTHER .	.	*Miss Evelyn Marthege*
COLONEL REDFERN	.	*Mr F. Randle Ayrton*

SCENE. *Miss Baines's parlour in Cranford, June* 1859

The Play produced by Mr Milton Rosmer

Later in the same year, 'Followers' was acted by Mr Milton Rosmer's Company at the Criterion Theatre, London.

Applications for permission to perform this play must be made to Samuel French Ltd, 26 Southampton Street, Strand, London, W.C.2, or to their authorized agents. The fee for each and every representation of the play by amateurs is one guinea. Upon payment of this fee a licence will be issued for the performance to take place. No performance may be given unless this licence has first been obtained.

FOLLOWERS

The scene is the parlour of Miss Lucinda Baines at Cranford, in June 1859. It is the room of an old maid of the period, over-crowded with fragile furniture, spattered with antimacassars and china. The room is filled with the bright light of a summer's morning. Bushes and green hedge are seen through the window, centre. The door is left.

Susan Crowther, a ruddy country girl of twenty-two, shows in Helen Masters, a young lady of the same age, in summer outdoor clothes.

SUSAN. Miss Baines says, will you please take a seat, Miss Masters, and she 'll be down in a minute.

HELEN. [*Not sitting.*] Susan, go at once and tell your mistress I shall be seriously offended if she has gone upstairs to change her cap on my account.

SUSAN. [*Severely.*] Miss Baines would not think of receiving a visitor without changing her cap, Miss Masters.

HELEN. I am not a visitor here, and, if I am, this is an early morning-call and——

SUSAN. [*Finally.*] Miss Baines is changing her cap and there 's an end of it. She won't be long.

HELEN. [*Defeated, sitting.*] Oh, I am sorry, but this was my only opportunity of seeing her. I return to London this afternoon

SUSAN. [*Awed.*] By the train, miss?

HELEN. [*Smiling.*] Yes.

SUSAN. You have more courage than I have.

HELEN. Tell me, Susan, your mistress keeps well?

SUSAN. She 's well enough. Will worry herself, you know. Solomon has been a great disappointment to her.

HELEN. Solomon? Who is Solomon?

SUSAN. Solomon is the cat. He had kittens, and the shock nearly sent Miss Baines to her bed.

HELEN. Oh, dear!

SUSAN. We still call her Solomon because she 's used to it, but things will never be the same again. Miss Baines feels that Solomon has deceived her.

D 947

HELEN. And you, Susan?

SUSAN. Oh, I am quite well. Miss—[*pausing awkwardly, then*] —Miss Masters!

HELEN. Yes. Nothing wrong?

SUSAN. No, but—Miss Masters—you are one the mistress listens to. She 's—there is one thing that sorely troubles me, and, if you would speak a word for me, I 'm sure——

HELEN. What is it, Susan?

SUSAN. Well, miss, when I came here ten years ago—straight from the charity school it was—Miss Baines said when she took me: 'Now, Susan, no followers,' she said, and I said: 'No, mem, never.' I passed my word when I was too young to know, and there 's many wouldn't keep it on that account, but——

HELEN. Do you want followers, Susan?

SUSAN. No, miss, I don't. Not followers. One follower at a time 's enough for any woman.

HELEN. You 've somebody in mind?

SUSAN. I 've seen James Brown look at me and I wouldn't say if it wasn't for my promise but that James——

HELEN. I see.

SUSAN. But I promised and I 'm not the one to break my word, only when I try to put it to the mistress it 's as if she saw it coming, and there 's something in her eye that stops me asking. And it 's not as if she never had a follower herself.

HELEN. [*Rising.*] Susan!

SUSAN. [*Defending herself.*] A body can't live ten years in Cranford without hearing that old story of Miss Baines and——

HELEN. Hush, Susan.

SUSAN. Well, it 's true, and, what 's more, he 's back from India now. I 've seen him.

HELEN. Mr Redfern is back?

SUSAN. You spoke his name, not I. Yes, he 's back.

HELEN. When?

SUSAN. I only know I was carrying the basket yesterday while Miss Baines bought the grocery in Mr Wilson's shop, and there was a gentleman inside when we went in, buying matches to light his cheroot——

HELEN. A cheroot in Cranford High Street!

SUSAN. Yes, miss, and he raised his hat to Miss Baines, and she gave a jump and held my arm hard, and just said: 'Mr Redfern'—gasping, like that—'Mr Redfern,' and went on giving her orders as if nothing had happened. She 's a brave

woman, though I say it that's her own servant. And, if she
had him once, why mayn't I have James Brown?
HELEN. I will see what I can do, Susan.

*Enter Lucinda. She is a fragile old maid of fifty, delicate in her
dress, with transparent complexion, grey clothes, and lace cap.*

LUCINDA. Helen!
HELEN. Dear Miss Baines. [*They kiss. Exit Susan.*] Pardon
this early call.
LUCINDA. You could not come too early, Helen. [*They sit.*
HELEN. This was my only chance. I arrived yesterday and
return to-day.
LUCINDA. Cranford will not see much of you now.
HELEN. Now!
LUCINDA. I have heard the great news, Helen. You are
betrothed.
HELEN. Yes, Miss Baines. [*Pause.*] You do not wish me joy.
LUCINDA. Child, I have always wished you every joy.
HELEN. I want you to know Harry, Miss Baines. He is here
with me, but I know no gentleman has entered your house as
long as I remember, yet I hoped you might make an exception
in my case.
LUCINDA. Helen, you are not asking me to receive your affianced
husband in this house?
HELEN. Forgive the recklessness of my desire. I have so great
a wish that Harry should see this room where you taught me
to work my samplers and to knit.
LUCINDA. I should take great pleasure in seeing him if I could
meet him out. Here, as you know, I have no apartment
suited for the entertainment of a gentleman. I should be in
agonies for the safety of my china. I was for long uneasy
about Solomon until I found that cats tread with the most
prudent delicacy. But men's movements are singularly lacking in grace.
HELEN. Harry is very gentle.
LUCINDA. Without doubt, my dear. But a man is so much
in the way in a house. He must himself feel out of
place.
HELEN. [*Smiling.*] Would you have them live in the stables?
LUCINDA. I make no rule for others, Helen. For myself, I am
quite decided.
HELEN. And for Susan too?
LUCINDA. Susan, my dear?

HELEN. Susan is in love, but she will not break the promise made to you.

LUCINDA. My dear, I said, 'No followers,' and I meant no followers. If Susan is in love she has her fortnightly evening, and I am broad-minded enough not to ask too closely with whom she walks to the Dorcas Meeting, but my kitchen is no place for Susan's sweetheart. Men of our own order speak habitually in voices too loud for a room, let alone one of Susan's class.

HELEN. [*Pleading.*] She finds it lonely, I am afraid.

LUCINDA. Susan has her work.

HELEN. Do you never feel lonely here in the dark winter-evenings?

LUCINDA. Lonely, child? I used to be afraid of loneliness, and once, when there had been some burglaries in Cranford, I did think how much safer I should have felt with a husband by my side. . . . Does it shock you to hear me talk of husbands?

HELEN. No, no. I try not to speak the word myself, because I know that one should not before the time, but it cannot really be immodest.

LUCINDA. Yes, I remember the time when I looked forward to being married as much as any one, but the person I once thought I might be married to went far away because I said 'No' when I didn't mean it, only he thought I did, and I don't know to this day why I did say 'No' when all of me was throbbing to say 'Yes.' Oh, Helen, Helen, be very happy with your Harry. Thank God *you* did not say 'No.'

HELEN. I hope I am a modest woman, Miss Baines. I said 'No' twice, but Harry asked three times, and at the third I thought it became me to yield.

LUCINDA. Mr Redfern asked but once and then he went away.

HELEN. Mr Redfern!

LUCINDA. That was his name. I did not mean to mention it. Pray forget I did so, Helen. Old memories are best forgotten.

HELEN. Mr Redfern. But . . . Miss Baines . . . there is still the future.

LUCINDA. No, there are ghosts of the past that are hard to lay, but for me there is no future. I have lived so long with my shadows that I should fear the light.

HELEN. Your shadows?

LUCINDA. Oh, you will not come to live in the shadow-world. There in the light your husband and your children are waiting and calling for you to come.

HELEN. You make me feel ashamed.

LUCINDA. Ashamed? Whatever for? Be proud of life and joy.

HELEN. I have so much. I want so much and you are contented with so little.

LUCINDA. I? Life is for the young, life and the golden day. For me, age and the shadows. Yes, Helen, I used to be afraid of loneliness. I used to weep because the days were long and the nights were longer still.

HELEN. And now?

LUCINDA. Now I have the children of my dreams. They are just like other people's children, Helen, only mine are all, all my own. They don't grow up. They don't grow big and clumsy. They are always small and neat, and beautiful and well-behaved. They come to me when I am alone, and then, you see, I am not alone. They sit upon those seats that I keep near the fire, so that in winter they can watch the glow—that is Mary's, and the little hassock there is John's—and their boots are never dirty, and they don't disturb the antimacassars, and their voices are soft and low. And in the night I have wakened with the clasp of their arms about my neck, and my darlings put up their little mouths to mine to be kissed just as I 've seen real babies do to real mothers.

HELEN. I wonder if it is better so.

LUCINDA. [With energy.] No, no. Never. Forget this, Helen. I have spoken things I did not mean to speak. Tell me more of your betrothal. Is your trousseau far advanced? You must have lavender from my garden. Lavender for one's dresses and rose-leaves for one's rooms. And I have both for you.

Enter Susan.

SUSAN. [Awkwardly.] Miss Baines.

LUCINDA. What is it, Susan?

SUSAN. There 's a gentleman at the door, and he is asking for you.

LUCINDA. A gentleman!

SUSAN. [Volubly.] Oh, Miss Baines, if you please, it 's the gentleman we saw yesterday in Mr Wilson's shop, only he is dressed grander still to-day. I told him you couldn't see him, but I might as well have talked at the wall of a house.

LUCINDA. [Pauses, then collects her courage.] I will see him, Susan, please.

SUSAN. [Staggered.] In here?

LUCINDA. Yes.

SUSAN. Save us, what goings-on!   *[Exit Susan.*

LUCINDA. Helen, stand by me. This is my hour of trial. Don't leave me, child.

HELEN. Not if you wish me to remain.

LUCINDA. My courage is not all I could desire. Thank God, you are here, Helen. It's a mercy you came and I changed my cap for you.

HELEN. You're looking splendid, dear; you have a colour.

LUCINDA. I am all of a twitter. Is my cap straight?

HELEN. You are perfect.

LUCINDA. Helen, what should I offer him? Do gentlemen take gooseberry wine? Do they drink tea in the morning? I don't know anything. I am so ignorant of men.

HELEN. He will not want anything but you.

    [Enter Susan, smirking, and Charles Redfern. Exit Susan without announcing. Redfern is a spare, soldierly figure of fifty-five, grey-haired, very brown, dressed carefully. He is shy, talking at one moment as if addressing a squad, then, remembering, is subdued for a time before resuming his usual commanding tone.

LUCINDA. *[Bowing.]* Mr Redfern.

REDFERN. *[Bowing.]* Colonel, madam, colonel, retired from the service of the East India Company.

LUCINDA. *[Introducing.]* Colonel Redfern. My goddaughter, Miss Masters.   *[They bow.*

REDFERN. Your servant, madam.

LUCINDA. Will you sit down, colonel? *[Redfern looks doubtfully.]* . . . er . . . That chair is stronger than it looks. I think you have no cause for apprehension.

REDFERN. *[Sitting.]* I thank you, madam.

    [It is a very low chair and his long legs make him acutely conscious of it.

LUCINDA. May I offer you refreshment, colonel? A little gooseberry wine, or——

REDFERN. I thank you, no. I do not like gooseberries.

    [He looks at Helen, resenting her presence. Pause.

LUCINDA. *[Embarassed but brave.]* You must find Cranford a dull place after your martial career, Colonel Redfern.

REDFERN. I find it very pleasant to be back in England.

LUCINDA. It is safer, I have no doubt. Did you find the Asiatics very fierce?

REDFERN. *[Glancing at Helen.]* I have not come here to talk about myself, Miss Baines.

LUCINDA. But yours has been an adventurous life. Surely——

REDFERN. Pardon me, madam, a soldier's tales are not for a lady's ear. My life is of less interest to you than yours is to me.

LUCINDA. Mine! But I——

REDFERN. [*Rising.*] Yes. That is what I have come to hear, and as Miss Masters is your goddaughter she must know all about you, and I fear it would only weary her to hear you telling me.

LUCINDA. I am sure Helen will not mind. I have nothing to tell.

HELEN. [*Rising.*] Yes, Colonel Redfern, I ought to leave you two old friends together.

LUCINDA. [*Rising, frightened.*] But, Helen! Colonel, your arrival interrupted us. Helen was telling me of her betrothal.

REDFERN. [*Bowing.*] I congratulate Miss Masters.

HELEN. Thank you, Colonel Redfern.

LUCINDA. Go on, Helen.

HELEN. Really, Miss Baines, there is nothing more to tell.

REDFERN. Ah! And so?

HELEN. May I have a word with Susan before I go?

LUCINDA. You are not going!

HELEN. I must.

LUCINDA. But——

HELEN. I will step in later on to say farewell. Good morning, Colonel Redfern.

REDFERN. [*Opening door and bowing.*] Good morning, Miss Masters, [*as she passes him*] and bless you for a sensible girl. [*Exit Helen. He turns from closing door and speaks commandingly.*] Now, Lucy.

LUCINDA. [*Faintly protesting.*] Colonel Redfern!

REDFERN. I remind you, Lucy, that my Christian name is Charles.

LUCINDA. I had not forgotten.

REDFERN. Nor the last time you called me by it, I warrant. This very room, wasn't it? I never had such a downfall in my life. In I came, found you alone, popped the question, and when you rapped out your 'No' I could have dropped through the floor for simple wonderment, I'd made so sure you were only waiting to be asked. I've taken some gruelling in my time, but I was never harder hit than on that day—how many?—twenty-five years ago?

LUCINDA. Twenty-five years, three months, ten days. It was March seventeenth, 1834.

REDFERN. Ah? So you 've not forgotten. No, nor I. Nor the way I cut and ran like a whipped dog with my tail between my legs—all the way to India as fast as sail and wind would carry me. And, do you know, Lucy, I 've been trying ever since the day I landed there to get home again. For twenty-five years I 've been trying. That 's why I never wrote. I always expected to be here myself as quickly as a letter. At first I couldn't get leave, and if I had I couldn't have paid my passage, and when I got leave I had fever, and when I recovered from the fever I 'd to go on active service—and when I was better from my wound——

LUCINDA. You were wounded!

REDFERN. A trifle that time, but it kept me there till the next affair, and so it 's gone on all these years till the Mutiny came, and I went through that without a scratch, and thought it time to send my papers in and make for home. And that 's the last word I 'll say about myself. Now, Lucy, what have you been doing?

LUCINDA. I? Living at home.

REDFERN. Do you know what home means to me? I used to hear the other fellows talk of home—mothers, sisters, sweethearts, wives, and children. Home meant something to us all. It meant Cranford to me.

LUCINDA. But you hadn't used to live in Cranford.

REDFERN. You did, and Cranford meant you. Lucy, don't you know why I have come home?

LUCINDA. Have you not reached the age for retirement?

REDFERN. Age? I am as young as on the day I went away. I 've come to ask you a question, Lucy. It 's the doubt that lay heavy on my mind the day I landed in India, and made me want to take the next ship home, and it 's not grown less since then. It 's this—suppose I hadn't listened to you, suppose I had asked again, would you still have told me 'No'?

LUCINDA. How can I tell what I should have said?

REDFERN. Come, Lucy, you had the date off pat. You 'd not forgotten that.

LUCINDA. It is all so many years ago.

REDFERN. You mean I am to let bygones be bygones.

LUCINDA. If you please, Colonel Redfern.

REDFERN. No, madam, I do not please. But I obey. The past is past—but there remains the future.

LUCINDA. Are you going to make your future home in Cranford, colonel?

REDFERN. I hope so, Lucy. I shall stay on at the 'George' until I 've looked round and then, I trust, anchorage.

LUCINDA. Then no doubt we shall have friends in common at whose houses we may chance to meet sometimes.

REDFERN. Other people's houses! You 're a cordial hostess, Lucy.

LUCINDA. Colonel Redfern, you have recalled the occasion when last you visited me. My father was already dead, and, since the day of your call, no gentleman has entered my house until to-day. Your coming here breaks all my rules.

REDFERN. Then I think it 's time you had a little male society.

LUCINDA. This is an old maid's house.

REDFERN. Old maid be hanged. I beg your pardon, Lucy. A soldier's bluntness. But I am seeing you now as I saw you then with your bonny face and those dear blue eyes with what I fancied was the love-light in them, though now I know that it was just the sunshine of your soul, and the smile that has made my fever-bed a thing of joy because I could lie still and think of you and—and—yes, madam, I will say it—the neatest ankle in the world peeping out below your petticoats. The Lord forgive me for recalling such a thing, but you wouldn't believe the comfort that ankle 's been to me in India.

LUCINDA. Colonel, hadn't you better rub your eyes?

REDFERN. Why, madam?

LUCINDA. To see me as I am.

REDFERN. I see no change. It might have been yesterday.

LUCINDA. You are laughing at me.

REDFERN. I do not laugh at my divinity.

LUCINDA. Then it is your pleasure, sir, to be gallant, and I suggest you find a better subject for your gallantry than a lean and wrinkled——

REDFERN. Lucy, have you a looking-glass?

LUCINDA. I see my wrinkles in it every day.

REDFERN. Your glass tells lies.

LUCINDA. Colonel, I am too old for compliments. May I ask you to state what is the object of your visit?

REDFERN. The object, madam? Upon my word, you are a little short.

LUCINDA. I find you, sir, a little long.

REDFERN. Very well, madam, I will be brief. It is not the custom of the Service to beat about the bush. I have an object, and the object is to ask you to be my wife. It 's the second time of asking, Lucy, and it 's a plaguy long time since

*D 947

the first, but that was not my fault. It 's the lady's privilege to change her mind. Won't you change yours?

LUCINDA. Yes, Charles, my mind is changed.

REDFERN. [*Approaching gladly.*] Lucy?

LUCINDA. [*Backing with hand up.*] You do not understand.

REDFERN. I understand that you have changed your mind, and——

LUCINDA. Charles, when I said 'No,' it was my lips that spoke. My mind, my heart were aching to say 'Yes'—five-and-twenty years ago. To-day I am all united when I answer 'No.'

REDFERN. Ah, but I 'll not take 'No' this time. I 'll ask and ask again until——

LUCINDA. Till what, Charles? Till I become a girl again? Your asking will not bring back my youth, nor yours.

REDFERN. Mine? Time does not matter if love keeps young.

LUCINDA. Has yours kept young?

REDFERN. It is young and fresh and strong as on the day I went away. It 's never flagged. It 's——

LUCINDA. And I will tell you why. Because you went away and had a great career in India. You put your love aside and filled your mind with other thoughts.

REDFERN. Not filled.

LUCINDA. Oh, sparing me a small recess, securely sealed, as I seal up my autumn plums. You took it out sometimes, that thought of me, to polish up and put it back in its recess until the next campaign was over and gave you leisure for another look. But I 'd no splendid wars to occupy my mind. I had no seal to put upon my love to keep it fresh. The pain was great until Time came to heal the open sore. Time put a halo round your love for me, but Time killed mine for you.

REDFERN. Lucy, it is not too late. Love doesn't die. It sleeps. Let me awaken yours to life.

LUCINDA. It has been too late for many years. Charles, I want you to understand. It is too late. I do not look for happiness. I have contentment.

REDFERN. And what have I?

LUCINDA. You have had your life, a full life, Charles, a man's life.

REDFERN. I have lived on hopes. I can't live on regrets.

LUCINDA. Change them to memories.

REDFERN. Of what?

LUCINDA. Of what? For you the years have brought a great career. For me catastrophe.

REDFERN. Then—then is there no hope for me, Lucy?

LUCINDA. None.

REDFERN. [*Moving towards door.*] In India, I have not known defeat.

LUCINDA. You are back in England now, colonel.

REDFERN. Colonel!

LUCINDA. [*Extending hand.*] Good-bye, Charles.

REDFERN. [*Taking it, appealingly.*] Lucy! [*She shakes her head.*] Good-bye.

> [*Exit Redfern. Lucy sits, opens the locket she wears on a chain round her neck and buries it against her face, kissing it.*
> *Enter Helen softly.*

HELEN. May I come in?

LUCINDA. [*Closing locket.*] Helen, did I disappoint you greatly when I said I could not receive your Harry?

HELEN. We both hoped very much that he might come.

LUCINDA. Helen, tell him from me that he may come, just once, if he will wipe his boots most carefully and sit there quietly in the centre of the room.

HELEN. Oh, thank you, Miss Baines. You can't tell how much pleasure you will give us both.

> [*Exit Helen. Miss Baines carefully straightens her anti-macassars. Susan knocks.*

LUCINDA. Come in.

> *Susan enters.*

SUSAN. [*Awed.*] Miss Baines!

LUCINDA. What is it, Susan?

SUSAN. The gentleman.

LUCINDA. Yes?

SUSAN. He gave me this. [*Showing sovereign.*] Am I to keep it, mem?

LUCINDA. Certainly, Susan.

SUSAN. He said it was for a new gown or—or a present for my sweetheart and—oh, miss, I do not want a gown, and I do so want a sweetheart and I don't care if it is forward to say it, for I do.

LUCINDA. You remember I said 'No followers,' Susan.

SUSAN. Yes, miss, I have not forgotten, nor likely to, neither.

LUCINDA. You are young, Susan.

SUSAN. Not me. I'm twenty-three in November.

LUCINDA. Yes, you 're young.

SUSAN. Too young for a sweetheart, miss?

LUCINDA. No, Susan. I did say you were to have no followers, but if you meet with a man you like and let me know, and I find on proper inquiry that he is respectable, I shall have no objection to his coming to see you once a week, if he will promise to move carefully in the kitchen and abstain from raising his voice.

SUSAN. [*Kneeling at Lucinda's feet.*] Oh, Miss Baines!

LUCINDA. [*Simply.*] God forbid that I should grieve any young hearts.

CURTAIN

A NIGHT AT AN INN

Lord Dunsany

DRAMATIS PERSONAE

A. E. Scott-Fortescue (*the Toff*),
   a dilapidated gentleman
William Jones (*Bill*)
Albert Thomas   } *Merchant Sailors*
Jacob Smith (*Sniggers*)
1st Priest of Klesh
2nd Priest of Klesh
3rd Priest of Klesh
Klesh

The curtain rises on a room in an inn

A NIGHT AT AN INN

Sniggers and Bill are talking, the Toff is reading a paper.
Albert sits a little apart.

SNIGGERS. What's his idea, I wonder?

BILL. I don't know.

SNIGGERS. And how much longer will he keep us here?

BILL. We've been here three days.

SNIGGERS. And 'aven't seen a soul.

BILL. And a pretty penny it cost us when he rented the pub.

SNIGGERS. 'Ow long did 'e rent the pub for?

BILL. You never know with him.

SNIGGERS. It's lonely enough.

BILL. 'Ow long did you rent the pub for, Toffy?

    [*The Toff continues to read a sporting paper; he takes no notice of what is said.*

SNIGGERS. 'E's *such* a toff.

BILL. Yet 'e's clever, no mistake.

SNIGGERS. Those clever ones are the beggars to make a muddle. Their plans are clever enough, but they don't work, and then they make a mess of things much worse than you or me.

BILL. Ah.

SNIGGERS. I don't like this place.

BILL. Why not?

SNIGGERS. I don't like the looks of it.

BILL. He's keeping us here because here those niggers can't find us. The three heathen priests what was looking for us so. But we want to go and sell our ruby soon.

ALBERT. There's no sense in it.

BILL. Why not, Albert?

ALBERT. Because I gave those black devils the slip in Hull.

BILL. You give 'em the slip, Albert?

ALBERT. The slip, all three of them. The fellows with the gold spots on their foreheads. I had the ruby then and I give them the slip in Hull.

BILL. How did you do it, Albert?

ALBERT. I had the ruby and they were following me. . . .

93

BILL. Who told them you had the ruby? You didn't show it?

ALBERT. No. . . . But they kind of know.

SNIGGERS. They kind of know, Albert?

ALBERT. Yes, they know if you 've got it. Well, they sort of mouched after me, and I tells a policeman, and he says, oh they were only three poor niggers and they wouldn't hurt me. Ugh! When I thought of what they did in Malta to poor old Jim.

BILL. Yes and to George in Bombay before we started.

SNIGGERS. Ugh!

BILL. Why didn't you give 'em in charge?

ALBERT. What about the ruby, Bill?

BILL. Ah!

ALBERT. Well, I did better than that. I walks up and down through Hull. I walks slow enough. And then I turns a corner and I runs. I never seen a corner but I turns it. But sometimes I let a corner pass just to fool them. I twists about like a hare. Then I sits down and waits. No priests.

SNIGGERS. What?

ALBERT. No heathen black devils with gold spots on their face. I give 'em the slip.

BILL. Well done, Albert.

SNIGGERS. [*After a sigh of content.*] Why didn't you tell us?

ALBERT. 'Cause 'e won't let you speak. 'E 's got 'is plans and 'e thinks we 're silly folk. Things must be done 'is way. And all the time I 've give 'em the slip. Might 'ave 'ad one o' them crooked knives in him before now but for me who give 'em the slip in Hull.

BILL. Well done, Albert.

SNIGGERS. Do you hear that, Toffy? Albert has give 'em the slip.

THE TOFF. Yes, I hear.

SNIGGERS. Well, what do you say to that?

THE TOFF. Oh . . . Well done, Albert.

ALBERT. And what a' you going to do?

THE TOFF. Going to wait.

ALBERT. Don't seem to know what 'e 's waiting for.

SNIGGERS. It 's a nasty place.

ALBERT. It 's getting silly, Bill. Our money's gone and we want to sell the ruby. Let 's get on to a town.

BILL. But 'e won't come.

ALBERT. Then we 'll leave him.

SNIGGERS. We 'll be all right if we keep away from Hull.

ALBERT. We 'll go to London.

BILL. But 'e must 'ave 'is share.

SNIGGERS. All right. Only let 's go. [*To the Toff.*] We 're going, do you hear? Give us the ruby.

THE TOFF. Certainly.

[*He gives them a ruby from his waistcoat pocket; it is the size of a small hen's egg.*

[*He goes on reading his paper.*

ALBERT. Come on, Sniggers.

[*Exeunt Albert and Sniggers.*

BILL. Good-bye, old man. We 'll give you your fair share, but there 's nothing to do here, no girls, no halls, and we must sell the ruby.

THE TOFF. I 'm not a fool, Bill.

BILL. No, no, of course not. Of course you ain't, and you 've helped us a lot. Good-bye. You 'll say good-bye.

THE TOFF. Oh, yes. Good-bye.

[*Still reads paper. Exit Bill.*

[*The Toff puts a revolver on the table beside him and goes on with his paper.*

SNIGGERS. [*Out of breath.*] We 've come back, Toffy.

THE TOFF. So you have.

ALBERT. Toffy—how did they get here?

THE TOFF. They walked, of course.

ALBERT. But it 's eighty miles.

SNIGGERS. Did you know they were here, Toffy?

THE TOFF. Expected them about now.

ALBERT. Eighty miles.

BILL. Toffy, old man—what are we to do?

THE TOFF. Ask Albert.

BILL. If they can do things like this there 's no one can save us but you, Toffy—I always knew you were a clever one. We won't be fools any more. We 'll obey you, Toffy.

THE TOFF. You 're brave enough and strong enough. There isn't many that would steal a ruby eye out of an idol's head, and such an idol as that was to look at, and on such a night. You 're brave enough, Bill. But you 're all three of you fools. Jim would have none of my plans and where 's Jim? And George. What did they do to him?

SNIGGERS. Don't, Toffy!

THE TOFF. Well, then, your strength is no use to you. You want cleverness; or they 'll have you the way that they had George and Jim.

ALL. Ugh!

THE TOFF. These black priests would follow you round the world in circles. Year after year, till they got their idol's eye. And if we died with it they 'd follow our grandchildren. That fool thinks he can escape men like that by running round three streets in the town of Hull.

ALBERT. God's truth, *you* 'aven't escaped them, because they 're *'ere.*

THE TOFF. So I supposed.

ALBERT. You *supposed?*

THE TOFF. Yes, I believe there's no announcement in the society papers. But I took this country seat especially to receive them. There's plenty of room if you dig, it is pleasantly situated, and, what is most important, it is in a very quiet neighbourhood. So I am at home to them this afternoon.

BILL. Well, you 're a deep one.

THE TOFF. And remember you 've only my wits between you and death, and don't put your futile plans against those of an educated gentleman.

ALBERT. If you 're a gentleman why don't you go about among gentlemen instead of the likes of us?

THE TOFF. Because I was too clever for them as I am too clever for you.

ALBERT. Too clever for them?

THE TOFF. I never lost a game of cards in my life.

BILL. You never lost a game!

THE TOFF. Not when there was money on it.

BILL. Well, well.

THE TOFF. Have a game of poker?

ALL. No, thanks.

THE TOFF. Then do as you 're told.

BILL. All right, Toffy.

SNIGGERS. I saw something just then. Hadn't we better draw the curtains?

THE TOFF. No.

SNIGGERS. What?

THE TOFF. Don't draw the curtains.

SNIGGERS. Oh, all right.

BILL. But, Toffy, they can see us. One doesn't let the enemy do that. I don't see why. . . .

THE TOFF. No, of course you don't.

BILL. Oh, all right, Toffy.   *[All begin to pull out revolvers.*

THE TOFF. [*Putting his own away.*] No revolvers, please.

ALBERT. Why not?

THE TOFF. Because I don't want any noise at my party. We might get guests that hadn't been invited. *Knives* are a different matter.

[*All draw knives. The Toff signs to them not to draw them yet. The Toff has already taken back his ruby.*

BILL. I think they're coming, Toffy.

THE TOFF. Not yet.

ALBERT. When will they come?

THE TOFF. When I am quite ready to receive them. Not before.

SNIGGERS. I should like to get this over.

THE TOFF. Should you? Then we'll have them now.

SNIGGERS. Now?

THE TOFF. Yes. Listen to me. You shall do as you see me do. You will all pretend to go out. I'll show you how. I've got the ruby. When they see me alone they will come for their idol's eye.

BILL. How can they tell like this which of us has it?

THE TOFF. I confess I don't know, but they seem to.

SNIGGERS. What will you do when they come in?

THE TOFF. I shall do nothing.

SNIGGERS. What?

THE TOFF. They will creep up behind me. Then my friends, Sniggers and Bill and Albert, who gave them the slip, will do what they can.

BILL. All right, Toffy. Trust us.

THE TOFF. If you're a little slow you will see enacted the cheerful spectacle that accompanied the demise of Jim.

SNIGGERS. Don't, Toffy. We'll be there all right.

THE TOFF. Very well. Now watch me.

[*He goes past the windows to the inner door right; he opens it inwards, and then under cover of the open door he slips down on his knees and closes it, remaining on the inside, appearing to have gone out. He signs to the others, who understand. Then he appears to re-enter in the same manner.*

THE TOFF. Now. I shall sit with my back to the door. You go out one by one so far as our friends can make out. Crouch very low, to be on the safe side. They mustn't see you through the window.

[*Bill makes his sham exit.*

THE TOFF. Remember, no revolvers. The police are, I believe, proverbially inquisitive.

[*The other two follow Bill. All three are now crouching inside the door right. The Toff puts the ruby beside him on the table. He lights a cigarette.*

[*The door in back opens so slowly that you can hardly say at what moment it began. The Toff picks up his paper.*

[*A Native of India wriggles along the floor ever so slowly, seeking cover from chairs. He moves left where the Toff is. The three sailors are right. Sniggers and Albert lean forward. Bill's arm keeps them back. An armchair had better conceal them from the Indian. The black Priest nears the Toff.*

[*Bill watches to see if any more are coming. Then he leaps forward alone (he has taken his boots off) and knives the Priest.*

[*The Priest tries to shout, but Bill's left hand is over his mouth.*

[*The Toff continues to read his sporting paper. He never looks round.*

BILL. [*Sotto voce.*] There's only one, Toffy. What shall we do?

THE TOFF. [*Without turning his head.*] Only one?

BILL. Yes.

THE TOFF. Wait a moment. Let me think. [*Still apparently absorbed in his paper.*] Ah, yes. You go back, Bill. We must attract another guest. Now are you ready?

BILL. Yes.

THE TOFF. All right. You shall now see my demise at my Yorkshire residence. You must receive guests for me. [*He leaps up in full view of the window, flings up both arms and falls on to the floor near the dead Priest.*] Now be ready.

[*His eyes close.*

[*There is a long pause. Again the door opens, very, very slowly. Another Priest creeps in. He has three golden spots upon his forehead. He looks round, then he creeps up to his companion and turns him over and looks inside each of his clenched hands. Then he looks at the recumbent Toff. Then he creeps towards him. Bill slips after him and knives him like the other, with his left hand over his mouth.*

BILL. [*Sotto voce.*] We've only got two, Toffy.

THE TOFF. Still another.

BILL. What 'll we do?

THE TOFF. [*Sitting up.*] Hum.

BILL. This is the best way, much.

THE TOFF. Out of the question. Never play the same game twice.

BILL. Why not, Toffy?

THE TOFF. Doesn't work if you do.

BILL. When?

THE TOFF. I have it, Albert. You will now walk into the room. I showed you how to do it.

ALBERT. Yes.

THE TOFF. Just run over here and have a fight at this window with these two men.

ALBERT. But they're——

THE TOFF. Yes, they're dead, my perspicuous Albert. But Bill and I are going to resuscitate them. Come on.

[*Bill picks up a body under the arms.*

THE TOFF. That's right, Bill. [*Does the same.*] Come and help us, Sniggers. [*Sniggers comes.*] Keep low, keep low. Wave their arms about, Sniggers. Don't show yourself. Now, Albert, over you go. Our Albert is slain. Back you get, Bill. Back, Sniggers. Still, Albert. Mustn't move when he comes. Not a muscle.

[*A face appears at the window and stays for some time. Then the door opens and looking craftily round the third Priest enters. He looks at his companions' bodies and turns round. He suspects something. He takes up one of the knives and with a knife in each hand he puts his back to the wall. He looks to the left and right.*

THE TOFF. Come on, Bill.

[*The Priest rushes to the door. The Toff knives the last Priest from behind.*

THE TOFF. A good day's work, my friends.

BILL. Well done, Toffy. Oh, you are a deep one.

ALBERT. A deep one if ever there was one.

SNIGGERS. There ain't any more, Bill, are there?

THR TOFF. No more in the world, my friend.

BILL. Ay, that's all there are. There were only three in the temple. Three priests and their beastly idol.

ALBERT. What is it worth, Toffy? Is it worth a thousand pounds?

THE TOFF. It's worth all they've got in the shop. Worth just whatever we like to ask for it.

ALBERT. Then we're millionaires now.

THE TOFF. Yes, and what is more important, we no longer have any heirs.

BILL. We 'll have to sell it now.

ALBERT. That won't be easy. It 's a pity it isn't small and we had half a dozen. Hadn't the idol any other on him?

BILL. No, he was green jade all over and only had this one eye. He had it in the middle of his forehead, and was a long sight uglier than anything else in the world.

SNIGGERS. I 'm sure we ought all to be very grateful to Toffy.

BILL. And indeed we ought.

ALBERT. If it hadn't 'ave been for him——

BILL. Yes, if it hadn't a' been for old Toffy.

SNIGGERS. He 's a deep one.

THE TOFF. Well, you see, I just have a knack of foreseeing things.

SNIGGERS. I should think you did.

BILL. Why I don't suppose anything happens that our Toff doesn't foresee. Does it, Toffy?

THE TOFF. Well, I don't think it does, Bill. I don't think it often does.

BILL. Life is no more than just a game of cards to our old Toff.

THE TOFF. Well, we 've taken these fellows' trick.

SNIGGERS. [*Going to the window.*] It wouldn't do for any one to see them.

THE TOFF. Oh, nobody will come this way. We 're all alone on a moor.

BILL. Where will we put them?

THE TOFF. Bury them in the cellar, but there 's no hurry.

BILL. And what then, Toffy?

THE TOFF. Why then we 'll go to London and upset the ruby business. We have really come through this job very nicely.

BILL. I think the first thing that we ought to do is to give a little supper to old Toffy. We 'll bury these fellows to-night.

ALBERT. Yes, let 's.

SNIGGERS. The very thing.

BILL. And we 'll all drink his health.

ALBERT. Good old Toffy.

SNIGGERS. He ought to have been a general or a premier.

[*They get bottles from cupboard, etc.*

THE TOFF. Well, we 've earned our bit of a supper.

[*They sit down.*

BILL. [*Glass in hand.*] Here 's to old Toffy who guessed everything.

ALBERT and SNIGGERS. Good old Toffy.

BILL. Toffy who saved our lives and made our fortunes.

ALBERT and SNIGGERS. Hear. Hear.

THE TOFF. And here's to Bill who saved me twice to-night.

BILL. Couldn't have done it but for your cleverness, Toffy.

SNIGGERS. Hear, hear. Hear, hear.

ALBERT. He foresees everything.

BILL. A speech, Toffy. A speech from our general.

ALL. Yes, a speech.

SNIGGERS. A speech.

THE TOFF. Well, get me some water. This whisky's too much for my head, and I must keep it clear till our friends are safe in the cellar.

BILL. Water. Yes, of course. Get him some water, Sniggers.

SNIGGERS. We don't use water here. Where shall I get it?

BILL. Outside in the garden.

[Exit Sniggers.

ALBERT. Here's to fortune. *[They all drink.*

BILL. Here's to Albert Thomas, Esquire. *[He drinks.*

THE TOFF. Albert Thomas, Esquire. *[He drinks.*

ALBERT. And William Jones, Esquire.

THE TOFF. William Jones, Esquire. *[The Toff and Albert drink.*
[Re-enter Sniggers terrified.

THE TOFF. Hullo, here's Jacob Smith, Esquire, J.P., *alias* Sniggers, back again.

SNIGGERS. Toffy, I've been a-thinking about my share in that ruby. I don't want it, Toffy, I don't want it.

THE TOFF. Nonsense, Sniggers, nonsense.

SNIGGERS. You shall have it, Toffy, you shall have it yourself, only say Sniggers has no share in this 'ere ruby. Say it Toffy, say it.

BILL. Want to turn informer, Sniggers?

SNIGGERS. No, no. Only I don't want the ruby, Toffy. . . .

THE TOFF. No more nonsense, Sniggers, we're all in together in this, if one hangs we all hang; but they won't outwit me. Besides, it's not a hanging affair, they had their knives.

SNIGGERS. Toffy, Toffy, I always treated you fair, Toffy. I was always one to say, give Toffy a chance. Take back my share, Toffy.

THE TOFF. What's the matter? What are you driving at?

SNIGGERS. Take it back, Toffy.

THE TOFF. Answer me, what are you up to?

SNIGGERS. I don't want my share any more.

BILL. Have you seen the police? *[Albert pulls out his knife.*

THE TOFF. No, no knives, Albert.

ALBERT. What then?

THE TOFF. The honest truth in open court, barring the ruby. We were attacked.

SNIGGERS. There's no police.

THE TOFF. Well, then, what's the matter?

BILL. Out with it.

SNIGGERS. I swear to God . . .

ALBERT. Well?

THE TOFF. Don't interrupt.

SNIGGERS. I swear I saw something *what I didn't like.*

THE TOFF. What you didn't like?

SNIGGERS. [*In tears.*] O Toffy, Toffy, take it back. Take my share. Say you take it.

THE TOFF. What has he seen?

> [*Dead silence only broken by Sniggers's sobs. Then stony steps are heard.*
> [*Enter a hideous Idol. It is blind and gropes its way. It gropes its way to the ruby and picks it up and screws it into a socket in the forehead.*
> [*Sniggers still weeps softly, the rest stare in horror. The Idol steps out, not groping. Its steps move off, then stop.*

THE TOFF. Oh, great heavens!

ALBERT. [*In a childish, plaintive voice.*] What is it, Toffy?

BILL. Albert, it is that obscene idol [*in a whisper*] come from India.

ALBERT. It is gone.

BILL. It has taken its eye.

SNIGGERS. We are saved.

A VOICE. [*off*] [*With outlandish accent.*] Meestaire William Jones, Able Seaman.

> [*The Toff has never spoken, never moved. He only gazes stupidly in horror.*

BILL. Albert, Albert, what is this?

> [*He rises and walks out. One moan is heard. Sniggers goes to the window. He falls back sickly.*

ALBERT. [*In a whisper.*] What has happened?

SNIGGERS. I have seen it. I have seen it, oh, I have seen it.

> [*He returns to table.*

THE TOFF. [*Laying his hand very gently on Sniggers's arm, speaking softly and winningly.*] What was it, Sniggers?

SNIGGERS. I have seen it.

ALBERT. What?

SNIGGERS. Oh!

VOICE. Meestaire Albert Thomas, Able Seaman.

ALBERT. Must I go, Toffy? Toffy, must I go?

SNIGGERS. [*Clutching him.*] Don't move.

ALBERT [*Going.*] Toffy, Toffy. [*Exit.*

VOICE. Meestaire Jacob Smith, Able Seaman.

SNIGGERS. I can't go, Toffy. I can't go. I can't do it.
[*He goes.*

VOICE. Meestaire Arnold Everett Scott-Fortescue, late Esquire, Able Seaman.

THE TOFF. I did not foresee it. [*Exit.*

CURTAIN

BIRDS OF A FEATHER

A Welsh Wayside Comedy

J. O. Francis

'And first concerning rivers; there be so many wonders re-
ported and written of them, and of the several creatures that be
bred and live in them, and those by authors of so good credit,
that we need not to deny them an historical faith.'—Izaak
Walton in *The Compleat Angler*.

The first performance of this play was given by the Welsh Society of the University of London, at the London School of Economics, on 2nd March 1923, with the following cast:

TWM TINKER . . .	*Emrys Lloyd-Davies*
DICKY BACH DWL	*Jack Davies*
JENKINS THE KEEPER . . .	*J. J. Jory*
THE BISHOP OF MID-WALES .	*Emrys Harries*

Produced by the Author

SCENE: *A roadside in rural Wales*
TIME: *About ten o'clock at night*

The play was also produced by Robert Atkins at the Coliseum, London, on 11th March 1929.

Welsh expressions in the play: *Twm*, Tom; *Dicky Bach Dwl*, Daft little Dicky; *Jawch*, the deuce; *Mawredd*, goodness; *Fach*, little, a term of endearment; *Darro*, dash it; *Iechyd da, iachi da*, good health; *Ach y fi*, an expression of disgust.

BIRDS OF A FEATHER

Throughout the play the stage directions are to be taken from the view-point of an audience.

The foreground of the stage is a country road. At the back are trees in summer foliage. Between the trees and the road is a low grassy bank which, half-way across the stage, is broken by a gap from which a pathway runs through the trees to the river near by. Moonlight is seen amidst the trees in the further parts of the stage. There is a wood fire in the foreground. To the right and to the left of the fire are boxes, both serving as seats. Near by is a third box, used as a store-table. On it are plates, knives, forks, a couple of tin drinking-mugs, packets of condiments, and a hurricane lamp. On the ground, near the fire, is another hurricane lamp; also, a frying-pan containing steak and onions. This part of the stage is lit by the two lamps and the glow of the fire.

The rise of the curtain shows Twm Tinker seated upon the box to the right, eating his supper with a plate balanced on his knees. Twm is a middle-aged man, weather-beaten and poorly clad. From his doleful examination of his empty cup, it is clear that his meal lacks drink. Putting down the cup with a sigh of resignation, he cleans his plate by wiping it round with a handful of grass from the bank and polishes it with some paper. Then, lighting his pipe, he settles down for an after-supper smoke.

Dicky Bach Dwl begins to sing on the road to the left.

Twm. Hullo, Dicky?
Dicky. [*Without.*] Hullo, Twm?
Twm. Got the beer?
Dicky. Yes.
Twm. Then hurry up, my boy, hurry up!

[*Dicky Bach Dwl comes in from the left, carrying a loaf of bread and a gallon jar. He is a young fellow dressed in ragged rustic clothing, with a battered soft hat set on his mop of unkempt hair. His facial expression shows a mind a little awry. There is, however, nothing unpleasant about him, but, rather, something pitiful and appealing.*

DICKY. [*Sniffing the air.*] Jawch, Twm, there's a grand smell on that steak and onions.

TWM. Your share is in the frying-pan. Hand over that jar, Dicky.

> [*Dicky puts the loaf with the other stores and gives the jar to Twm, who pours out a mugful of ale and drinks with large appreciation. Dicky holds the frying-pan over the fire, enjoying the odour.*

DICKY. A-a-h! H'm! Lovely! Have you set the night-lines, Twm?

TWM. Yes. [*With a gesture towards the back of the stage.*] They're tied to that willow tree at the bottom end o' the pool.

> [*A dog whimpers on the road to the right.*

DICKY. [*Concerned.*] There's the little bitch crying.

TWM. Yes. I put her in the cart out o' the way. If Jenkins the keeper or Powell the policeman should come along, it's best they don't see the dog.

DICKY. [*Consolingly, as if to a fellow-creature.*] Lie you still, Floss fach. It will be safer for us. [*The dog begins to bark happily, hearing his voice.*] Quiet! [*The dog stops at once.*] Where's the donkey?

TWM. I tethered him down by the bridge. Give him a call to be sure he's there.

DICKY. [*Calling on a special note.*] Ned-dy!

> [*The donkey brays a friendly reply from the right.*

TWM. Hark at him—yes, answering you back like a Christian in a pair of trousers. The understanding you've got for animals—well, boy, it's beyond me quite.

DICKY. [*Beginning to transfer the viands from the frying-pan to his plate*] Aay, and I've got a pretty tidy understanding for a bit o' steak and onions, too.

TWM. Here—steady, my lad! Take half and leave half.

DICKY. [*Reluctant.*] Leave?

TWM. Yes, just for safety. You know the character we've got for poaching. Well, if anybody dangerous comes along [*suiting the action to the word*] then I pop the frying-pan over the fire—like this—and here we are, Twm Tinker and Dicky Bach Dwl, a proper picture o' two law-abiding tinkers eating their bit of honest supper.

DICKY. [*Doubtful.*] Well, p'raps people would believe it. They might.

> [*The raucous note of a corn-crake is heard from the distance on the left.*

Twm. The old corn-crake there doesn't seem to think much of it either. Did you see Price when you fetched the beer?

Dicky. Yes. [*Producing a note.*] Oh! He asked me to give you this.

Twm. About that salmon, I expect. [*Reading by the light of one of the lamps.*] 'Castle Hotel, Pontewyn. Private and Confidential. Dear Twm Tinker, this is to let you know that everything is arranged now about the luncheon party that Mr Venerbey-Jones is giving to-morrow to the clergymen who are coming for the opening of the new schoolroom at St David's Church.' [*With a fierce air of grievance.*] Venerbey-Jones? I wish that bunch of parsons would give *him* a lunch—and begin by pouring half a pint o' prussic acid down the old devil's throat!

Dicky. Hear, hear, Twm! I've only got three ha'pence; but I'd pay it willing just to hold the bottle to his lips.

Twm. [*Reading again.*] 'The party will be given here in this hotel, so please don't forget that I am relying on you for a salmon and will pay you tenpence a pound for it. Sincerely yours, Robert Price.'

Dicky. Tenpence a pound? Jawch, Twm, there's money for you!

Twm. [*Putting the letter in his pocket.*] I'll keep this in case o' dispute. We promised him a salmon, Dicky, and a salmon he shall have. This pool of Venerbey-Jones's has always got the pick o' the river. [*Pointing away.*] Look, Dicky. There's banks of cloud coming up. Good! We shall have a bit o' dark for the water. The wind's gone round sou'-west.

[*There is a rustling in the trees.*

Dicky. Aay, sou'-west. D' you hear her? A grand wind she is, Twm—a dark old wind. Come on, wind. Send up the clouds. That's right—up and up, to shut the eyes o' the moon. Let's go to the river, Twm. I can't wait any longer.

Twm. Yes. We'd better get ready. Swaller down your vit'ls, Dicky.

Dicky. [*Hastily polishing off his supper.*] I'm swallering, Twm. I'm swallering. Have you got the things to make a torch?

Twm. Yes. I hid them behind this bank. [*Producing the articles.*] Stick, rag, paraffin oil. [*Producing a trident.*] And here's my spear.

Dicky. [*Suddenly tense.*] H'sh!

[*He bends forward listening.*

Twm. What is it?

DICKY. Footsteps.

TWM. Where?

DICKY. [*Pointing to the left.*] In the wood.   Twm, it 's Jenkins the keeper.

TWM. Him?   Mawredd Moses!   Let 's get these out o' sight. [*He hides the poaching implements.*] Tell the little bitch to lie still.

DICKY. Right.   [*He whistles a low warning note.*

TWM. Seems to me, Dicky, you can smell a keeper or a policeman a mile off.   Where 's that blessed frying-pan?   Ah! [*He picks up the frying-pan and sits down, holding it over the fire.*] Sit down, Dicky, and put on a look as mild as milk. [*Sitting peacefully by the fire, they compose their faces to an expression of seraphic virtue.*

DICKY. [*Whispering.*] Here he is.

TWM. [*Loudly.*] Yes, Dicky, you 're quite right.   Davies Ty Isha ought to have offered more than sixpence for mending that bucket. [*Jenkins the Keeper comes in from the left.   He is a stalwart, middle-aged man, dressed in clothes appropriate to his calling.*

TWM. [*With a start of pretended surprise.*] Oh, Jenkins the keeper!   Good evening, Jenkins.

DICKY. Good evening, *Mister* Jenkins.

TWM. [*Generally.*] Taking a stroll after supper?

JENKINS. I don't want any soft soap from you two.   What are you doing here, Twm Tinker?

TWM. Frying steak and onions.

JENKINS. Whose onions, I wonder?

TWM. [*Angrily.*] Whose onions?   My onions.   Dicky's onions. *Our* onions!

JENKINS. [*Sarcastically.*] Indeed!

TWM. What d' you mean, Jenkins!   What are you hinting at?

JENKINS. I 'm not hinting at anything.   What I 've got to say I 'm going to say straight out: I want to see you and this Dicky Bach Dwl off Mr Venerbey-Jones's land.

TWM. Who 's on Venerbey-Jones's land?

DICKY. Aay, who 's on it?

TWM. Is this the public road, or is it not?

JENKINS. Public road it may be; but the land on either side of it is Mr Venerbey-Jones's land.   The game on it is Mr Venerbey-Jones's game.

TWM. That 's as may be.

JENKINS. The fish for a mile and a half of that river are Mr Venerbey-Jones's fish.

TWM. So you say.

JENKINS. Yes, on this estate, fur, fin, and feather, everything is Mr Venerbey-Jones's. And don't you forget it.

TWM. I know what this means, Jenkins. That boss o' yours has been complaining that you haven't got enough pluck for your job.

JENKINS. What?

TWM. Oh, yes—I 've heard! So you 're beginning to stir things up by persecuting two peaceful, hardworking tinkers.

JENKINS. Yes, a bright pair of beauties you are. The police don't know one-tenth of the mischief you do—sleeping out in that cart like a lot of thieving gipsies.

TWM. [*Highly indignant.*] Gipsies? Gipsies, you say?

DICKY. Too bad, Twm. And you a Calvinistic Methodist, too.

JENKINS. In the workhouse you ought to be, you young vagabond.

DICKY. No. No walls for me—never.

JENKINS. And, as for you, Twm Tinker, your proper place is the County Gaol—and a great pleasure to me it will be to get you there.

TWM. You never will, Jenkins, though you 've been trying hard for twenty years.

JENKINS. I 'll have you one of these days—the pair of you. And now, before I go home, I want to see you off this estate.

TWM. We 'll move from this spot just when we like, Jenkins, and not a moment sooner.

DICKY. Not a moment, Twm.

TWM. If anybody had better be moving, it 's you, Jenkins, for fear I should happen to let fly with this frying-pan.

JENKINS. Well, remember: I 've told you.

TWM. Thank you for nothing, Jenkins. Good night and sweet repose to you.

JENKINS. Trash—rodneys—pah!

[*He goes away to the left.*

DICKY. [*Watching Jenkins go.*] If there 's one thing on earth worse than a weasel, it 's a keeper.

TWM. We promised a salmon to Price—Jenkins or no Jenkins.

DICKY. He said he was going home. H'sh! Yes—he 's walking back through the wood. Come on, Twm. Let 's chance it. I can't wait now. Don't you feel the old river drawing

you — aay, drawing and drawing? The moon's going,
Twm.

Twm. Very well, we 'll chance it. I 'll get the things out again.
   [*He produces the poaching tackle. The moonlight begins to
   fade into darkness as the clouds cover the sky.*

Dicky. [*Moving to and fro excitedly and laughing with delight.*]
Ha, ha, ha! So long, old Man in the Moon. Good-bye, you
little white stars. And, if you should happen to be peeping,
I hope you won't see anything short of a sixteen-pounder.
Ha, ha! Ho, ho!

Twm. [*Giving the things to Dicky.*] Here you are—stick, rag,
paraffin oil. Make yourself a torch.
   [*Twm practises a few movements with his spear, while Dicky
   improvises a torch by wrapping the rag around the end of
   the stick.*

Dicky. [*Pouring oil over the rag.*] Now the paraffin.

Twm. Got matches?

Dicky. [*Rattling a match-box.*] Yes, plenty.

Twm. Good.

Dicky. Ha, ha, ha! Spear and torch once again—aay, this is
the time when I 'm happy. Happy? Darro, Twm—I can't
tell you. It 's—it 's—oh, it 's like as if there 's a lot o' little
birds all singing inside me. [*Dancing a few steps.*] I can't keep
still—no, not I. [*Suddenly downcast.*] But, Twm—that talk
o' me being put in the workhouse—it comes over me something dreadful on times. If I was in the workhouse, Twm,
and somebody was to come to me on a night like this and
whisper the word 'salmons'—only just whisper it—O mawredd,
Twm, I think I 'd lie down and die broken-hearted!

Twm. Well, my lad, let 's hope we 're neither of us in jail before
to-morrow's breakfast. [*Moving towards the back of the stage.*]
Come along.

Dicky. [*Turning to the right.*] Wait. There 's somebody else
coming now.

Twm. Damn the people! Isn't a man ever to have peace to
get on with his business? [*Once again he puts the poaching
tackle into hiding.*] Where's that frying-pan? [*He resumes his
former position at the fire.*] Who is it this time, Dicky?

Dicky. [*Listening.*] I don't know that step. It 's a stranger.
[*He peers into the darkness.*] Aay, there he is. Jawch, Twm,
it 's a curate!

Twm. Curate?

Dicky. Aay, with a top hat and leggings on him.

TWM. Curate? At this time o' night? Any danger, I wonder? Sit down Dicky, and try to look as if it was Sunday.

[*They again assume the role of blameless tinkers cooking supper by the roadside. To meet the special occasion, Twm begins to hum a Welsh hymn-tune, with which he is but loosely acquainted. Dicky joins in.*

[*The Bishop of Mid-Wales comes in from the right, carrying a suit-case and trudging wearily. He is dressed in episcopal attire, his gaiters being stained with dust. He is a benign, white-haired old gentleman of a very friendly disposition. For a moment he pauses, blinking through and over his glasses in the manner of a very short-sighted person.*

BISHOP. What's this? Ah yes, thank heaven—humanity at last! Good evening, friends.

TWM. [*Non-committally.*] Good evening.

DICKY. [*Touching his forehead.*] Good evening, sir.

BISHOP. Can you tell me, please, if I am anywhere near the vicarage?

TWM. You mean Mr Owen Matthews's place?

BISHOP. No. Mr Lewis Pugh's.

TWM. Pugh? But that's in the next valley.

BISHOP. [*Horrified.*] What?

DICKY. Yes, sir—four miles away.

BISHOP. Four miles? Oh, dear, dear, dear! I can't do it.

DICKY. Lost your way you have, sir?

BISHOP. Yes. I reached Pontewyn on the last train, and I've been wandering about for over two hours. [*Mopping his brow.*] I'm quite worn out.

TWM. [*Putting down the frying-pan, assured that the Bishop is harmless.*] But didn't anybody meet you at the station?

BISHOP. No. You see I wrote to my friend Pugh. [*Producing a letter.*] But I've just found that I've had the letter in my pocket all the time.

[*The Bishop's sad plight and his obvious good nature begin to win over Twm and Dicky.*

DICKY. Twm, p'raps the gentleman would like to sit down?

TWM. Sit you down, mister, and welcome.

BISHOP. Thank you very much. I feel rather faint.

DICKY. [*Offering his box.*] Here you are, sir. Rest your poor feet. [*The Bishop sits down with a sigh of relief.*

BISHOP. [*Sniffing the air.*] I seem to—— Do I? Or do I not? Yes, a pleasant aroma.

DICKY. It's the frying-pan, sir—steak and onions.

BISHOP. [*In a spasm of desire.*] Steak and—did you say steak and onions? [*Sighing longingly.*] Oh, dear!

TWM. Two hours' walking, with that heavy bag? [*Suddenly magnanimous.*] Dicky, he must have what's left o' the steak and onions.

DICKY. [*Heartily.*] Aay, Twm, so he must.

BISHOP. [*In polite but feeble demand.*] No, really—er—no. I oughtn't to deprive you of——

TWM. That's all right, sir. We've had our supper. Dicky, pass that plate.

[*Dicky holds out a plate on to which Twm tips the contents of the frying-pan.*

DICKY. That's it, Twm, gravy an' all. [*Giving the plate to the Bishop.*] There you are, sir. Now, a chunk o' bread.

BISHOP. Thank you. I really am most grateful. The fact is I'm quite famished.

[*He begins to eat hungrily.*

DICKY. Would you like a nice drop o' beer, sir?

BISHOP. [*With an anticipatory smile.*] Beer?

TWM. [*Aside, doubtful as to their guest's views on total abstinence.*] Er—Dicky——

DICKY. That's all right, Twm. Church the gentleman is, not chapel.   [*He pours out a mugful of ale.*

BISHOP. Precisely! The older institution, the more catholic outlook, the more tolerant philosophy. [*Taking the mug from Dicky.*] Thank you, my boy. Well, iechyd da!

TWM and DICKY. Iachi da, sir.

BISHOP. [*Growing expansive.*] Ah—h'm—excellent! Yes, most refreshing. And now—may I ask your names, my good friends?

TWM. Twm Tinker I'm known as.

DICKY. And Dicky Bach Dwl they're calling me.

BISHOP. Dicky Bach D——? [*Catching Twm's informative gesture towards his head.*] Er—yes—quite so! Well, I shan't forget this little roadside party.

TWM. I wouldn't boast of it, mister, if I was you.

DICKY. No. You see, sir, we've got a bad name—somehow.

BISHOP. A bad name?

DICKY. Yes, for poaching.

TWM. [*Warningly.*] Er—h'm——

DICKY. Don't be afraid, Twm. You can tell from the gentleman's face there's a kind heart in him.

Twm. P'raps I ought to say one thing to you, sir, as man to man: it won't do you any good as a parson to be seen sitting here, chatting with me and Dicky.

Bishop. But I enjoy sitting here, chatting with you and Dicky.

Dicky. [*Surprised*] Enjoy it, sir?

Bishop. Yes. I must explain that I 've just come straight from a conference at Llandrindod.

Dicky. What do they do at a conf'rence, sir?

Bishop. [*With gloomy recollections.*] Make speeches, my boy— and usually long ones! Admirable people, of course; irreproachable people; people for whom I have the highest respect. But now, after four whole days with the saints, it 's quite a pleasant change to sit down and talk to a couple of sinners. [*Looking around.*] After the crowded conference, it 's rather strange to me to be here, just three of us alone.

Dicky. Alone, sir? Oh, no! We ain't alone.

Bishop. [*Peering here and there.*] Not alone? But——

Dicky. All round us, sir—they 're watching.

Bishop. Watching?

Dicky. Aay, eyes in the dark.

Bishop. Eyes in the dark? Dear me!

Dicky. There 's rabbits by the score.

Bishop. [*Beginning to grow interested.*] Yes, of course—the rabbits.

Dicky. [*With a shout.*] Hyp! B-r-r-r! Hop it, rabbits! [*With his low, chuckling laugh.*] Now, it 's tails up, sir, and they 're all scurrying off, as if the Day o' Judgment had come on 'em sudden.   [*A fox barks in the distance on the left.*]

Bishop. There 's a dog.

Dicky. Dog? That 's a fox.

Bishop. Really? A fox?

Dicky. Aay, slipping along the top edge o' that wood—and thinking hard, I expect, o' somebody's chickens.

Bishop. Eyes in the dark—I never thought of them before. [*Kindling.*] This isn't merely pleasant; it 's—it 's quite exciting.

[*The corn-crake is heard.*

Dicky. There 's that old corn-crake down on the marsh. Very often when he begins, there 's no hope o' stopping him.

Bishop. It reminds me of Llandrindod.

Dicky. On that slope, there 'll be a couple of hedgehogs nosing about for sure; and here, in this field o' corn, there 's the little squeaky fellers.

BISHOP. And who are the little squeaky fellows?

DICKY. The mice, o' course; and they 're nibbling, nibbling, nibbling. Aay, I 've got a great feeling for them little squeaky fellers. I 'm a bit of a nibbler myself.

[*An owl hoots near by.*

BISHOP. I know what that is: an owl.

DICKY. Yes. [*Calling loudly and clapping his hands.*] Look out, all you little fellows. There 's owls after you. I like to warn 'em, sir.

BISHOP. Quite right, my boy. [*Concerned and clapping his hands also.*] Look out there.

DICKY. Ach y fi, them old owls! They 're no better than Jenkins the keeper and Powell the policeman.

BISHOP. [*A lure beginning to grip him.*] Those watching eyes! The thought of them stirs me—yes, most strangely.

DICKY. [*Eager and joyous.*] Ha, ha, ha! You feel it, too? It 's the way o' the night, sir. It 's the wind and the dark getting hold of you.

BISHOP. [*Uneasy under his pleasure.*] Well, something 's getting hold of me; that 's certain.

DICKY. Ha, ha! Wait you, sir—just wait.

TWM. Curate or not, mister, take care how you listen to Dicky Bach Dwl. There 's times when he 'd make a gang o' poachers out of the Twelve Apostles themselves.

DICKY. Are you fond of a bit o' sport, sir?

BISHOP. Sport? Well, I was something of a sportsman up at Oxford.

[*Dicky goes to the Bishop. His silent, swift-footed motion is now, in itself, a fascination. He is a-quiver with an eager, joyous stealth, and his voice is low and seductive.*

DICKY. P'raps you 'd like a bit o' sport in the river to-night?

TWM. [*Aside, anxiously.*] Dicky, Dicky!

DICKY. But, Twm, don't you understand? He 's half one of us already. Listen, sir. I 'll just whisper. [*Into the Bishop's ear.*] Twm and me are going after a salmon.

BISHOP. A salmon?

DICKY. Yes, there in Venerbey-Jones's pool. [*Producing the spear and the torch.*] Here are the things. [*Offering the spear to the Bishop.*] Now, you take the spear.

BISHOP. But, my boy——

DICKY. It 's only pretending. Take it.

BISHOP. [*The old Adam waking in him, as he grasps the spear.*] What do I do with it?

DICKY. Suppose we 're going into the water.

BISHOP. [*His diocese forgotten.*] Right in? Dear me!

DICKY. There 's only the torch in the darkness and the big, big shadders all popping about. And you 're waiting—like this—h'sh!—as quiet as a stone. And then—there 's the salmon.

BISHOP. Yes, the salmon.

DICKY. Just you think of it, curate or not. Can't you picture his nose coming up towards the light?

BISHOP. His nose—yes! And then?

DICKY. Then you lift up the spear [*showing the movement*] slow and careful, like this.

BISHOP. [*Imitating the movement.*] Like this? I see. Well?

DICKY. [*Dropping his voice.*] Up he comes—nearer, nearer. Then you can see his back. It 's all shiny in the water. And you take your aim—just behind his head. [*Aloud.*] Now! [*With a swift stroke.*] Swish! Down comes the spear.

BISHOP. [*Again imitating.*] Swish!

DICKY. [*Making another illustrative movement.*] And then, with a twist, you throw him out on the bank.

BISHOP. [*With a similar movement.*] You throw him? So!

DICKY. Oh, there 's fun it is! Fun, sir? Aay, fit for the kings o' the world. You 'll come along?

BISHOP. I? Well, really, perhaps I——

DICKY. Yes, you must come, if it 's only to watch us.

BISHOP. Of course, if it 's only to watch—yes. The spear goes this way, you say? [*With the appropriate movement.*] Swish!

[*The corn-crake is heard again.*

BISHOP. [*Suddenly dashed.*] Ah—the voice of conscience and Llandrindod!

DICKY. You 're coming with us? You *are* coming?

BISHOP. No, Dicky, certainly not. [*He puts down the spear.*] How could you suggest such a thing? And to a clergyman of all people.

TWM. [*Judicially.*] Still, he pretty nearly had you, sir.

DICKY. Trying to show kindness I was. If you won't come after a salmon, sir—well, p'raps you 're fond of a feed o' trout?

BISHOP. Trout? Yes, a pleasant dish at breakfast.

DICKY. Twm, those night-lines—fast to the willows, you said? Wait you a minute, sir, if you like trout.

[*He hurries away through the trees at the back.*

TWM. A tidy little feller is Dicky, sir, though o' course, he 's counted a bit daft in the head.

BISHOP. Daft? And who amongst us shall say that he knows all the ways of God's wisdom? Poor Dicky! I like him—yes, very much.

TWM. He's terrible afraid o' being caught red-handed one o' these nights. There's talk o' putting him in the workhouse. [*Hesitating and uneasy.*] O' course, sir, after all he's told you, you know enough now to set the police on our track.

BISHOP. Don't be alarmed, my friend. I know enough to do that for people whose names would surprise you.

[*Dicky comes back, bringing a few trout.*

DICKY. Here you are, sir. Look at these trout. Beauties they are, sir—fresh off the hook. For you, sir. Take 'em.

BISHOP. I'm afraid they're stolen goods, Dicky.

DICKY. You won't take 'em, sir?

BISHOP. I'd—I'd—er—better not.

TWM. Don't you understand, Dicky? The gentleman is in the Church. Hand me them fish, Dicky. I'll find a good use for 'em.

[*He takes the trout and puts them in his pocket.*

DICKY. Excuse me offering 'em, sir. I thought p'raps you wouldn't be so religious on a week-night. Curate you are, sir, o' course?

BISHOP. Well, I was once.

DICKY. You was once? [*Sympathetically.*] Did they give you the chuck-out?

BISHOP. Not exactly, Dicky.

TWM. A vicar now, maybe?

BISHOP. I've been a vicar, too.

DICKY. Well, what are you *now*, sir?

BISHOP. At present I'm a bishop.

TWM and DICKY. [*Staggered.*] Eh? What?

DICKY. A bishop?

TWM. Well, I'll be d——

BISHOP. [*Hastily.*] H'm—er—yes. I'm the Bishop of Mid-Wales.

TWM. But a bishop can't go wandering about the roads like a stray cat. Why don't you go to Mr Venerbey-Jones's, sir? He's the big man in these parts.

BISHOP. Venerbey-Jones? I don't like him—a man of wrath. No. I'm going on to Mr Lewis Pugh's place. I thank you for all your kindness.

TWM. Oh, that's nothing! The road you want is the second after crossing the bridge down there.

BISHOP. Thank you. Well, my friends, good night to you both.

TWM and DICKY. Good night, sir.

[*The Bishop, carrying his bag, begins to move away.*

DICKY. And mind you don't fall into the river, sir.

BISHOP. If there's a river about, I shan't be surprised to find myself in it. Good night to you. Good night.

TWM and DICKY. Good night. [*The Bishop goes off on the right.*

DICKY. Mawredd, Twm, we've got something to tell 'em in the blacksmith shop to-morrow! What do they say for a bishop, Twm? Your Worship?

TWM. Even an ordinary mayor gets that much.

DICKY. I know what to call him.

TWM. What?

DICKY. His Holy Highness.

TWM. Very right and proper it sounds, too.

DICKY. [*Eagerly.*] And now, Twm, what about that salmon?

TWM. [*Taking up the spear and the torch, giving the latter to Dicky.*] Yes. Here's your torch. [*Looking to the right.*] What's that noise?

DICKY. Only His Holy Highness. He frightened the donkey.

TWM. I hope the old chap hasn't gone into the river. Now, Dicky.

DICKY. [*In great delight.*] Ha, ha, ha! Spear and torch and the river once again! [*Beginning to cut capers.*] Ha, ha! O darro, Twm—I feel I want to go there dancing.

TWM. Steady, my lad, steady. Come along.

[*They go off through the trees at the back, Dicky laughing to himself.*

[*There is a short pause.*

[*Jenkins the keeper comes in from the left, moving stealthily.*

JENKINS. [*Whispering, with a gesture to people without.*] H'sh! Stay there, all four of you. Don't show yourselves till I blow my whistle.

A VOICE. [*Without, in a whisper.*] Righto, Jenkins.

JENKINS. [*Advancing and noting the things near the fire.*] Ah! [*Returning to talk to his companions.*] They mean to come back here—and with fish or game, you can be sure. [*Suddenly crouching and looking to the right.*] H'sh! Who's that on the road? He—yes, he's carrying a bag. One of Twm Tinker's poaching pals, I've no doubt. I'll tackle this fellow myself. Get to your places.

[*There is a brief murmur without, then silence. Jenkins,*

*E 947

*bending low, moves round in the shadows to a position
from which he can pounce upon the newcomer.*
[*The Bishop comes in again from the right, and, struggling
along, loaded up with his bag and odd items of attire, he
makes a sorry spectacle. His clothes are wet; his collar
is limp and stained; his hat is gone. He has taken off his
coat and is carrying it on his arm. He has also removed
his gaiters, and a few inches of underpants are to be seen
above his old-fashioned grey socks.*
BISHOP. [*Muttering as he comes in.*] Dear, dear, dear! [*Aloud.*]
Excuse me. [*To himself.*] Gone!
JENKINS. [*Springing upon him.*] I 've got you, you rascal!
BISHOP. [*Startled and dropping his things.*] Oh! [*Struggling.*]
Let go! How dare you?
JENKINS. Let go, indeed? [*Tightening his grip.*] Not of your
sort—you thieving scoundrel!
BISHOP. Scoundrel? Thieving? I? [*Wriggling hard.*] I 've
never heard such a——
JENKINS. Keep still, I tell you.
BISHOP. I will *not* keep still.
JENKINS. Then I 'll make you. [*Striking him.*] Now!
BISHOP. [*Angry.*] A blow! Heavens above—a blow! [*He wrenches
himself free and faces Jenkins with fists raised in good boxing
style.*] Don't think I can't defend myself. I 'm not afraid of
any village hooligan—not I!
JENKINS. [*Trying to seize him again.*] You 've got to——
BISHOP. [*Beating him off.*] Ah! You would, would you? [*Ex-
changing blows, not without credit.*] Take that, you black-
guard—yes, and that. Don't think you can frighten me—
just because I 'm a clergyman.
JENKINS. [*With a shout of surprise.*] What? [*Drawing back.*]
Clergyman? Did you say 'clergyman'?
BISHOP. Yes, clergyman. Can't you see? No, perhaps you
can't. I fell into the river. But here—look at my collar.
JENKINS. Yes—your collar; your way of speaking, too——
BISHOP. And who are you to dare to carry on in this fashion?
What 's your name?
JENKINS. Jenkins. I 'm head keeper to Mr Venerbey-Jones.
BISHOP. [*Snorting.*] Oh—him?
JENKINS. A clergyman? Well, well, well! [*Still a little suspicious.*]
But what are you doing in such a state——
BISHOP. [*Sharply.*] State?
JENKINS. And at this time of night, too?

BISHOP. [*Who thoroughly dislikes Jenkins now.*] That's no business of yours, my man.

JENKINS. P'raps not. Well, I'd better move along. I'm sorry for laying hands on you, sir.

BISHOP. [*Preening himself a little.*] You got as good as you gave, I think.

JENKINS. Good night, sir.

BISHOP. [*Curtly.*] Good night. [*Jenkins goes away on the left.*
[*The Bishop shakes the water from his coat and puts it on. He sets his gaiters by the fire to dry. Opening his bag, he takes out his night-shirt, which is soaking wet, wrings it and spreads it upon one of the boxes by the fire. As he begins to recover from his ducking and from the exertion of his fisticuffs, his native cheerfulness comes back to him.*
[*A breeze stirs the leafage. He listens with a smile of pleasure. An owl hoots near by.*

BISHOP. [*Clapping his hands and shouting.*] Look out, you little fellows! [*Smiling and murmuring to himself.*] Poor Dicky! Where are—— [*Turning towards the trees.*] Yes, I suppose so —the river. [*Recalling the allurement of Dicky's talk, he stirs uneasily.*] How does it—— [*He raises his hand and brings it down in the movement of spearing.*] Swish! [*A smile flits over his face and he sighs—enviously.*] Ah well! [*He gets up and paces to and fro, fighting down the subversive appeal.*] I? No, no, no—NO! [*His pace slackens and he pauses to peer through the trees.*] Still, just to watch—— [*With another movement.*] Swish! [*The corn-crake sounds its note.*
[*Starting violently.*] No, certainly not—not for a moment!
[*He falls to pacing to and fro again.*
[*Dicky and Twm come back. Dicky carries a large salmon. Twm has the spear and the Bishop's hat, which he has recovered from the river. For a moment the newcomers do not see the Bishop, whose march of self-conquest has carried him into a patch of shadow. Dicky reaches a position near the fire before the Bishop is aware of their return.*

BISHOP. [*Delighted.*] Ah—my hat!

DICKY. [*Frightened.*] Oh! [*He drops the salmon near the fire.*

TWM. [*Promptly getting rid of the spear.*] Darro!

DICKY. [*Relieved.*] It's only His Holy Highness.

BISHOP. I'm sorry to trouble you again, but I walked into the water. [*Noticing the salmon.*] What's this, Dicky? Still more fish?

DICKY. [*Smiling and at ease.*] Well, you see, sir—we'd had an offer of—— [*Starting in alarm.*] Twm?

TWM. Well?

DICKY. Over there—it's Jenkins the keeper.

TWM. Jenkins?

BISHOP. [*Annoyed.*] That fellow again?

DICKY. And there's a man in that gateway. It's Powell the policeman.

TWM. Somebody behind us, too, Dicky—we're surrounded.

DICKY. I'll pick up the salmon.

TWM. [*Stopping him.*] No. P'raps they haven't seen it yet.

DICKY. What shall we do?

TWM. I don't know.

DICKY. They're moving. Yes—there's Jenkins.

BISHOP. I detest that man.

TWM. Blazes, Dicky—here's my pocket full o' trout!

BISHOP. T-t-t!

TWM. Yes, and Price's letter on me somewhere.

DICKY. They're closing in on us.

TWM. It's jail for me, boy; workhouse for you.

DICKY. Workhouse? Oh, no, no, no! [*To the Bishop.*] Can't you help us?

BISHOP. I?

DICKY. Oh, sir, them walls all round!

BISHOP. [*In sudden resolve.*] One moment! The evidence against you is this fish?

DICKY. Yes.

BISHOP. [*Going to the box near the fish.*] If you have sinned with your hands, I've sinned also in my heart; so I may as well see this through.

TWM. What are you going to do?

BISHOP. Suppress the evidence! Now. [*Suiting his action to his words.*] If I sit down and take my night-shirt—so.

DICKY. Well?

BISHOP. I can hold it to the fire—so.

DICKY. Well?

BISHOP. And drop it on to the fish—so.

TWM. And then?

BISHOP. Then I wrap it round the fish—so.

TWM. [*Joyfully.*] Dicky!

BISHOP. And I put the lot in my bag—so.

[*He locks salmon and night-shirt in his bag.*

DICKY. Safe in his bag—well, I'll be blowed!

BISHOP. No keeper would dare to search a bishop.

TWM. [*In a whisper.*] Here's Jenkins. [*Aloud.*] Yes, sir, we'll take you up to Mr Lewis Pugh's place with pleasure. With pleasure, sir.

[*Jenkins comes in from the left.*

BISHOP. So *you*'re here again, are you?

JENKINS. What were you doing in the river just now, Twm Tinker?

TWM. [*For a moment at a loss.*] The river?

JENKINS. Yes. You had a light there. What were you doing?

TWM. [*Holding out the Bishop's hat as an answer comes.*] Fetching this gentleman's hat.

JENKINS. Hat? [*To the Bishop.*] Did you lose your hat?

BISHOP. I certainly did lose my hat.

JENKINS. Don't think, Twm Tinker, that you can put me off with a tale of a hat. [*To the Bishop.*] So you're a friend of this pair, after all? Yes, a fine sort of clergyman, I'll be bound. We'll take charge of the lot of you.

[*He raises his whistle to his lips.*

BISHOP. If you blow that whistle, you'll regret it.

JENKINS. Regret it? Shall I, indeed? And who are you, I'd like to know?

DICKY. [*Sonorously.*] His Holy Highness, the Bishop of Mid-Wales.

JENKINS. [*Taken aback.*] Bishop?

BISHOP. Precisely! If you doubt it, let me see what I have in my pockets. [*Producing envelopes.*] Look at these. They're addressed to me.

JENKINS. [*Reading.*] 'The Right Reverend the Lord Bishop of Mid-Wales.'

DICKY. [*Aside.*] Mawredd, Twm—a lord!

JENKINS. [*Forced to acceptance.*] So you really *are* a bishop?

BISHOP. [*Taking back the envelopes.*] I know your employer. In fact, one of these letters is an invitation from him to a luncheon to-morrow.

DICKY. What? Ha, ha, ha! Twm, it's the Castle Hotel. From what I hear said, they're buying a grand big salmon for that party. [*To Twm, aside, looking towards the bag.*] Twm, ha, ha, ha! The salmon!

BISHOP. I dare say you'll be glad to earn an honest shilling, Dicky. [*Significantly.*] Take charge of my bag, will you?

DICKY. Take charge? [*Gleefully seizing the bag.*] Oh, yes, I'll take charge of the bag!

TWM. [*Picking up the lamps.*] Our things will be safe enough till we come back, Dicky. Now, my lord, we 'll have the donkey harnessed up in half a jiffy; and then, my lord, we 'll drive you over to Mr Lewis Pugh's, my lord.

BISHOP. Thank you, Twm. [*Coldly.*] Good night, keeper.

JENKINS. [*Sullenly, helpless though still a little suspicious.*] Good night.

DICKY. [*With sly malice.*] Good night, *Mister* Jenkins.

TWM. Good night, Jenkins. And, in the way o' kindness, let me tell you this: you 're one o' those that 's up and doing a bit too soon.   [*He moves off to the right.*

BISHOP. [*Following Twm.*] Yes, too soon, my good man—too soon!

[*The corn-crake is heard on a violent note.*

BISHOP. [*Pausing, with a wave of the hand.*] Too late, my good bird—too late!

[*Twm, the Bishop, and Dicky go out on the right.*

THE CURTAIN FALLS

THE SPELL

Mary Kelly

The first performance of this play was given at the Village Drama Society's Drama School at Wells, Somerset, in 1928, *with the following cast:*

AN OLD WIDOW WOMAN, very poor . *Elizabeth Ramsden*

HER DAUGHTER . . . . . *Rhona Wingfield*

The play is written in the dialect of North Devon, but may be given in any other rural dialect.

SCENE. *The kitchen living-room of a very poor cottage in a lonely moorland part of North Devon. Door up centre. An open hearth, on which a peat fire is burning, left. A plain wooden table with a chair beside it, right. On the upper side of the fire is an old wooden grandfather chair, in which an old woman is crouching, muttering to herself over something hidden in her lap. There is no light in the room but the subdued glow of the fire.*

THE SPELL

There is a second's pause after the curtain rises. Then the door opens, and a younger woman enters, in a weary, dispirited manner. She is carrying a lantern, which she puts on the table.

YOUNG WOMAN. 'Er 've a-gone.

OLD WOMAN. [*Lookin up.*] The cow?

YOUNG WOMAN. Ees . . . 'er 've gone dade.

OLD WOMAN. Was the calf living?

YOUNG WOMAN. 'Twas born dade.

OLD WOMAN. There idn' nort left now.

YOUNG WOMAN. [*Suddenly roused.*] 'Tis terr'ble, mother, 'tis terr'ble! What shall us do? . . . If us was rich vokes 'twouldn' matter so much; us could lose a cow, and the pegs, and the chicken, and us 'd still have some'in left . . . but there idn' nothen, nothen. . . .
    [*She flings herself down on the chair with her arms on the table, and gives way to her grief.*]

OLD WOMAN. No, there idn' nothen left, to be sure. [*A short silence, broken only by the younger woman's sobs.*] But there idn' no use in carryin' on like that there—that won't call the bastes back. . . . There 's some'in that must be *done!*

YOUNG WOMAN. You 'm talking silly, mother, there idn' nort that us can do . . . us can't make they live again.

OLD WOMAN. No, us can't make they live again, for sure. . . . Lookee, my dear, what have all this yer trouble come upon us for?

YOUNG WOMAN. [*Sullenly.*] 'Tis the will of the Lord, I sim.

OLD WOMAN. Ah, you 'm wrong there—tidn' the Lord! Us have a-been to chapel regular forty year, and us haven't never done nort to be 'shamed of. He wouldn' a-laid His hand upon us like this yer. . . . No, 'tidn' the Lord, 'tidn' the Lord!

YOUNG WOMAN. Who be it then?

OLD WOMAN. Ah, who be it? [*With sudden fierceness.*] I tell 'ee, 'tis the Devil, and he hath his servants in this yer parish, same as the Lord!

YOUNG WOMAN. What do 'ee mane?

OLD WOMAN. What day did they pegs die?

127

YOUNG WOMAN. Mondav.

OLD WOMAN. And the chicken?

YOUNG WOMAN. Tuesday and Wednesday—they was all dade Wednesday evenin' time.

OLD WOMAN. Ah . . . and who was it come up yer last Sinday?

YOUNG WOMAN. Only old Sally Endicott, that I know by— Mother! do 'ee mane——?

OLD WOMAN. I didn't name her name, nor I wouldn't name no names, but I knaws how to find out for certain sure, and I be 'bout doin' of it.

YOUNG WOMAN. Mother . . . what be 'bout?

OLD WOMAN. I knaws . . . I knaws . . . [*She chuckles.*

YOUNG WOMAN. [*In dread.*] What have 'ee got in your lap?

OLD WOMAN. Bullock's heart.

YOUNG WOMAN. [*Her dread increasing.*] What vor? . . . Oh, mother, I don't like this yer . . .

OLD WOMAN. I be putting of the pins in, my dear, and I be putting of it in the turves to bakey, my dear [*bending to the fire*], and I be covering of it with the ashes . . .

YOUNG WOMAN. Mother!

OLD WOMAN. And when her beginn'th to bakey, my dear, us 'll knaw . . . us 'll knaw . . . [*Chuckles.*

YOUNG WOMAN. [*In terror.*] Don't 'ee do it, mother, don't 'ee! 'Tis devil's work!

OLD WOMAN. Us 'll knaw, sure as gospel. . . . When her beginn'th to bakey, the one as ill-wished us will come to the door.

YOUNG WOMAN. Oh, don't 'ee do it, mother! I be veared!

[*She seizes the tongs, and tries to draw the heart out of the fire, but the old woman pushes her back in sudden fury.*

OLD WOMAN. Lave un bide, you fule! If you don't lave un bide, I won't never spake to 'ee no more, and I 'll lave my curse upon 'ee when I do die! [*The young woman cowers back against the table, right.*] I be gwain to knaw our enemy, and nothen shan't hold me! [*She bends over the fire, muttering to herself. A short silence. Knocking at the door. The young woman gives a stifled scream, and throws her apron over her face. The Old Woman raises herself in her chair, and fixes her eyes on the door. Knocking again. The Young Woman rushes across to the fire, and flings herself on her knees, burying her face in her mother's lap. The Old Woman shakes her angrily.*] Get up, you fule! [*Knocking again, rather fainter.*] Who is it, then? Come inside? [*Silence.*] Open the door, you gurt fule!

YOUNG WOMAN. [*In hysterical tears.*] I can't . . . I can't . . .
don't ask me, mother!

OLD WOMAN. [*Seizing her arm.*] Open the door to wance! [*The Young Woman gets up slowly and reluctantly, and goes to the window near the door in obvious fear. She peers out, then gives a sudden scream and rushes back to the Old Woman.*] What is it, then?

YOUNG WOMAN. There's someone lying out there to the door!
[*The Old Woman takes the lantern and goes to the door. She kneels, holding the lantern over something outside on the ground. She rises and comes inside, centre. The Young Woman crouches by the fire, her back to the audience, watching her.*

OLD WOMAN. Her's dade, sure 'nough.

YOUNG WOMAN. [*In a strained whisper.*] Who is it, mother?

OLD WOMAN. [*With hardly concealed triumph in her voice.*] Sally Endicott!
[*The Young Woman gives a gasping scream, and sinks to the ground.*

CURTAIN

.

COUNT ALBANY

AN HISTORICAL INVENTION

DONALD CARSWELL

This play was produced at the Arts Theatre, London, 22nd and 29th January and 12th March 1933, with the following cast:

PRINCE CHARLES EDWARD .	*George S. Wray*
THE CARDINAL YORK . .	*Dennis Arundell*
FATHER MACKINTOSH . .	. *John Laurie*
CLEMENTINA WALKINSHAW .	. *Elliot Mason*
A SERVANT . .	. *Murray MacDonald*
A STRANGE GENTLEMAN .	*Robert Eddison*

Production by Tyrone Guthrie

Previous Productions: Scottish National Players, Glasgow, Christmas 1927–8; Liverpool Repertory Theatre, Easter 1931, and Easter 1932.

The production by the Midland Bank Dramatic Society won the Howard de Walden Cup in the final of the British Drama League Festival, 1938.

Count Albany can be performed quite effectively in curtains, but as a curtain set often rules out a fireplace, the stage directions should be modified accordingly and Mackintosh's opening lines should be altered to read as follows:

MACKINTOSH. 'Ohe! Jam satis est, ohe libelle!'
    [*He sands the document vigorously, and then crosses to the door, etc.*

The Gaelic word *Dhia!* (God!) is pronounced 'Eea.' *Slainte mhor!* (very good health!) is pronounced 'slanche vore'—with the nasal French n.

The costumes call for some care. Mackintosh wears the ordinary cassock and bands of a priest, a rusty grey 'Dr Johnson' wig, and silver buckles on his shoes. York wears a scarlet cassock just clearing the ground and *without mantle.* The cloak he wears on entering is black. Lace ruffles may be worn. His well-powdered wig is small and neat, with rows of curls running right round, but no queue. Clementina wears a heavy velvet travelling dress and a Pompadour wig. Charles Edward's clothes are ordinary period, but must suggest seediness.

COUNT ALBANY

*The Cardinal York's study in the Cancelleria in Rome on the
evening of 1st January 1766.
It is a typical Italian palace chamber, lofty and sombre. The
entrance is at the back through a tall rather narrow folding door.
On the right, beside the large open fireplace with its glowing wood
fire, are a high-backed arm-chair and a small table on which are a
flask of wine, a wineglass and a plate of dried fruit. A door
leading to the Cardinal's bedchamber is on the same side, but
farther back. On the left, at a large desk table littered with
papers, the Cardinal's secretary, Father Mackintosh, is writing
diligently. He is a short, sturdily-built man of fifty, black-
haired, ruddy-complexioned and lively in his movements.
Presently he sits up, pushes his quill pen behind his ear, and rubs
his hands vigorously.*

MACKINTOSH. [*Crossing over to the fireplace and throwing on logs.*]
      'Dissolve frigus, ligna super foco
      large reponens.'
[*He warms his hands for a few moments, then crosses quickly
to the door and listens. Reassured, he returns to the desk
and unlocks a drawer from which he takes a flat black
bottle, and then, taking the wineglass from the small table,
pours out a generous tot of whisky.*]
'Nunc est bibendum.' [*Drinks.*] My first this day and God
knows I need it. [*He makes as if to fill up his half-empty glass,
then changes his mind.*] 'Ne quid nimis.' Let your modera-
tion be known to all men. And moreover, when will I be
getting another bottle when this is finished? [*Suddenly he cocks
an ear and listens intently.*] Och, Dhia!
[*He gulps down the rest of his drink, thrusts the bottle back into
drawer, replaces the wineglass after giving it a hasty wipe
with the hem of his cassock, and gets back to his place at
the desk. The door opens and the Cardinal York enters,
followed by a man-servant. York is a man of forty, but
looks more. His clear-cut features have that gentle,
rather futile aspect that never changes into anger but only*

*peevishness when things go wrong.   He is wearing cap
and cloak.   Mackintosh rises as he enters.*

YORK. No change, Mackintosh.

[*The servant takes his cloak and retires.*

MACKINTOSH. Is His Majesty conscious at all?

YORK. [*Sitting down wearily in the arm-chair.*] He comes and
goes.   He has been able to make his confession and receive
the sacraments.   He asked for—for my brother. . . . I'll
take a glass of wine, Mackintosh.   I am very tired.   No sleep
last night and little the night before. . . . Thank you.
[*Drinks.*] I am not to go there again to-night unless they
send for me.

MACKINTOSH. His Majesty's physicians do not apprehend——?

YORK. He may go at any moment.   He may linger on for a
week.   That is all they say.   But we Stuarts do not die
readily.

MACKINTOSH. Barring cold steel.

YORK. True.   Cold steel is our hereditary ailment.   Very fatal,
too.   Otherwise we are good for our fourscore as a rule.   So
I am going to rest a little.

MACKINTOSH. Your Eminence's bed is ready.   It is warmed
for your Eminence.

YORK. No, I won't go to bed.   My brother arrives to-night.

MACKINTOSH. It is possible his Royal Highness may arrive.

[*A pause, during which Mackintosh writes diligently.*

YORK. Of course the roads are bad at this time of year.

MACKINTOSH. There is nothing wrong with the roads.

YORK. [*With a gesture of irritation.*] Confound the fellow!   Confound all Scotsmen!

MACKINTOSH. It is not for a Stuart to say such a thing.   Your
Eminence's brother would not have said it.

YORK. Perhaps not.   Scotsmen may be excellent in their own
place.

MACKINTOSH. [*Bridling.*] My lord Cardinal——

YORK. No more, I beg you.   I am tired.

MACKINTOSH. I crave your Eminence's pardon.

[*A distant clock strikes nine.*

YORK. Nine o'clock.   He will be here before midnight if the
roads are good.

MACKINTOSH. The roads will be all right for them that will
travel them.

YORK. [*Sharply.*] What do you mean, man?   You think my
brother is not coming?   Is that it?

MACKINTOSH. [*Laying down his pen and speaking very deliberately.*] I think nothing. I only ask myself. And what I ask myself is this. When your Eminence dispatched the courier to Florence, did your Eminence entrust the courier with sufficient funds to defray the expenses of his Royal Highness's journey?

YORK. I should not care to insult my brother by offering him his coach fare. I have always kept him well supplied.

MACKINTOSH. Ay, and there's hardly a tavern in Florence that Bonnie Prince Charlie can show his face in for the score that is chalked up against him.

YORK. Mackintosh, you forget yourself. You have the faults of your nation. Still, no man knows what he can do till he tries. Prayer and fasting—who knows? One day, by the grace of God, you might even be redeemed from being a Scotsman. With God all things are possible.

MACKINTOSH. I am obliged to your Eminence.

YORK. Not at all. [*Pause.*] I grant you know a good deal more about my brother than I do.

MACKINTOSH. I have had dealings with him.

YORK. Quite so. For the last twenty years my dealings with him have been confined to communications through my bankers. Twenty years! A long time, Mackintosh, and a full time, too. I'd like to see Charles again. Whether he will care about seeing me is another question. He does not like me much, though he takes my money punctually enough. But whom does Charles like? Poor Clementina, perhaps. I suppose he likes her after a fashion.

MACKINTOSH. It is hard to say.

YORK. A deplorable business, truly deplorable. The Holy Father feels very strongly about it.

MACKINTOSH. The Holy Father is not the only one.

YORK. And yet one can't help being sorry for the wretched woman. We were children together, she and I. Used to play in the Borghese Gardens. I haven't see her since. I don't want to. Have you heard anything about her lately, Mackintosh? You are more in the way of hearing things than I am.

MACKINTOSH. The last letter I had from my cousin in Florence informed me that the Countess Albany ——

YORK. I presume you mean Signora Walkinshaw?

MACKINTOSH. As your Eminence pleases. Signora Walkinshaw, my cousin informs me, is in the best of health and spirits—

especially spirits; but the *consortium vitae* that she and his Royal Highness have maintained these many years seems to be drawing to a close.

YORK. [*Startled.*] What? Separating? Why?

MACKINTOSH. The Signora Walkinshaw, my cousin says, feels that at her time of life her constitution is unable much longer to support the privilege of being thrashed at least thrice *per diem* by her exalted consort.

YORK. [*Starting up angrily.*] It 's monstrous! I won't hear it. You eat our bread and laugh at us and gloat over the filthy gossip your blackguard cousin sends you from Florence. It 's *scandalum magnatum.* It 's worse. It 's a treasonable correspondence. You 're a traitor, a dirty spy. You 're drunk, too. I 'll have you unfrocked, pig of a Scotsman, I 'll——

MACKINTOSH. [*Angrily thrusting the Cardinal back into his chair.*] Sit you down there, man, and hearken to me. I had four brothers, as fine men as ever stepped on heather. Lachlan, the youngest, fell at Prestonpans. Duncan's carcass has long since rotted to bits on the gallows at Carlisle. Alistair and John, they helped to break the Butcher's left at Culloden, and there they sleep. And I—I should be with them where they are gone, all young and fresh in their sins—God have mercy upon them—but for having to skulk about in a black petticoat and not much to show for it. These men died for your brother, gave their good lives for the Stuart cause, and you call me traitor and spy, and drunken pig of a Scotsman! By Christ, my lord Cardinal, there was a time before I put on these rags when the man that said the hundredth part of that would have had to face me on ten foot of grass with good chance of staying there till Judgment Day . . .

YORK. [*Whose fits of temper are soon over.*] Basta, basta, Mackintosh mio——

MACKINTOSH. . . . unless somebody had the charity to give his dirty body Christian burial.

YORK. Per l'amor di Dio——

MACKINTOSH. Traitor, is it? Drunken rascal? Pig of a Scotsman? Unfrock me, would you? Och, Dhia, the man is daft. 'Tis only the black coat of me keeps my fingers off him.

YORK. No, no, perdonatemi. I am extremely sorry. You understand? Very sorry. I apologize. We are both rather hasty, Mackintosh. Don't hit if you can help it. It would be so unpleasant—for you, I mean.

MACKINTOSH. Does your Eminence withdraw every word?

YORK. Si, si, sicuro.

MACKINTOSH. And it is utterly false that I am not devoted, body and soul, to your Eminence's illustrious family?

YORK. Quite.

MACKINTOSH. Moreover, you said I was drunk. I never was drunk in my life, so I was not, though I could drink more in a day, had I a mind to it, than your Eminence and the whole Sacred College could drink in a month.

YORK. I know, I know. Everybody knows that, Mackintosh. Of your charity, enough.

MACKINTOSH. Well, I am a gentleman. And being an ordained priest of God I hope I am a Christian. I forgive you. From the bottom of my heart I forgive you. I will shake your Eminence's hand. [*He holds out his hand.*

YORK. [*Taking Mackintosh's hand limply.*] Thank you.

MACKINTOSH. [*Returning to his desk and picking up a document.*] Will your Eminence be good enough to peruse this draft?

YORK. [*Waving him away peevishly.*] I won't peruse anything, I am tired. Leave it there. Leave me in peace—that is all I want. [*Rising wearily.*] I 'll lie down for a few minutes. Call me at once the moment his Royal Highness arrives.

[*He goes into his bedchamber.*

[*Mackintosh resumes his work at the desk, humming 'The White Cockade' as he begins to copy a document. Presently there is a tap at the door.*

MACKINTOSH. Avanti!

SERVANT. Riverenza——

MACKINTOSH. [*Pointing towards the bedchamber.*] S-sh! [*The servant whispers in his ear with many excited gesticulations.*] What 's that? [*The servant continues to whisper.*] Are you crazy, man, or have you been drinking? Tell her to go away.

SERVANT. She won't go, riverenza.

MACKINTOSH. You goddam fool! Chase her off. Shut the door in her face.

[*He starts hustling the servant out of the room, but as they reach the door a lady in cloak and hood steps in, and the servant slips out smartly, closing the door behind him. Mackintosh stares at the stranger, quite at a loss.*

THE LADY. I want the Cardinal York. You are not a cardinal.

MACKINTOSH. No, signora, not exactly. His Eminence is having a little repose and must not be disturbed on any account whatever. I am his Eminence's secretary. My name is Mackintosh, at your service, signora, and if I can——

THE LADY. I like your name. How do you like mine—Walkinshaw, Clementina Walkinshaw? Not much I see.

MACKINTOSH. [*After an embarrassed pause, during which he casts his eyes towards the ceiling, looks on the ground, takes snuff, blows his nose, and clears his throat.*] Madam, as to the *suppositio materialis* of your name, if you know what I mean——

THE LADY. I don't.

MACKINTOSH. [*Avoiding her gaze, putting the tips of his fingers together judicially and swaying his body back and forth.*] Then I will leave that point and pass to what presents itself to me, if I may make so bold as to say so, as the immediate issue. I will be frank. We were not expecting *you*, madam, but seeing you are here it may be that a certain exalted personage is not far distant.

CLEMENTINA. He is below in the coach, and likely to stay there unless you bail him out.

MACKINTOSH. I don't take you, ma'am.

CLEMENTINA. I say his Royal Highness is a prisoner in the coach we hired at Florence. The postilions swear they won't part with him till they get their money. I can't blame them, but it's devilish uncomfortable for Charles. . . . I'll sit down, though you haven't asked me to.

MACKINTOSH. [*Greatly agitated.*] I beg your pardon, ma'am. [*He rummages in his desk.*] And wasn't that just what I told his Eminence? And I don't believe there's sufficient money in the house. How much did you say it would be?

CLEMENTINA. I didn't say anything. I've no idea. A good deal, I imagine. One can't come to Rome from Florence for nothing, though some people seem to think so.

MACKINTOSH. Dhia, Dhia! Have ye no money at all, at all?

CLEMENTINA. Not a soldo. I gave my last crown to your servant to get him to let me upstairs.

MACKINTOSH. [*Furiously.*] God's curse on the dirty black devil! [*Picking up a small bag of money.*] Well, well, here's something anyway. I'll see to it.   [*Rushes from the room.*

CLEMENTINA. [*Bawling after him.*] Don't be afraid to bring Charles up, father. He is fairly sober now.

YORK. [*Outside.*] Yes. What is it? [*He re-enters hurriedly, adjusting his wig.*] . . . Mackintosh! . . . Where's Mackintosh? Mackint—— [*Clementina quickly leaves her chair and drops on her knees before him. He stares at her in sleepy bewilderment.*] In the name of God, who are you?

CLEMENTINA. A despised but faithful friend of the House of Stuart.

YORK. [*Recoiling and crossing himself.*] Get thee behind me, Satan!

CLEMENTINA. Ay, that's you Stuarts all over. You take our heart's blood—ay, and more, if it's a woman—but will you give anything? No, not so much as your blessing, though it costs you nothing and is worth just as much.

YORK. [*Puzzled and rather nervous.*] M-yes. . . . Quite so. . . . You seem to be acquainted with our family, madam, but I do not know you. Who are you, and how did you get here?

CLEMENTINA. [*With malicious archness.*] Not know me! Oh, Henry, how can you forget? The sweet days of long ago! Your little sweetheart and all the funny little houses we used to play at in the Borghese Gardens! Oh, Henry!

YORK. [*With a gasp.*] Clemmy! [*Slowly and sadly, distressed by her appearance.*] Sacramento! [*Then after a slight pause, coldly.*] You have come with Charles? Is Charles here? Where is Charles?

CLEMENTINA. [*Clutching his robe.*] Charles, Charles, always Charles. Never a thought for poor Clementina.

YORK. Let me go, woman.

CLEMENTINA. I will not let thee go unless thou bless me! [*Rises quickly and pushes him into his chair.*] Sit down, man. He will be here in a moment. Father Mackintosh is bringing him up. [*She drops on her knees again.*

YORK. [*Feebly.*] I don't understand.

CLEMENTINA. All in good time. Talk to me first. Aren't you going to give me your blessing? [*She pauses. York makes no sign and she gets up.*] Very well, then. Keep it and be damned to you. I'll have a brotherly kiss, though, which is better.

[*Before York can prevent her she throws herself on him and kisses him heartily.*

YORK. [*Struggling to his feet.*] This is an outrage!

CLEMENTINA. Tut, tut, tut! What's the matter? Nobody is going to hurt you. [*Pushes him back into his chair again.*] There now, that's a good little Henry. [*Smoothing out and arranging his robes.*] Sit still and be dignified. A prince of the Church should never look ruffled.

YORK. Have you no shame?

CLEMENTINA. [*Looking at him grimly and speaking with growing passion.*] Once I had what was better—innocence. Youth, too—health, good name, peace of mind, friends, faith in God

and man. I had all these once. The Stuarts have taken
them all. So I have the virtue—the Christian virtue—of
sacrifice.

YORK. [*With downcast eyes.*] It is true. I was wrong. The
shame is not yours, but ours.

CLEMEMTINA. People like you can afford to be ashamed. You
are not naked, like me. Better to be unashamed if you are
naked. The fig-leaves didn't save Adam and Eve from being
turned out of Paradise. Tell me, Henry, why are people such
fools as to believe in things?

YORK. You scoff at faith because you have lost it.

CLEMENTINA. Isn't the parson clever? Too clever for a poor
woman. Listen. I hear Charles's footsteps. Nice and
steady, aren't they? I 've listened for these footsteps night
after night for twenty years. There 's a school of faith for
you—the kind you don't lose.

[*With these last words Clementina returns to her chair. The
door opens. Mackintosh enters and ushers in Charles
Edward—dishevelled, haggard, and doubtfully sober.*

MACKINTOSH. His Royal Highness Charles Edward, Count of
Albany and Prince of Scotland.

[*Charles advances slowly. York stares at him, silent and
horrified.*

CLEMENTINA. Aren't you going to kiss your long-lost brother,
Henry?

YORK. [*Stammering.*] Charles! . . .

CHARLES. How 's little Harry? Damn it, what are you staring
at? Changed a bit, am I? Of course I am. So are you.
So is everybody. So is everything. Now don't let us waste
time gaping and gushing. Business is business, as you,
Harry, in those nice brotherly letters of yours, have often
reminded me. In the first place, about His Most Sacred
Majesty, our revered father James by the grace of God,
etcetera. Our reverend friend here tells me he is still
with us.

YORK. He is *in extremis*. He received the sacraments to-day.
He has asked for you more than once.

CHARLES. Has he, though? Poor old soul! Born unlucky.
. . . Well, that 's one point clear. The next point is—have
you anything to drink in the house?

CLEMENTINA. Don't give him a drop, Henry. He has had as
much as is good for him and more.

CHARLES. Hold your tongue. And, mark you, none of your Henrys to his Eminence. You forget your station, madam.

CLEMENTINA. Oh, do I? And so do other people. Even Princes of the Church, let alone other kinds of princes. You should have seen Henry and me before you came in, Charles. He tried to kiss me.

CHARLES. [Amused, leering at York.] Oh, you dirty dog——

YORK. [Indignantly.] I need hardly say, Charles——

CLEMENTINA. [Maliciously.] Just like the sweet old days in the Borghese Gardens.

YORK. Really, madam——

CHARLES. Shut up, both of you. You 're both liars anyway. Clemmy, sit down there and don't speak again till you are spoken to. . . . Henry, you haven't answered my question. Have you anything in the house to drink?

YORK. [Sulkily.] There is some vin santo there.

CHARLES. I said something to drink—brandy.

YORK. No, certainly not. I never touch it.

CHARLES. You wouldn't. Haven't the guts. But you might have the decency to think of other people. Nice hospitable house. After twenty years I visit my one and only brother and he offers me vin santo. My God!

MACKINTOSH. [Anxious to be tactful.] Begging your Royal Highness's pardon, his Eminence's wine is famous of its kind. It is strong, moreover.

CHARLES. [Turning to him with sudden interest.] Ah, my reverend Scottish friend, I had almost forgotten you. Your name, pray. I 'm afraid I didn't catch it before.

MACKINTOSH. Mackintosh. James of that name—a good name, —at your Royal Highness's service—a poor adherent.

CHARLES. [Rising and shaking him warmly by the hand.] Mackintosh! Of course! I know you, father. I know your family. Good friends—the best.

MACKINTOSH. We did what we could. I had four brothers— your Royal Highness will doubtless remember—as fine men as ever stepped on heather. Lachlan—that was the youngest, but your Royal Highness may not call him to mind—he fell at Prestonpans. Duncan's corpse has long since rotted to bits on the gallows at Carlisle—that much your Royal Highness will have heard. Alistair and John lie under the earth at Culloden—but I needn't be telling your Royal Highness that. And myself would have been with them but for having to skulk about in a black petticoat and——

CHARLES. I saw them fall. If flesh and blood could have saved that day the Mackintoshes would have done it. [*Lowering his voice confidentially.*] A word with you, father.

[*He draws Mackintosh aside and whispers in his ear. Mackintosh listens with growing anxiety on his face.*

MACKINTOSH. I would gladly oblige your Royal Highness, but——

CHARLES. [*Turning away.*] As you please. If you won't, you won't.

MACKINTOSH. Not a drop has passed my lips since——

CHARLES. [*Sniffing.*] Say no more, father. I understand. I did think that Charles Edward Stuart could count on a Mackintosh. However . . . Clemmy, as the reverend father refuses supplies I must come on you. Turn out your reticule.

CLEMENTINA. [*Clutching the reticule tightly.*] Indeed I will not.

CHARLES. Turn it out, I tell you.

YORK. Charles, I beg you——

CHARLES. [*To York.*] Mind your own business. [*To Clementina.*] Do as you are told.

MACKINTOSH, [*Who has been fumbling at his drawer.*] It had quite escaped my recollection, but [*producing his bottle and, with an agonized glance at the Cardinal, offering it to Charles*] there is a modicum here that your Royal Highness is very welcome to.

CHARLES. Behold, a miracle! Better than the loaves and fishes. Henry, this must not go unrecorded. When you make Mackintosh a saint you shall find it given under our hand and seal that in the year of grace one thousand seven hundred and sixty-six, his prince being like to die of thirst, the Blessed James Mackintosh did miraculously produce a bottle of Scotch whisky from his desk, where it is quite certain there was no such thing before, he himself having said so.

[*He fills a wineglass with the neat spirit.*

YORK. [*Controlling his anger with difficulty.*] When you have done being profane, Charles, perhaps you will tell me what is to be done with this lady.

CHARLES. What about her?

YORK. She cannot stop in my house.

CLEMENTINA. [*Sardonically.*] Ha, ha!

YORK. I mean no discourtesy, madam, but you must understand the impossibility . . .

CLEMENTINA. Oh, perfectly! I quite understand I am in the way. Poor Clemmy is always in the way when she has served her turn. Would his Royal Highness be here now if it hadn't been for Clemmy? Would he have left Florence yet if it hadn't been for Clemmy? Would he be even as sober as he is if it hadn't been for Clemmy? But now he is safely here, Clemmy isn't good enough for his Eminence's house. She isn't respectable. She can go into the streets.

CHARLES. Where she belongs.

YORK. Charles! [*To Clementina.*] Madam, you are unjust. This is a Churchman's house. There are proprieties, canonical proprieties——

CLEMENTINA. So there are, Henry. You are a Christian priest, I a sinner. How appropriate! What a chance to show your Christianity. Let me stay. I 'll promise not to kiss you again.

MACKINTOSH. [*Coming forward.*] Begging your Eminence's pardon, but I think I could procure a suitable lodging for Mistress Walkinshaw in the very near neighbourhood. Would your Eminence wish me to . . .

YORK. [*With a gesture of weariness.*] Do. See to it.

CHARLES. Excellent fellow! Admirable Mackintosh! Saint Jamie of Speyside! [*Raises his glass.*] Slainte mhor, father!

MACKINTOSH. And meanwhile, as the lady will no doubt wish to rest and refresh herself, perhaps say a prayer for His Majesty, my own humble chamber is at her disposal.

YORK. Is that agreeable to you, madam?

CLEMENTINA. Nothing is agreeable to me. But have it your own way. I wash my hands of everything. [*With a significant glance at the bottle, which Charles is rapidly emptying.*] Look after Charles yourself. [*To Mackintosh.*] I 'm ready, father.

YORK. [*As the two are leaving.*] And before you do anything else, go to the Palazzo Muti and say that his Royal Highness is here.

MACKINTOSH. [*Bowing.*] As your Eminence pleases. His Majesty's servants shall be informed with all speed.

CLEMENTINA. [*Curtsying low.*] I leave your Royal Highnesses to your momentous conference.

[*Exeunt Clementina and Mackintosh.*

YORK. [*Almost inarticulate with rage.*] It—it—it comes to this.

CHARLES. [*Drinking.*] What 's that?

YORK. Why did you bring that woman?

CHARLES. I didn't bring her. She brought me.

YORK. I toil and plan and humiliate myself, and this is the thanks I get—to sit and listen to this kind of thing—to be subjected to the insults of that woman—before my own servant. I warn you, you may drive me too far. I am tired of it all, tired and . . . sick.

CHARLES. [*Pushing the bottle across.*] Have some. Nothing like whisky when you are sick.

YORK. If it were only myself . . . but all Rome will have it to-morrow to grin and mouth over. I suppose that never occurred to you? And so from Rome to London. Don't you know this wretched place is crawling with spies and scandal-mongering vermin who 'll do anything for a half-dollar? The whole disgusting story will be off by the next post. A pretty thing for your fine Tory squires to guffaw over in their news-letters—how the last moments of the Old Pretender were cheered by the happy arrival of the Young Pretender from Florence in a hired coach, accompanied by the faithful Walkinshaw, both parties being well in liquor. Pah!

CHARLES. Little Harry, he threw away his little wooden sword because his naughty big brother had a bigger one. But the Holy Father said: 'Who is going to be a good lad? And he shall have a nice little red hat and a nice red frock and lots and lots of pretty pennies and never play with nasty swords any more.' Bah! I tell you I 'll take my trollop where I please, and when I please I 'll drink. Never a Tory squire will think the worse of me for that. I 'm a soldier, not a snivelling priest. You go to hell.

YORK. The Holy Father will hear of it. He will speak to me. What am I to say?

CHARLES. The Holy Father, I suppose, is a Christian and a gentleman?

YORK. If you will pardon me, Charles, that is a most improper observation.

CHARLES. Oh well, you know best. I was giving him the benefit of the doubt. However, if he isn't a gentleman he is at least Christian—*ex officio.* Very well, then. Remind him he is a Christian. It is the duty of a Christian to forgive. Nobody can forgive more than the Holy Father and nobody needs more forgiveness than I do. Each one according to his need. Ergo, it is the duty of the Holy Father to forgive me. Q.E.D. Logic, Henry, my boy, logic and sound religion found together for once. Put it to him. He 'll see it—perhaps.

[*He gulps down more whisky.*

YORK. [*Moaning.*] All my work wasted!

CHARLES. [*Sharply.*] Had His Holiness promised to do anything for me?

YORK. One cannot exact promises from His Holiness, but a certain atmosphere can be created. That, so far as lay in my power, had been done. There were good grounds for hope. I——

CHARLES. Grounds for hope! Grounds for humbug. Will he *do* anything? No, not till he is taken by the scruff of the neck, and that is hardly in your line, Henry. You would rather just talk, create atmospheres.

YORK. Will you?

CHARLES. Will I what?

YORK. Take the Holy Father by the scruff of the neck? [*Charles makes a gesture of impatience, but says nothing.*] Quite so. I just talk and you just talk. The only difference between you and me is that my talk is couched in terms that are at least respectful to the Vicar of Christ. But then I have never apostatized from the Faith.

CHARLES. [*Shouting angrily.*] Can't you leave that alone? Isn't it all dead and done with? It was imperative that I should consolidate the Tory party in my interest, and how could I do that without turning Church of England for a bit? It was an essential part of the system, and a damned good system too, if you, Henry, hadn't spoiled it all with your vanity and selfishness, grabbing at the tassels of Cardinal's hat. [*Mockingly in baby-talk.*] Oh, pretty, pretty, pretty—like the blasted silly baby you are. However, don't let's argue. You had your way. Nobody can say I'm not a good Catholic now.

[*He has been rummaging in his overcoat pocket and produces a dirty 'cutty' clay. Finding some tobacco still in it, he tears a strip off Mackintosh's draft, makes a spill of it, and lights up.*

YORK. [*Coldly.*] The Church's difficulty, Charles, is not that you are weak in the Faith—that might always be adjusted—but weak in the head. The Church cannot mend that. What I have just called, perhaps harshly, your former apostasy is a case in point. You say it was a measure of expediency, as no doubt it was, an essential part of your system. I say nothing about the system. I want to be fair. It may have been right or it may have been wrong. I don't say. But it could only be justified on the score of—of—ah—ah—how shall I express it?—a high *prima facie* potentiality of practical consequence. Do I make myself clear?

CHARLES. [*Puffing a cloud of smoke into York's face.*] Perfectly.

YORK. [*After a fit of coughing.*] Very well, then. It was, you say, your system, but it was a system in which we were not included. We could have told you that no results—no good results—were possible, but without a word to us you must go and make a laughing-stock of yourself. The Young Pretender abjuring the Pope and rallying the Protestant boys to his drum! The English may be rogues and heretics, but they 're not fools. Did the Tory squires lift a little finger to help you in '45?

CHARLES. They did more. They lifted their elbows a dozen times a day.

YORK. And stayed at home to do it, and locked up their silver when they heard Charlie's Scotsmen were coming.

CHARLES. [*Banging the table.*] That 's it. We should have been in St James's to-night if brother Henry had had the business in hand. You wouldn't have done much with the Scots. The Scots have their own ideas of what a Stuart should be, and, with all respect, Harry, you wouldn't have filled the bill. But who cares for the Scots? The English are the people who count, and they would have loved you—what 's more, approved of you. You are the only Stuart that was ever known to make money. You must be very well-to-do, Henry.

YORK. I had need be.

CHARLES. A single man, no vices, not even a mistress, I suppose. But an expensive father and me for a brother. Well, you 'll be relieved of the one before many hours are past, and perhaps the other mayn't trouble you long. [*Pauses.*] You 'd be all right then, with Charlie in his coffin. You 'd be king—*in partibus.* My God! King Henry the Ninth! Bluff King Hal! You old hypocrite, how many wives have you had? [*Roaring angrily.*] Damn it, man, can't you say something?

YORK. I could say much, but—— [*He shrugs his shoulders.*

CHARLES. You are a fox, so quiet, so mim there, making out you haven't said a word. But I don't forget. You called me a fool just now. Weak in the head—that was it—weak in the head. The Church Infallible has spoken. Charles Edward Stuart is weak in the head—extinct—blotted out— non-existent—a dead fancy—a rumour that 's past. . . .

YORK. If you had listened to me——

CHARLES. You call me a fool! By God, I am a fool—such a fool that I not only believe in myself but have made countless other men believe in me too. Suppose I were a wise man, a prudent man, a respectable man, a godly, money-making man —a man like you, Henry. Should I have been loved as never Prince was loved before? Would thousands of men have

died for me and thought themselves happy? Fools to die
for a fool? I have set a whole nation singing. When did
wisdom make anybody sing? I have made history. What is
history but the handiwork of fools? Do wise men make
history? No, all they can do is to write it—write it down
on paper—all wrong. Can you deny it? No, you can only
sit on your backside and sneer. You sneer at my naked
caterans. Quite right. We were the raggedest, lousiest regi-
ment that ever marched, but we marched to win a kingdom.
We had no guns, we had oumoney, we had no food. But we
had what was better—loyalty to the death, love stronger
than death—all the things that only fools believe in. It was
a fool's game, but it was a great game.

YORK. A lost game.

CHARLES. But a game that was nearly won—ay, and will be won
yet. There's still a hand to play. The fool will have his
revenge. This is not the end.

YORK. Not yours conceivably. But what of the others—the
fools that died? Who is to give them their revenge?

CHARLES. God help the mole! What do they want with revenge whose death was a consummation? But that is all
nonsense to you, so much meaningless talk. You poor worm,
wriggling blind and slimy through your earth of policy and
prudence, what can *you* know of the eagle's way? Ah, my
eagle, my sign from Heaven—would to God I had followed
no other guide! Did I ever tell you about the miracle,
Henry?

YORK. Miracle?

CHARLES. Ay, miracle. Sorry. I forgot. You're a Churchman. Churchmen don't believe in miracles. What prudent
man does? But fools know better. . . . It was when the
Doutelle first sighted Scottish land. I had been sea-sick for
a week, a solid week. Know what that means? A great
spiritual experience, Henry. A lesson in humility. No
proud prince strutting the quarter-deck in gold lace. Shivering in a seaman's watchcoat, clutching the taffrail—my legs
were damnably shaky and there was a nasty sea running—
that was I. Old Tullibardine (God rest his soul) told me to
look. 'Scotland,' he said, and the tears were running down
his cheeks. 'Where?' I asked. 'There,' said he, pointing.
'Yon's Barra and yon's South Uist. Your Royal Highness is
home.' Home! I wish you could have seen that low huddle
of barren rocks. You'd have pitied me. But you'd have

been wrong. I was sick, trembling, dejected, frightened nearly to death; but I was never less to be pitied than then. In my soul I *believed*. Do you know anything about the soul, Henry? It 's your business.

YORK. Only God knows the soul.

CHARLES. I should have said something graceful and gracious to poor old Tullibardine, but I was too cold and wet—and shocked. The Hebrides! Rain and a wicked sea! Enough to shock any man. God, the very thought of it makes my bones rattle. [*Pours out more whisky and gulps it down.*] Then the miracle. Mind you, I had no hope at that moment—not a scrap. But I had faith. Miracles are a matter of faith, eh?

YORK. So the Church teaches.

CHARLES. Good, I 'm no heretic. The sun broke through—a poor pale pretender of a sun, casting a wan glance of sympathy on his little brother below. Suddenly Tullibardine starts dancing. 'Look!' he shouts, pointing to the maintop. 'A royal welcome!' And there, circling round us high in the tempest-torn heavens, an eagle! I tell you my spirits rose to the heavenly greeting. On that eagle's wings I was borne to Holyrood.

YORK. But not to St James's. At Derby the eagle's wings failed.

CHARLES. [*Banging the table.*] No. The eagle's way was the right way, if only I had followed it. But I didn't. Too many owls about. The fool was fool enough to listen to the wise men. You say I didn't consult you. Good God, I 'm sick of you and your kind! They were always about me, and at Derby they were too strong. And so Culloden Moor. Would to God I had died at Culloden! . . . I don't know if you ever heard. When the day was lost, I would have charged Cumberland's greasy Germans myself—ay, alone I would. But they held me back by main force. . . . And even then, Henry, even at Culloden, we could have won. We had always won before, and why not then? And we should have won if I had had my way. I 've always said so. I say so still. Consider the st-strategical situation. [*He swings round in his seat and begins to indicate a plan on the table.*] Here was the idea. . . .

YORK. I consider the moral situation. William of Cumberland was the butcher, but it was a Stuart that drove the sheep to the slaughter.

CHARLES. There was no driving. We had to fight, man, and

we fought. Cousin Billy had the guns—God rot his fat ugly carcass!—and he made the most of them. He ploughed up our lines and our bodies with his bloody guns. But we did the fighting. I don't know how those Highlanders stood it. But for all Billy's guns our right was unshaken. The Mackintoshes, the Camerons, the men of Appin—they gave our cousin a riposte he didn't expect. They sent his left reeling. They'd have smashed it in, if they had been supported. I said that then. I say it now. But what could I do? Nothing but watch their bodies being piled up three and four deep.

YORK. For the love of God, Charles——

CHARLES. Those were the fellows. Just give me their like again. Knowing what I know now——

YORK. This *I* know, that the voice of our brother's blood crieth out from the ground.

CHARLES. [*Staring at him.*] Eh?

YORK. You speak of things I try to forget. You speak of them as if with pride, but me they fill with shame and fear. What right had we to send these men to death? The justice of our cause? Will God take that answer? How dare I say at God's altar 'Lavabo manus meas inter innocentes'?

CHARLES. [*With a sneer.*] *Your* hands are clean enough, curse you.

YORK. If one is guilty all are guilty. The burden of the House of Stuart——

CHARLES. [*Laughing noisily.*] Oh, but haven't you got the family failing, Harry! Vanity and vainglory! You call it conscience, a nice Churchman's name, but it is just vulgar vanity and vainglory for all that. I ought not to laugh so in the present melancholy circumstances, but before God I can't help it. Eh, it's a rare jest. 'The Stuarts,' says he, 'the burden of the Royal House of Stuart!' [*Turning on York fiercely.*] And who the hell do you suppose cares a tinker's curse for the House of Stuart? Nobody. Nobody but you and half a dozen other old women, mostly doited. Shall I tell you something?

YORK. You're drunk.

CHARLES. Granted, granted. I am not prepared to dispute the proposition. But hear a drunken man tell the sober truth. Listen. I'll tell you something worth knowing. Henry, my boy, hark to me. There is no Royal House of Stuart. Have you taken that in? No? Then I'll say it again. There are no Stuarts. None at all anywhere. Once there were. Not

now any more. You, Henry Benedict Maria Clement,
Cardinal Duke of York, you think you exist, but you don't.
You were invented by the Whigs to keep the Tories out of
office—oho! I know more about English politics than you
think—and I tell you you are not a man. You are only a
vulgar superst—superst—[*he cannot articulate 'superstition'
and compromises*] . . . myth. That's where you and I are
different, Henry. I'm no more a Stuart than you are. But
I'm *real*. The Whitehall devils believe in me and tremble.
They know. Would the clans have drained their life-blood
for the name of Stuart? You flatter yourself. Vanity and
vainglory. Listen. When I first arrived in Scotland Boisdale told me to go back—MacDonald of Boisdale—and he
spoke for his people. The clans were quite content to be
George's men. Do you blame them? George is a German.
What are we? Nobody knows and nobody cares. Stuart!
For all the good it did me I might as well have called myself
Fitzwarmingpan. It was for Charlie the clansmen died,
Bonnie Prince Charlie, and that's me. You'll never be king,
Harry, any more than poor old Jamie Stuart over there—no
not if you had all Billy's guns on top of your prudence and
policies. But I was born to be king. I have the divine right
of kingship.

YORK. By your birth alone.

CHARLES. I say I have the divine right, the right that is mine
and mine only. It comes not after the flesh, but by the grace
of God.

YORK. Must you blaspheme?

CHARLES. Yes, by God, for my very existence must needs be a
blasphemy in your eyes. Does it not give the lie to you and
all that you stand for? But how about *your* blasphemies? I
tell you mine will be forgiven sooner than yours. You would
cage the eagle, would you? You would stand for the divine
right of a Stuart and crush with all the curses of the Church
the divine right of a man, an individual, myself that am
myself. You would make me cringe on the backstairs of the
Vatican and rule my conduct to suit some paltry priests' in-
trigue. . . . Do you know who I am? I am the Young
Chevalier. I am that prince for whose sweet sake Balmerino
said he would have given a thousand heads. It was on Tower
Hill he said it, at the end. He wore his regimentals, my
regimentals, blue turned up with scarlet, and his shroud
underneath. He had but one head, poor devil, and not

much in it. But he had a heart, and if I never wear another crown I was crowned that day before all the world—Charlie, the King of Hearts. . . . What have you to say to that? Nothing. It is beyond your comprehension. You can only hate it and me. [*He pours out the last of the whisky.*

YORK. Put that bottle away.

CHARLES. [*Tossing the empty bottle into the fire.*] There, not a drop left! Poor old Mackintosh, he must be given another, a full one. Oh, don't pretend you don't hate me, Henry. Prince of the Church and Prince of the Blood, your soul is the soul of a slave. But don't think I hate you. I care no more for you than for Mackintosh's empty bottle. The king-soul neither hates nor loves. It is its own end, its own fulfilment. It is God.

YORK. So has the Devil always spoken.

CHARLES. The Devil! That reminds me of something. Wait . . . I have it. It was at Holyrood, one night after Prestonpans. I could not sleep. There was a book of English plays in my room—good plays—one about the Devil. There was a line . . . one moment . . . yes, it was this: 'Myself am hell, nor am I out of it.' Damned good. Wish I could remember the man's name. 'Myself am hell.' D' you understand what that means?

YORK. [*In a low voice.*] I believe I do.

CHARLES. [*Furiously.*] Speak up, can't you? [*Gets up unsteadily and shakes York by the shoulders.*] Speak up and look me in the face. Do I look like a king or do I not?

YORK. [*Agitated.*] Leave me, Charles, leave me. I should not have sent for you. I——

CHARLES. [*His mood changing.*] You wish I were dead. I know. Have I not wished it too? But I am not dead. I ought to have been a hundred times. A price was set on my head—good money. Wish I had it in my pocket now. Yet here I am alive. Why is that? Because my destiny must be fulfilled. There can be no other reason. . . . Now I'm going to tell you something good. I've told you the bad. Now the good. But it's a secret, mind. Moidart. Aha, Moidart! There are caves in Moidart, brother, big caves that George's redcoats don't know. Clanranald, good friend of ours—he has told me all about them. Not a word, though, not a whisper even to His Holiness. But one day—not to-morrow, but one day—the caves will give up their secret, and the world will get a surprise. The dragon's teeth will

yield their fruit; ten thousand armed men will spring from
the rocks and the heather; and Charlie will come again.

Clementina bounces into the room.

CLEMENTINA. [*Shrilly.*] While your Royal Highnesses settle the
affairs of the universe I may perish of cold and hunger.
My lord Cardinal, your hospitality overwhelms me.

CHARLES. Ah, the sweet gentle Clementina!   [*Sings.*
'Si le roy m'avait donné
Paris, sa grand' ville,
Et qu'il me fallût quitter
L'amour de ma mie,
J'aurais dit——'

CLEMENTINA. [*To York.*] I knew it. Have you no sense, no
decency, but you must let himself fill himself up again?

YORK. It has been very difficult——

CLEMENTINA. Difficult! What do *you* know of difficult? Did
you bring him from Florence? He was middling sober when
he arrived. I saw to that. And this is my thanks! A fine
figure for a royal father's death-bed!

CHARLES. [*Singing.*] 'J'ai un long voyage à faire,
Je ne sais qui le fera.'

CLEMENTINA. He can't go to the Palazzo Muti like that to-night.

YORK. To-night there may be no need. To-morrow. . . .

CLEMENTINA. To-morrow! But anything may happen before
to-morrow. . . . I see what it is. A plot. A dirty priest's
plot. You and that cross-eyed Highlandman, you hatched
it between you. I see it all.

YORK. Madam, you don't know what you are saying. No
doubt you are overwrought——

CHARLES. Don't mind her, Henry. She is—you know—a little
from the reticule. [*Sings again, making gestures of drinking.*
'Les belles dames font comm' ça,
Et puis encore comm' ça.'

YORK. For God's sake, Charles . . . My dear, good woman . . .

CHARLES. She isn't a good woman. She 's a whore.

CLEMENTINA. And your Royal Highness is no gentleman.

CHARLES. [*Staggering to his feet.*] You dare insult me! Get out
of my sight. I 'm sick of you. Leave the room—leave the
house before I throttle the life out of you, you old harridan. . . .
[*He rushes at her.*

YORK. [*Struggling with Charles.*] Charles! Charles!
[*There is a sharp knocking at the door. York drags Charles*

back to his chair. Clementina, who has fallen in the scuffle, scrambles to her feet. York glances round anxiously and then opens the door, revealing Mackintosh and a strange gentleman, who wears the ribbon of the Thistle. At the sight of the latter York starts, then composes himself and motions him to enter.

YORK. The King? [*The Stranger bows. There is a pause while York and Mackintosh mutter a prayer. Charles has not moved. He lolls in a stupor, his head sunk on his chest.*] Your Lordship will understand. . . . His Royal . . . my brother is extremely fatigued after his long journey.

[*He goes over to Charles and shakes him by the shoulder. Charles looks up stupidly. The Stranger advances towards him and makes a low bow.*

CHARLES. Eh! What 's the matter. Who the devil are you? What d' you want?

THE STRANGER. [*Kneeling.*] I have to present my humble duty to Your Majesty and to announce the death of King James the Third, which occurred this evening at ten o'clock. Requiescat in pace. God save the King!

[*Charles stares, only half comprehending, but presently, seeing his brother kneeling before him, he slowly holds out his hand to be kissed. The others also kneel and kiss hands—first the Stranger, Mackintosh next, and Clementina last.*

CHARLES. [*Rising and speaking with difficulty.*] The death of our beloved father . . . deeply afflicts us . . . though in the course of nature . . . we must . . . we are comforted by . . . loyalty . . . your loyalty which—— Harry. . . . Help me . . . I 've forgotten. I knew it all once, but I 've forgotten. Oh, God, I 've forgotten how to be a king.

[*He sinks back into the chair in a fit of weeping.*

CURTAIN

PROGRESS

St John Ervine

'Progress' was performed for the first time at the Little Theatre, London, on 3rd April 1922. *It was produced by Lewis Casson, with the following cast:*

PROFESSOR HENRY CORRIE, D.Sc.	*Lewis Casson*
MRS MELDON	*Sybil Thorndike*
HANNAH	*Cecily Oates*

The terms for the performance of this play may be obtained from the author at 'Honey Ditches,' Seaton, Devon, to whom all applications for permission should be made. No performance or public reading may be given without written permission.

The play is published separately by Messrs Allen & Unwin Ltd.

PROGRESS

The scene of the play is laid in the study of Professor Henry Corrie in a remote village in the north of England on a spring day in the year 1919. *The room is tidy enough, with the tidiness of a house dominated by a bachelor who is dominated by his work rather than by domestic comfort; and on the large table near the centre of the room there is a litter of scientific apparatus employed by Professor Corrie in the experiment in which he is now engaged. On the walls of the room are a number of diagrams, showing sections of very large bombs. There is a model of a big bomb on a stand underneath one of these diagrams. There are sectional diagrams of aeroplanes and airships to be seen, and also fairly large models of aeroplanes and airships.*

Professor Henry Corrie, aged between fifty and sixty, is sitting at the centre table watching a chemical process in a large retort. He has cold, humourless eyes, and his mouth, if it were not concealed by a thickish beard, would be seen to have cruel lines about it. He does not, however, impress the casual visitor as a cruel man—indeed, he seems to be a harmless, kindly, inconsequent person, completely absorbed, of course, in his work. It is when he is angry that something of his cruelty is observable—he is inclined to utter wolfish snarls if he is thwarted or hindered in any way. But the most certain sign of his fundamentally cruel character is his absorption in his scientific work. Nothing is of greater importance to him than that, and a human being is of less consequence to him than the success of even a minor experiment.

He regards the retort very closely, muttering to himself as he does so. Sometimes his mutterings are of satisfaction, sometimes of anxiety, and once of rage that turns again to satisfaction. A knock is heard on his study door, but he does not hear it. It is repeated. He leans forward to glance more closely at the retort, and then, with a shout of pleasure, rises up and contemplates it. The knock is heard for the third time.

CORRIE. [*Bending over the retort and ending the experiment.*] Ah, at last, at last! By Heaven, I've done it at last. [*A very loud*

157

knock on the door. He turns round in a puzzled fashion.] Eh? Oh, oh! Come in! *Come* in!

[*The door opens, and an elderly servant enters.*

SERVANT. Mrs Meldon . . .

CORRIE. Yes, yes, Hannah, what is it?

HANNAH. Mrs Meldon wants to know whether you'll come downstairs to tea or have it up here?

CORRIE. Has she got back?

HANNAH. Yes, sir. She expected you to meet her at the station, sir. She waited a long time in the cold, and then got Marshall to drive her up.

CORRIE. I meant to go, but I was busy, and then I forgot. But she's quite capable of coming home by herself.

HANNAH. Yes, sir. Will you come downstairs to tea, sir, or have it up here?

CORRIE. The drawing-room's so cold! . . . Tell Mrs Meldon I'll have it up here. I've news for her. Tell her I've good news for her. My experiment is ended, and it's a success.

HANNAH. Is it, sir?

CORRIE. Yes—but it's no use telling you about it. You wouldn't understand.

HANNAH. No, sir.

CORRIE. But I'm a proud man, Hannah. Perhaps you'll understand that. Go and tell Mrs Meldon.

HANNAH. Yes, sir.

CORRIE. Don't forget to tell her that my experiment is a success. Or, no!—you'd better not tell her. I'll do that myself. You're sure to make a mess of it. She'll be as pleased as I am.

HANNAH. She's not very happy to-day, sir.

CORRIE. Not happy! Why? I'm happy, aren't I?

HANNAH. Well, you see, sir, it's three years ago to-day since her son was killed in the War! . . .

CORRIE. [*Almost forgetting his grievance.*] Oh, yes! I'd forgotten that! Of course, one can't keep on thinking about these things! . . .

HANNAH. She does, sir.

CORRIE. I'm sorry I didn't meet her at the station. But I had to attend to my experiment, Hannah. I wish she wouldn't dwell on Eddie's death. It's not right for the living to think so much of the dead. She's a woman, of course, and a mother —a bereaved mother. We must make allowances, Hannah. That's all. Now if I tell her about my successful experiment, how would that do?

HANNAH. [*Dubiously.*] I don't suppose it would make her
feel any worse than she is now, sir.

CORRIE. Well, tell her to come up here and have her tea with me.
See? And I 'll tell her about my experiment.

HANNAH. Very good, sir. [*She turns to go.*

CORRIE. Oh!—and, Hannah, tell her I 'm very sorry I couldn't
meet her at the station. That 'll break the ice a bit. Then
when she realizes how important my work is and how much
depends on it, she 'll be all right.

HANNAH. Very good, sir. [*She goes towards the door. Then she
stops and turns towards him.*] She really isn't happy, sir. Her
nerves aren't at all right. You see, she can't forget, sir!

[*But the professor is back at his table, intently regarding his
experiment, and, except for a grunt, he does not reply.
Hannah goes out. The professor makes some calculations
on paper, and then sits back in his chair regarding them
with delight. His manifestations of joy are interrupted
by the entrance of his sister, Mrs Meldon, aged about
forty-three. She is dressed in black, partly because she
is a widow, but chiefly because of her son's death. She is
a sensitive-looking woman, now plainly suffering deeply
from her memories, but her nervous sensibilities give her a
strength on occasions which is hardly credible. She is not
a fretful, complaining woman who behaves as if she were
the only person in the world who had suffered a bereave-
ment, and when, in the course of the play, she speaks of
her loss she does so with grave and beautiful dignity.*

MRS MELDON. Henry!

CORRIE. Eh? [*Turning.*] Oh, my dear Charlotte, I 'm sorry I
did not meet you at the station! . . .

MRS MELDON. [*Seating herself by the fire.*] It doesn't matter,
Henry. Only I thought you were coming—you said you
would—and I waited a long time in the cold! . . .

CORRIE. Yes, I 'm sorry about that, but, you see, I was busy,
Charlotte. I 've succeeded at last. I 've got just exactly
what I wanted, Charlotte. Absolutely *the* thing. This will
bring fame and fortune to me. I shall be rich now, but
more than that, I shall be famous. My name will live for
ever. When I saw how well the experiment was going, I
said to myself, 'Charlotte won't really expect me to meet
her just when everything 's going so right, and after all, she 's
a grown-up woman and she knows the way home as well
as I do!' So I didn't go. I stayed here and did my work.

I knew you'd understand. And it's a success, Charlotte, the greatest and most wonderful success I've ever had.

MRS MELDON. Oh, yes.

CORRIE. [Dashed.] Well, you don't seem very excited about it.

MRS MELDON. Of course, I'm glad it's a success, Henry, whatever it is, but, you see, you've never told me anything about it.

CORRIE. No, that's true. I've always believed in keeping secrets to myself. Tell no one anything until you are obliged to, that's my principle. No one knows that I have been working at this thing—except myself. The secret of successful invention, Charlotte, is reticence! But now, I can tell you what is is. The component parts are still my secret and will remain such until I can get a binding offer from some government! . . .

MRS MELDON. Government! Is it a government matter?

CORRIE. I should think it is. I shall offer it first to the British Government, of course, but if they won't pay my price, I'll offer it to somebody else. Too many inventors have been let down by the British Government, Charlotte. But they will not let me down. No. I can take care of myself. But then, when they hear what my invention is, they'll jump at it.

MRS MELDON. Will they?

CORRIE. Of course they will, though you're quite justified in feeling sceptical about them. It was very hard to get them to use tanks in the War—very hard. These cavalry generals had to be forced to use them. They ought to be horse-knackers, instead of soldiers. And tin hats, too! Look what a time it was before that damned War Office could be persuaded to use 'em! . . . But I'm sorry, Charlotte. I ought not to be talking about the War to you—especially to-day.

MRS MELDON. I don't mind, Henry. And, after all, the War Office isn't the War!

CORRIE. No, that's true.

MRS MELDON. What is your invention, Henry?

CORRIE. Ah, Charlotte! There's something interesting to talk about.

[Hannah enters with a tea-tray.

HANNAH. Here's the tea, sir.

CORRIE. Damn! Oh, all right! Put it down there!

[Hannah arranges the tea-tray in front of Mrs Meldon.
[The professor, meantime, is back at his table and his retorts and his formulae. Now and again he exclaims to himself.

MRS MELDON. Has everything been all right, Hannah?

HANNAH. Yes, ma'am. Gage, the gardener, brought up the wreath you ordered for the War Memorial, ma'am. I 've got it in the kitchen now. Shall I fetch it for you?

MRS MELDON. Yes, do, please, Hannah.

[*And then Hannah, having finished with the tea-table, goes out.*

MRS MELDON. Come and have your tea, Henry!

CORRIE. All right!   [*But he does not stir.*

MRS MELDON. Come along, Henry!

CORRIE. Eh? Oh, all right! In a minute!

MRS MELDON. Your tea will get cold if you don't come now!

CORRIE. [*Getting up and coming to the tea-table.*] Oh, how women do fuss! Your sex is most extraordinary, Charlotte. Always willing to break off things for other things. No application. No concentration. No capacity for complete, impersonal devotion. That 's why no women have ever been great artists or scientists. Because they will not forsake everything and follow—well, whatever it is they ought to be following!

[*Hannah returns, carrying a bunch of flowers to which a label is attached.*

HANNAH. Here it is, ma'am.

CORRIE. What 's that?

MRS MELDON. [*Taking the flowers from Hannah.*] I ordered it from Gage to put on the War Memorial. It 's for Eddie! . .

CORRIE. Oh, yes, yes!

MRS MELDON. I shall take it down there after tea. Will you come with me?

CORRIE. I 'd like to, of course, but I really must finish up these things.

MRS MELDON. Very well, Henry. [*To Hannah.*] Thank you, Hannah. I 'll keep the flowers here.

[*Exit Hannah.*

MRS MELDON. [*To her brother.*] They 're very beautiful, aren't they, Henry?

CORRIE. Oh, yes! Quite nice! You know, Charlotte, this invention of mine——

MRS MELDON. Will you have some more tea, Henry?

CORRIE. [*Vaguely.*] Oh-h-h-h! [*Then definitely.*] Yes. Half a cup!

[*He hands the cup to her, and she fills it and returns it to him while the following speeches are uttered.*

CORRIE. I was saying this invention of mine will revolutionize warfare.

MRS MELDON. Will it abolish warfare?

CORRIE. Abolish war! . . . My dear Charlotte, don't be childish!

MRS MELDON. I 'm very interested in that subject. It seems to me more important than anything else in the world, Henry. You don't realize how deeply women like me feel about this . . . this organized butchery of boys. Look at me! I had a husband and a son when the War began. I had neither when it was over. I am a most lonely woman . . . cruelly alone! . . .

CORRIE. [*A little annoyed by what seems to him sentimental harping on one string.*] I know, of course, that the War hit you very badly, Charlotte—what with Eddie being killed and Tom taking his death so badly! . . .

MRS MELDON. Tom died of a broken heart, Henry. That may sound sentimental and unscientific to you, but it 's true. I sometimes wonder why I was not granted the mercy of death— why I should be compelled to live on alone! . . .

CORRIE. Oh, come, come, Charlotte! Not alone! No, no, not alone! You 're happy enough with me, aren't you? Your only brother! . . .

MRS MELDON. You 're not a very good substitute for a son, Henry!

CORRIE. Well, no, I suppose not, but, still, there 's no need for despair. Let me tell you about my invention.

[*He puts his cup down and prepares to explain.*

MRS MELDON. Will you have some more tea?

CORRIE. No, thanks! Now, Charlotte, when I say that war ought to be revolutionized, I mean that it ought to be made more expeditious. The war we 've just had lasted for a ridiculous period. Five years—or nearly five years. Perfectly preposterous. It ought not to have lasted more than five weeks.

MRS MELDON. Have you invented a means of restricting the duration of wars?

CORRIE. Well—yes, I think you might put it like that. What the combatants ought to aim at, in war, is to get the first blow in so hard that the other side immediately succumbs to it.

MRS MELDON. I see.

CORRIE. That means that the weapons of war must be made immeasurably more horrible and devastating than they now are.

MRS MELDON. More horrible! Is that possible?

Corrie. Yes. Oh, yes! We haven't yet reached the limits of horror in war! Oh, dear me, no!

Mrs Meldon. My son was nineteen, Henry, and he was killed in a fight of which he knew very little. That seems to me a horrible thing!

Corrie. Oh, a mother's feelings, of course, but look at the matter from a broad point of view. Put your own feelings aside! . . .

Mrs Meldon. I can't do that, Henry. The whole war for me comes down to this one thing, that my son, a boy new from school, was taken away from me, just when his life was beginning to open out, and killed. I'm not a clever woman, Henry. I can only feel things as they touch me and mine. Eddie was my only son, my darling, my heart's joy! I expected so much from him—and he's gone, and there's nothing . . . nothing . . . nothing!

Corrie. [Being very gentle with her.] Yes, I know, Charlotte, but you really ought not to dwell too much on your sorrow. It isn't good for you. You ought to take a broad point of view. Imagine yourself a statesman! . . .

Mrs Meldon. If Eddie had been a statesman, he would not have gone to the war. He would have compelled some other person to go.

Corrie. Oh, now, don't be bitter, Charlotte; don't be bitter!

Mrs Meldon. My dear Henry, I'm beyond being bitter. Do you know what I discovered to-day?

Corrie. No.

Mrs Meldon. You know I've never really known how Eddie died. I found out to-day.

Corrie. I wish you wouldn't think so much about it.

Mrs Meldon. [With sudden passion.] I must think about it. I can't help thinking about it! . . . I met a young man in town to-day who had been in the same battalion as Eddie, and he told me about it. Poor lad, it slipped out before he realized that I hadn't known before! . . .

Corrie. People oughtn't to talk so much about the War. Much better forget about it!

Mrs Meldon. [Recovering herself.] You remember the C.O. of the battalion wrote to me and said that Eddie had been killed by a piece of shell and that he had been buried behind the line somewhere?

Corrie. Yes, I remember.

Mrs Meldon. That comforted me very much. It made things

easier to think that he wasn't . . . mutilated . . . that even
when he was killed he was still my dear and beautiful boy . . .
a soldier, buried by soldiers, in a soldier's grave! . . . But he
wasn't buried, Henry!

CORRIE. Wasn't buried?

MRS MELDON. No! There was nothing to bury. The shell
came and . . . and . . . there was nothing. [*They are silent for
a moment or two.*] Don't you think *that* is horrible, Henry?
There was no decency in his death! . . . Oh, my God! my
God! You tell me to take a broad point of view about that!
My son! . . . They'd been in a little, shallow trench, Eddie
and his men, sitting there for eight days and nights, waiting
and waiting and waiting; and then a shell came right into the
middle of a group of them and destroyed them . . . utterly
destroyed them. Five of them . . . nothing left . . . nothing
left!

[*She sits back in her chair and both of them are silent. Then
the professor goes to his table and sits down before his
papers and retorts.*]

MRS MELDON. What is your invention, Henry?

CORRIE. Oh, I think we'd better not talk about it! You're
upset! That chap ought not to have told you about Eddie.

MRS MELDON. He thought I knew. What is your invention?

CORRIE. I'll tell you another time.

MRS MELDON. I'd like to know now. Something to make war
more expeditious! To end it quickly!

CORRIE. [*Swinging round to her.*] Really, Charlotte, this is a
most humanitarian invention. I don't believe, mind you,
that wars will ever end. No. We're altogether too pug-
nacious, we human beings. So the only thing to do then is
to make war so horrible that no nation will engage in one
unless absolutely driven to it. That's where I come in.
I'm going to make war horrible, *really* horrible!

MRS MELDON. Yes.

CORRIE. I've got something here, Charlotte . . . the formula
for a bomb that will make war not only stupendously horrible,
but will end it almost as quickly as it began.

MRS MELDON. On that table?   [*She rises and goes to him.*]

CORRIE. Yes. I've made tests and I've worked out the
formula with mathematical precision, and I've discovered
a combination of gases and explosives that will obliterate
thousands at once. Thousands!

MRS MELDON. Thousands?

CORRIE. Yes.

MRS MELDON. Obliterate them . . . just like Eddie.

CORRIE. Oh, my dear Charlotte, you really must not be so morbid. We've got to deal with the world of fact, and if this country is going to maintain her position in the world, she will have to use every device she can employ to keep her there. I consider that I'm performing a highly patriotic act in offering this discovery to my country. Now, listen! By means of my formula, we can make a bomb, a big bomb, not one of those little footling things the Germans used to drop on London, but an enormous bomb, full of corrosive gas, which will be dropped from a powerful aeroplane or airship—that has to be settled yet—but it's not really my job. Now, when the next war breaks out! . . .

MRS MELDON. The next war?

CORRIE. Yes, I should say we'd have another in twenty or thirty years, wouldn't you? Not more than fifty, anyhow. Well, when it comes, our ultimatum will consist of a number of airships or aeroplanes dropping these big bombs on the country with which we're at war—just in the way the Japanese declared war on the Russians by blowing their ships to pieces. Only ours will be much more effective than that. The Japs only sank a few ships. We'll utterly obliterate whole cities . . . perhaps a whole nation.

MRS MELDON. Yes.

CORRIE. When this bomb falls, the explosion will devastate a wide tract of the district in which it falls, and at the same time will release a powerful, spreading gas, without colour or smell, which will spread over a wide area and poison every person who inhales it. They won't know that they've inhaled it until they see their bodies rotting. And nothing will save them then! With a single bomb we could wipe out the population of a city as big as Manchester. Single bomb, Charlotte!

MRS MELDON. But that would mean everybody—men and women and children.

CORRIE. Oh, yes. After all, nowadays, there is no logical distinction between a civilian and a soldier. What's the difference between the girl who makes munitions and the man who uses them in the trenches? You know, Charlotte, it's a terrific thought, to think that I can sit here at this table, with a formula written out on those sheets of paper which will enable a few men to go up into the air and wipe out a whole city. And I'm the only man in the world who knows how to do it.

MRS MELDON. Aren't there men like you in other countries using their brains for the same purpose?

CORRIE. Yes, but I don't imagine any one will discover as powerful a weapon as this. If I had made this discovery in 1914, the War would have been over before the end of that year, and there probably wouldn't be any Germans left now. They'd be an extinct race.

MRS MELDON. Perhaps an enemy of this country might make a similar discovery, Henry, and use it on us.

CORRIE. We'll have to take the risk of that. Anyhow, my discovery will be available to our people, and if a war does come along, we've only got to get our bomb dropped on them before they get theirs dropped on us, and the trick's done.

MRS MELDON. I suppose it was someone like you who invented the kind of shell that destroyed Eddie . . . that obliterated him!

CORRIE. [Rising and patting her on the shoulder.] Now, now, don't go back to that subject, Charlotte. Come over here by the fire, and try and take a more cheerful view of life.

MRS MELDON. Cheerful view! My dear Henry, I sometimes wonder whether, in spite of your cleverness, you aren't really the stupidest man on earth.

CORRIE. Oh, come!

MRS MELDON. I'm not clever. It seems odd that I should be your sister, a quite ordinary, commonplace woman, with nothing in my life but my love for my husband and my son. But when I hear you telling me to take a broad statesmanlike view of my son being blown to pieces, I begin to think that you're a fool, Henry—just a dull, unimaginative, bloodless fool. And when you ask me to rejoice because you've invented a bomb that will destroy a whole city in a few minutes, I think you're . . . you're mad—wickedly, horribly mad.

CORRIE. My dear Charlotte! . . .

MRS MELDON. One moment, Henry. I want you to try and realize my point of view, the point of view of an ordinary woman without any pretensions. Think of Eddie as I think of him! . . .

CORRIE. This isn't good for you.

MRS MELDON. Oh, yes, it is. I go back now to the very beginning, and I think of Tom and me, very young and foolish, I suppose, but very happy, too, Henry, and our queer pleasure and fright when we knew that Eddie was coming. And I think, too, of myself, sometimes at night, awake, with Tom lying asleep beside me; and how I thought about the little child I was going to bear him, and how I loved it and loved him for being its father, and how sure I was that it would be a boy! I was frightened, too, sometimes, because I thought I might die and never know my son, who would grow up and have no knowledge of me. And then he was born, such a dear, little, clutching child, so terribly dependent on me. Tom was very pleased and proud, but never so pleased and proud as I was. We both watched him grow—you know how handsome he was!

CORRIE. Yes, he was a good-looking lad.

MRS MELDON. And we made plans for him. He was to be great and liked—people did like him; even you liked him, Henry, didn't you?

CORRIE. Yes, I . . . I liked him. He was an attractive boy. But don't you think——

MRS MELDON. And then he was ill. You remember how we all thought that he would die, and Tom, poor Tom, who never could express himself very aptly, went about as if he were stunned. I can't tell you what I thought then, Henry. I just can't tell you, but oh! I prayed for him, Henry—prayed for him so that my whole mind was a prayer. Well, he got better, and seemed to grow stronger, and at school he did very well. I can see him now, the first time he played in a cricket match, very pleased with his blazer, and how excited he was when he came to tell me that he had made ten runs. Ten runs he made, my little son, in his first cricket match. All the other boys of his age were very respectful to him, and I was so glad when he let me walk about with him, just as if he hadn't had a triumph. And Tom was frightfully pleased, too, and gave him a sovereign! . . . [*Her tears overcome her, and she raises her hands to her lips in a gesture of grief.*] My little boy! . . .

CORRIE. This is distressing you, my dear. Don't talk about it any more.

MRS MELDON. [*Recovering herself.*] He hadn't been at Oxford long when the War began, and then he went off and enlisted. We didn't know whether to be proud of him or to be angry with him, but chiefly we were proud. I loved him in his clumsy uniform and his great, rough boots, just as much as I loved him later on in his officer's uniform. And when he went off to France, I tried to be worthy of my son and not to cry. It was frightfully hard to smile, Henry, but I did smile. I felt that that was what Eddie would wish me to do, not to shame him before the other people, and so I smiled and made a little silly joke about the fear of the Germans when they heard of his arrival. But I was in terror, Henry, and all the time that he was away I was in terror. The sight of a telegraph messenger made my heart sink! . . . And then he came home on his first leave, and my little son wasn't my little son any more, but a strangely grown man, young to look at, but full of extraordinary knowledge. I felt shy with him. He'd seen so much and knew so much. And then I think I felt prouder of him than ever before, because he was a man and I could depend upon him. We were very happy during that leave, Henry, so happy that I hardly had time to be miserable because it would so soon be over, and when he went back, although I cried a little when he wasn't looking, I didn't mind so much as I thought I should, because I persuaded myself to believe that he wouldn't be killed. When he had his second leave and was a captain, I was sure that he would come home to me, quite safe. Even Tom, who had always felt we should lose him, began to believe that he'd come home again. But he didn't. Immediately he got back to France, he had to go into the line, and eight days later he was killed—just obliterated, as you say, by men who had never seen him, who didn't even know that they'd killed him. And all my years of love and hope and desire and pain—gone! I'd nursed him and cared for him and taught him little lessons and been proud of him—and then in a moment my beautiful son was . . . obliterated, Henry! [*There is a slight pause while she recovers herself.*] You see, don't you, Henry, that I can't take a broad view of that. I can only see my son's body mutilated and destroyed. That's all.

CORRIE. Well, of course, I quite see your point of view, Charlotte. It is hard. I admit that. But we have to keep our feelings under control. And after all, there's the consolation that Eddie did his duty to his country. I dare say he accounted for a good many Germans! . . .

MRS MELDON. That doesn't comfort me, Henry. I can't get any pleasure out of the thought that some poor German woman is suffering just as I'm suffering. No, Henry, I feel that I should want to take sides with her against men like you!

CORRIE. Men like me!

MRS MELDON. Yes. People with broad views. Because you 're such fools. Someone like me, not clever, creates a beautiful thing like my son, and you, with all your cleverness, can only destroy it. That's why I think you 're a fool, Henry.

CORRIE. [*Nettled.*] Well, of course, Charlotte, with your views, I can hardly expect you to appreciate me or my work, but I fancy that my countrymen, if they have any sense, will know how to value me. My bomb will make my name known to the most ignorant men in the country. People will talk about the Corrie bomb, just as they used to talk about the Mills bomb during the War. I shall have to ask for a large lump sum in payment of the invention, because a royalty wouldn't pay me at all. Mills got a royalty on each of his bombs, but then they were small and hundreds of thousands of them were used. My bombs will be big, and one of them will suffice for a city. Yes, I shall have to ask for a large lump sum. Now that they 're spending several million pounds on a battleship that is generally believed to be useless, I 'm entitled to ask for a very large sum for my bomb which will certainly decide the war. I wonder how much I ought to ask for? Charlotte, how much ought I to ask for? They won't give me what it 's worth, that 's absolutely certain. They might pay a quarter of a million. Charlotte, what would you ask for if you were me?

MRS MELDON. I should ask for my son.

CORRIE. Now, now, now, Charlotte, not again, please. Not again. We must think of the future, not of the past. I don't want to ask for too much, because I shan't get it, and I don't want to ask for too little, though I shall probably get that anyhow. What do you think, Charlotte? Do you think it would be better to let them name a price?

MRS MELDON. I don't know.

CORRIE. Well, you might take a little interest in the matter. It 's very important to me. They ought really to give me a title, too. Supposing I say a couple of hundred thousand pounds and a peerage! . . .

MRS MELDON. Why not say thirty pieces of silver?

CORRIE. [*Thoroughly angry.*] Really, Charlotte, you 're insufferable! You 're absolutely insufferable! I put up with a great deal from you because you 're in distress, but there are limits to endurance, you know. You haven't congratulated me, even perfunctorily, and you 've made yourself and me thoroughly miserable by this . . . this moaning over what can't be helped. You 've even made Hannah miserable. My dear Charlotte, I 'm talking to you now for your good. You really ought not to let your mind dwell on things in the way you do. It isn't good for you, and it 's very unpleasant for me and for others who associate with you. Your boy was killed—so were other people's boys—but we can't spend the rest of our lives in lamentation. I have my work to do! . . .

MRS MELDON. Your bomb?

CORRIE. Yes.

MRS MELDON. Which will make the bodies of men and women and little children rot if it does not blow them to pieces.

CORRIE. The fortune of war, my dear Charlotte. After all, what does it matter to a man whether he is blown to pieces by a bomb or stabbed to death by a bayonet? As a matter of fact, the bomb is the more merciful of the two. It isn't any use being sentimental about these things. The purpose of war is killing, and the side which kills the most people in the shortest time is going to win the wars of the future. My bomb will enable those who possess it to conduct a war in a rapid and efficient fashion. No reasonable person can deny that I have performed a service to my country in inventing this bomb for its use, and even you, if you were not distracted by what you heard this morning and the fact that this is the anniversary of Eddie's death, would agree with them.

MRS MELDON. No one but you knows the secret of your invention, Henry?

CORRIE. No—not that I am aware of.

MRS MELDON. If you were to destroy your invention, never reveal its secrets, thousands of boys like Eddie might live without fear of being destroyed?

CORRIE. Oh, I don't know. It 's a fantastic thought, that, but there 's nothing in it. Other people will invent things even deadlier than my bomb.

MRS MELDON. But, Henry, if you were to suppress your invention!

CORRIE. Suppress it!

MRS MELDON. Yes, if you were to destroy your formulae, and people were to know what you 'd done, perhaps you 'd do a great deal to change people's hearts! . . .

CORRIE. My dear Charlotte, most sensible people would think I 'd gone off my head. A few cranks and religious maniacs might praise me, but the average person would think I was a fool—besides being damned unpatriotic.

MRS MELDON. Henry, I beg you to destroy your invention.

CORRIE. You what?

MRS MELDON. I beg you to destroy it. Let that be your memorial to Eddie! . . .

CORRIE. My dear Charlotte, I begin to believe that grief has unhinged your mind. Destroy my invention! . . .

MRS MELDON. Your bomb will destroy life, Henry. I beg of you to destroy it! . . .

CORRIE. Rubbish, woman, rubbish.

MRS MELDON. Then I will destroy it for you! . . .

[*She goes to the table where the retorts are and hurls the table over so that the retorts are smashed.*

CORRIE. What the hell are you doing?

MRS MELDON. I'm destroying your foul invention.

CORRIE. [*Laughing harshly.*] That won't destroy it. I've got it all in my head. All that you've done, Charlotte, is to make a mess on my floor. Damned silly, I call it.

[*He stoops down and begins to clear up the mess.*

MRS MELDON. [*Standing behind him.*] It's all in your head!

CORRIE. Of course it is. Anybody but a fool of a woman would have realized that. Making a confounded mess like this! . . .

MRS MELDON. It's all in your head?

CORRIE. Yes, yes. Don't keep on repeating yourself, but come and help to clear up this mess you've made.

MRS MELDON. Henry, won't you do what I ask you?

CORRIE. Don't be a fool. [*Looking round.*] Give me that cloth over there so that I can mop up this stuff.

[*He continues to collect the pieces of broken glass, etc., while she goes towards the table where the cloth is. When she reaches the table, she sees a long knife lying there, and half unconsciously she picks it up and looks at it.*

CORRIE. [*Impatiently.*] Hurry up. What on earth are you doing?

MRS MELDON. I'm looking at something—this knife!

CORRIE. Well, you can look at it afterwards. Fetch the cloth now. Here's Eddie's wreath under the table. You've made a mess of it, too!

MRS MELDON. Eddie's wreath!

[*She comes towards him, the knife in her hand*

CORRIE. Yes.

MRS MELDON. If you were to give up your invention, Henry, I

wouldn't mind about the wreath. Your offering would be better than mine.

CORRIE. Well, I shan't. Give up my invention for a lot of damned sentiment! Not likely!

MRS MELDON. It'll destroy life, Henry.

CORRIE. What's that got to do with it? Give me that cloth.
  [*He snaps it out of her hand, but does not see the knife in her other hand.*

MRS MELDON. You won't destroy it, Henry?

CORRIE. [*Almost in a snarl.*] NO!

MRS MELDON. [*Raising the knife above him.*] Then I . . .
  [*With a queer moan of despair, she drives the knife into his back. He sways a moment, uttering a choking sound, and then, clutching at the air, he pitches forward on to his face.*
  [*She stands above him, looking down on his body in a dazed way. She is crying hysterically, and suddenly she stoops and picks up the broken wreath. She holds it to her breast, and stares distractedly in front of her.*

MRS MELDON. Eddie, dear, I had to, I had to, Eddie! . .

CURTAIN

THE MAN WHO WOULDN'T GO TO HEAVEN

F. Sladen-Smith

'*The Man who wouldn't go to Heaven*' was first produced by The Unnamed Society, Manchester, at The Little Theatre, Lomax Street, Salford, on 24th March 1928, with the following cast:

THARIEL	*G. Bernard Smith*
MARGARET	*Betty Crosthwaite*
RICHARD ALTON . . .	*. John Wardle*
BOBBIE NIGHTINGALE . .	*Bertram E. Smith*
ELIZA MUGGINS . . .	*Beatrix Preston*
SISTER MARY TERESA . .	*Dorothy Crosse*
MRS CUTHBERT BAGSHAWE .	*Elsie J. Crosse*
HARRIET REBECCA STRENHAM	*. D. Walton*
REV. JOHN MCNULTY . .	*L. Oppenheimer*
TIMOTHY TOTO NEWBIGGIN	*. J. Edward Roberts*
DERRICK BRADLEY . .	*. Norman F. Taylor*

Produced by the Author. Decorated by Eric Newton

A NOTE ON THE ANGELS

A number of masked Angels may strike producers as a difficult problem, but, if masks are out of the question, the Angels could be seen dimly, through a curtain at the back. Whether masks or transparent curtains are used, not many Angels are actually necessary to get the required effect, especially if the stage is small. The lighting at the end should be soft and glowing, in contrast to the clear, hard lighting of the rest of the play.—F. S-S.

THE MAN WHO WOULDN'T GO TO HEAVEN

SCENE. *A gateway leading to Heaven. A flight of steps leads to a white-curtained archway. In front of this archway sits Thariel at a small table towards the left. On the table is a large book. Thariel's wings and raiment are magnificent. The characters enter from a small archway on the extreme left. On the right is a long bench.*

As the curtain rises, Thariel is talking to a young girl.

GIRL. And then I go up those steps?

THARIEL. Yes.

GIRL. And never see any one again?

THARIEL. Why should you think that?

GIRL. Because [*looking round*] it all seems so lonely.

THARIEL. [*Indicating bench.*] Perhaps you would like to wait until someone comes? There is sure to be someone in a moment.

GIRL. Oh, no, no, please. There is only one I would——

THARIEL. But he might not come just yet.

GIRL. Oh—then you know——?

THARIEL. Yes, I know.

GIRL. Oh, I suppose you do. [*Eagerly.*] But, when he does come, you'll be very nice and kind to him, won't you? I mean, he is bound to be a little shy and nervous. [*With a smile.*] He is so funny when he's shy!

THARIEL. Is he? Then we'll do our best with him. Pass up those stairs, please.

GIRL. What is beyond?

THARIEL. So many things; all so different.

GIRL. But he won't be different when he comes, will he? I couldn't bear that! I shall wait so patiently—will he have changed?

THARIEL. Why do you all make yourselves unhappy by perpetual questioning? Pass along.

Enter Alton.

THARIEL. Name, please.

ALTON. Well, I'm blowed!

GIRL. [*Ascending the steps and turning round.*] He will come some day?

THARIEL. Certainly; possibly very soon. But I am not allowed to tell people when others are coming.

ALTON. Well, I'm blessed!

GIRL. [*At the top of the steps.*] But when he does come you'll be very kind to him and send him to me?

THARIEL. Very kind to him and send him to you. Yes. [*Girl disappears through curtain.*] Now then, name, please.

ALTON. Well, I never!

THARIEL. So you keep on saying. Why?

ALTON. Do you expect I expected——? Do you imagine I imagined——? It can't be true—it can't! I must have gone off my head!

THARIEL. Do I surprise you?

ALTON. You? I should think you did! I—I—— No, I simply *can't* believe in you.

THARIEL. In that case you must disbelieve in me. Name, please. [*Opens book.*

ALTON. Richard Alton. What is in that book?

THARIEL. Your name, and a good many others. All I expect at this period.

ALTON. You mean to-day.

THARIEL. [*Writing in book.*] There is no day.

ALTON. What do you mean?

THARIEL. [*With quiet impatience.*] Well, how can there be?

ALTON. Look here, you know, I never believed in a hereafter, or any such nonsense. You know quite well there is no such place as Heaven—or at least, there ought not to be.

THARIEL. There is a great deal in what you say, but, still, here you are.

ALTON. But I need not put up with it! Unless it is all a silly dream—which, mind you, I think it may be—unless it's a dream, I'm dead, I suppose. *Am I dead?*

THARIEL. Technically, yes. For the sake of argument, yes.

ALTON. Well, then, I can't be, because, like every sensible man, I've always believed in utter extinction.

THARIEL. Do you feel utterly extinct?

ALTON. No: so I must be delirious or dreaming. But to dream of Heaven and angels! That beats me. The place I've laughed at all my life, and now I imagine I'm bang in it.

THARIEL. I would not go so far as to say you were in Heaven; at least, not yet. But, technically, you understand, you will be if you go up those steps.

ALTON. I 'm sure it 's all rot. I 'm delirious.

THARIEL. You 're not.

ALTON. I 'm dreaming.

THARIEL. No.

ALTON. Then some trick is being played on me. I won't have it, do you hear? [*Brings his fist down on Thariel's book.*] I 'll have no tricks played on me!

THARIEL. Well, go and say all that when you 've passed up those steps.

ALTON. You *don't* suppose I 'm going up those steps?

THARIEL. Why not?

ALTON. Do you imagine, after half a lifetime spent in writing and talking against such rubbish, I 'm going to start climbing idiotic stairs supposed to lead to an idiotic Heaven? Where do those steps really lead to?—tell me that!

THARIEL. Pass along and see.

ALTON. I refuse, unless you answer my questions. You know very well Heaven is a sheer impossibility.

THARIEL. If I explained further you wouldn't understand, so pass along there, *please.*

ALTON. I will not.

THARIEL. [*With a sigh.*] Then go and sit on that seat. [*Indicating bench on the right.*] I haven't time to argue with you at present: here is somebody coming.

Enter Nightingale.

ALTON. I tell you, nothing shall make me go up those silly steps and enter your silly Heaven.

THARIEL. Very well. [*To Nightingale.*] Name, please.

NIGHTINGALE. Nightingale, Bobbie Nightingale. I say, is this the box-office for Heaven?

ALTON. No, it 's not!

NIGHTINGALE. All right, old man, but surely this impressive-looking gentleman knows best. I may be wrong, but the whole get-up of the place smacks of sanctity.

THARIEL. [*Who has been examining his book.*] Robert Nightingale. Yes. Any remark to make before you pass up those steps?

NIGHTINGALE. 'Cept that, if this is really anywhere near Heaven, it 's the last place I expected to get to.

THARIEL. [*Smiling.*] So many people say that.

NIGHTINGALE. But are you sure it's all O.K.? I wouldn't like to get you into trouble. Fact is, I've been a little—little—you know.

THARIEL. [*Referring to book.*] Yes; so I see.

ALTON. Don't you believe him. It's all put on. You bet he knows nothing about you.

NIGHTINGALE. I say, are you the Devil's Advocate?

ALTON. My name's Richard Alton. You may have heard of me. Free-thinker Dick, I used to be called. Went up and down the country exposing religion; had a great following at one time, I can tell you. Started life as a miner and worked myself up. I don't know what all this foolery means, but I'm jolly well not going to give way to it. Do as I do; be a sensible man. Refuse to go up those steps.

NIGHTINGALE. Well, considering everything, you've got some courage.

THARIEL. He always had courage; that is why he is here before his time.

Enter Mrs Muggins.

THARIEL. Name, please.

MRS MUGGINS. Eliza Muggins, Mr Angel, sir, good morning. Well, I'm in Heaven after all! And consequently no chance of meeting Muggins, thank God! But me in Heaven! Not that I ever did anything wrong, Mr Angel, far from it. As I always said, more sinned against than sinning, and by a long chalk; but still it is a surprise! I bet it's me health that's got me here. The doctor, he says, never imagine yourself well, he says, and I didn't, and here I am!

THARIEL. Any further remarks to make before you pass on?

MRS MUGGINS. Oh, Mr Angel, sir, I don't fancy no passings on just yet. I've had enough of passings on; in a manner of speaking my life's been all passing on. You'll look well and you'll feel well, the doctor says, but never imagine yourself well, he says, and I didn't, and here I am!

THARIEL. Then, if you don't feel like passing on just yet, perhaps you'll join these two gentlemen.

MRS MUGGINS. Oh, with pleasure, Mr Angel; I was always fond of the company of gentlemen, except perhaps Muggins, not that he was a gentleman, by no means! And I see I've got my Sunday dress on just as if I was going to a party.

ALTON. Come along, Mrs Muggins, and we'll smash the whole blooming thing.

MRS MUGGINS. Why, it's Free-thinker Dick! My daughter Maud, she once went to one of your lectures and came back believing nothing, something shocking. And the next week she saw the story of the Bible at the pictures, and believed so many things we had to call in the doctor. How are you feeling now you've got here, Mr Alton? Bit of a surprise for you, ain't it?

ALTON. I don't believe in it any more than I did on earth.

MRS MUGGINS. No, I dare say you wouldn't.

[Sits down beside him.

NIGHTINGALE. Hanged if I know what to do. Of course I could go straight on—if you're sure it's all right. On the other hand . . . say, old man, do you expect any—any——

THARIEL. There is sure to be a pretty girl up here before long.

NIGHTINGALE. Thanks, then I'll certainly wait.

[Sits down on the other side of Mrs Muggins.

NUN. [*Entering.*] I suppose this must be the Gate of Heaven. Oh, how wonderful! Oh, how glorious! It is just what I expected it to be like.

THARIEL. Glad to hear you say that. We always try to please people. [*Opening book.*] You are——?

NUN. Sister Mary Teresa of the Holy Angels.

THARIEL. Right. Do you wish to say anything before you go forward?

NUN. To say anything? Oh, how dare I speak?—besides, I have nothing to say, it is all so wonderful. It is so wonderful to see you, a real angel! But would you please tell me—shall I suffer much?

THARIEL. What's that?

NUN. Shall I suffer much? Because, of course, I know there will be a long, long purification before I am fit to enter the humblest Gate of Heaven.

NIGHTINGALE. Shame!

NUN. [*Turning to him.*] I beg your pardon?

NIGHTINGALE. I said 'Shame,' my dear; I said it loudly.

THARIEL. Do you want to suffer?

NUN. I know I ought to. . . . Mother Mary Joseph said we ought to love suffering. She said she did.

ALTON. And did she?

NUN. It was a little difficult to see just what suffering she had, but I am sure whatever it was it was great and she will go straight to Heaven.

THARIEL. But what makes you think *you* will not go straight to Heaven?

NUN. Oh, I am not so proud and vainglorious as that! I know this is only a brief space of rest before my trials begin.

NIGHTINGALE. Shame!

NUN. Please will you tell me why this gentleman is so ashamed?

THARIEL. He is not. He never felt ashamed in his life. What he would term your beauty is having an effect on what he calls his heart.

NIGHTINGALE. You 're right there, old boy. It makes me boil all over to think of a pretty creature like that being shut up.

NUN. But I wanted it. I threatened to throw myself into the river if they did not let me enter a convent.

ALTON. Simply one more case of sex-repression.

MRS MUGGINS. Now come, Mr Alton, you didn't ought to say such things in front of a religious lady.

THARIEL. Then your ideal of happiness is a convent?

NUN. Not now. Oh, I ought not to have said that! But I feel so strange. May I go further, please, if I 'm supposed to go further?

THARIEL. Certainly. Just up those steps.

NUN. Thank you. [*Ascends the steps. Suddenly.*] Oh, all saints and martyrs pray for me!

ALTON. What is the matter?

NUN. I am afraid! I am afraid! I know fortitude is always necessary, but——

NIGHTINGALE. The poor child is frightened to death. [*To Thariel.*] Can't you possibly say something decent to her?

THARIEL. Of course, of course. My poor child, there is nothing whatever to be afraid of. Go straight forward.

NUN. But, although I renounced so much on earth, still it *was* earth—this is so strange, and I feel I must renounce still more. And there are so many things I have not tasted! Ah!

[*Sways slightly.*

NIGHTINGALE. Good heavens! [*Rushes forward and seizes her in his arms.*] My pretty little white bird, before you die again, let me kiss you and kiss you that you may know love if only for a moment!

[*Kisses her passionately. From the other earthlings comes an involuntary cry of horror. Suddenly the Nun and Nightingale break away from each other and look scaredly at Thariel, who is calmly writing in his book. A slight pause.*

THARIEL. [*Without looking up.*] Have you finished?

NIGHTINGALE. Damn you for a spoil-sport!

THARIEL. What did I spoil?

NIGHTINGALE. Oh, we felt you there all the time.

THARIEL. You felt something more important than me.

NUN. [*Suddenly.*] Oh, I am cursed for evermore! An eternity of Hell awaits me!

THARIEL. Nonsense! Of course it doesn't. Don't be so primitive.

MRS MUGGINS. Don't take on so, dearie. I 've been cursed something terrible in my time, but here I am!

NIGHTINGALE. [*To Thariel.*] Is she cursed for evermore? [*A pause.*] Say something, you coward!

THARIEL. I cannot discuss these trivialities.

NIGHTINGALE. Do you call sending a nun to Hell because she 's had a good, thumping kiss, trivial?

THARIEL. [*Wearily, to Nun.*] Will you please go forward now?

NUN. But I am in mortal sin! Mother Mary Joseph would say——

THARIEL. Mother Mary Joseph may not be here for some time yet. I 'm sorry to disappoint you both.

MRS MUGGINS. I don't see any reason why they should be disappointed, Mr Angel. It was a good, hearty kiss, past denying.

THARIEL. It was singularly ineffective.

NIGHTINGALE. There 's something very beastly about you.

ALTON. Hear, hear!

NUN. Oh, for courage to go forward!

THARIEL. [*With a strange shade of meaning in his voice.*] You have gone forward already.

NIGHTINGALE. What do you mean?

[*But the Nun has slipped quietly through the curtains.*]

MRS MUGGINS. Well, it 's all queer, but fairly comfortable, isn't it? Not that that 's anything to go by. The doctor, he says to me, you 'll feel comfortable, he says, and you 'll look comfortable, he says, but never imagine——

ALTON. Comfortable! With that fool sitting there in fancy dress, and saying evasive, meaningless things to the poor creatures who come before him? But I 'm not taken in by him. He 's not going to put me in what he calls Heaven, like some dog in a kennel. I 'm not a child.

THARIEL. That 's just the pity of it.

NIGHTINGALE. I feel a perfect fool standing here while you two argue. I may as well slip in and see how Sister Mary 's going on, unless—say, old man, when 's the next pretty girl coming along?

MRS MUGGINS. It 's a proper shame the way some of 'em 's took off sudden. Why is it allowed, Mr Angel?

ALTON. A good question.

THARIEL. What a lot you think about death, down there!

ALTON. It has a knack of obtruding, you know. When you realize——

NIGHTINGALE. If you are going to start again, I 'll take the plunge. Anything to avoid an argument. [*Ascending the steps.*] So long, everybody. By Jove, I don't wonder that poor girl felt a bit queer. It 's distinctly atmospheric up here. You know nothing seems to matter, somehow. One begins to feel very simple, like some bally child. [*Ascending a step.*] I 'm sure I 'm about to be executed!

MRS MUGGINS. [*Greatly interested.*] Is he really, Mr Angel? I never thought I should live to see an execution!

THARIEL. He can be anything he likes later, but not just yet. Pass along there, *please.*

NIGHTINGALE. Damned if I want to, after all. [*Tries to step back.*

THARIEL. [*Sharply.*] Sorry, but you can't do that.

NIGHTINGALE. Why can't I?

ALTON. Don't be bamboozled by their conjuring tricks. Make an effort; come back if you want to.

MRS MUGGINS. Yes, make an effort, Mr Nightingale, make an effort!

NIGHTINGALE. I say, can't I really come back for a moment? I don't much want to go forward, you know. I 've been a bit thick, sometimes, you know.

THARIEL. It matters supremely little what you 've been. Pass along there, please.

ALTON. Do nothing of the kind!

NIGHTINGALE. Look here, old man, if you were on these steps you 'd sing a very different song. I 'd like to come back, but somehow I can't. And yet, dash it, I feel much more real than you.

ALTON. Don't be a fool.

Enter a fat, fussy female.

FEMALE. [*Amazed.*] Oh, dear, oh, dear! How shocking, how surprising!

THARIEL. Name, please.

FEMALE. Mrs Cuthbert Bagshawe, Emilia Stubbins that was, you know. Oh, dear, if only Mr Bagshawe were here, but I left rather suddenly, and I see I 've got my new silk blouse on, the one the vicar preferred. Oh, dear, wherever am I? I 'll do anything you like, sir—within reason, of course—but I 'm not at all used to being alone; Mr Bagshawe was always with me, in fact I was hardly ever out of his sight, which makes one so dreadfully dependent, doesn't it? However, I 'm certainly out of his sight now, and as I always said——

THARIEL. Pass along, please, up those steps.

MRS BAGSHAWE. I should love to, of course, but if only Mr Bagshawe——

THARIEL. There is a gentleman on the steps waiting to conduct you forward.

MRS BAGSHAWE. Oh, but how kind, how——

NIGHTINGALE. [To Thariel.] Look here, are you suffering from a sense of humour?

THARIEL. Not after all these aeons.

NIGHTINGALE. But considering the way I 've carried on—and I really *have*, you know—to send me into Heaven with——

MRS BAGSHAWE. [Arriving beside Nightingale.] I don't know you, of course, but I 'm sure that under the circumstances Mr Bagshawe would be only too——

NIGHTINGALE. Oh, but I say——

THARIEL. Robert Nightingale, will you please conduct Mrs Bagshawe forward?

NIGHTINGALE. All right, old man, I apol. Sorry to have been such a trouble to you. [Taking Mrs Bagshawe's arm.] So long, everybody. Now, Mrs Bagshawe, we 're in for it!

[Arm in arm they disappear.

MRS MUGGINS. I must say that 's a nice, comfortable gentleman. My daughter, Maud, once went for a week to Brighton with a gentleman like that.

ALTON. Damn shame such things happen.

MRS MUGGINS. Not it! She badly needed a bit of polish.

[A strong-minded woman in shooting attire strides in.

WOMAN. [To Thariel.] Here, you. If this is Heaven, as I strongly suspect, there 's been a mistake.

MRS MUGGINS. There 's honesty, now.

THARIEL. Most people expect Hell. Name, please.

WOMAN. Harriet Rebecca Strenham. But there 's been a blunder, I 'll take a bet on it.

THARIEL. Why do you think there has been a mistake?

*G 947

HARRIET. Well, fact is, I did myself in. Got fearfully fed up, seized a gun—always a good shot—well, I expect it's in the papers. Unsound mind, you know, and all the rest of it. Damn rubbish! Never was more sane in my life—like most people who do themselves in. [*Calling loudly.*] Bob!

THARIEL. You're here, nevertheless.

HARRIET. Yes, but of course it's a mistake. Never expected to go to Heaven. Fact is, between you and me, never expected there *was* a Heaven.

ALTON. There isn't.

HARRIET. Oh, is that so? Bob!

THARIEL. Would you mind telling me why you keep shouting 'Bob'?

MRS MUGGINS. The poor dearie's calling for her husband. It's pathetic, it is.

HARRIET. Indeed I'm not, my good woman. I'm not the marrying kind—had troubles enough. Bob's my dog. Fine little fellow, devoted to me.

THARIEL. But why should you think he is here?

HARRIET. Well, strictly between ourselves, you know, I did him in also. Just before myself. Saw no use in him moping and pining without me. And, if I've got here, surely that little fellow won't be kept out. Worth twenty of me—always was. Bob!

ALTON. You're the kind we want; come and take a seat here. We want people of character on this bench.

THARIEL. Wouldn't you rather go forward?

ALTON. No, don't give way to him! Come here and help us.

HARRIET. But how the deuce can I help you?

ALTON. They're obviously making fools of us in some way, and it's up to people of sense not to be taken in by it. I want to get to something definite: stay here and help me.

HARRIET. [*Going to him.*] Well, I don't mind resting for a moment. Besides, I'm not going into Heaven without the dog. Bob!

FREE CHURCH MINISTER. [*Arriving.*] To whomsoever is here, peace.

MRS MUGGINS. That's the best up to now.

FREE CHURCH MINISTER. [*Advancing to Thariel.*] I take it you, reverend sir, are in charge of this little gathering of holy souls?

ALTON. [*To the others.*] Damn funny.

THARIEL. I am in charge here. Name, please.

FREE CHURCH MINISTER. McNulty. The Reverend John McNulty, who has at last left a world of sin and suffering and is content. This is Heaven, I suppose? It is a blessed thought that, if there is a Heaven, there is also a Hell.

THARIEL. Do you find that a blessed thought?

McNULTY. I do indeed. My constant preaching on the subject has not been in vain. There is a Hell, there is a Hell! [*With satisfaction.*] Hell!

MRS MUGGINS. Well, I never thought to hear such language when I was a spirit!

LUNATIC. [*Arriving.*] I am here.   [*Strides forward.*

THARIEL. Quite so. Your name?

LUNATIC. Timothy Toto Newbiggin.

THARIEL. Why?

LUNATIC. Why? Because I thought of it as I came along. It's better than my real name, now isn't it?

THARIEL. [*After a moment's reference to his book.*] It's a matter of opinion. Now, Mr McNulty, any remarks to make before you go forward?

McNULTY. I presume no one here is in need of a word of comfort?

ALTON. Much good your croaking about Hell will do us.

McNULTY. [*Turning round—horrified.*] Good gracious! It is Alton, the unbeliever! I should never have thought it possible. Then this must be—this must be *Hell!*

HARRIET. I was certain there'd been a mistake.

McNULTY. This explains all. These peculiar people, that woman smoking——

HARRIET. [*Taking her cigarette out of her mouth in amazement.*] My good man, where *have* you been vegetating?

MRS MUGGINS. Oh, Mr Angel, surely he's wrong? This isn't one of them there fool's paradises, is it?

LUNATIC. [*Sitting down cross-legged at Thariel's feet.*] No one takes any notice of me, although, bless you, *I* don't mind where I'm put.

McNULTY. I have preached on Hell; I have meditated on Hell; I turned my own son out of doors because he did not believe in Hell. And now the presence of the man Alton convinces me that this must *be* Hell.

HARRIET. I believe you hope it is.

MRS MUGGINS. Well, the doctor said I couldn't have too much warmth. You'll look warm, he says, and you'll feel warm, he says, but never imagine——

McNULTY. I hoped for better things, I admit it; in sinful pride

I hoped for better things. But, oh, what a comfort to know that Hell exists!

ALTON. As if all this mummery were anything at all.

McNULTY. Mummery!

MRS MUGGINS. But it can't be Hell. I don't smell no fire or smoke.

LUNATIC. And there are no little nondescript monsters, are there?

McNULTY. I cannot imagine that man in Heaven.

ALTON. And yet you cannot imagine yourself in Hell. It 's a good joke. [*They laugh.*

LUNATIC. [*To Thariel.*] Why don't you laugh?

THARIEL. Our notions of humour here are different. Any remarks to make before you go further?

LUNATIC. Yes. [*Rises.*] Ever heard of the Euroquillo?

THARIEL. Why?

LUNATIC. [*Archly.*] It is a very bitter bird.

THARIEL. No doubt.

LUNATIC. [*His forefinger on his nose.*] That is, a bird renowned for its bitterness.

MRS MUGGINS. Surely the poor dear 's not right in his head.

LUNATIC. What wonderful powers of observation you possess, madam. I 've not been right in my head since—[*to Thariel*] how long ago will it be?

THARIEL. [*After a brief reference to his book.*] It will be about ten years now. It was just after you took up politics.

LUNATIC. You see, he knows. He is a very knowing man—that is, a man renowned for his knowingness. They were just going to make me an M.P. when I discovered it was more blessed to be the Queen of Sheba. May I tell you more about the Euroquillo?

THARIEL. I am too busy. Go and tell the others about it before you pass on.

MRS MUGGINS. Surely we don't want a poor lunatic among us, Mr Angel? We 've got enough queer creatures here as it is.

McNULTY. No lunatic will help us solve these knotty problems.

LUNATIC. [*Going to them.*] But I love knotty problems, that is, problems renowned for their——

MRS MUGGINS. [*Making him sit down, and patting him.*] Yes, dearie, we know.

THARIEL. [*To Alton, with a smile.*] I 'm sure you 'll find him a great help.

ALTON. Of what use are a madman's words?

THARIEL. You consider your own more useful? [*A Boy arrives at the gate.*] But I know you have a sharp division down there between what you call the sane and the insane. Most curious.

BOY. Hullo!

THARIEL. Hullo!

BOY. [*Entering.*] So I 've arrived, have I?

THARIEL. It looks like it, doesn't it? Are you surprised?

BOY. [*Looking round.*] It 's a bit quaint, isn't it?

THARIEL. Most things are.

BOY. And what a lot of people! Good morning!

HARRIET. Say, young man, did you happen to notice a little dog on your way here?

MRS MUGGINS. Now don't worry the poor dear. It 's a bit flurrying to be took off sudden.

BOY. It wasn't so sudden. [*To Thariel.*] Why am I dressed up in these things?

THARIEL. [*Smiling.*] They are the clothes in which you felt happiest while on earth. They 'll soon vanish.

ALL, EXCEPT ALTON AND LUNATIC. What?

[*Harriet and Mrs Muggins rise.*

HARRIET. Look here, what *do* you mean?

MRS MUGGINS. Am I going to look like a picture by Halma Tadema any moment?

MCNULTY. I knew it was Hell.

LUNATIC. [*Rising, and producing a pack of cards.*] I 'm sure it will all be very different. Let 's play Snap to keep ourselves warm.

ALTON. Fools! You believe anything he says.

[*Harriet, Mrs Muggins, and Lunatic sit down again, the Lunatic quietly playing Snap by himself—one hand against the other—on the extreme right.*

BOY. I appear to have created a disturbance.

THARIEL. Don't apologize. Anything disturbs them. They 're still dreadfully human.

ALTON. And why the hell shouldn't we be?

HARRIET. A damn good question.

MRS MUGGINS. The cussing and swearing that goes on up here is the limit. Why don't you answer their questions, dearie, I mean Mr Angel?

THARIEL. If I did there would be more cussing and swearing than ever. We 've noticed human beings hate answers to questions. [*To Boy.*] I haven't had your name yet.

BOY. Oh, sorry. Bradley. Derrick Bradley.

THARIEL. [*Looking in book.*] Yes, I promised just now to be very nice and kind to you.

BOY. Did you really? Then I wish you'd tell me something; I won't kick up a row, I promise you.

THARIEL. [*Rather wearily.*] What do you want to know?

BOY. To put it bluntly, what's it all for down there? It used to puzzle me no end, and I always made up my mind that if there were any—any hereafter—I'd ask that question as soon as I arrived. What's it all for—the misery, the struggle, everything?

ALTON. At last we've got a sensible man. [*Pointing to Thariel.*] But he won't answer that question, you'll see.

THARIEL. Was there much misery for you?

BOY. Not much, I suppose—until—— You see there was someone I was very fond of—— It was all rather wretched, and one couldn't help feeling—— I wish I knew what it was all for. [*Turning to the others.*] After all, it *is* a bit thick down there, now isn't it?

HARRIET. Most people haven't got a dog's chance. Bob!

MRS MUGGINS. Life don't bear thinking about, dearie, and that's a fact.

McNULTY. The world is a vale of tears, and it is a sin to think it anything else.

THARIEL. It's a pity you thought about it so much.

ALTON. How dare you sit there and say such things? Do you mean we ought to accept everything that is thrown at us by an evilly disposed fate, and neither rebel nor think about it? I suppose you call that being dreadfully human?

MRS MUGGINS. But how can we help being dreadfully human, Mr Angel?

THARIEL. You can't possibly help it.

BOY. Then, if we can't help it, what's it all for?

HARRIET, ALTON, MRS MUGGINS. Yes, what's it all for?

THARIEL. That's precisely what it is for.

ALTON. [*Rising.*] Damn you, give a plain answer to a plain question!   [*Goes up to the table.*

BOY. [*Going up to the table.*] Yes: why was I born?

THARIEL. Because the human species has a knack of propagating itself.

MRS MUGGINS. Now, Mr Angel, don't be so common.

LUNATIC. [*Waving a hand to Thariel.*] I knew you were a humorous man, that is, a man renowned—— Snap!

HARRIET. Must say, this kind of thing rouses me. [*Going to table.*] It 's up to you to give some kind of answer. Hang it all, you ought to know!

MRS MUGGINS. [*Rising and going to the table.*] I 'm, sure, Mr Angel, if I was to tell you about my daughter Maud——

McNULTY. [*Trying to restrain them.*] My friends, it is better to submit even in Hell than to argue.

LUNATIC. It is. Come and play Snap.

[*Minister indignantly refuses.*

BOY. Now, there 's my immortal soul—I heard a lot about that in the past.

THARIEL. Well, you 'll hear nothing whatever about it in the future.

BOY, HARRIET, McNULTY. Why not?

MRS MUGGINS. Do you mean we 're going with nothing on to hextinction?

THARIEL. Oh, you are so silly and so tiresome! What you call your immortal soul is only one of many curious tortures you invent for yourselves. Extinction, immortality, soul; all words invented to cover your supreme ignorance.

BOY. If these things are so silly, why are you all dressed up as an angel?

THARIEL. How do you know I am? You think you are all dressed up in a cricketing suit. [*With a strange smile.*] That is not how I see you.

HARRIET. Tell us more about that.

THARIEL. I cannot. There has been too much uproar already. Nothing will alter your ideas or your vision at present; pass up those stairs and learn a little wisdom.

ALTON. Not until we know something definite. [*Turning to the others.*] Stand by me, all of you. The whole time we were on earth we were tormented with doubts and problems impossible to solve. And if we asked questions some vague nonsense was preached to us. Now we 've arrived somewhere—goodness knows where—and the same game goes on. But we can resist; we need not be baffled by mysteries for ever. Will you all stand by me?

HARRIET. I don't mind standing by you. This gentleman [*indicating Thariel*] is a bit too indeterminate for me.

MRS MUGGINS. Of course, Maud would want me to be on your side, Mr Alton.

BOY. I 'm with you all right.

McNULTY. They are all with you, my friend. The human heart is ever rebellious and stubborn.

LUNATIC. Snap!

ALTON. You see; weak, dreadful creatures that we are, we still have courage left.

THARIEL. I never said you were weak. I said you were dreadful, and so you are. But you have powers of which you know nothing. You are stronger than I. It makes me laugh to think you do not realize it.

ALTON. It 's all very well to sit there laughing at us, and writing in a silly book, and sending lunatics to talk to us, but we are fresh from a world whose grey realities make this trumpery show and your meaningless remarks disgusting and infuriating. What do you know of the misery of most of the people who come up here? How can you realize the hopeless problems they have left behind—*unsolved?* How would you go on down there, I should like to know? As this boy says, what 's it all for? God, I wish you could see the slum I died in! God, I wish you could smell it! There you sit saying: 'Pass along there, please,' with a silly smirk on your face, hurrying poor wretches on to fresh misery. All their lives someone has said: 'Pass along there, please,' and—God help us all—most people have passed along, to be killed in mills, factories, and offices, or blown to pieces because a few old fools somewhere have quarrelled. You 're worse than our blasted kings and queens and presidents, curse me if you 're not! What do you know of the horrible questioning that comes to us as we struggle down there? What does it matter to us if you see us now in some queer way that we cannot understand? It is *down there* which counts, and the people we have left struggling behind us, not all the mysterious bunkum up here. It is down there we think of! I wish you could see it, I wish you could hear it; I wish you could hear, as I 've heard so often, the buzzers hooting on a bitter December morning, calling the slaves to work. [*Leaning over him in sudden passion.*] Hear it, you figure of fun, and with it all the misery of a wretched world!

[*From very far away comes a curious and rather terrible sound. There is the hooting of buzzers, the roaring of machinery, and, most of all, a strange, prolonged, sobbing wail, insistent and vitally distressing.*

ALTON. Good God, what is that?

THARIEL. Isn't that what you intend me to hear?

ALTON. Are you making this happen to fool me?

THARIEL. You are too busy fooling yourself for any one else to fool you. I told you human beings have strange powers,

especially when they come here. You want me to hear this.
I hear it. I have heard it before.

Mrs Muggins. Oh, Mr Angel, that sound does bring back the
shocking sights I 've seen in my time. You know there 's a
lot in what Mr Alton says: I wish you could see a little of what
goes on, I really do. [*Wiping her eyes.*] I 've always thought
that, if only you gentlemen in Heaven could see a bit more of
what goes on, you just couldn't help trying to alter it a little.

Thariel. I see it and hear it.

Harriet. Of course, Heaven 's all very well, but there are sights
and sounds on earth that would surprise you.

Thariel. I hear them and see them.

McNulty. The groans, tears, and pains of humanity rise up in
expiation of the wrath of God.

Thariel. I hear them and see them.

Boy. Then why don't you *do* something about it?

Alton. He either can't or won't. [*The sound dies away.*] All he
can say is: 'Pass along there.' I wish I 'd been able to stop the
others who came while I was here.

Harriet. Let 's have 'em back. He says we have remarkable
powers, and your buzzer stunt was most successful. See if
you can call 'em back—they may be able to tell us something.

Mrs Muggins. O—O—O! It fair gives me the creeps to hear
you talk like that! I 'm sure it hadn't ought to be done.

McNulty. Beware, rash man, of blasphemy.

Lunatic. [*Looking up from his game.*] I thought we 'd got
beyond blasphemy long ago.

Alton. It 's a splendid idea. [*Goes to centre of stage.*] All you
who have passed up the stairs since I came, come back, come
back. [*A pause.*] Come back!

[*The stage swiftly darkens : when the light returns, the Girl,
the Nun, Nightingale, and Mrs Bagshawe are seen stand-
in motionless on the top of the steps. They are grave, and
there is something a little unreal about their appearance.*

Nun. [*Stepping forward after a short silence.*] Why have you
called us back?

Alton. Come down and thrash the matter out.

Nun. We cannot come down: you must come to us.

Alton. Why?

Nun. Because there is no going back. You should have learnt
that before coming here. There is no going back.

All those with her. There is no going back.

Boy. [*Suddenly.*] Margaret!

THARIEL. Silence!

BOY. But it *is* Margaret! I can see her—Margaret, I am here!

NUN. The earth! The earth speaks!

> [*They appear distressed. Swift darkness. When the light returns they have gone.*

BOY. It was Margaret, I saw her!

THARIEL. [*Really annoyed.*] I am tired of you all. You shriek and rave. You see all things with your dreadful, earthly eyes. I am tired of you. [*Closes book.*] You have no simplicity in you.

ALTON. Your simplicities are no use to us. Of course, I 'm not at all sure they were really the same people who——

THARIEL. Oh, why won't you go up those stairs and quarrel with someone else?

ALTON. I have told you we are not going up those steps at your bidding. You say we have mysterious powers; well, we are going to exercise those powers. [*A man appears at the gate.*] Send that man away! No one shall enter here until we 've learnt more.

THARIEL. [*Waving his hand to man.*] Another gate.

> [*Man disappears.*

ALTON. And shut the gate. [*Gate shuts with a heavy clang.*

HARRIET. Now, my boy, you 've done it!

McNULTY. Heaven or Hell, I cannot possibly approve of this.

ALTON. I don't care a damn who approves and who does not. It is time there was a revolt here. [*To Thariel.*] Get out of this, I 've had enough of you [*Thariel rises with a smile*]—and take that book and your silly smile elsewhere.

> [*Thariel goes with dignity up the steps. As he goes it gradually becomes dark, with the exception of the curtain and archway at the back.*

MRS MUGGINS. Oh, Mr Alton, now you 've been and gone and behaved really stupid. They 're eclipsing something to frighten us!

McNULTY. There has been grave blasphemy. We are in exterior darkness: there shall be weeping and gnashing of teeth.

HARRIET. Of course this sort of thing is all very well, but they have the whip-hand, you know.

BOY. I don't mind what happens if I may see Margaret again.

LUNATIC. [*Still quietly playing Snap.*] Mr Alton is a man renowned for his masterfulness, but nothing will make him realize it is so different here.

ALTON. All my life I have been in revolt against power, and I am still in revolt. I loathe mystery and veils. No one has ever solved my problems or helped me. I can only fight and smash and hate! Why should I go to a Heaven that is obviously as perplexing and foolish as the earth? I will fight and smash and hate it!

MRS MUGGINS. [*Going to the foot of the steps.*] Oh, Mr Angel, it 's gone a bit too far now, hasn't it? A joke 's a joke, but don't you go thinking we are all as silly as Mr Alton. I don't mind much where I 'm put so long as I 'm put somewhere, I 'm always at home, I am. If it 's Heaven, I 'm ready any old time; if it 's Hell, well, let 's get down to it and make the best of things. But teeth-gnashing in hexterior darkness isn't in my line at all, and the sooner I 'm out of it the better.

[*The Nun appears.*

NUN. Come, Mrs Muggins, I 've been sent to fetch you.

MRS MUGGINS. And I 'm, coming, dearie, with all my heart, and proud to be in good company. [*Turning round as she reaches the steps.*] Now, Mr Alton, give up worrying and cursing, and take whatever comes like a good boy. It 's quite comfortable up here, wish I 'd come before, but, as Maud always said, you can't help listening to that Mr Alton. Why aren't I more frightened, dearie, now I 'm close to Heaven?

NUN. [*Kissing her on the forehead as they enter.*] Because you 've never been very far away from it.

[*Hardly have they gone when Nightingale appears, very little altered.*

NIGHTINGALE. [*Beckoning to McNulty.*] Come along.

MCNULTY. Have they sent *you* to fetch me?

NIGHTINGALE. They have. Don't ask me why. I seem to be expected to chaperon the most impossible people.

MCNULTY. [*With conviction.*] I was right. This is the beginning of my torments. But I accept. My consolation is that I spoke the truth; Hell exists; my belief is justified.

NIGHTINGALE. Glad to find you 're determined to look on the bright side of things. [*Helping him up.*] Now come along up those stairs, and [*going through curtain*] here we are!

[*They disappear.*

HARRIET. [*Striding forward.*] Well, I 'm not going to wait until some footling person is sent to fetch me; I 'll go now. [*At bottom of steps.*] Now look here, Alton, we 're up against it. No use fighting forces we know nothing about. Thought I should end the whole idiotic muddle as far as I was concerned by doing myself in, but I can't see it 's made much difference. All I 've done is to lose my dog. However, perhaps they 'll put that straight. [*Pushing open curtains and shouting in stentorian tones.*] Bob! [*She disappears.*

[*The Boy goes to the steps and calls.*

BOY. Margaret! [*The Girl appears.*] By Jove, it is good to see you again! May I come now!

GIRL. Yes, yes. I seem to have waited so long already.

BOY. [*On first step.*] I say, it won't all be different up there, will it? I mean we shall still know each other?

GIRL. [*Holding out her arms to him with a smile.*] Come and see.
[*He runs up the steps, into her arms. The curtains cover them.*
[*Darkness descends on the stage with the exception of a light that plays on Alton and the Lunatic in the foreground.*
[*A pause. Alton turns and looks at the Lunatic, who, sitting cross-legged, cards in hand, looks up at him.*

ALTON. Well?

LUNATIC. The Euroquillo is a very bitter bird.

ALTON. Aren't you going also?

LUNATIC. That is, a bird renowned for its bitterness.

ALTON. I said, aren't you going also?

LUNATIC. Wouldn't that be rather unsporting?

ALTON. What do you mean?

LUNATIC. You might feel a bit lonely.

ALTON. I have been lonely all my life.

LUNATIC. Because you think such a lot. It would have been so much better if you 'd played Snap more and thought less.

ALTON. Curse you for a fool!

LUNATIC. Quite so—come and play Snap.

ALTON. Do you suppose I 've nothing better to do than to play Snap with a lunatic?

LUNATIC. What have you better to do? You 've refused to go up the steps, you 've frightened every one but me away—what is there better to do? Oh, how I laugh when all the thought in the world proves useless, and the only thing left is to play the fool! It 's no good arguing with me because I shouldn't understand you, but I can play Snap and so can you. [*Dealing out the cards.*] Let 's begin.

ALTON. I wish I could make you realize——

LUNATIC. I 'd so much rather you didn't. I 'm sure you were most effective while on earth, but it 's so different here: you 'd better play Snap until you realize it. Come, be a sport; I stayed behind to play with you.

ALTON. [*Sitting down.*] God knows, I do this to please you, not to please myself.

LUNATIC. [*Gravely.*] It is not improbable, God knows you are pleasing Him considerably more in consequence.

[*They play intently, calling out 'Snap' at frequent intervals. Alton gradually becomes engrossed in the game and distinctly more cheerful. Sometimes he laughs. It grows lighter, and shadowy forms are seen. The light returns : steps, table, and archway have gone : the players are surrounded by magnificent masked Angels, standing, serene and silent, watching the game.*

ALTON. By Jove! I'd no idea I should enjoy this foolery so much. Snap! I feel positively young!

LUNATIC. I have never managed to feel positively old. Snap!

ALTON. Snap! I've won! I've won!

[*Looks up : is transfixed with astonishment.*

LUNATIC. [*Rising and bowing.*] We have a distinguished audience.

[*The Angels part in the centre : Thariel advances in glory.*

ALTON. Now what's the matter?

THARIEL. I regret to inform you that you have entered Heaven.

ALTON. [*Rising.*] I did not go up those steps!

THARIEL. No, there was no need, after all.

LUNATIC. I told you it was better to play Snap with a lunatic than to spend your time cursing.

ALTON. But I won't have it! I won't have it, do you hear? [*Breaking down completely and hiding his face in his hands.*] Oh, why can't you let me alone? I've always been alone before.

THARIEL. [*Very quietly, gazing at him compassionately.*] As if these earthlings ever were alone.

ALTON. [*Jumping up.*] But, now I am here, take care! I shall hate and smash and rebel as much as ever. You may have caught me, but you have not tamed me. I shall never forget the injustice and cruelty of the earth. I shall never cease to curse the powers that could do so much, and do—nothing! I shall smash—[*gazing at the Angels his voice grows faint*] and hate—[*his voice grows fainter*] and rebel——

[*His voice dies away. The Angels, calm, benignant, stand watching him. There is a curious sense of power, of mystery about them. Alton is motionless.*

LUNATIC. [*Going up to him, softly.*] I told you it would be so different.

CURTAIN

CULBIN SANDS

GORDON BOTTOMLEY

'The Culbin Sands, which lie along the line of the south coast of the Moray Firth, west of the River Findhorn, form a remarkable scene of desolation and dreariness . . . a greater it would be impossible to conceive. For four long miles, and occupying a space of two miles broad, you have nothing but a great sea of sand, rising, as it were, in tumultuous billows. . . . The solitude is absolute and unbroken. And if a whispering sound does reach you for a moment, you find it is but the hissing of the sand as it pours down the hillsides in its work of desolation. . . .

'The estate of Culbin was the finest and the most fertile in Moray. . . . It was called the garden and granary of Moray. . . . We know that the occurrence of the great sand-drift was connected with changes in the coast-line, and that the sand which overwhelmed Culbin came from the west, in the autumn of 1694. And it came suddenly and with short warning. . . . The drift, like a mighty river, came on steadily and ruthlessly, grasping field after field, and enshrouding every object in a mantle of sand. . . . In terrible gusts the wind carried the sand amongst the dwelling-houses of the people, sparing neither the hut of the cottar nor the mansion of the laird. . . . A lull in the storm succeeded, and they began to think they might still have their dwelling-houses, though their lands were ruined. But the storm began again with renewed violence, and they had to flee for their lives, taking with them only such things as they could carry. . . . On returning . . . not a vestige, not a trace of their houses was to be seen. . . . From that time to this, the estate of Culbin has been completely buried by the sand, and so far as can be judged will never be free of it. . . .

'Young Kinnaird had only just come into possession of the estate. . . . He escaped on the night of the catastrophe with his wife and child, attended by a nurse. . . . Shortly afterwards we find him applying for personal protection against his creditors. . . . Both he and his wife died a few years after. The faithful nurse took the child to Edinburgh, and supported him and herself on needlework.'—GEORGE BAIN, *The Culbin Sands*, pp. 16–25. (The *Nairnshire Telegraph* Office, Nairn.)

This play was first performed by the London Verse Speaking Choir at the London Polytechnic Theatre, Regent Street, on 1st and 2nd May 1931.

THE WINDS
{ *Phoebe Polishuk*
Lucy Story
Mary MacAuley
Lucy Summers
Marion Welham
Sybil Wayman
Daisy Dykes
Mabel Ogle
Cleonike Paschali }

THE TREES
{ *Catherine Barry*
Winifred Hudson
Anna Ormerod
Elizabeth Richards
Margaret Boulton
Eva Lane
Doris Fowler
Alice Martin
Ann Barber }

ALISON BRODIE
{ *Louise Cottam* (1st May)
Catherine Barry (2nd May) }

THE LADY
Winifred Hudson

WITCHES OF AULDEARN
{ *Geoffrey Simpson*
Denzil Pickering
Allan Keeling
William Richards }

Grouping and movement arranged by Rita Nahabedian
Stage Manager: Kathleen Stone
Costumes by Rita Nahabedian and Kathleen Stone
Produced by Marjorie Gullan

CULBIN SANDS

A.D. 1698

Eight men, winged figures of The Winds, enter and range themselves across the stage.

CHORUS OF THE WINDS. Wind is a spirit, flying.
SECOND AND FOURTH WINDS. Sighing.
THIRD, FIFTH, AND SEVENTH WINDS. Crying.
EIGHTH WIND. Dying.
CHORUS OF THE WINDS. Wind is the power of The Will
 That is everywhere and still,
 Dark and still and unknown.
FIRST WIND. Secret.
FOURTH WIND.   Silent.
EIGHTH WIND.   Alone.
CHORUS OF THE WINDS. It has no body; it is born
 As the Will chooses, and dies
 As the Will changes: its horn
 Is sounded by no lips,
 It is a spirit's sound,
 At once the horn and the player,
 The pain and the heart that cries
 Out against the pain.
SECOND, FOURTH, AND SIXTH WINDS. Yet it breeds fury and has
        whips;
 It has all the passion of the hunting hound
 As well as the cry of the hunted beast.
 When it sounds in its zest it hears no prayer;
 It rushes; it surges; it can sunder and tear.
CHORUS. And whether it pities, or injures in zest,
 It does not look back again.
    [*The Winds part and move round to each side in a curve,
    revealing six women in the guise of Pine Trees with
    downward-spreading boughs for arms.*
CHORUS OF THE TREES. Between the tide and the great heights
 There was a fair land
 At Culbin in Moray-side.

It heard the sea on still nights:
Its corn was full; its ancient life
Was kind and calm, the oldest wife
Knew no tale but a tale of peace.
And a singing river that came from the knees
Of the great heights swept down to the seas
And the desolate, shelterless sand,
The lonely, innocent sand.

THE TREES. FIRST SEMICHORUS. The loveliness of a land
   Comes by its trees;
   And this was a region of pines
   That give a voice to the lightest air
   And change the sound of the wildest storm
   To something wilder, wilder; and where
   There are no men make sounds and signs
   Of life and mysteries.

THE TREES: SECOND SEMICHORUS. There is strange life in trees
   And the instinct of their form:
   It comes from the earth and the air.

FIRST WIND. [*Quietly.*] Whispering.
FOURTH WIND. [*Quietly.*]   Wakening.
EIGHTH WIND. [*Quietly.*]   Stirring.

THE TREES: SECOND SEMICHORUS. Only the birds know our
         secrecies,
   Nesting in us, moving with us,
   In and out floating and fluting and whirring,
   Part of our purpose awhile.

THE TREES: FIRST SEMICHORUS. Not even the timorous,
   Restless and ever-changing birds,
   That flutter without a wind and defile
   Reverend trees that cherish them,
   Can understand our sounds that are words
   To warn and guide:
   There is one that will ride
   The leaping bough when agony
   Is in the wind, and sing and sing
   As though a rapture of song could tame
   The dangerous winds that scatter and bring
   The deadly foam of the sea——

THE WINDS. [*Quietly.*] And the sand, the moving sand,
   The ever-moving sand that flows
   Wherever the streaming wind-flight goes——

THIRD WIND. [*Not quietly.*] Sweeping.

FIFTH WIND.   Swirling.
SEVENTH WIND.   Rising.
THE TREES. The wind begins, the force of the air
   Awakes and is sounding
   Beyond the tide, in the mountains where
   Its voice is hounding
   The ruffled eagle, the fellow wind.
   It is renewing
   Its search for the haven it cannot find,
   Its anger that it should still be blind,
   Its old pursuing.
   It has remembered that it can tear us,
   Leaping, surprising——
FIRST WIND. We have passed the whitening waves: beware us.
SECOND WIND. Stooping like the hunting bird.
FOURTH WIND. Swooping between the rollers ranging.
SIXTH WIND. [*Stealthily.*] And the sand, the little sand, has
      heard
   As it never heard before.
EIGHTH WIND. The harmless sand has heard;
   It has felt our touch, its films are stirred
   In sheltered stretches of shore.
FIRST, FOURTH, AND EIGHTH WINDS. It is a vapour, and earth
      no more.
SECOND, THIRD, AND SEVENTH WINDS. Eàrth nò mòre.
THE WINDS. The wind is its shaper, its place is changing:
   It is one with the wind, the lift is darkening.
   It swathes all things in a stinging veiling.
   There is no more any space for seeing.
THE TREES: FIRST SEMICHORUS. [*Bending sideways, as though
      before a storm.*] Is it not thinning? The darkness is
      paling.
THE TREES: SECOND SEMICHORUS. [*Bending sideways.*] It is
      denser and thinner; and denser; and dimmer.
   The ploughman has run from his plough; the reaping
   Ends as the unbound sheaf goes sweeping
   Up the brown air, and sickles glimmer
   Briefly under the falling sand
   That is spreading like spent waves over the land
   And over every form of being.
THE WINDS. [*Passing in a mazy dance in and out among the
      Trees.*] Trees, I am here: tall trees, are you hearkening?
THE TREES. You we have known: we have feared your embracing,

Torturing, strengthening, in age overthrowing:
But what is this beyond our knowing?
THE WINDS. From a nèw plàce in the mountains racing,
The low-flying cloud and the great gull chasing,
I leap and come.
Thwarting the waves, stripping their cresting;
Raising the sand from an age-long resting;
Labouring against it, heaving and lifting,
Heavy in flight with it, panting and breasting
A moving wall of it settling and drifting——
THE TREES. [*Crouching to the floor, each shielding her head with a
lifted arm and sleeve.*] The storm-cock is dumb.
The sand is rising
From bole to bough.
THE WINDS. And man hides in fear, but the sea and I sing;
And the corn-lands are hidden by dry sand now.
THE TREES. Light and wounding
Is the sand's touch.
THE WINDS. It does not matter: the wind is yet sounding
And the sand is to cover you overmuch.
THE TREES. [*Faintly.*] Bark, needles, and next year's bud
It strips, and we bleed. . . .
THE WINDS. The sand still rises and pours in flood,
And that is all the healing you need.
[*As the dance of the Winds closes, they range themselves in front
of the Trees, concealing them. The Tree Chorus goes
out unseen.*
THE WINDS. [*Continuing.*] The eagle in all its heavenly pride
At last must descend;
And the wind, that it cannot master and ride,
Has also its end.
The air is dark no more with the mixture
Of wind-divided soil;
The deceitful earth that seemed without fixture
Is still again for man's toil.
[*The succeeding speeches are to be said more and more quietly,
ending in no more than a murmur that dies slowly.*
FIRST WIND. By day and night on a dreary shore,
SECOND WIND. Now, and seeming for evermore,
THIRD WIND. There is no life but the passing bird's,
FOURTH WIND. No sound but its cry, or a lost man's words;
FIRST WIND. Or a breath that calls a change in the dance
SECOND WIND. Of small sand-spires that swirl by chance,

FIFTH WIND. And again are quiet, and again awaken.
SIXTH WIND. Slurring and sliding——
SEVENTH WIND. Gliding——
EIGHTH WIND. And shaken.
FIRST WIND. A quiet rustling.
SECOND WIND. A susurrant shudder.
THIRD WIND. A sound forsaken.
FIRST WIND. Shoaling or sheer,
THIRD WIND. The shifting sand
FOURTH WIND. Is shapeless and streaming.
SECOND WIND. Seedless and share-less,
FIFTH WIND. The stretching sand
SIXTH WIND. Is shadowless, shivering, seeming
THIRD WIND. Afloat in the sighing air——
SEVENTH WIND. Hushing and sighing——
EIGHTH WIND. Dying, and of dead things dreaming. . . .

[*The Winds retire to the back of the stage and, crouching low, align themselves there, revealing a middle-aged woman standing alone, travel-worn and poorly dressed in clothes of the late seventeenth century.*

THE WOMAN. My name is Alison Brodie.
I was born at Darklass near here, on Kinnaird's land.
I have not seen Culbin since I was a girl.
I have come from Virginia, I shall reach home to-night
At last, my home at last, my dear home.
My father was shot by troopers of Montrose
For faithfulness to God and His Covenant,
Standing against the gable of his house:
I was there in my mother's arms, I believe I remember—
Though I do not remember falling down with her.
He was always shining among the saints in my mind,
And I prayed to enter the radiance of such glory
By the same fire flaming its benediction at me.
Claverhouse came in his turn, as Montrose had come;
I believed my eagerness and heat of prayer
Had brought him seeking me, unknown to himself.
I have worn a thumbscrew, my blood has dripped on the soil
From my back, but my God denied me my father's death.
The thing I had never thought of came to me:
I was shipped like a quey to America and driven
To labour in cotton-fields among bad women
With a dark man over us, and a long whip.
Only the bad women were good to me.

It is over now: I am free.   When I was loosed
I could only think of Culbin in Nairn, and a ship
To take me to Glasgow.   That is over too,
And I am near again to the first things I knew,
To the holy land of my longing, the places of my spirit.
Yet the old way is farther than I thought.

[*She seeks here and there, as though she had lost her way.*

THE WINDS: RIGHT HALF. She does not know
What the wind has done:
She cannot go
To her minnie's home,
For it lies under her
Deeper than a grave,
And sand-waves sunder her
As the ocean-wave.

THE WINDS: LEFT HALF. Now she is ill at ease:
She believes she has lost her way.
She looks for familiar trees,
Something she cannot say
Troubles her throbbing mind.
'What has been taken away?'
She is asking herself now.
She does not know that the wind
Is telling her slowly and low,
A little at once, to be kind——

THE WINDS: RIGHT HALF. To beseech her to go
Before she must know.

ALISON. I have trodden this road in my heart nearly thirty years,
I have seen it every day with shut, wet eyes;
Yet I did not remember the way was so far from Dyke.
I never thought I could miss it:
Yet now I am lost among sandhills.
I must be near the sea—
But I cannot hear the tide.
I do not know where I am—
There are sandhills at Mavistoun,
But that is miles away from where I am.

[*She goes out, still seeking,*

[*A Lady enters from the opposite side, cloaked and hooded and
carrying a child in her arms.   She crosses the stage, goes
out, and returns slowly.*

THE WINDS: LEFT HALF. Who is this?

Is her scent on the air?
Is she living, or is
She something that has no share
In life and its brief ways?
Air touches her;
But not a tress does it raise,
Nor her cloak stir.

THE WINDS: RIGHT HALF. She is living, she comes again—
The one who is always here.
In the sun, in the rain
She is quiet, changeless, and near;
As though the vital centre
Of her being should lie
Here, and nothing content her
But endlessly
To enter and re-enter
A place she must be leaving
Yet must be nigh—
Existing but for grieving.

THE WINDS: LEFT HALF. Who knows her home? Not I.

THE WINDS: RIGHT HALF. Nor I.

THE LADY. [*On her return.*] It is the hour when every one
Upon this side of doom
Turns homeward and is not alone;
And even the wind sighs 'Home!'
I have no home, I have no rest:
No love awaits me there.
I have only a baby in my breast,
And a heavier inward care.
I was beloved and a lady of lands,
With plentiful gear of my own:
Now I have nothing but empty sands,
And I wear my sister's gown.
My love has left me, my love has gone,
Tired, to a deep grave;
But his home is buried deeper down,
Our home that he could not save.

Alison enters from the side at which she went out.

The House of Culbin is my home,
The sand has buried it deep:
To what lonely rest shall I ever come,
And where shall my baby sleep?

H 947

ALISON. [*Addressing the Lady.*] I am seeking the way to Culbin:
     will you help me?
   I knew it once: I seem to have forgotten
   Something that was in me to guide me there.
THE LADY. This is the way to Culbin. That is why
   You find me here when nightfall is so near.
   Culbin is my home: where is your home?
ALISON. Are you the Laird's wife, Kinnaird's wife?
   I cannot see your face.
THE LADY. [*Lifting her head.*] What do you know of Alexander
     Kinnaird
   Or of his lonely wife?
ALISON. Not Alexander, not the young Laird.
THE LADY. This is the young Laird whom I have in my arms.
ALISON. You speak of someone whom I do not know.
   I have been long away.
   My name is Alison Brodie: oh, tell me, tell me,
   Is Janet Mackay of Kincorth Wester still there?
   John Brodie's wife and my mother. Oh, tell me now.
THE LADY. Where is she now? She is not under the sand.
   There is nothing under the sand except my heart.
   Even my loved one is not lying there:
   We had better have stayed there, and be lying there now
   Together; together. . . . Together.
ALISON. Under the sand? What is there under the sand?
   You do not understand me. It is Culbin I seek.
   Who are you? You seem to be a stranger here.
   Have you too lost your way?
THE LADY. Yes, I have lost my way for ever and ever.
   I want to go home to Culbin.
ALISON.   And I too;
   I want to go home to Culbin.
THE LADY.   But there 's no way.
   The bonny holms of Culbin are under sand.
   My husband took me away from here with him,
   Me and my baby; then my husband died.
   You will see I had to return to Culbin then:
   I could not find it, and they took me away.
   And then I came again, but they took me away.
   Yet I return: if you will come with me
   We will go to Culbin together, for I must find it.
ALISON. What do you mean? Who are you?
THE LADY. I am Grisel Rose of Clava, Kinnaird's wife.

No, no—O God, O God—Kinnaird's widow.

ALISON. Then surely you know where Culbin is.   What ails you?

THE LADY. What is your name?

ALISON.   Alison Brodie.

THE LADY.   Yes—Brodie:

Then you are not a stranger, and I can trust you.

Come, Alison, I will take you to Culbin with me.

  [*She holds out a hand, as though to a child : Alison takes it, and*
  they go out together.

THE WINDS. It is not wise of them to be about on the sand

When night is coming: it is not wise of them

To wander farther away toward the strand

And the long desolation at the Old Bar.

The wind is secret: it knows of others who came

Looking for something or someone and going too far

When a gale was breeding-in on itself in the west

And the sand was above them like a tossing crest,

Blinding them and falling where they still are.

The Four Witches of Auldearn enter.

FIRST WITCH. [*While entering, and as though continuing a con-*
    versation.] And now the light is failing: yes, yes, we
    have lost

Too much good time.   As my name is Isobel Goudie,

I 'll have no more to do with any of you

If you disobey me again and think for yourselves.

SECOND WITCH. I will not come here again while the wind is
    rising:

We have sense for three among us—and that, thrawn woman

Is more than you have—and we were all for waiting

Till last night's storm had properly quieted down.

THIRD WITCH. Is there not a face at every window-side

When we go down Auldearn street by daylight?

FIRST WITCH.   Owl!

THIRD WITCH. Very well, owl: the owl has lessons for us—

It flies without a sound, it can see in twilight.

Tibby knows better than you: we do not want

The watching neighbours to see us turn off for Culbin.

FIRST WITCH. Owls—owls—You tell where you are by your
    hooting.

I tell you, when you would go to Culbin Sands,

Set out when the wind is in fury: then no one believes

You have gone to that dangerous airt.   On the other side

Of little Loch Loy wait till the storm goes down:
You can then be first to find the new bare places
And look for the ancient money that is lying there.

FOURTH WITCH. I have had enough of you. When we go out,
Huddling together at the height of the wind,
It takes our clothes up over our heads or spreads
Our mauds and cloaks flying like dark wings,
And there is always someone watching then
To say we are riding the air on an evil purpose—

SECOND WITCH. Ay, that we are off to meet the Cromarty
witches,
Who are such terrible witches they can cross the water,
For a gathering of the witches of the north
On Culbin Sands——

THIRD WITCH.   On the dreaded, unnatural sands
That Isobel Goudie and we and the Cromarty witches
Have piled up higher than Kinnaird's lost house
On the fair holms of Culbin, mile after mile,
Because Kinnaird had driven us off his land—
Calling us witches.

FOURTH WITCH. Someone is ready with that dangerous word
Everywhere!

FIRST WITCH. And is it not a trùe wòrd?
Where is your pride, to fear it?   Where is our power,
That is not small, except in the dreadful word?
Have there not been witches in Auldearn
Since those who prophesied King Duncan's death
On Hardmuir yonder to his murderer—
And who knows now how long before in the darkness?
Mother to daughter, they say, mother to daughter—
A noble tale to have lasted hundreds of years
Along with the terrible knowledge passed on to us
That we must keep alive.

FOURTH WITCH. Slander your own mother if you will:
Let mine alone, she was a decent woman
And did not guess that I should listen to you
And let you teach me your dirty ways. . . .

FIRST WITCH.   Mysie!
Take care of yourself: I still know more than you.

FOURTH WITCH. [With rising, excited voice.] Goudie, I shall go
to the minister
And tell him——

FIRST WITCH.   You dare not tell, you shrieking carrion!

SECOND WITCH. Hush, Mysie: that talk is dangerous to us all.

THIRD WITCH. [*Threateningly.*] The first one who says to the
  minister the things
He thinks of us and has not dared to say
Will light a fire that we shall have to burn in.
                    [*The Three cluster angrily about the Fourth.*

FIRST WITCH. I shall quieten you——

SECOND WITCH.   Mysie, take care, she can hurt you.

THIRD WITCH. It is time for someone to hurt her.

FIRST WITCH.   More than time,
  More than time.

FOURTH WITCH.   Wait, wait until I get home,
And you shall see. . . . Don't. . . . Let me alone. . . .
  Don't: don't. . . .

FIRST WITCH. And what will you do if you never reach home?

FOURTH WITCH. [*Hysterical.*] Don't!

THIRD WITCH.   Goudie, it was only four years ago
That the sand came down upon Culbin deep and for ever;
Yet I heard in Forres that the gale last month
Uncovered a woman's bones this side of Binsness.

FIRST WITCH. A stranger lost on the sands when the wind was
  rising
And the air was full of sand that blinded her;
Choked her; and buried her.

THIRD WITCH. Goudie, if our poor Mysie's bones are found
In a few years from now, her delicate ribs
Still hàlf fùll of sand, our neighbours will know
That the tale we are going to tell them is sadly true
Of her folly in stealing off to the sands alone
Before the wind had dropped.

FOURTH WITCH.   God, hear me and help me!

THIRD WITCH. Another fault: she has sworn not to call upon
  God.

FIRST WITCH. The tale will be plainly true. There is a hollow
And a lochan in it a little further on:
Bring her down there.

FOURTH WITCH.   Help, help me!

ALISON. [*Entering from the side she went out by.*] Who is here?

FIRST WITCH. [*Stepping forward.*] We are bound for Kincorth,
  and in the fading light
We have lost our way. The sands are always strange,
Always changing, always man's enemy.

THE WINDS. After sunset the wind begins its old unease.

FIRST WITCH. [*Continuing.*] Where there is no path there is no safety—
And the wind is beginning behind us, the treacherous wind.
THE WINDS. There is danger here in this slight stirring of a breeze.
FIRST WITCH. [*Continuing.*] Do you come from east or west? Where does Kincorth lie?
THE WINDS. It has a peaceful sound; but its significance is not peace.
ALISON. The God of my father has sent you in my need:
Tell me, I beseech you, whom you know at Kincorth—
Or is it, indeed, Kincorth Wester you seek?
SECOND WITCH. [*In an undertone and taking the Fourth Witch by the hand.*] Come away, Mysie: now.
[*The Second and Fourth Witches go out on tiptoe in the opposite direction from Alison.*]
FIRST WITCH. Kincorth Wester! Where do you come from, woman?
Kincorth Wester is under the sand.
ALISON.   The sand?
The other woman could only talk of the sand:
What do you mean? What did she mean? Where am I?
Where, where is Culbin?
THIRD WITCH.   This is Culbin.
ALISON.   This?
But this is Moray shore.
FIRST WITCH.   Ay, once it was—
Before it went up the sky and came down here.
It has been in more places than one, this quiet sand.
ALISON. Will you not tell me where I am?
FIRST WITCH.   At Culbin.
Four years ago a wind came over the firth,
Lifted the beach from the Carse of Ardersier
To the Old Bar, and spread it over Culbin
And four miles more—over the House of Culbin,
Over the church, and the farmsteads. And the House,
The House of Culbin is voided and ended and dark.
ALISON. Oh, tell me what became of Janet Mackay
Of Kincorth Wester: is she under the sand?
FIRST WITCH. There is no one under the sand: there was bare time
For men and women to save themselves, so they left
Their sheep and kye and horses, and saved themselves.

But who are you who ask for Janet Mackay,
Who died the winter that Claverhouse took her girl,
And only old women remember? Who are you?
Come, turn your face to the west, where the last light is.
ALISON. She died of my loss. I knew. Why have I come...?
FIRST WITCH. [*Laughing.*] I know your face. Cummers, look
    here at her:
This is Alison Brodie, the holy girl,
Who got herself flogged by Claverhouse for Christ's sake
And a free passage to the plantations and hell.
ALISON. You know me; but I only know your voice.
I am conscious in my heart why I have come:
The hòpe thère was not to find my mother,
But someone . . . someone . . . You who know my face.
Perhaps you know my heart. Now tell to me—
Shall I find David Fraser at Feddan still?
FIRST WITCH. [*Skirling with laughter.*] Hark, hark ye now at the
    ways of God with men,
And more especially women, and the treasure
He lays up for His well-beloved. Alison,
David Fraser left his plenished farm
Twenty yèars syne and went to sea
In the Virginia trade before the mast,
To look for you—and when his ship returned
He did not sail in her. Have ye not seen him?
And Àlisòn, Àlisòn, have ye no mind
Of Isobel Goudie and your cursing of her?
ALISON. The wòrst witch there ever was in Auldearn,
Who offered me a charm to slip into the Cup
Of Communion when I passed it to David Fraser?
FIRST WITCH. I am Isobel Goudie, Alison:
Have you prospered without my charm in your sour cup?
ALISON. [*Rapt and inattentive.*] How is all taken from me by
    The Beloved
Above all other beloved.
I am accepted of Him.
My mother and my lover have gone out,
My home is erased from the record of man's places;
Yet it is now I feel no longer alone.
I need not try to divine the Holy Will:
It is prepared for me: I learn to wait,
And not be anxious for the time and the place.
How blessed am I. And, even above this blessing,

How blessed am I in the place to which I am brought
To wait in this holiness poured over me.
My desolated home!
Nothing is left but the air that I first breathed;
Yet here, oh, here, joy has returned to me.
I am sent into the wilderness; and it is my own place.
Here I am one with my longing, here the servitude
That is my God's intention becomes my own desire;
For now no longer shall I weary for freedom or to be elsewhere.
I shall come here with the light and see again
Mountains and summer snow and dark waters;
I shall watch Findhorn in spate, with my heart in spate;
And at another time I shall hear familiar voices
Making the only music I love; and all I feel
Or receive into my being will be part of my home.
Holiness is mine: it is all holy to me!
Holy! Holy! And Holy!

FIRST WITCH. Beautiful . . . beautiful . . .

THIRD WITCH. Beautiful.

FIRST WITCH. I am Isobel Goudie, Alison.
I wish you no evil for your ancient cursing,
Although you called me witch. You are welcome home.
You will have brought something with you over the sea
To help your mother with?

ALISON. [*As though awaking.*] Nothing great, but enough to
serve.

FIRST WITCH.   Yes. Yes.
You will be needing a roof awhile, maybe,
Until you can find one? Come with me to-night.
But maybe you have met with other friends,
And one is expecting you at nightfall?

ALISON.   No:
I have met no one but Kinnaird's wife.

BOTH WITCHES. Kinnaird's wife?

ALISON. I had forgotten: she must be near us still:
I only left her when I heard your cry.

THIRD WITCH. Kinnaird's wife? . . . Grisel Rose of Clava?

ALISON. She called herself that name.

THIRD WITCH. But she's not here. The dòomed Hòuse of
Culbin
Is under its height of sand, and no one is there.

FIRST WITCH. Kinnaird went off to Edinburgh with his wife,
And broke his heart there for his bonny holms.

THIRD WITCH. [*Bitterly.*] In the secrets of existence there are ways
  To show these great men what their greatness is.
FIRST WITCH. His widow is in Edinburgh with her child,
  The landless Laird of Culbin—a helpless Laird,
  Yet not more helpless than his father was
  For all his pitiless pride.
ALISON.   But I have seen them.
BOTH WITCHES. Them? Who?
FIRST WITCH.   The dèad Làird?
ALISON.   The mother and child.
  She came to me here a little before you came:
  She was kind and lovely, and said she would take me with her
  To Culbin and her home. . . .
THIRD WITCH. Can she also be dead; and walking?
FIRST WITCH.   We should have heard:
  There would be news at Clava if she were dead.
  I have heard that she would not settle and came back,
  And took to her sister's baby, that she thought was her own;
  And was hard to persuade that nothing can be done
  And that she could be happier far away.
ALISON. Poor, beautiful lady; I know more than that.
  She is happier here, and I have all the reasons
  For that sad happiness in my own spirit.
  But living people can walk where their longing is,
  Apart from the body; and this may be a wraith. . . .
  I wonder if I touched her: I cannot remember. . . .
  The lonely lady may have returned unknown,
  And be lost on the sands all night if we do not find her.
THIRD WITCH. Searching at nightfall is too dangerous:
  And where would you begin?
FIRST WITCH. [*With deliberation.*] There is one place
  Where we might look before we must go home.
THIRD WITCH. I know it: a likely place.
FIRST WITCH.   There is a hollow
  And a lochan in it a little further on:
  Bring Alison down there before we go.
THIRD WITCH. Yes, a good place: take hands with each of us,
  Alison, it is darker as we go.
    [*The two turn to go, with Alison between them. They are
    hidden by the Winds, who have filed down each side of the
    stage and now range themselves across it—but not so far
    forward as at first.*
  *H 947

First Wind. For evermore,
 There will no one come here to remain;
 Neither the sea nor the shore,
 Neither the hill nor the plain
 Have part in the place:
 It is for death and the wind,
 And the wind smooths over each trace
 That death would leave behind.
 Then the wind is alone again.
The Winds. But those who die here remain.
 The place has its dead—
 A stately house and a race.
 As a tree's last leaves are sped
 By the wind to a far-off place,
 The broken man
 Whom the wind ruined lies afar:
 The house had a longer span
 But it lies where dead things are—
 In darkness, with no space
 To fall as a house that is done
 Falls when its race has gone.

   The Lady enters with her child in front of the Winds
       and pauses.

The Lady. [*As though alone.*] There was a braw house long ago
 That was builded upon sand:
 Men called its builder fool not to know
 That his house could not stand.
 Tempest shook it, flood took it;
 It was ill-founded and fell.
 It was ill-founded, it has no story,
 There was nothing more to tell.
 Oh, whatna a house shall I build myself,
 Oh, whatna a house and hall?
 And what foundation shall I delve
 If my house is not to fall?
 I had the brawest house of my own,
 With love alight therein:
 It was founded deep on earth and stone,
 And long its story had been:
 But it might as well have been built upon sand,
 For the sand sought it and rose
 About its doors and windows and walls—

It is as lost as a house that falls,
In its grave that no one knows. . . .
Busk ye, busk ye, my maidens all;
Let go your clothing and gear;
Shield your eyes from the sand with a shawl,
And hurry away from here.
    [*During the preceding stanza she goes out through the rank of
       the Chorus, which closes behind her. She continues
       unseen.*

And say you to my little son's nourice
She shall throw her bundle away:
She cannot save both it and him,
Breathing sand in a light so dim
That we lose and lose our way. . . .
    [*As she speaks the Third and First Witches enter left in front
       of the Chorus, stealthily and as though fearing to be
       observed, cross the stage, and go out right. The Third
       Witch carries a bundle of clothing that is recognizably
       Alison Brodie's ; the First Witch counts money into a
       money-bag.*

Where is he now who brought me here
And called me Culbin's bride?
We turned away from all that was dear
Except each other, and he cried.
               [*She sounds to be speaking farther away.*

He goes with me; yet he left me alone
Behind a stranger's door.
I must seek him in the place of his own
To see him any more.   [*Her voice is lost in distance.*

FIRST WIND. No more.
SECOND, THIRD, AND FOURTH WINDS. No more.
THE WINDS.   No more.
FIRST, SECOND, THIRD, AND FOURTH WINDS. Shall we uncover
    the house?
FIFTH, SIXTH, SEVENTH, AND EIGHTH WINDS. We do: we never
    undo
The thing we have done. If we rouse
The sand and cast it elsewhere,
Does it matter to us or to you
If it lies here, or there?
FIRST, SECOND, THIRD, AND FOURTH WINDS. Let it lie: let us go
    anywhere.
The wind has no care.

THE WINDS. Everything has gone.
The sand is alone.
FIRST WIND. [*With a shiver.*] Except for something dead.
THE WINDS. The wind smooths over each trace
That death would leave behind:
No one will know the place.
And no one will ever be kind
To the lonely woman who fled,
And who has to return and return
Because she can only yearn
To enter the buried house. [*They begin to withdraw.*
FIRST WIND. Leave her with night that knows
Hòw to calm and restore,
Until she comes and goes
No more.
FIFTH, SIXTH, SEVENTH, AND EIGHTH WINDS. [*As they go.*] No
more.
THE WINDS. [*As the last withdraws.*] No . . . more. . . .

CURTAIN

UNNATURAL SCENE

KATHLEEN DAVEY

'Unnatural Scene' was first performed on 4th March 1933 at Richmond by the Surbiton High School Old Girls' Association, with the following cast:

Miss Brown (Principal)	*Mervyn Pocock*
Miss Conway (Principal's Secretary) .	*Ruth Collins*
Miss Fletcher (Shorthand Instructor) .	*Gwenfra Williams*
Miss Tomkinson (Typewriting Instructor) .	*Grace Pooley*
Miss Ellis (Languages Instructor) . . .	*Gwen Davies*
Miss Stewart ⎫ Students . . .	*⎧Lenore Dickie*
Miss Gilchrist ⎭	*⎩Alicia Phipps*

Producer: Phyllis White

The scene is the secretary's office in the St Mary's Secretarial College for Gentlewomen

The fee for each and every representation of this play by amateurs is half a guinea, payable in advance to Samuel French Ltd, 26 Southampton Street, Strand, London, W.C.2, or to their authorized agents. Upon payment of this fee a licence will be issued for the performance to take place. No performance may be given unless this licence has first been obtained.

UNNATURAL SCENE

The secretary's office has the atmosphere of cold discomfort which is peculiar to such places. A door up centre leads into the principal's office; another door up left opens bleakly into a passage. The window right is closed to keep out a London fog, and the fire-place down left adds to the gloom by being neither ornamental nor in use. The secretary's desk is right. There is a somewhat uncomfortable arm-chair, left, and by the side of it a table; four wooden chairs are placed at intervals round the room. Another smaller table with a typewriter on it is up right. Down stage a large safe stands against the right wall. There is, of course, a clock. A reprint of a well-known old Italian master—it is so well known that we think it should be the 'Mona Lisa'—hangs on the centre wall to the right of the door leading to the principal's room. The wall left of this door is decorated with a poster bearing the words 'There's No Fun Like Work,' rather splendidly written in Old English lettering, but somewhat inadequately suspended by three drawing-pins. Other signs that someone, presumably the principal, in addition to being a woman of affairs, has an eye for the artistic (as opposed to the beautiful) are a pair of candlesticks at either end of the mantelpiece, and a large earthenware jug—empty—on the table by the arm-chair.

It is about 8.50 on a Tuesday morning in November. As the curtain rises, Miss Conway is standing by her desk, sharpening a pencil. At first sight she is certainly attractive, although it is difficult to say exactly why. Then we look at her a second time—she is that sort of person—and realize that she is not as young and carefree as at first we thought she must be. All the same, we are surprised that she should be there, for something about her does not fit in with the general atmosphere. Miss Conway herself does not appear to feel this. She begins to open the morning's post with an efficiency born of long practice, and arranges the letters in two neat piles—those she has to deal with, and those for the eyes of Miss Brown. While she is doing this, the door up left opens and lets in Miss Tomkinson, small, elderly, and distinctly worried. In her left hand she carries an order book, in her right a large handbag. She looks nervously at the far door before speaking.

MISS TOMKINSON. [*Cautiously.*] Has she come yet?

MISS CONWAY. Not yet. Do you want her?

MISS TOMKINSON. Yes, to sign an order. It's an urgent one.

MISS CONWAY. Oh, dear, what's happened?

MISS TOMKINSON. [*Seizing the opportunity of unburdening herself.*] My spare typewriter—the new student's jammed the roller. Pure carelessness, as I told her. And I shall get the blame, of course. Miss Brown doesn't realize how difficult it is to prevent these little accidents. It's the sort of thing that might happen to any one—except her.

MISS CONWAY. Poor old Tomkinson! Don't get so wrought up about it, though.

MISS TOMKINSON. I can't help it. Miss Brown always makes me feel so incapable. [*Defiantly.*] And I'm not. Even if I'm not so young as I was.

MISS CONWAY. [*Comfortingly.*] We all feel like that at times. It's because Miss Brown has such a high standard. It takes a lot of living up to. But think how lucky we are to be working for someone like her.

MISS TOMKINSON. [*Sighing.*] Yes, very lucky. [*After a pause, she looks anxiously at the clock. Miss Conway unshrouds her typewriter, cleans it, then settles down at her desk and begins to make entries in one of the ledger books.*] I wish she'd come and let me get it over. Another day to be got through. [*Sighs again.*] The sooner it begins the sooner it's over is the way I look at it now. If only it were Friday. . . .

[*To take her mind off the coming interview, she crosses to Miss Conway's desk and fills her fountain pen. Miss Fletcher enters rather as though she had come to pay an afternoon call. She is unusually well dressed, has a most attractive voice and charming manners.*

MISS FLETCHER. Is Miss Brown here yet, Conway?

MISS CONWAY. [*Looks at the clock.*] No. She's late—for her.

MISS FLETCHER. Oh! Shall I disturb you if I sit down here and look at something until she comes?

MISS CONWAY. Please do.

MISS FLETCHER. [*Sitting down in the arm-chair and opening one of the latest novels.*] Thanks. She sent me an urgent note yesterday, asking me to see her at four o'clock. When I arrived, she was entertaining a reporter from the *Feminine Outlook*—a man, of course. I think he was collecting material for his next article on 'How the Modern Woman combines Efficiency with Charm.' You know the sort of thing—'The future of England depends on England's daughters. I try to train these daughters to take a practical part in the work of the world without losing any of their feminine appeal'—and so on.

MISS CONWAY. [*A little reprovingly.*] She was free by a quarter to five, if you had waited.

MISS FLETCHER. I dare say, but I did *not* wait. I had something better to do.

[*Miss Conway, without answering, takes a pile of letters from her desk and carries them into the principal's room.*

MISS TOMKINSON. [*Enviously, with the typewriter interview on her mind.*] I wish I had your nerve.

MISS FLETCHER. [*Noticing her for the first time.*] What's the matter, Tomkinson? You look ruffled.

[*Miss Conway returns and settles down to copying out a foolscap list.*

MISS TOMKINSON. [*Coming centre and unburdening herself again, thankfully.*] It's the Remington—the spare one. It's been broken, and I do so dislike having to tell Miss Brown.

MISS FLETCHER. [*Bored.*] Oh, is *that* all? I thought it might be something serious.

MISS TOMKINSON. [*Before whom it is looming more largely than even the end of the world could.*] But it *is* serious.

MISS FLETCHER. [*Sarcastically.*] It's serious here if one uses too many sheets of blotting paper a week. It is a criminal offence to underline in black ink instead of red. [*Looking thoughtfully at Miss Conway, who has deliberately withdrawn from the conversation.*] If one of the staff were to fall down dead from overwork, I suppose the incident would pass unnoticed. [*Ironically.*] It hardly seems worth while cultivating a sense of proportion, certainly.

MISS TOMKINSON. [*Aghast.*] Well!! [*She looks at Miss Conway for support, but the latter is apparently busy with her work. Miss Tomkinson decides to ignore the remark and reverts to her main theme.*] It's not like Miss Brown to be so late. I hope nothing's happened to her.

MISS FLETCHER. [*Flippantly.*] Nothing could. It wouldn't dare.

MISS TOMKINSON. With all this traffic on the roads, one can't help being nervous.

MISS FLETCHER. My dear Tomkinson, it always seems to me rather careless of people to let themselves get run over—anyway, it's a sign of some human weakness. Our much respected principal hasn't any, so you may rest assured she will arrive intact.

MISS CONWAY. [*Quietly, looking up from her work.*] Come all over Somerset Maugham this morning, haven't you, Fletcher? Why this attack on Miss Brown?

MISS TOMKINSON. [*A little flustered, but doing her best.*] Yes, I don't think you *ought* to speak in that sneering way about her. I know we all find her a little difficult at times, but after all she *is* a wonderful woman.

MISS CONWAY. [*Stops working and warms to the theme.*] Yes. Look what she's done for this college—the reputation it's got. All the big professional men come to us for their secretaries. And without her it wouldn't exist. She's given her whole life to it for fifteen years.

MISS FLETCHER. Very laudable, I dare say.

MISS CONWAY. She was here till after seven last night working at the Loan Fund Report.

MISS FLETCHER. [*Quietly.*] How do you know that, Conway?

MISS CONWAY. [*Falling into the trap.*] I was here too.

MISS FLETCHER. [*Triumphantly.*] Exactly! Her work is her life, and she would like to make it ours, too.

MISS TOMKINSON. [*Scoring for once.*] Well, I must say she doesn't succeed in your case, Miss Fletcher.

MISS FLETCHER. No. My instinct of self-preservation is still healthily active, thank heaven. [*More seriously.*] But I'm not sure about yours, Conway. You're becoming a perfect glutton for self-sacrifice.

MISS CONWAY. What rubbish you talk, Fletcher.

MISS FLETCHER. Is it rubbish? I'm not so sure. It seems to me that you're working here late every evening, and then you're too tired to do anything but go straight home to bed.

MISS TOMKINSON. And very sensible too. There's nothing I like better than to have a hot bath at nine o'clock, pop into bed, and get a nice long read.

MISS FLETCHER. [*Dryly.*] Very cosy, I've no doubt. All the same, I don't like to see you succumbing to the Bath-Bed-and-Book routine, Conway. You're far too young, my child. Look here——

[*But at this moment the telephone rings.*

MISS CONWAY. [*Speaking into the telephone.*] St Mary's Secretarial College. Miss Brown's secretary speaking. Yes, I'll hold on.

MISS FLETCHER. [*Crossing to Miss Conway's desk, and continuing from where she left off.*] Will you come round to my flat this evening, Conway?

Miss Conway. [*To Miss Fletcher.*] I—— [*Into the telephone.*]
Yes? I 'm afraid not. No. Not any time to-morrow. Will
you say that Miss Brown is booked up all day? Thank you.
Miss Fletcher. [*Unusually persistent.*] Will you come, Conway?
I 've got some friends coming—quite amusing people. I 'd
like you to meet them.
Miss Conway. [*Looking up from the telephone.*] I couldn't
possibly, thanks very much.
Miss Fletcher. Oh. I 'm sorry.
    [*The atmosphere is becoming uncomfortable and Miss Tom-*
    kinson begins to wish she were not there. Trying to make
    herself inconspicuous, she creeps quietly towards the back
    of the room.
Miss Conway. [*Into the telephone.*] Yes? You 'll ring up again
next week? Very well. Good-bye. [*Puts down the receiver.*
To Miss Fletcher.] Please don't think me rude. I don't mean
to be. It 's just that I——
Miss Fletcher. I know. It 's just that you always like to be
within reach in case there 's a sudden Call to Duty. You can
never forget this office for one single moment——
Miss Conway. There 's really no need for you to get so agitated
about me, Fletcher. I happen to enjoy my work.
Miss Fletcher. I see. [*Turning away, she catches sight of Miss*
Tomkinson, who has ended up in front of the poster, which she
has been studying intently. There is an awkward pause. Then
Miss Tomkinson, whose neat little soul is offended by the missing
drawing-pin, looks for it and finds it on the floor. Thankful that
she can put something right, she picks it up and pins it in the
corner. Miss Fletcher, noticing the effort, goes up to the poster.]
'There 's No Fun Like Work.' You and Mr Selfridge seem to
have had the same Great Thought, Conway.
Miss Conway. [*Realizing that earnestness can be rather ridiculous.*]
I 'm sorry. That was terribly smug of me. May I change my
mind, Fletcher, and accept for to-night?
Miss Fletcher. *Do.* I want you to come. [*She crosses to her*
arm-chair, sits down, then adds casually.] There 's a rather
interesting man coming. He 's just had his first novel
published.
Miss Conway. [*Transformed.*] Oh, how exciting! What is it
called?
Miss Fletcher. [*Tolerantly.*] *The Doom of Youth*, or *Age* can
wither her, or something else quite young. But he 's a dear,
really. [*Clinching matters.*] That 's settled, then. I 'll expect

you along about seven. Oh, and Conway—do you think you could stifle your conscience sufficiently to enjoy a quite frivolous evening?

Miss Conway. [*Laughingly.*] I 'll try.

[*Miss Ellis enters, carrying a blue paper money-bag. She is middle-aged, dictatorial, completely satisfied with herself and her environment, which is obviously the right one for her. If we add that her creed is summed up in the word 'Efficiency,' we have said all there is to say.*

Miss Ellis. [*Briskly.*] I 've brought you the last of the Loan Fund subscriptions, Miss Conway. [*Holding out the blue bag.*] It 's in here—three pounds, five shillings. A list of subscribers is here, too, so it 's quite straightforward for you.

[*She hands Miss Conway the list.*

Miss Conway. Thank you. I 'll put it in the safe now.

[*She unlocks a drawer in her desk, takes out a key, and rises to go to the safe.*

Miss Ellis. [*Fussily.*] Check it, check it, Miss Conway, if you please.

Miss Conway. [*Keeping her temper.*] Certainly, if you wish it.

Miss Ellis. I 'm not fussy, I hope, but one must be business-like.

Miss Conway. [*Counts it over.*] Absolutely O.K. I can't accuse you of appropriating a single penny.

[*Miss Ellis does not respond to this. Miss Conway goes over to the safe, unlocks it, puts the bag in, and relocks it.*

Miss Ellis. Oh, and Miss Conway, if it 's not troubling you too much, could we have the balance sheet ready a little earlier this year?

Miss Conway. Not before Friday, I 'm afraid. I 've got an awfully busy week.

Miss Ellis. It 's so inconvenient for others when it 's left till the last minute.

Miss Tomkinson. [*Rushing in.*] Oh, Conway dear, do let me do it for you. [*Every one seems so surprised at this offer that Miss Tomkinson feels she has been a little rash to make it, but she goes bravely on.*] You know I love anything to do with figures. And Miss Brown herself put me in charge of the accounts for the sale of work last year.

Miss Ellis. Wasn't that the time there was a serious error in one of the totals?

Miss Tomkinson. It was only a typing mistake. Every one understood.

MISS CONWAY. Of course. It 's sweet of you to offer, Tommy. Thank you so much.

MISS ELLIS. [*Horrified.*] Really, Miss Conway! I think you are making a mistake. It is asking too much of Miss Tomkinson.

MISS CONWAY. [*Indignantly.*] Nonsense! She 's good at figures.

MISS TOMKINSON. [*Crushed, and with her former hang-dog expression.*] No. She 's right, Conway. I don't get much responsibility given me now. [*Turns away dejectedly.*] I oughtn't to have offered.

MISS CONWAY. [*Firmly.*] Rubbish, Tomkinson; of course you can do it.

MISS ELLIS. In any case, I 'm sure Miss Brown wouldn't approve. I 'm not fussy, but I shouldn't like it myself if the tasks I gave to certain people were redelegated without my consent.

MISS CONWAY. [*Impatiently.*] As though Miss Brown would quibble about a detail like that!

MISS FLETCHER. [*Who has been making abortive attempts to get on with her novel. Into space.*] Miss Conway has been here all this time and can still talk in that light-hearted way about a detail. Ye gods!

MISS CONWAY. No, but seriously, Fletcher, you don't see any reason why Tomkinson——

MISS FLETCHER. *Reason* has nothing to do with it, my dear Conway. Surely you know by now that Miss Brown does not react favourably to any attempt at initiative on the part of her staff.

[*She and Miss Conway look at each other for a moment. Then the latter turns away with a slight shrug.*

MISS CONWAY. She couldn't possibly mind a thing like this.

MISS TOMKINSON. Then I *may* do it?

[*There is a pause while Miss Conway decides.*

MISS CONWAY. Of course. [*She sits down at her desk.*

MISS TOMKINSON. [*At once becoming self-confident.*] Thank you so much. I shall love to. And you can trust me not to do it carelessly. I never mind how much trouble I take over any work Miss Brown wants done. I could begin it in my free time this morning if I could get at the account books. Do you think you could let me have the key of the safe, Conway?

MISS CONWAY. [*Hesitatingly.*] Well—I don't usually let any one take it away.

MISS ELLIS. I should think not, indeed. Really, Miss Conway, what has come over you this morning?

MISS TOMKINSON. But, you see, so often when we come in for

something, you 're in there [*pointing to the inner door*] and we can't get at you.

MISS CONWAY. Very well, I 'll take a chance and let you have it. [*Hands it to her.*] But hang on to it [*mock-seriously*] as you value your life!

[*Miss Ellis watches the incident curiously. Miss Fletcher is making better progress with her novel. Miss Tomkinson crosses right of the desk, holding firmly on to the key.*

MISS ELLIS. Well, I hope events will prove you right, Miss Conway, that 's all I can say. [*Looks at Miss Fletcher disapprovingly.*] Some of us don't seem to be very busy this morning. I have enough work for two people to get through, so I mustn't stay gossiping here.   [*Goes off.*

MISS FLETCHER. My God!

[*There is a knock at the door, which opens a little way, and Miss Stewart's head appears round it.*

MISS STEWART. Good morning, Miss Conway. May we come in and wait for Miss Brown?

MISS CONWAY. Yes, do.

Miss Stewart and Miss Gilchrist enter.

MISS TOMKINSON. [*All smiles and self-possession.*] She hasn't come yet. We 're waiting for her, too. Quite a crowd of us, isn't there, waiting for an audience with her?

[*She laughs nervously ; no one else joins in.*

MISS STEWART. [*She is unsophisticated and rather charming.*] She wanted to see us about the Loan Fund.

MISS TOMKINSON. Oh, yes, of course, you 're trying to think of a new way of raising money, aren't you?

MISS STEWART. Yes, we are. Always.

MISS GILCHRIST. [*Who likes to be thought a Bright Young Thing. We find her rather too self-assured.*] I expect it will be the same old story in the end.

MISS TOMKINSON. What 's that, Miss Gilchrist?

MISS STEWART. Oh, she means a dance.

MISS GILCHRIST. [*Bored.*] Yes, without men. I ask you!

MISS TOMKINSON. [*Innocently.*] Well, I can't see anything wrong with that. It 's nice healthy exercise just the same.

MISS GILCHRIST. Oh, too frightfully healthy for words. And so exhilarating. Like a Y.M.C.A. cocktail.

MISS STEWART. Shut up, Gilchrist.

MISS GILCHRIST. Oh, it 's so stupid the way Miss Brown insists on these dreary, let's-all-be-girls-together affairs. Of course nobody comes, and we don't make any money. If we can't have a *proper* dance, why can't we think of something else— a sweepstake, for instance?

MISS STEWART. Yes, I think a sweepstake would be an awfully good idea. Do you think we dare suggest it, Miss Tomkinson?

MISS TOMKINSON. [*Rather taken aback.*] I—I hardly think she would approve.

MISS GILCHRIST. It's a perfectly normal way of raising money for charity. I vote we suggest it.

MISS STEWART. All right—as long as you do the suggesting.

MISS GILCHRIST. [*Airily.*] Righto, I will. I shall just put it to her quite reasonably——

[*At this moment Miss Brown enters, carrying a bunch of autumn leaves. She is tall and striking-looking, and speaks as one having authority. Her bright, brisk, beginning-of-the-morning manner is rather attractive, but somehow we wonder how long it will last. At her entry the students subside, somewhat awed, and Miss Tomkinson's self-confidence immediately vanishes. Miss Fletcher rises, but otherwise remains unmoved. Miss Conway, on the other hand, stands up eagerly.*]

MISS BROWN. Good morning, every one. [*With an attempt at playfulness.*] Dreadful of me to be so late, isn't it? But I've been interviewing Mrs Carter. The kitchen staff seem to need so much looking after. Just put these leaves in water for me, will you, Miss Conway. [*She goes into her room to take off her hat and coat, and conducts the conversation for the next few minutes from behind the door. Meanwhile Miss Fletcher sits down again.*] Have there been any messages for me?

MISS CONWAY. [*Used to this sort of thing.*] Yes. King's Employment Bureau were on the 'phone, and wanted an appointment for to-morrow afternoon——

MISS BROWN. Not to-morrow—my free Wednesday? Oh, Miss Conway! I hope you warded them off?

MISS CONWAY. Yes, I told them you were booked up every minute, and they must ring up again next week.

MISS BROWN. [*Emerging, and rewarding Miss Conway with a smile.*] Thank you! You do look after me, don't you? [*Miss Conway, obviously touched by the praise, goes off with the leaves. Miss Brown proceeds to deal with those who are left.*] Oh, good morning, Miss Fletcher.

MISS FLETCHER. [*Rising.*] You asked me to speak to you, Miss Brown——

MISS BROWN. I *sent* for you, yes. [*Miss Fletcher is not affected by the attempted reproof.*] Just wait one moment, please. [*Miss Fletcher retires gracefully to the back of the room. Miss Brown takes up her stand by the arm-chair. To the two students.*] Are you two waiting to speak to me?

MISS STEWART. [*Coming forward rather shyly.*] Yes, Miss Brown, you told us to come to you about raising money for the Loan Fund.

MISS BROWN. Oh, of course, I remember. We are going to have a dance for all the students before Christmas, are we not? Well, first of all, there's the question of date. [*She takes out her diary.*] It must be a Saturday, of course. [*Miss Fletcher wonders why.*] As far as I am concerned, it could be either the third or the seventeenth. No, not the third. I shall be away that week-end. The seventeenth, then? How does that suit you?

MISS GILCHRIST. [*Uncomfortably.*] Well, you see——

MISS BROWN. You have something else arranged for that evening? A college fixture?

MISS GILCHRIST. Oh, no.

MISS BROWN. If it's a personal engagement, I think you must be prepared to break it. It is impossible to arrange an entertainment for such a large number unless the organizers are prepared to make sacrifices. You do see that, don't you?

MISS STEWART. [*Unhappily.*] Yes, of course. We didn't mean that.

MISS BROWN Very well, then. The seventeenth. Now don't leave the arrangements till the last minute. The music, for instance. We don't want to go to the expense of hiring a band, of course. Last year one of the old students played for us—Millicent Reade, I think it was.

MISS GILCHRIST. [*Desperately.*] But, Miss Brown, we aren't quite sure whether——

MISS BROWN. [*Brushing the effort aside.*] Not now, Miss Gilchrist, I have a very busy morning before me. Come to me when you have thought out your plans more fully. I shall be most interested to hear them. [*She sweeps the students off, and notices Miss Tomkinson standing in an agony of apprehension.*] Oh, Miss Tomkinson, [*resignedly*] you want me, too?

MISS TOMKINSON. [*Stammering in her extreme agitation.*] Y-yes, Miss Brown, it's about an order for a——
  [*As she comes forward, in her nervousness she knocks a pile of cards from the index drawer off the table.*

MISS BROWN. Oh, *really*, Miss Tomkinson, and those cards had just been arranged in alphabetical order. No, no, leave them *alone. [As Miss Tomkinson, who has hastily picked them up, tries fumblingly to rearrange them.]* You'll only make them worse. Miss Conway will have to do them again.

MISS TOMKINSON. *[Almost in tears.]* I'm so sorry. I can't think how I could——

MISS BROWN. *[Relenting.]* Never mind, Miss Tomkinson, just try to keep quite calm. *[She sits down in the arm-chair and waits so patiently for Miss Tomkinson to speak that the latter is far from being encouraged.]* And now, what is your difficulty? Be quick, please, because I am busy.

MISS TOMKINSON. *[Hastily.]* Yes, I won't keep you a minute, Miss Brown. If you would just sign this repair order.
                                                    [Hands out the order book.

MISS BROWN. But you know I never sign these orders indiscriminately. I must know all about it. And I haven't time to go into the matter now. You must come back later.

MISS TOMKINSON. *[Thankful this time for a reprieve.]* Certainly, Miss Brown.

MISS BROWN. *[As Miss Tomkinson goes hurriedly off.]* Poor Miss Tomkinson! But she is so clumsy! *[Miss Brown now settles down to enjoy the last of her encounters. She is at last meeting a foeman worthy of her steel.]* Well, sit down, Miss Fletcher, I may as well speak to you in here. *[Miss Fletcher chooses a chair, brings it opposite Miss Brown, and sits down.]* I'm not going to keep you a moment. *[She pauses to collect her thoughts, which are becoming a little confused. She is having a busy morning.]* It's about the waste of stationery that I wanted to see you. We really must put a stop to it. This, I think, especially applies to the Shorthand Dictation Classes.

MISS FLETCHER. Very well, Miss Brown, I will see that as little as possible is used.
      [There is another pause, and she rises to go, thinking that the interview is at an end.

MISS BROWN. One moment, Miss Fletcher. *[She has now come to the real reason for the interview. Miss Fletcher again sits down.]* I was in the Library last Tuesday, and I noticed that some of the students were taking down shorthand—in pencil. Surely they should have been using ink?

MISS FLETCHER. *[Indifferently.]* I don't think it matters, Miss Brown. Either is equally satisfactory.

MISS BROWN. But I've always heard that the ink method is the

correct one. It makes it easier to differentiate the outlines.
I believe it is compulsory in most Technical Colleges.

MISS FLETCHER. [*Coldly.*] In *Technical* Colleges. Oh, possibly.

MISS BROWN. You mean——?

MISS FLETCHER. [*Still detached, yet choosing her words carefully.*]
One feels, surely, that the students here are being trained on
rather different lines. They *ought* to be able to choose their
own methods—up to a certain point. I encourage them to
use their initiative in such small matters as these.

MISS BROWN. [*Jumping to a new attacking ground.*] Ah, that is
exactly what I have been meaning to discuss with you. How
far, Miss Fletcher, do the staff, as subordinates here, act in
direct opposition to me, as Principal of this College?

MISS FLETCHER. [*Bewildered at the sudden change of argument.*]
I'm afraid I don't understand you, Miss Brown. I thought
we were discussing a small and relatively unimportant point
—the question of ink or pencil for shorthand outlines. There
was no question of anything else.

MISS BROWN. It comes to the same thing, it seems to me.
[*Leaning forward and speaking almost hysterically.*] This may
seem an unimportant matter to you, Miss Fletcher, but *I*
realize its significance. To me it appears one of the many
ways in which my authority in this building is beginning to
be disregarded.

MISS FLETCHER. [*Entirely unmoved.*] I'm afraid I cannot agree
with you. The matter as I see it is a purely impersonal one.
For me it is a question of which of two methods will give the
better result. That and nothing more.

[*In the pause that follows they face each other. Then Miss
Brown, realizing that she has lost, smiles disarmingly, and
speaks in her former matter-of-fact-tone.*]

MISS BROWN. Well, of course, it is a great relief to hear you say
that. It was, perhaps, a false impression of mine.

MISS FLETCHER. [*Firmly.*] Entirely false, Miss Brown.

[*Miss Conway enters with the jug of leaves and carries it into
Miss Brown's room.*]

MISS BROWN. I see. Then I need not keep you any longer.
But I'm so glad to have had this talk with you. It's been
most helpful.

[*She rises. Miss Fletcher, having brought the interview to a
successful close, rises too. She is about to press her
advantage home, when Miss Conway re-enters. She has
a large delivery note in one hand.*]

MISS CONWAY. The new cupboard has just come, Miss Brown. It's for the students' common room, isn't it. Miss Keith is showing the carter where to——

MISS BROWN. [*Who misguidedly believes that 'if you want a thing done properly, you must do it yourself.'*] Oh, I'd better go down myself and see to it, or there will be some mistake. Just one moment, before I forget. Are you free this evening, my dear? [*She does not notice Miss Conway's face, but continues in an almost pathetic attempt to impress Miss Fletcher.*] The editor of *Feminine Outlook* wants to print my speech—the one I made on Foundation Day. He seems rather impressed with my remarks about the modern young woman being thoroughly well-equipped for her work without losing any of her feminine charm. Rather an important problem, don't you think, Miss Fletcher? [*Miss Fletcher makes a diplomatic gesture. She probably feels that other matters, such as the rate of exchange on the Continent or the latest Aldous Huxley novel, are equally important.*] I've only got a few rough notes, as I always speak extempore—I feel it's so much more effective. [*To Miss Conway.*] But if you would come round to my house to-night, I could dictate it to you at the typewriter.

MISS CONWAY. I *am* sorry, Miss Brown, I'm afraid I can't possibly——

[*She stops as she sees Miss Brown's look of surprise.*

MISS BROWN. You realize that it is a great honour for me to have my speech published in such a famous journal—a wonderful tribute to the college?

MISS CONWAY. Yes, I should be proud to help. But to-night I've promised to go out, and I——

MISS BROWN. [*Brusquely.*] I see. Very well.

MISS CONWAY. I will do it for you to-morrow, without fail.

MISS BROWN. [*A pained note in her voice.*] It must be posted to-night, I am afraid. I shall have to write it out myself by hand, that's all. [*Playing her trump card.*] Obviously the reputation of the college does not mean as much to you as I hoped it did.

MISS CONWAY. [*Giving in.*] I'll come. It just means that I shall have to alter my plans. I can go out another time, I expect.

[*She looks appealingly at Miss Fletcher, who is gazing into space as though the whole affair had lost interest for her.*

MISS BROWN. [*All smiles again now that she has won.*] Thank you so much, my dear. It 'll be made up to you later, I promise you.

[*She is hurrying off to her cupboard, but is recalled by Miss Fletcher.*

MISS FLETCHER. [*Coldly, but as though the last incident had never taken place.*] Oh, Miss Brown, then I am to understand that the students *may* use pencil for their shorthand outlines?

MISS BROWN. [*Who is no longer concerned with this problem.*] If you think it better, Miss Fletcher. I must leave it to your judgment entirely. [*Half-way through the door.*] I don't want to interfere. [*She goes off.*

MISS FLETCHER. [*Flippantly, to ease the situation.*]

'Behold, the heavens do ope,
The gods look down, and this unnatural scene
They laugh at . . .'

Or is it—weep? [*Casually.*] I can't remember.

MISS CONWAY. I can see her point of view. It *is* important for her speech to be published.

MISS FLETCHER. Nothing excuses her behaving like *that*. The woman 's inhuman.

MISS CONWAY. [*Turning and facing Miss Fletcher.*] What do you mean?

MISS FLETCHER. If she sets her mind on something, she 'won't be happy till she gets it.'

MISS CONWAY. That seems to me rather human.

MISS FLETCHER. Rather—childish, shall we say?

MISS CONWAY. No, I don't think that 's fair. Miss Brown is ruthless, I know. But she has to be—to achieve what she set out for—to make this college famous for turning out the best kind of student. That 's a big thing to do. And she 's succeeded.

MISS FLETCHER. [*This is more than even she can bear.*] For heaven's sake, Conway, don't get lyrical about this place.

MISS CONWAY. Well, let 's stop the discussion altogether. I 've got some work to do this morning. [*She begins to settle down at her table.*] Won't you—finish your novel?

MISS FLETCHER. Thank you, I find real life more interesting at the moment.

[*Rising, she puts her chair back against the wall, and, crossing the stage, stands behind Miss Conway's chair.*

MISS CONWAY. [*Noticing the cards which Miss Tomkinson has upset.*] What on earth 's happened to these?

MISS FLETCHER. Oh, another of Tomkinson's little accidents.

MISS CONWAY. Poor old Tomkinson!

MISS FLETCHER. Yes—but not only poor old *Tomkinson*. She's not the only victim.

MISS CONWAY. I don't know what you mean.

MISS FLETCHER. [*Quietly.*] I'll tell you. If you're not careful, Conway, you'll be another of the lambs on the altar. In ten years' time you'll be exactly like Tomkinson. [*Lightly, as she crosses to the arm-chair.*] She's one of the Awful Warnings here. [*Miss Conway sees quite clearly, for one brief moment, what this means. Miss Fletcher, realizing this, continues much more seriously.*] That's why you must get away now, Conway, before you're content to take all this for granted.

MISS CONWAY. But what do you expect me to do? Throw up my job and go out into the wide, wide world without a penny? Oh, come, Fletcher, one must be practical.

MISS FLETCHER. Is it practical to refuse to look facts in the face —to drift into accepting conditions that you know will never make you happy? [*Sitting down as comfortably as possible in the arm-chair.*] Tell me, Conway, didn't you expect to get something better out of life once?

MISS CONWAY. I suppose so, when I was very young. Yes, I did think it was all going to be rather wonderful. [*With enthusiasm.*] I knew what I wanted then.

MISS FLETCHER. What was that?

MISS CONWAY. I wanted to do one perfect thing. It might be quite small and unimportant. That wouldn't matter, as long as it was perfect—like—like——

[*She stops because it is difficult to talk like this without feeling embarrassed.*

MISS FLETCHER. [*Who does not seem to mind this sort of conversation.*] Go on.

MISS CONWAY. Oh—like a dance in the Russian Ballet, or one of those trees that Cézanne puts in the centre of his pictures—do you remember them?—or even a quite perfect baby——[*Becoming self-conscious again.*] What a fool I am to talk like this!

MISS FLETCHER. I think you're just beginning to talk *sense*.

MISS CONWAY. [*After a pause, in which she wakes up completely to all that Miss Fletcher is trying to do to her.*] Can't you see you're making it much more difficult for me?

MISS FLETCHER. Yes, that's exactly what I'm trying to——

MISS CONWAY. [*Speaking her most serious thoughts aloud.*] I want to believe that I've found a purpose in life—the work I was meant to do. I must have something I can believe in

—something so much worth while that the petty scenes that happen incidentally—don't matter.

MISS FLETCHER. They *wouldn't* matter—if they *were* incidental.

MISS CONWAY. [*In a last attempt to avoid reality.*] I try to believe they are. It's only sometimes—when I'm watching Tomkinson and Miss Brown together, or when Ellis is being exasperatingly efficient about nothing at all—that I wonder whether it isn't all rather unnatural—whether we aren't forgetting the main objective.

MISS FLETCHER. Is there a main objective for them? I wonder. But for you, Conway——?

MISS CONWAY. [*Slowly, as though she has only just discovered what it is.*] Freedom. That's the only thing that matters, I think. To be free from the idiotic futility of it all, so that I can create something worth while—that's what I wanted from here. [*Flippantly.*] It seems a little late in the day to begin the search all over again somewhere else. And, anyway, I expect I'm crying for the moon.

Miss Tomkinson enters. It is at once clear that she is extremely agitated about something.

MISS TOMKINSON. Oh, Conway, have you found it? Did I leave it here after all?

MISS CONWAY. [*Her thoughts still on the moon.*] Leave what here, Tomkinson?

MISS TOMKINSON. [*Breathlessly.*] Why, the key.

MISS CONWAY. Not—the key of the safe?

MISS TOMKINSON. [*Tremblingly.*] Yes.

[*The pause that follows this confession brings home to her the enormity of her crime.*

MISS FLETCHER. [*Impatiently.*] Good heavens, Tomkinson, it didn't take you long to lose it, did it?

MISS CONWAY. [*Quickly.*] No, don't bait her, Fletcher. Now, think, Tomkinson. What did you do with it after I gave it you?

MISS TOMKINSON. Well, I *thought* I put it in my bag.

MISS FLETCHER. It's probably there still. [*Authoritatively.*] Let me look, Tomkinson. [*Miss Tomkinson hands her the bag.*] You're so excitable.

[*Methodically she takes out the miscellaneous collection of articles that fill Miss Tomkinson's shabby black bag. Then, with the eyes of the other two fixed anxiously upon her, she turns the empty bag upside down and shakes it out, but with no success.*

MISS TOMKINSON. [*Despairingly.*] You see, I *knew* it wasn't there.

MISS CONWAY. You may have dropped it out of the bag.

MISS FLETCHER. Quite easily, I should think. Just look! [*Holding it up to show how it gapes.*] It's a wonder that anything stays in it.

MISS CONWAY. Where were you standing?

MISS TOMKINSON. [*By the safe.*] Over here.

MISS CONWAY. Perhaps it's on the floor.

[*They both look. Miss Tomkinson gets down on her hands and knees to feel on the carpet.*

MISS FLETCHER. [*Rising and crossing to the safe.*] Where did you go when you left here?

MISS TOMKINSON. Only to the cloakroom, and then to the typing class. I've looked in both places, *and* on the stairs and everywhere. Oh, I *am* unlucky.

MISS FLETCHER. Do get up, Tomkinson. You look so ridiculous grovelling about on all fours.

MISS TOMKINSON. [*With unexpected spirit.*] Ridiculous, am I? That's nothing to what I shall look if Miss Brown discovers the key's missing. It's all very well for you to laugh, Miss Fletcher, but you know what she'll say—all that money in the safe, and the key lying about for any one to pick up and help themselves.

MISS CONWAY. [*More cheerfully than she feels.*] Don't worry. We'll soon find it.

Miss Brown enters. Miss Tomkinson, still on her hands and knees, remains unconscious of her entrance.

MISS BROWN. [*Smoothly.*] You appear to have lost something, Miss Tomkinson. May I ask what?

MISS TOMKINSON. [*Scrambling to her feet.*] Oh, nothing, Miss Brown, nothing.

MISS BROWN. Indeed? [*Sarcastically.*] You are playing some kind of game, then? [*There is a pause, in which Miss Tomkinson feverishly tries to think what she can say next.*] Won't you enlighten me, Miss Tomkinson? You are obviously looking for something.

MISS TOMKINSON. [*Cornered.*] It's nothing—really important. Just something personal—I thought I might have dropped it in here.

MISS BROWN. I see. And Miss Fletcher is very kindly helping you to look. Do you think you ought to keep her from her work like this?

Miss Fletcher. [*Glancing at the clock.*] There are still five minutes before the advanced shorthand class begins.

[*She meets Miss Brown's eye blandly, and remains where she is.*

Miss Brown. At any rate, Miss Conway, I think, might be better employed. [*Miss Conway goes to her desk and sits down.*

Miss Tomkinson. [*Miserably.*] I'm sorry. I'll go.

[*She takes her bag up and is crossing to the door when Miss Brown speaks.*

Miss Brown. One moment, Miss Tomkinson. You are sure it is something belonging to you that you have lost? It isn't by any chance this key? [*She has opened her bag and taken out the missing key. Miss Tomkinson, gazing at it, gives a little gasp. She has indeed been unlucky.*] So that *was* it. Miss Ellis found it beside your books in the staff cloakroom. She very rightly brought it to me. First of all, I must remind you of the rule that no keys may be left about the building. In the second place, this is the key of [*she pauses dramatically*] the *safe*! In that safe, Miss Tomkinson, we keep *money*. Perhaps you did not realize that? Nor that this money was at the disposal of any one who happened to pick up the key? [*This sarcasm is somewhat lost on Miss Tomkinson, who is too frightened to take anything more in. Miss Brown sits down in the arm-chair and proceeds with the cross-questioning.*] And now I shall be glad if you will tell me how it came to be in your possession.

Miss Conway. [*Rising.*] It is entirely my responsibility, Miss Brown. I gave her the key. She is doing a little job for me, and she needed it.

Miss Brown. May I know what piece of work Miss Tomkinson has—undertaken?

Miss Conway. [*Quietly.*] The balance sheet for the Loan Fund Committee. Miss Ellis wants it out earlier this year, and as I am very busy this week, Miss Tomkinson offered to do it for me. It was extremely kind of her to——

Miss Brown. Extremely kind, or extremely interfering, shall we say? [*Cuttingly, to Miss Tomkinson.*] After all these years on my staff, Miss Tomkinson, you ought to know that when I give a certain piece of work to one of you, I strongly object to its being taken away from her in this high-handed manner.

Miss Fletcher. [*Protesting for her weaker brethren.*] Surely it is beside the point whether Miss Tomkinson or Miss Conway does this work. All that matters is that it should be carried out efficiently.

MISS BROWN. [*Twisting the meaning to her own advantage.*] Exactly! And I consider myself the best judge of those who are efficient and [*she looks at Miss Tomkinson*] those who are not.

MISS TOMKINSON. [*Pitifully.*] I only wanted to *help*.

MISS BROWN. [*And now she makes use of the worst form of cruelty.*] To help! That is really rather amusing. I feel I must let you know, Miss Tomkinson, that your carelessness and general incompetence have made me seriously consider lately whether your services were worth retaining. I suggest that you concentrate in future on improving your own standard of efficiency. That is all the help that is required from *you*. Please go away now and leave Miss Conway to get on with her own work. There have been enough interruptions already this morning. [*Miss Tomkinson clutches her bag and stumbles out, a humiliated little figure. Miss Brown is not really aware of all that she has done.*] Really, Miss Tomkinson must not be so touchy.

[*During this scene Miss Conway has been holding herself in with difficulty. Miss Brown's last comment on Miss Tomkinson is too much for her.*

MISS CONWAY. It's not that. Can't you see what you've done to her?

MISS BROWN. [*Majestically.*] Miss Conway! I think you forget yourself.

MISS CONWAY. I'm sorry. I didn't mean to be rude. [*Forgetting again.*] But didn't you see how awful she looked—when you spoke to her like that—— [*She stops, for Miss Brown is looking at her in complete astonishment. Limply.*] I'm sorry.

MISS BROWN. [*Impatiently.*] What *is* the matter with you this morning, Miss Conway? You seem to be acting extremely foolishly. What on earth possessed you to hand over the balance sheet to Miss Tomkinson?

MISS CONWAY. I'll tell you. I let Miss Tomkinson do it because I was sorry for her, and she was so anxious to help. She isn't often given any responsibility, is she? You call her incompetent, but if she is, it's because of you—you've made her feel futile and ineffectual—made her [*bitterly*] a failure.

MISS BROWN. [*Rising.*] That will do, Miss Conway. I must ask you not to say anything more until you can control yourself.

MISS CONWAY. [*Going up to Miss Brown.*] I must say one thing more. I must ask you to accept my resignation.

I 947

MISS BROWN. [*Coldly.*] That is an understood thing.   After this
extraordinary outburst, no other course is open to you.

MISS CONWAY. [*Turning away.*] I can't stay here any longer.

MISS BROWN. [*After waiting a moment to make her next remark as
impressive as possible.*] I would just remind you of something
which, in your present exalted state, you may have overlooked.
You will probably find it extremely difficult to get other work.

MISS CONWAY. [*Quietly.*] Yes, I realize that.

MISS BROWN. Without an adequate testimonial from me, it
might be impossible.

MISS CONWAY. I know.

MISS BROWN. [*Pausing, this time before an attempt at a reconcilia-
tion.*] I don't wish to be hard on you, Miss Conway.   I can
only think that you are ill.   I suggest that you go away and
lie down.   When you are yourself again, if you feel like making
a full apology——

MISS CONWAY. [*Turning and facing Miss Brown.*] Oh, no, I don't
regret anything.   I am seeing it all clearly for once, and I
couldn't do anything else.   I am so terribly glad to be free.
To know that I shan't ever have to look at *that* again. [*She
points to the poster, and the irony of the words strikes her so
forcibly that she is moved desperately to do something about it.*]
I 've always hated it, and now I know why. [*Going up to the
poster, she tears it down, comes down stage, and holds it out before
Miss Brown.*] Look at it! [*More bitterly than she has yet
spoken.*] It 's bunk! [*She crumples it up and throws it on the
floor.   But somehow she feels now that it is useless.   She is
shouting to someone who lives on a different continent, and she
can't make herself heard.   Yet she has to go on.   Her voice
becomes flat, dull, completely unemotional.*] What pleasure do
we get out of our work?   Not the pleasure that comes from
creating something.   You don't allow us that.   You want us
to work like machines—to make *you* successful. [*Desperately,
her voice rising again.*] It doesn't really matter about the
college at all.   You only want us to satisfy your sense of
power.   As long as we do that, you don't care what you do to
us—waste our energy, crush our self-respect—you don't even
stop at that.   You 'd destroy everything in us which might
have become fine and splendid——

MISS BROWN. [*Savagely, completely losing her self-control.*] Get
out—get out of this room at once.

[*Miss Conway is afraid for a moment that she is going to faint,
but by making a great effort she steadies herself and walks*

*unfalteringly out of the room. It is obvious that Miss
Brown is badly shaken. She sits down wearily in the
arm-chair. Her face looks haggard, and she has lost
momentarily her self-assurance. Then she remembers
that she is not alone. Miss Fletcher, of all people, is
there with her. The situation, she realizes, cannot be
left as it is.*

MISS BROWN. Oh, Miss Fletcher, I am sorry you have been
subjected to this disgraceful scene. I can only stress more
firmly what I said to you this morning. I am relying on your
loyal co-operation.

MISS FLETCHER. [*Choosing her words carefully.*] You can always
rely on me to do my *work* properly, Miss Brown. [*She goes
towards the door, but noticing the poster, she stoops to pick it up.
Politely.*] Where would you like me to put this? Back on the
wall, or— [*looking at its torn condition*] in the waste-paper
basket?

MISS BROWN. Oh, pin it up, please, Miss Fletcher. [*Miss Fletcher
takes drawing-pins from the desk and does so.*] And as you go,
will you find Miss Stewart and tell her to come to me?

MISS FLETCHER. Certainly.

[*She exits, not forgetting to take her novel with her. Miss
Brown is glad to be alone. She leans back in her chair
and puts her hand to her head. In a few seconds there is
a knock at the door. She pulls herself up with a jerk.*

MISS BROWN. Come in.

Miss Stewart enters.

MISS STEWART. Miss Fletcher said you wanted me, Miss Brown.

MISS BROWN. [*Almost her natural self again.*] Oh, yes, of course.
Come and sit down over there, Miss Stewart. [*She points to the
chair at the table, formerly occupied by Miss Conway.*] I want
you to take down a speech in shorthand at my dictation. It
will be a good test for me to see what progress you are making.
And this afternoon I will see that you are freed from your
classes, so that you can come here and type it out neatly.
You can use Miss Conway's machine. Have you got your
note-book with you?

MISS STEWART. Yes, Miss Brown. [*She opens her note-book and
plays rather nervously with her pencil.*] I was on my way to
Miss Fletcher's speed class.

MISS BROWN. Good. Are you ready? [*She rises, and paces about
the room. As the speech proceeds, she gradually recovers her*

sense of power, her faith in her own efficiency.] Mr Chairman,
my lord, ladies, and gentlemen—— [*Stops. To herself.*] Or
shall I leave that out? No, better put everything in. [*To
Miss Stewart.*] Begin again, please, Miss Stewart. [*Clears her
throat.*] Mr Chairman, my lord, ladies, and gentlemen. It is
with much pleasure that I present to you my report for the
past year. After fifteen years' work at this college, I feel
that I may be pardoned if I begin by speaking for a few
moments—— [*Breaks off.*] Am I going too fast, Miss Stewart?
You must tell me if I am. I don't want you to miss a single
word.

MISS STEWART. No, it's all right, thank you.

MISS BROWN. —for a few moments on the aims of my work here.
In the first place, I have always put before both the staff and
the students a high standard—I may say a very high standard
—of efficiency. And here I would like to pause and pay a few
words of grateful tribute to my loyal, efficient, and devoted
staff—— [*She stops as though she has remembered something.
Then she sees Miss Stewart taking advantage of the pause to
look up at her admiringly, and, annoyed with herself for her
foolishness in hesitating, she continues more firmly.*] There is
no member of it who is not prepared to make every sacrifice
to maintain this high standard that we have set ourselves——
[*Again she pauses. Miss Stewart, who in ten years' time, we
imagine, will be very like Miss Conway, looks up, 'Oh, how
splendid!' on her lips, her eyes shining at this picture of noble
women. Miss Brown, thus encouraged, becomes once more
completely self-confident, and she finishes her sentence with a
flourish.*]—this high standard that we feel is worthy of
achievement, whatever the cost. . . .

THE CURTAIN HAS SLOWLY DESCENDED

PANDORA'S BOX

A PLAY IN VERSE AND MIME

ROSALIND VALLANCE

PERSONS OF THE PLAY

THE LEADER OF THE CHORUS ⎫
THE CHORUS   ⎬ *Speaking*

PANDORA   ⎫
EPIMETHEUS ⎬ *Miming*
HERMES   ⎭

The scene throughout is Pandora's garden

PANDORA'S BOX

The Chorus (about twelve persons) enter from left and right, forming an arc at the back of the stage. The Leader comes through the entrance at the centre back. The Chorus greet her by raising their right arms. The Leader returns their salutation.

LEADER. Are ye come forth, glad hearts, to greet the sun?
CHORUS. The world is new, the world has just begun.
ONE OF THE CHORUS. The merry birds are singing in the trees.
A SECOND. The little clouds are ships upon the breeze.
A THIRD. And the brook murmurs like the pipes of Pan.
LEADER. The gods are good, and happy every man
And every woman. Young Apollo's fire
Lights up the world, and Pan, with soft desire,
Pipes to the dance.
                Where is the child of joy,
Dark-eyed Pandora, and the lovely boy?
CHORUS. Pandora, Pandora, come into the sun;
Pandora, Pandora, the day has begun.
   Pandora comes dancing on left, throwing an imaginary ball, in time with the verse. She keeps the centre of the stage.
High and low, high and low,
A golden ball for Pandora to throw;
Low and high, low and high,
But the gods have the moon and the stars in the sky.
   Epimetheus runs on right. Pandora and he throw the ball to each other—Pandora left, Epimetheus right.
FIRST SEMI-CHORUS. [*While they play.*] Lalla leerie, lalla lo,
To and fro, to and fro,
The gods look down on the world below,
Lalla leerie, lalla lo.
SECOND SEMI-CHORUS. Lalla leerie, lalla lo,
The sun is ashine and the river's aflow,
And the world is young as the flowers that blow,
Lalla leerie, lalla lo.
   [*During the last verse the Leader has been looking preoccupied, as though seeing and hearing things unseen and unheard by the others.*

LEADER. What scent is this that floats upon the air?
And music too?
              Do ye not hear it? There!
It comes again.   [*All listen.*
          A wind-borne melody.
The herald of the gods.
    [*She goes to the centre opening and looks out ; then cries softly.*
                  Dear sisters, see,
'Tis he indeed, Hermes, the Silver-shod,
Far, far away, like a bright bird of God.
                 [*She stands looking out, unmoving.*
CHORUS. Speak, for thou seest where we cannot see:
Whence has he come, and whither goeth he?
LEADER. From high Olympus he has flown,
   Over the mountains where the moon
   Gleameth white on endless snow,
   Past the vales where olives grow,
   Over the rippling Alpheus river,
   Over the pastures, pausing never.
    [*She watches him in silence a moment. Then she looks within,*
       towards the Chorus again, crying joyfully.
He comes to bless this green pleasaunce,
And sweet Pandora in the dance,
And Epimetheus, lovely boy:
White Hermes loves to see their joy.
[*To the Children.*] Gentle mortals, of your grace
Dwellers in this fairy place,
Greet him well with lifted hand,
For Hermes comes at Zeus' command.
    [*Pandora and Epimetheus stand left, shyly. Enter Hermes,*
      lightly, carrying an imaginary box on the finger-tips of his
      right hand. He crosses to the centre. The Children and
      the Chorus greet him with right hand uplifted and head
      slightly bent. Hermes smiles at the Children and holds
      out his box. They look at it with great interest. The
      Chorus also lean forward to look.
CHORUS. Hermes of the silver sandal, Hermes of the silver wing,
   Hermes of the twining serpents, white-foot, light-foot, what
     dost bring?
LEADER. A box of sandalwood. Lo, sisters, see,
   With carven faces smiling curiously,
   And writhing snakes around it, fold on fold,

And on the lid an amulet of gold:
Fearful and beautiful.

[*Upon her last words, the Chorus indicate their feelings of
growing awe and wondering delight. The hands are
raised with the fingers together and the palms forward, one
held a few inches from the chin, the other a little lower and
farther forward : the head and upper part of the body are
drawn back, away from the box, but the eyes gaze upon the
wonder as though fascinated. The gesture may be taken
simultaneously, or one player may follow another, but
there should be symmetry in this, as in every one of the
stage pictures, and the position should be held until the
exit of Hermes.*

ONE OF THE CHORUS. I scarcely dare
To breathe the scent that floats upon the air.
A SECOND. Ambrosia from the fields of Paradise
Lies in the box.
ALL.   Pandora, veil thine eyes!

[*Pandora draws back, a little awed, but continues to gaze at the
box in fascination. Epimetheus, who has shown more
nervousness all the time, moves back left. Hermes puts
the box down in the centre. Pandora offers to come
nearer and examine it, but Hermes holds up a warning
hand, and she retreats. Hermes, smiling mysteriously,
glides out, centre.*

CHORUS. Hermes of the silver sandal, Hermes of the silver wing,
Hermes of the twining serpents, hast thou fled? [*Turning
each to her neighbour.*] What means this thing?
LEADER. In mystery, in mystery,
Secret as night the great gods be,
And who can guess the power of them,
Or who foretell the hour of them?
He leaves his treasure here awhile;
Mayhap he has full many a mile
Over the earth to float and run
Before the setting of the sun.

[*To the Children.*] Come, children, dance! Come, children, play!
Hermes the swift has flown away.

[*Epimetheus invites Pandora to play again. She consents
half-heartedly, and the ball game is renewed. Pandora's
attention keeps wandering to Hermes' box.*

CHORUS. Lalla leerie, lalla lo,
The sun is ashine and the river 's aflow,

*I 947

And the world is young as the flowers that blow,
Lalla leerie, lalla lo.
  [*Epimetheus throws the ball out left and runs out after it.
    Pandora is about to follow, but when she reaches the wings
    she turns, looks back at the box, and stands irresolute.*
ONE OF THE CHORUS. Pandora does not move, and, sisters, see,
  The carven faces smile more curiously,
  And closer still the writhing serpents fold,
  And brighter shines the amulet of gold,
  As if to draw her near.   But she 'll not stir.
CHORUS. [*Fearfully.*] Oh, has bright Hermes laid a spell on her?
  [*Suddenly Pandora hears a voice from the box, speaking to her.
    She stands very still, listening intently.*
LEADER. Listen: I heard a voice cry: 'Open wide!
  For thine own joy, Pandora, look inside!'
  She hears it too—behold her trancèd face,
  And limbs in eager stillness, with the grace
  Of living marble.   Call her all we may
  She will not heed.
CHORUS.   Pandora, come away!
  [*Pandora does not heed them, but moves slowly, as though
    entranced, towards the box.*
CHORUS. Hermes of the silver sandal, Hermes of the silver wing,
  Hermes of the twining serpents, was it evil thou didst bring?
  [*Pandora lifts the box and gazes longingly at it.   She listens
    intently to the voices within.*
ONE OF THE CHORUS. The subtle serpents seem to be alive,
  They seem to speak, and evermore they strive
  To loose themselves.   She peers into their eyes,
  And startles back in fear, they are so wise,
  Subtle and sly.
A SECOND.   Their little eyes are clear
  With knowledge.
A THIRD.   Come away, Pandora dear.
A FOURTH. Knowledge of evil things, alas, alas!
LEADER. Evil must dwell with good, ere it can pass,
  And they are evil voices that she hears.
  I hear them cry: 'Pandora, calm your fears,
  And open, open!'   [*Pandora is about to open the box.*
CHORUS. Hermes, Hermes fleet,
  Come back on thy wingèd feet.
  [*Pandora, suddenly determined, opens and peers into the box.
    Almost immediately she lets the lid fall to again.   But the*

Troubles have escaped like a cloud of winged insects, and begin to attack her. Epimetheus comes running in. He is overcome with surprise and fear. Both try to beat the Troubles off. This is done in rhythmic movement while the Leader speaks.

LEADER. Ah me, ah me,
What misery,
Evil, and fear
Are loosened here!
What pain and misery!

[*The Troubles, having been beaten off, fly away, leaving their victims in misery. Epimetheus looks angrily and reproachfully at Pandora, who at first attempts a show of defiance, and finally hangs her head in shame. They fall on their knees on either side of the box, covering their faces with their hands. There is a moment's complete silence —the Children kneeling like statues with bowed heads on either side of the box, the Chorus also standing with lowered heads and grieved looks. At last, one of them gives voice to their sorrow.*

ONE OF THE CHORUS. O lost for ever,
Thou crystal river
Of peace and heavenly innocency:
Farewell, thou treasure
Of Love's sweet pleasure,
And spirits moving in harmony.
A SECOND. O Guardians four
Of the holy door,
Rivers that rose to the sound of singing,
He passed you over,
The fleet-foot rover,
Hermes the baneful, and ill was his bringing.
A THIRD. And now ye are sunken,
Wasted and shrunken
Into the earth, and the wilderness wild
Has passed the border
And sown disorder,
And the heart of a child is no longer a child.

[*There is another pause before the Leader speaks.*

LEADER. Speak, if ye can, some comfort to her heart,
For I have none: I needs must draw apart

A little space, to seek the truth that dwells
In solitude's most precious healing wells.
[*She retires, and stands back centre, looking out, as she did
previously.*
ONE OF THE CHORUS. [*Stepping forward, near to Pandora.*] Had
I the power
To seize Time's wheel, and turn it back an hour,
Or work some spell,
Pandora dear,
Thou 'dst not be weeping here,
Thou know'st full well.
A SECOND. [*Coming forward to Epimetheus.*] Had I the grace
To reach the gods in their immortal place,
Unhappy boy,
I 'd pray for thee
They 'd spare thy misery
And give thee joy.
CHORUS. But far, oh far
Away from us, where the high mountains are,
The great gods dwell.
And will they move
For pity or for love?
We cannot tell.
LEADER. [*Returning.*] Something, I know not what, my heart
has heard:
Only a whisper, but my soul is stirred
To answer: 'Yes.'
What mortal hope is there,
Unless the gods, who ride upon the air
And walk the waters, hold our little lives
In their great hands? But still the young heart strives
Against its doom—still it must dare and know
More than the gods allow, and that is woe.
CHORUS. Woe for Pandora, then, alas, alas!
LEADER. Evil must dwell with good, ere it can pass!
CHORUS. Evil must dwell with good, ere it can pass!
[*Pandora suddenly lifts her head and seems to be listening to
another voice from the box.*
LEADER. [*Observing her.*] But it *will* pass. Pandora lifts her
head.
See, see, her eyes grow bright.
O house of dread,
Ambrosial box, mother of mysteries,

What last sweet voice is thine? Arise, arise,
Ye grieving ones, for Grief herself is dying!
CHORUS. Who speaks? What spirit is this?
LEADER.   I hear one crying,
'Open the box and find me.
Open! I will not blind thee,
Nor sting, nor wound nor curse thee,
But comfort thee and nurse thee.'
  [*Pandora leans over towards the box, and so does Epimetheus.
  Kneeling on one knee, Pandora takes the box in her hands,
  and, summoning all her courage, opens it again. All
  draw back, fearful of some fresh evil, but joy replaces fear
  as they look upwards at Hope, who has fluttered out of the
  box and hovers in the air above it.*
CHORUS. [*In ecstasy.*] Oh, who is this? What lovely fairy
  thing?
LEADER. 'Tis Hope, my children, Hope, with iris wing!
And hark, she sings, 'Lift up your hearts again,
I am the Rainbow shining after rain;
I am the Flower that springs where Grief has trod;
I am the Future. I am the Voice of God.'
  [*Pandora, Epimetheus, and the Chorus have all been looking
  upward and listening with delight as the Leader interprets
  the song of Hope. At the close, the Chorus join hands,
  while the Children embrace.*

CURTAIN

BROTHER SUN

A Little Play of St Francis

LAURENCE HOUSMAN

PERSONS OF THE PLAY

THE SOLDAN
CAPTAIN OF THE GUARD
EMIRS
COUNCILLORS
A SWORDSMAN, SOLDIERS, NUBIAN SLAVES,
    ARAB SERVANTS, *and*
ST FRANCIS
BROTHER ILLUMINATO

*Applications regarding the amateur acting rights of this play
should be made to the Secretary, The League of Dramatists, 84
Drayton Gardens, London, S.W.10.*

BROTHER SUN

SCENE. *The camp of the Saracens before Damietta, looking out
eastward over the sands and lagoons.*

*In a large circular tent, gorgeously hung with arras of gold and
scarlet, the Soldan sits enthroned on a high dais. Upon the steps
to right and left, in order of rank, stand his emirs and councillors.
Before the entrance are armed soldiers and around the tent-walls
Nubian slaves and Arab servants. Against the pole of the tent
stands the Soldan's sword-bearer. The door is wide open,
revealing the red glare of an eastern day now nearing its end.
Before the Soldan stands the Captain of the Guard.*

SOLDAN. Two men, you say, captain? What like are they?

CAPTAIN. Beggars, Soldan, to look upon: ragged, bare-foot, and
very weary.

SOLDAN. Whence come they?

CAPTAIN. From the camp of the Infidel—so they say.

SOLDAN. Had they arms?

CAPTAIN. No, Soldan.

SOLDAN. How came they in?

CAPTAIN. They were in our midst before we knew. Because
the hand of heaven seemed on them, our outposts had let
them pass.

SOLDAN. The hand of heaven?

CAPTAIN. As being of those afflicted ones on whom Allah bids
us have pity, Soldan.

SOLDAN. Madmen?

CAPTAIN. Such I took them to be when first I saw them. But
now, having questioned them, I am in doubt.

SOLDAN. Wherefore?

CAPTAIN. Because, though their speech is sane, what they do
is contrary.

SOLDAN. Ay? How?

CAPTAIN. They seem to make mock of us, Soldan; and of the
peril they stand in. When I warned them of death they did
but smile; when we used them roughly, they seemed grateful
to us; when we put chains on them they laughed and sang.

Some say they be magicians, Soldan, and would have no
dealings with them.

SOLDAN. Said they for what cause they came?

CAPTAIN. To bring thee peace, Soldan.

SOLDAN. Peace? Are they ambassadors?

CAPTAIN. I know not, Soldan. Their message, they said, was
for thee.

SOLDAN. Well, I will see for myself. Bring them in.

[*The Captain goes, followed by his guard. The emirs and
councillors show perturbation.*

COUNCILLOR. O Soldan, is it forgiven if now we speak?

SOLDAN. Speak, any who will.

COUNCILLOR. Have a care, dread king! For though these men
be not armed, they may have power of evil.

SOLDAN. Very like. Has not the Most High commanded us to
fight evil?

COUNCILLOR. But these having no arms, Soldan, how canst thou
fight them?

SOLDAN. How can they fight us?

COUNCILLOR. By evil enchantments, Soldan.

SOLDAN. And have we none wiser that can withstand them?
See to it. To your charge I commit me. Do ye your office,
while I do mine.

COUNCILLOR. Commander of the Faithful, it shall be done.

[*One of the councillors, taking from his finger a ring, threads it
upon a red cord; the cord is drawn across the front of the
dais, the ring suspended upon it during the scene that
follows. A sound of chains is heard, and the tread of
the guard approaching. The voice of the Captain outside
cries 'Halt!' The Captain enters.*

CAPTAIN. The prisoners are here, Soldan.

SOLDAN. Bring them. [*Francis and Brother Illuminato are
brought in, and kept closely guarded at a safe and respectful
distance from the Soldan's person.*] Who art thou?

FRANCIS. Thy lover and servant, Soldan.

SOLDAN. Who is this with thee?

FRANCIS. He also is thy lover and servant, Soldan.

SOLDAN. Whence come ye?

FRANCIS. From the camp of thine enemy.

SOLDAN. Of whom, also, ye are?

FRANCIS. We are of the same race, Soldan.

SOLDAN. Wherefore, then, come ye here?

FRANCIS. To set thee free, O King.

SOLDAN. From whom?

FRANCIS. From fear.

SOLDAN. Fear? I fear no man.

FRANCIS. Thou bearest arms, Soldan. He that is without fear bears none.

SOLDAN. Why then, in the camp of the Christians also there is fear!

FRANCIS. Ay. Very greatly they fear thee, Soldan.

SOLDAN. They do well.

FRANCIS. They would do better if they did not fear thee.

SOLDAN. Dost not thou fear me?

FRANCIS. No, Soldan.

[*This causes no little stir among the emirs and councillors. The swordsman's hand instinctively takes a better grip on his weapon, as with sidelong glance he waits the word of command.*]

SOLDAN. Come! What art thou here for?

FRANCIS. To take thy chains from thee.

SOLDAN. I have no chains.

FRANCIS. O Soldan, are not these thy chains?

SOLDAN. [*Grimly amused.*] Ay: but *thou* wearest them.

FRANCIS. He that putteth chains upon others is chained also.

[*A murmur of angry astonishment comes from the assembled councillors.*]

AN EMIR. When is this man to die, Soldan?

SOLDAN. Not at thy bidding, emir. At mine.

COUNCILLORS. [*In a fierce whisper of impatience.*] Ay!

SOLDAN. Come hither! [*The guard bring Francis to the foot of the dais.*] I said not '*bring* him hither.' Stand back! [*The guard fall back. The Soldan comes down from his throne, takes hold of the fetters, and weighs them in his hand.*] So these are *my* chains that thou wearest?

FRANCIS. Very willingly, Soldan.

SOLDAN. [*Sarcastically.*] I thank thee. . . . Thinkest thou that I am in fear of thee?

[*Francis looks from Soldan to suspended ring and back again; and there is a suspicion of amusement in his tone as he answers.*]

FRANCIS. I know not, Soldan.

[*The Soldan snaps the thread. The ring falls. Francis stoops, picks up the ring, and hands it to the Soldan.*]

COUNCILLOR. Beware, Soldan!

SOLDAN. [*Returning to his place.*] Take from him his chains:

his also. [*The chains upon Francis and Brother Illuminato are struck off.*] Stand away! Do not hold them! . . . Prisoner, . . . where are my chains now?

FRANCIS. Upon thy heart, Soldan; yea, and upon thy soul. To us thou hast been gentle and gracious; but not unto thyself. For though thou givest freedom to others, to thine own self thou art yet a prisoner.
[*The Soldan lays by the talisman he has been holding.*

SOLDAN. And from this prison wherein I am—who shall set me free?

FRANCIS. Thou Prince of Majesty, holder of power and glory, give thyself into my hand, and I will lead thee.

SOLDAN. Whither?

FRANCIS. To thy Lord and my Lord which died for us.

SOLDAN. *My* Lord, thou sayest!

FRANCIS. Ay; for though thou see it not, His Light is already in thee. This is the Light which lighteneth every man that cometh into the world.

SOLDAN. And thou, also, art a Christian?

FRANCIS. God knows I would I were worthy to be called so.

SOLDAN. Is the way, then, so hard?

FRANCIS. Nay; but most sweet, and easy, and comforting. And yet I stray!
[*There is a pause: outside the light of day begins to fail.*

SOLDAN. How wouldst thou make me—a Christian?

FRANCIS. I would show thee Christ, Soldan. Or, if by that name thou know Him not, then by His other name which is Love, wherein also dwell Joy and Peace. This have I come— to show.

SOLDAN. Yea: speak!

FRANCIS.
Oh, hearken, for this is wonder!
Light looked down and beheld Darkness.
'Thither will I go,' said Light.
Peace looked down and beheld War.
'Thither will I go,' said Peace.
Love looked down and beheld Hatred.
'Thither will I go,' said Love.
So came Light, and shone.
So came Peace, and gave rest.
So came Love, and brought Life.
And the Word was made Flesh, and dwelt among us.
Then was He betrayed, and given up into the hands of

sinful men: Light to the darkness of Death, Peace unto the pains of Hell, Love to the separation of the grave. And because the power of Evil prevailed not against Him, these henceforth He holdeth, and they are His. So out of Darkness He wrought Light, and Peace out of the pains of Hell, and out of the prison-house of Death he bringeth us Life Eternal.

SOLDAN. Knowest thou this of thyself, or did others tell it thee?

FRANCIS. O Soldan, were it not true, wouldst thou not already have slain me?

SOLDAN. I may slay thee yet, prisoner: for I have not let thee go.

FRANCIS. What I have spoken thou hast heard. How wilt thou fear me less when I am dead?

SOLDAN. *I . . .* fear *thee?*

FRANCIS. When I am dead, Soldan, thou wilt remember me.

SOLDAN. Go on, prisoner. Say what thou hast to say, while yet there is time.

[*It begins to get dark.*

FRANCIS. Soldan, as I came hither, there met me in the way a great army of ants—many thousands of them, all hither and thither running without rest. What was their toil, whose word they obeyed, I could not tell; but they were all very full of it—in a world of their own. So I stood and looked at them; but though very plainly I saw them, they saw not me. I was nothing to them. Yet, had I so wished, I could have killed every one of them.

SOLDAN. Wherefore dost thou tell me this?

FRANCIS. Because thou art a great king, Soldan, and I am in thy power; and which of us is to die first—thou or I—we know not. But God, whom we see not, knows.

SOLDAN. Which is to die first?

FRANCIS. Ay.

SOLDAN. Knowest *thou* not?

FRANCIS. No, Soldan: nor dost thou. For thou art in His hands, even as I am; and He careth for both alike, having for each of us the same compassion.

SOLDAN. As thou also for the ants?

FRANCIS. Yes, Soldan. And they may have had kings among them—yet I could not tell which *was* their king—they being all so much alike—even as we are.

SOLDAN. [*To an attendant.*] Slave, bring in the lamps. . . . Thou and I alike, dost thou say?

FRANCIS. In the eyes of God, Soldan; ay, and of men also. For

look!—thou hast hands, and feet, and so have I: and on each
hand five fingers, and to each finger three joints; and at the
end are nails. So also our bodies—search as thou wilt, we
are made alike. Also what thou seest, I see; and what thou
hearest, I hear. In all these things we are alike, Soldan, because God has so willed who made us.

[*Lights are brought in ; over the Soldan's throne is set a lamp.
Round the wall stand torchbearers. The outer air goes
dark.*

SOLDAN. That is true. Stand near, Brother Ant! I would
look on thee, and see more of that likeness to myself whereof
thou speakest . . . Ay; thou hast a face and eyes, which
now see; thou hast limbs, and there is blood in them; thou hast
flesh that can feel pain; and thou hast a head and a neck, even
as I have. But for all we be so much alike, hast thou power
to do presently what I shall do?

FRANCIS. No, Soldan. Many things thou canst do which I
cannot.

SOLDAN. Whence comes that?

FRANCIS. From God, Soldan: not from thy feet, nor thy hands,
nor thy head. That which a man does comes from his heart.

SOLDAN. Truly said.

FRANCIS. And thy heart and mine are two, not one. We be
fellow-men, but separate; we look upon each other as strangers.
But it is not so that God sees. For we see each with a
difference; but He, looking within, sees we are alike.

SOLDAN. How alike?

FRANCIS. In heart we are alike, Soldan.

SOLDAN. Canst thou be sure of that?

FRANCIS. Since God made us to the same end, that we might
serve Him.

SOLDAN. I serve not thy God, Christian!

FRANCIS. Many *do* serve Him, not knowing.

SOLDAN. The service which I do is—different.

FRANCIS. Many wait on *thee*, Soldan, whose services are different.
But for each there is a place, and all labour to one end. So
thou and I—serving God.

SOLDAN. What if I serve God by slaying thee?

FRANCIS. Even so as, when good servants are hasty, platters get
broken. Yet if thou break this poor platter, God shall pardon
thee; and thou wilt still serve Him, though how I know not.

SOLDAN. And what says the platter, when it is broken?

FRANCIS. I am willing to be broken, great king, if it make thee more careful of others. Many hast thou broken, and little good has it done thee. Peace comes not yet; and all thy breakings shall not bring it thee.

SOLDAN. Swordsman, draw! [*The swordsman draws his sword, and stands ready.*] Emirs, councillors, judges, servants of the prophet, ye have heard this man and what he saith. How say ye? Is he innocent or guilty?

ALL. Guilty, O king.

SOLDAN. Unto what penalty?

ALL. Death.

SOLDAN. His offence?

COUNCILLOR. Great Soldan, this man is a dog and a blasphemer. Against thee, Sword of the Prophet, he hath said evil things, denying thy kingship and power. Also against our holy faith he hath spoken falsely.

SOLDAN. What saith the Prophet concerning him?

COUNCILLOR. That all Infidels must perish.

SOLDAN. Even so, let it be. Swordsman, hither. Have ready thy sword. Make the prisoner to kneel down. [*Francis kneels. Brother Illuminato kneels also, looking towards Francis with a face full of joy.*] Brother Ant, I have heard thee. Hast thou said all thou wouldst say? . . . If not, now speak!

FRANCIS. O Soldan, while I have breath needs must I plead. For I have short life, and little wisdom, and my tongue is feeble. But He, whose messenger I am, is almighty, and infinite, and eternal; and His glory is not as the glory of kings —being without end. So, if I begin to tell of it, how may I finish?

SOLDAN. [*Pointing to an hour-glass beside him, the sands of which are nearly run.*] A little time I yet give thee. While the sands in this glass still run, speak on!

FRANCIS. [*Stretching out his arms.*] As the sun be the king's reign! The wisdom of God be thy rule: the love of God thy possession: the Peace of God, which passeth all understanding, be with thee, Soldan, when thou also comest to die!

SOLDAN. [*To the Swordsman.*] Man, put up thy sword! Loose him: and go! Take with you that other prisoner: do no harm to him. Councillors and judges, what I do now, I do of myself. Go, all of you! [*They all go out. The Soldan remains seated, with Francis kneeling before him.*] Brother, come hither. . . . Sit near me. . . . Through all the world I have sought thee. Now, in the camp of mine enemy, I find thee! Oh, wherefore didst thou come?

FRANCIS. To be thy lover and servant, Soldan.

SOLDAN. That is well: I have great need of thee. In my service thou shalt have power, and riches, and great honour; for I will exalt thee, and make thee a ruler; also thou shalt be taught the truths of our holy faith, and become a believer.

FRANCIS. That cannot be, Soldan. Power is of God, not of kings. Serving all, I rule none, and naught have I of possessions save poverty. . . . Disband thine armies, Soldan. Fight not against the living God. Sheathe thy sword, and possess thy land in peace.

SOLDAN. Peace? Who offers peace?

FRANCIS. He against who thou fightest, Soldan.

SOLDAN. 'Tis of thy God thou speakest? Say then: [*he rises*] and speak truth! If I seek Him in the camp of mine enemies —shall I find Him?

[*Francis bows his head, for it is a question he dares not answer.*

FRANCIS. Seek Him in thine own heart, Soldan. There shalt thou find peace.

SOLDAN. Thou hast answered well. . . . And yet thou art still one of them!

FRANCIS. I came to them a traveller from my own land, Soldan.

SOLDAN. To fight for them?

FRANCIS. Ay: even as I have fought for thee, saying the same words: 'Disband your armies; fight not against God; sheathe your sword; go back to your own land in peace.'

SOLDAN. And they?

FRANCIS. They were like the ants, Soldan—very full of themselves.

SOLDAN. Not heeding thee?

FRANCIS. No man can heed that which he sees not—neither with eyes nor with heart.

SOLDAN. [*With a touch of the visionary.*] What, then, have *I* seen? . . . Nay, I know not. Yet to my ears hath come a voice.

[*The torches and the torchbearers have gone; and the only light now in the tent is the lamp which burns above the dais. Soldan sits in thought; and for a while there is silence. Presently, as the voice of his reverie, Francis begins speaking.*

FRANCIS. Look, Soldan, how bright in this tent shines the light! See, on walls, and roof, and armour, and jewels, how it glitters. But yonder at the door stands night, and thou seest naught of it—neither the beauty, nor the spaces of heaven which lie over it, nor the stars which are contained there. Because this light has made a covering to thine eyes, therefore do the heavens look dark. [*Francis has risen, and stands looking out into the night.*] O Soldan, in thine own heart seek wisdom! The flame of kingship and power is brief, and short-reaching, and by a breath it is put out. And with it shall depart the honour and fear and obedience and service which men render thee. These go, but thou remainest. Then, as a sleeper, that awakens when the lamp in his chamber is quenched, sees the door (which was darkness) changed to a window of light, and with his eyes searches the night, beholding the great spaces of heaven, and the stars that are hung in it, so in that day shalt thou see the standing of thy soul, and the home of thy inheritance to which thou travellest. [*The Soldan has risen, and coming down from the dais, he stands beside Francis.*] God is great, and infinite, and full of compassion. Thou art but a little thing: yet in His hand He holdeth and loveth thee. O Soldan, in that day of thine awakening, remember me, thy little lover and servant, and pray for me!

SOLDAN. [*Drawing him to the light.*] Come; ay, closer; for again would I look upon thy face, and know more of thee. . . . [*They stand eye to eye under the lamp, silent awhile.*] Well said, Brother Ant. When I come to die, I shall remember thee. [*He mounts the dais, strikes a bell, and puts out the lamp. The night grows luminous without. Presently in the doorway two attendants are seen standing motionless.*] There is thy road; there is thy star, and thy heaven! Go, thou art freer than I. Alas, that in my kingdom never shall I see thee again!

FRANCIS. In the Kingdom of God, brother, I pray that I shall see thee.

SOLDAN. There, when thou comest, look for me in thine own heart. If thou find me, there shall I be.

FRANCIS. Amen, Soldan. So—if God will!

SOLDAN. Take this signet, show it to the captain of the guard. Let him give command that thou and thy companion return in safety—to the camp of mine enemy.

FRANCIS. Alas, then, for peace have I failed!

SOLDAN. Who knows! . . . Farewell, Brother Ant.

FRANCIS. Farewell, great and gracious king, brother-servant of my Lord!

[*Francis goes out, followed, at a signal from the Soldan, by the two attendants. The Soldan stands looking after him.*]

SOLDAN. Farewell, Brother Sun.

[From outside comes the cry of the Muezzin calling the faithful to prayer : 'There is one God, Allah, and Mahomet is his Prophet!' *The Soldan bares his feet, stands looking toward Mecca, and prays.*

CURTAIN

THE PARDONER'S TALE

A Morality

Adapted from Geoffrey Chaucer

JAMES BRIDIE

PERSONS OF THE PLAY

AN OLD INNKEEPER
DUNCAN ELLIOT ⎫
HANDASYDE GRANT ⎬ Three second-rate bucks from
PHILIP MACGILLIVRAY ⎭   Edinburgh

SCENE. *A changehouse on the Perth Road. Night*

TIME. *Early eighteenth century*

Application for the performing rights of this play should be made to Messrs Curtis Brown Ltd, 6 Henrietta Street, London, W.C.2.

THE PARDONER'S TALE

*The scene is a dilapidated changehouse between Edinburgh and
Perth. The time is early in the eighteenth century. It is winter.
The room has two doors: one at the back opening on the road and
another, right, leading to the tap. The wainscoting has fallen
from the bare walls years ago; and the furniture is a table, a
window-seat below a mullioned window, some of whose panes
have been broken and stuffed with rags, and two or three rickety
chairs of different periods. There is a fine chimney-piece in bad
repair, and in front of a poor log fire there sits an old man
thinking. The room is lit by a storm lantern, but candles are
standing ready.*

*The old man gets up, pulls a green log from under the window-seat,
and mends the fire. As he does so, the noise of beating on the
door is heard. He opens the door, after lighting his candles, and
three horsemen with snow on their cloaks fall out of the darkness.*

FIRST HORSEMAN. Cock's body, it's cold. St Judas Iscariot,
what a house you keep! Where's the ostler?

OLD MAN. I am ostler and chambermaid and host in this house
these two years, sir.

FIRST HORSEMAN. Hell's guts, and do you tell me that? Blast
my eyes, on a nicht that would freeze the liver out of Beelze-
bub to stumble on a damned charnel-house the like of this!
See the horses stabled, then, and back with you like the
hammers of hell with a stoup of aqua-vitae. Run, or I'll
cut the spine out of ye!

OLD MAN. Speedily, sir, speedily.

*[He goes out. The first horseman flings off his cloak. The
second rider reels to the fireside and sits down. The
third sits on the window-seat and buries his head in his
hands. All three horsemen are dressed like gentlemen.
The first two are briefless advocates, the third a student.
The first is a big red-headed fellow, Duncan Elliot, a bully,
the soberest but noisiest of the party. The second,
Handasyde Grant, is a little blackavised man, all tipsy*

267

*ingratiatingness but with a cur's bite below his cringing.
The third, Philip Macgillivray, is the only decent-
looking fellow of the lot—a debauched Galahad, fair-
headed, with a Highland accent and the remnants of a
Highland gentility. He is sick and nearly exhausted.
Elliot sings in a loud brutal voice, beating time on the
table with his riding-crop.*

ELLIOT. 'It's Geordie he sat down to dine,
  And wha came in but Madam Swine;
  Grump, grump, quo' she, I'm come in time,
  I'll sit and dine wi' Geordie!
  The sow's tail is till him yet,
  The sow's birse will kill him yet . . .'

GRANT. In the name of God, man! Stop. Stop. Stop. Do
  you want us all hangit?

ELLIOT. Hangit, by Satan!... 'The sow's tail is till him yet...'

GRANT. Now, Mr Elliot. Now, Dunny, now. Now, now, now.
  There's songs that's decent among gentlemen, and there's
  songs that give offence, in a way of speaking, if ye see what I
  mean. You ken I'm a loyal subject. And I ken you're
  a loyal subject. And Philip's loyal subject, too. All loyal
  subjects King Geordie. Now, I say nothing against you.
  You're my friend. Very well then, you say nothing against
  Geordie. That's fair speaking. Forbye you're making the
  poor young doctor sick.

ELLIOT. Cock's body, I forgot about him. How is it with you,
  my poor wee yaud?

PHILIP. Let me alone.

GRANT. Let me alone! There's a hearty good fellow for you!
  There's the life and soul of the festive round! Whae ordered
  the horses, now, and led us hell-for-leather out on the Perth
  road on a nicht as black as a sewer and onding of snaw?

ELLIOT. And the claret birling fine and the doxies growing
  kinder every minute. Gog's wounds, I never saw a man
  whose guts led his heid such a dance. What for did you do it?

PHILIP. Oh, that hot room, and the hot claret and the hot
  wenches! And poor Andrew out there cold and coffined in
  the frost. I couldna, man, I couldna. I needed the wind in
  my face. Poor Andrew!

GRANT. [*Shaking his head in maudlin solemnity.*] A good lad
  was Andy. A good lad.

ELLIOT. Aye, and hotter at this minute than you and I above
  ground in this blasted, rotting, forfechan midden of a change-

house. Curse my lungs, what a drab's kitchen! Where 's
auld St Patey wi' the aqua-vitae?

PHILIP. He was a bonny singer, was Andy.   [*He weeps.*

GRANT. He was good company. The best of the whole boiling
of us. I wonder, Duncan, you have the heart to flyte.

ELLIOT. By St Paul's breeks, and isna flyting the only thing?
There 's poor Andra, a fine, swearing, randan, lechering,
drinking, guttling young bully-be-damned it did your heart
good to see ruffling down the Canongate wi' the beaver of
him cockit. None of your pinched Psalmists, yon. Full of
blood, the boy was. And Death comes creeping up behind
him and grips him by the thrapple in his cups. Andrew, no
less. Nae snivelling Whig, like Sneckie here. But a bull of
a lad wi' forty years' hard boozing and fornicketing before
him. What can we do but flyte?

[*The Old Man has come through the door of the tap with
brandy and glasses. He puts them on the table while
Elliot is speaking.*

PHILIP. Lord in heaven, see me some of yon! [*He reels to the
table and pours himself a drink. The others drink too, and do
honour to his toast. They become quieter and steadier. The
effect is most pronounced on Philip, but there is madness in his
eyes.*] Death, boys, Death? Here 's damnation to Death!
. . . You don't honour the toast, Mister Innkeeper?

OLD MAN. No. . . . No. Death is a coarse companion, but he
sees you home, and aye pays your reckoning.

PHILIP. Damn your companion! D' ye hear? My mother was
a bonny lady, and Death bloated her like a drooned dog and
took her away raving like a fishwife. My father was a kind
man, who prayed each night for Death to take him in a glen
with four or five Whigamores at his claymore's point. The
false thief, Death, chokit him with a bloody flux in a strange
wife's house in Amiens. Lily-white maids and wee croodling
weans that never did harm to any, the foul butcher clutches
and slays and rots awa their brightness. And he 's cut in twa
the heart of the best friend I ever had. . . . [*He drinks again.*]
You 're old. The old ken Death. Day by day they see him
face to face. Show me Death, you wizened dog. Show me
Death. I 've twa-three accounts to settle with him.

[*He draws his hanger.*

OLD MAN. Keep your hands off me, young sir. I 'm over old
to be feared.

[*Philip has shot his bolt for a while. He staggers and almost falls. The Old Man leads him to the fireside chair, takes off his cloak, and spreads it over his knees. The other two look at them, pulling heavily at the brandy. The Old Man goes to the window-seat and sits down. A pause.*

ELLIOT. [*With a hoarse laugh.*] Faith, there's a ploy for you! Hunting Death! There's a kittle bit fox now.

PHILIP. Death's a man. There's nothing else in earth or sky could be so bitter bad.

GRANT. That's true. That's a true word you say, Philip Macgillivray. There's them that have seen him, though there's few see him and live. An old grey man, they say . . . like yon.   [*He points with the bottle at the Old Man.*

ELLIOT. Hey! You'll no be Death, then, Methusalem?

OLD MAN. No. Oh, no.

ELLIOT. Are you acquaint with him, then?

OLD MAN. No, to my sorrow. The long days I've walked the world, restlessly, seeking him! But he will not have my life. Do you ken the verse, you three scholars?

> 'Thus walk I like a restless caitiff wight,
> And on the ground which is my mother's gate
> So knock I with my staff, early and late.
> And call to her, "Love, Mother, let me in!
> Lo, how I vanish, flesh and blood and skin!
> Alas! When shall my body be at rest?"''

Gentlemen, you're young. There are happier ways than the gate you have chosen. And for the nicht there is poor cheer for you between these walls. I rede you go home to your beds and pray. And God be with you.

[*He gets up and walks towards the door of the tap.*

GRANT. Amen. Here endeth the lesson.

[*Philip springs up in another gust of passion and gets between the Old Man and the door.*

PHILIP. No, nor ends! Are you thinking to turn us back, with your sly soft words? Do you think that we are drunk? You wear the white crest of Death on your head. You're in league with him against all youth. Show us our enemy!

ELLIOT. [*Rising.*] Ay, by the Black Plague! There's a fight worth fighting, now. We three against Death, and the deil tak' the chicken-guts! Show us Death, gaffer, or we'll clap your hurdies on your ain bit fire. You'll burn like parchment, cock's body!

OLD MAN. Sit ye down, gentlemen. Wild words are like the

wind in the chimney to me. I 'm old, ye understand. Sit
down. I 'll tell ye a thing about Death.

GRANT. Pray silence for Methusalem. Methusalem 's going to
give us a bawr. A wee bit bawdy in it, Methusalem. Haud
your peace, Mr Elliot, for Methusalem 's bawr. Sit down,
Doctor Macgillivray, if you 're no better at standing than
that. The court is open.

OLD MAN. Death 's in this room. . . . [*A pause.*] I had this
house from the heirs of Alec Bain; and Alec Bain was found
deid in this room with his heid in the ashes. There. His
elder brother, Big John, was pistolled by a highwayman in
that chair you sit in. They were taking a dram thegither.
Their father, Archibald of the Garse, hanged himself from
yon beam. Auld Archie, the great-uncle, who built the place
lang syne, died in yon chair too, and it is said the devil took
his saul. He hid a peck of siller some place, but it was never
found, and it has been an ill job seeking it. It was seeking it
that the Bains died. Every man. . . . And now, gentlemen, I cannot refuse you shelter. I have nae beds but my
ain, and I 'll betake mysel' there now. The logs are under
the settle. God be with you, young gentlemen.

[*He goes, taking the lamp with him and closing the door of the
tap behind him.*

PHILIP. If Death should be in this room!

ELLIOT. I 'm thinking there 's a hantle mair in this room than
auld Blood and Banes. Watch the door, Sneckie, and hit the
ault carlin on the heid if he comes back. Did ye lippen tae
his story?

GRANT. [*Glass in hand at the taproom door.*] Me? I heard nae
shtory. Just an ould ballant to nae tune.

ELLIOT. [*Examining the chimney-piece.*] Stash your gab. . . .
So Death came to the Bains at their ain fireside. Now, was
not that a droll place for Death to come for the Bains? At
their ain fireside. And is 't no a droll fireside for the Bains
to be at when Death came sleeking in at their back-sides?
And is Death no the sly old dog to come aye to the same
fireside to drench his garb in blood? Ay, the same fireside.
Cock's body, there are more things in heaven and earth . . .
And a gey queer bit bastard of a fireside. Master Philip,
did they teach ye architecture at the Coallege of Edinburgh?
Nay, hogswounds. Naething so useful. Wining and wenching they teach you at the Coallege in Edinburgh. Have ye
found Death yet, Philip Adonis Aesculapius, my sweetheart?

K 947

Ye're a great wee cocksparrow to be ruffling wi' Death.
Mors, pallida mors. Atch! Come oot, ye besom! And
there's the reason what wey Death came for the Bains at
their ain fireside! [*He has levered out a large stone with his
dagger. He drags a heavy ironbound box from the cavity.*] Ay,
by Calvary, a droll place for Death to come for the Bains!
    [*He crouches on the floor, forcing the lock of the box.*
PHILIP. Duncan! How did ye ken of this?
ELLIOT. Have I been so long time with you and yet thou hast
    not known me, Philip? Ratiocination, Philip. Besides, I
    have a keen nose for the siller. . . . Charlies, by Satan! In
    bags. There's the bonny, poxy phiz of old Rowley. Yellow
    wi' the jaundice. Gold, Whig, gold! Cock your snout,
    Whig! Now comes in the sweet o' the night. [*Grant joins the
    group, his eyes starting out of his head.*] Look now. Away
    you, Philip, and saddle the beasts, if your unruly members
    will tak you that far. We maun be at the Port of Leith by
    cock-crow. Haste ye, man. Sneckie and me'll burn the
    papers and dispose the bags about us. Then we'll settle wi'
    auld Methusalem. What was his word? 'Death aye pays
    the lawing.' He'll pay it well this night, mine host! Haste
    ye, Philip. [*Philip goes out to the road, leaving the door half
    open.*] Look you, Sneckie. Yon lad's owre unchancy ballast
    for the course we're setting. When he comes back I'll put
    twa bags in his hands and you'll come on him behind and
    put a knife between his ribs. Are ye sober enough?
GRANT. Ay, I'm sober.
ELLIOT. Then ye'll do it?
GRANT. Ay, I'll do it.
ELLIOT. Then we'll awa ben and let out the auld runt's life
    before he wakes. You're sure ye ken what to do?
GRANT. Ay, I ken.
ELLIOT. You heard his talk, the night? He's no companion
    for a gentleman of fortune. I'd liefer have the hangman.
    'Show him Death!' Set him up. He's owre long in the
    tongue. Come.
    [*They go into the taproom. Philip comes in. He has been
    hiding behind the door. He is rubbing a handful of snow
    on his shoulders and face. He is in a foggy, vicious state
    of drunkenness, but moderately steady in his movements.*
PHILIP. So. So, my gentlemen. There's friendship! The
    knife! I heard ye. I heard ye. You'd murder me, you
    think, you deil's bitches. Wait. Wait. Bide a wee while.

They teach you other matters than wining and wenching at Edinburgh College, Mr Duncan Elliot.   Where have I it now? Ah, here.   Ah, here!   Death!   Here's Death in a wee box. There you lie, Atropos, the beautiful lady; drown yourself in the brandy. [*He pours the contents of the box into the half-finished glasses of the two murderers.*] Oh, wait you, now, Duncan Elliot, my learned brother.   It's the great drinker of spirits you are, certainly, and the fine boastful man of his potations.   We'll see how you like the deadly nightshade. The deadly nightshade. . . . Saddle the beasts, says you, Philip Macgillivray, you bloody stable-boy!   That'll warm your heart, Duncan, for the long ride to the Port of Leith. Ha, ha, ha!   It's a bonny port, the Port of Leith!
> [*The murderers re-enter. Elliot wipes his dagger on the table-cloth. Neither can keep his eyes off Philip, and neither can meet his eye.*

ELLIOT. You are very joco.

PHILIP. I'm fine.   I'm a man again.   Let us drink.   Let us drink to Death.   Good old Death!   Come.   Drink.   Drink to Death.
> [*He goes to the table and fills up glasses for Elliot and Grant. He is about to take them up when Elliot grips his wrists and pins them to the table.*

ELLIOT. Now, Sneckie. [*Grant stabs Philip under the left armpit. Philip makes no sound, but drags himself free from Elliot and falls forward into the fireplace.*] Tchach!   What butcher's work.   That was well struck, Sneckie.   He never gi'ed a grunt.   Come.   A deoch an doris, and we'll bundle and go.

GRANT. Goad!   I need it too.   Save us all, what a fine like end to an ambrosial night!
> [*They stand at opposite sides of the table and drink in great gulps. Suddenly they put down their glasses and look at each other with fear in their eyes.*

CURTAIN

HANDS ACROSS THE SEA

A LIGHT COMEDY

Noel Coward

PERSONS OF THE PLAY

Lady Maureen Gilpin (*Piggie*)
Commander Peter Gilpin, R.N., her husband
The Hon. Clare Wedderburn
Lieut.-Commander Alastair Corbett, R.N.
Major Gosling (*Bogey*)
Mr Wadhurst
Mrs Wadhurst
Mr Burnham
Walters

*The action of the play takes place in the drawing-room
of the Gilpins' flat in London.*

Time: Present Day

HANDS ACROSS THE SEA

*The scene is the drawing-room of the Gilpins' flat in London. The
room is nicely furnished and rather untidy. There is a portable
gramophone on one small table and a tray of cocktail things on
another; apart from these, the furnishing can be left to the discretion of the producer.*
*When the curtain rises the telephone is ringing. Walters, a neat
parlourmaid, enters and answers it. The time is about six p.m.*

WALTERS. [*At telephone.*] Hallo—yes—no, her ladyship's not
back yet—she said she'd be in at five, so she ought to be here
at any minute now—what name, please?—Rawlingson—Mr
and Mrs Rawlingson—— [*She scribbles on the pad.*] Yes—
I'll tell her——
  [*She hangs up the receiver and goes out. There is the sound of
  voices in the hall and Lady Maureen Gilpin enters,
  followed at a more leisurely pace by her husband, Peter
  Gilpin. Maureen, nicknamed Piggie by her intimates,
  is a smart, attractive woman in the thirties. Peter is tall
  and sunburned and reeks of the Navy.*

PIGGIE. [*As she comes in.*] —and you can send the car back for
me at eleven-thirty—it's quite simple, darling, I wish you
wouldn't be so awfully complicated about everything——
PETER. What happens if my damned dinner goes on longer than
that and I get stuck?
PIGGIE. You just get stuck, darling, and then you get unstuck
and get a taxi——
PETER. [*Grumbling.*] I shall be in uniform, clinking with
medals——
PIGGIE. If you take my advice you'll faint dead away at eleven
o'clock and then you can come home in the car and change
and have time for everything——
PETER. I can't faint dead away under the nose of the C.-in-C.
PIGGIE. You can feel a little poorly, can't you—anybody has
the right to feel a little poorly—— [*She sees the telephone pad.*]
My God!

PETER. What is it?

PIGGIE. The Rawlingsons.

PETER. Who the hell are they?

PIGGIE. I'd forgotten all about them—I must get Maud at once—— [*She sits at the telephone and dials a number.*

PETER. Who are the Rawlingsons?

PIGGIE. Maud and I stayed with them in Samolo, I told you about it, that time when we had to make a forced landing— they practically saved our lives—— [*At telephone.*] Hullo— Maud—darling, the Rawlingsons are on us—what—the RAWLINGSONS—yes—I asked them to-day and forgot all about it—you must come at once—but, darling, you *must*— Oh, dear—no, no, that was the Frobishers, these are the ones we stayed with—mother and father and daughter—you must remember—pretty girl with bad legs—— No—they didn't have a son—we swore we'd give them a lovely time when they came home on leave—I know they didn't have a son, that was those other people in Penang—— Oh, all right—you'll have to do something about them, though—let me ask them to lunch with you to-morrow—all right—one-thirty—I'll tell them—— [*She hangs up.*] She can't come——

PETER. You might have warned me that a lot of colonial strangers were coming trumpeting into the house——

PIGGIE. I tell you I'd forgotten——

PETER. That world trip was a grave mistake——

PIGGIE. Who can I get that's celebrated — to give them a thrill?

PETER. Why do they have to have a thrill?

PIGGIE. I'll get Clare, anyway—— [*She dials another number.*

PETER. She'll frighten them to death.

PIGGIE. Couldn't you change early and come in your uniform? That would be better than nothing——

PETER. Perhaps they'd like to watch me having my bath!

PIGGIE. [*At telephone.*] I want to speak to Mrs Wedderburn, please—yes—— [*To Peter.*] I do wish you'd be a little helpful—— [*At telephone.*] Clare?—this is Piggie—I want you to come round at once and help me with the Rawlingsons—no, I know you haven't, but that doesn't matter—— Mother, father, and daughter—very sweet—they were divine to us in the East—I'm repaying hospitality—Maud's having them to lunch to-morrow and Peter's going to take them round the dockyard——

PETER. I'm not going to do any such thing——

PIGGIE. Shut up, I just thought of that and it's a *very* good idea—— [*At telephone.*] All right, darling—as soon as you can—— [*She hangs up.*] I must go and change——

PETER. You know perfectly well I haven't time to take mothers and fathers and daughters with bad legs round the dock-yard——

PIGGIE. It wouldn't take a minute, they took us all over their rubber plantation.

PETER. It probably served you right.

PIGGIE. You're so disobliging, darling, you really should try to conquer it—it's something to do with being English, I think—as a race I'm ashamed of us—no sense of hospitality—the least we can do when people are kind to us in far-off places is to be a little gracious in return.

PETER. They weren't kind to me in far-off places.

PIGGIE. You know there's a certain grudging, sullen streak in your character—I've been very worried about it lately—it's spreading like a forest fire——

PETER. Why don't you have them down for the week-end?

PIGGIE. Don't be so idiotic, how can I possibly? There's no room to start with and even if there were they'd be utterly wretched——

PETER. I don't see why.

PIGGIE. They wouldn't know anybody—they probably wouldn't have the right clothes—they'd keep on huddling about in uneasy little groups——

PETER. The amount of uneasy little groups that three people can huddle about in is negligible.

[*Alastair Corbett saunters into the room. He is good-looking and also distinctly Naval in tone.*

ALLY. Hullo, chaps.

PIGGIE. Ally, darling—how lovely—we're in trouble—Peter'll tell you all about it——

[*The telephone rings and she goes to it. The following conversations occur simultaneously.*

ALLY. What trouble?

PETER. More of Piggie's beach friends.

ALLY. Let's have a drink.

PETER. Cocktail?

ALLY. No, a long one, whisky and soda.

PETER. [*Going to drink table.*] All right.

ALLY. What beach friends?

PETER. People Maud and Piggie picked up in the East.

*K 947

PIGGIE. [*At phone.*] Hullo!—Yes—Robert, dear—how lovely [*To others.*] It's Robert.

ALLY. Piggie ought to stay at home more.

PIGGIE. [*On phone.*] Where are you?

PETER. That's what I say!

PIGGIE. [*On phone.*] Oh, what a shame!—No—Peter's going to sea on Thursday—I'm going down on Saturday.

ALLY. Rubber, I expect—everybody in the East's rubber.

PIGGIE. [*On phone.*] No—nobody particular—just Clare and Bogey and I think Pops; but he thinks he's got an ulcer or something and might not be able to come.

PETER. We thought you might be a real friend and take them over the dockyard.

ALLY. What on earth for?

PETER. Give them a thrill.

PIGGIE. [*On phone.*] All right—I'll expect you—no, I don't think it can be a very big one—he looks as bright as a button.

ALLY. Why don't you take them over the dockyard?

PETER. I shall be at sea, Thursday onwards—exercises!

PIGGIE. [*On phone.*] No, darling, what is the use of having her— she only depresses you—oh—all right! [*Hangs up.*] Oh, dear——

PETER. It's quite easy for you—you can give them lunch on board.

ALLY. We're in dry dock.

PETER. They won't mind. [*To Piggie.*] What is it?

PIGGIE. Robert—plunged in gloom—he's got to do a course at Greenwich—he ran into a tram in Devonport—and he's had a row with Molly—he wants me to have her for the week-end so that they can make it up all over everybody. Have you told Ally about the Rawlingsons?

PETER. Yes, he's taking them over the dockyard, lunching them on board and then he's going to show them a sub-marine——

PIGGIE. Marvellous! You're an angel, Ally—I must take off these clothes, I'm going mad——

[*She goes out of the room at a run. There is the sound of the front-door bell.*

PETER. Let's go into my room—I can show you the plans—

ALLY. Already? They've been pretty quick with them.

PETER. I made a few alterations—there wasn't enough deck space—she ought to be ready by October, I shall have her sent straight out to Malta——

ALLY. Come on, we shall be caught——
[*They go off on the left as Walters ushers in Mr and Mrs Wadhurst on the right.*
[*The Wadhursts are pleasant, middle-aged people, their manner is a trifle timorous.*
WALTERS. Her ladyship is changing, I 'll tell her you are here.
MRS WADHURST. Thank you.
MR WADHURST. Thank you very much.
[*Walters goes out. The Wadhursts look round the room.*
MRS WADHURST. It 's a very nice flat.
MR WADHURST. Yes—yes, it is.
MRS WADHURST. [*Scrutinizing a photograph.*] That must be him.
MR WADHURST. Who?
MRS WADHURST. The commander.
MR WADHURST. Yes—I expect it is.
MRS WADHURST. Sailors always have such nice open faces, don't they?
MR WADHURST. Yes, I suppose so.
MRS WADHURST. Clean-cut and look you straight in the eye—I like men who look you straight in the eye.
MR WADHURST. Yes, it 's very nice.
MRS WADHURST. [*At another photograph.*] This must be her sister—I recognize her from the *Tatler*—look—she was Lady Hurstley, you know, then she was Lady Macfadden and I don't know who she is now.
MR WADHURST. Neither do I.
MRS WADHURST. What a dear little boy—such a sturdy little fellow—look at the way he 's holding his engine.
MR WADHURST. Is that his engine?
MRS WADHURST. He has rather a look of Donald Hotchkiss, don't you think?
MR WADHURST. Yes, dear.
MRS WADHURST. I must say they have very nice things—oh, dear, how lovely to be well off—I must write to the Brostows by the next mail and tell them all about it.
MR WADHURST. Yes, you must.
MRS WADHURST. Don't you think we 'd better sit down?
MR WADHURST. Why not?
MRS WADHURST. You sit in that chair and I 'll sit on the sofa.
[*She sits on the sofa. He sits on the chair.*
MR WADHURST. Yes, dear.
MRS WADHURST. I wish you wouldn't look quite so uncomfortable, Fred, there 's nothing to be uncomfortable about.

MR WADHURST. She does expect us, doesn't she?

MRS WADHURST. Of course, I talked to her myself on the telephone last Wednesday, she was perfectly charming and said that we were to come without fail and that it would be divine.

MR WADHURST. I still feel we should have telephoned again just to remind her. People are always awfully busy in London.

MRS WADHURST. I do hope Lady Dalborough will be here, too— I should like to see her again—she was so nice.

MR WADHURST. She was the other one, wasn't she?

MRS WADHURST. [*Irritably.*] What do you mean, the other one?

MR WADHURST. I mean not this one.

MRS WADHURST. She 's the niece of the Duke of Frensham, her mother was Lady Merrit, she was a great traveller too—I believe she went right across the Sahara dressed as an Arab. In those days that was a very dangerous thing to do.

MR WADHURST. I shouldn't think it was any too safe now.

[*Walters enters and ushers in Mr Burnham, a nondescript young man carrying a longish roll of cardboard.*

WALTERS. I 'll tell the commander you 're here.

MR BURNHAM. Thanks—thanks very much.

[*Walters goes out.*

MRS WADHURST. [*After a slightly awkward silence.*] How do you do?

MR BURNHAM. How do you do?

MRS WADHURST. [*With poise.*] This is my husband.

MR BURNHAM. How do you do?

MR WADHURST. How do you do? [*They shake hands.*

MRS WADHURST. [*Vivaciously.*] Isn't this a charming room— so—so lived in.

MR BURNHAM. Yes.

MR WADHURST. Are you in the navy, too?

MR BURNHAM. No.

MRS WADHURST. [*Persevering.*] It 's so nice to be home again— we came from Malaya, you know.

MR BURNHAM. Oh—Malaya.

MRS WADHURST. Yes, Lady Maureen and Lady Dalborough visited us there—my husband has a rubber plantation up-country—there 's been a terrible slump, of course, but we 're trying to keep our heads above water—aren't we, Fred?

MR WADHURST. Yes, dear, we certainly are.

MRS WADHURST. Have you ever been to the East?

MR BURNHAM. No.

MRS WADHURST. It 's very interesting really, although the

climate's rather trying until you get used to it, and of course the one thing we do miss is the theatre——

MR BURNHAM. Yes—of course.

MRS WADHURST. There's nothing my husband and I enjoy so much as a good play, is there, Fred?

MR WADHURST. Nothing.

MRS WADHURST. And all we get is films, and they're generally pretty old by the time they come out to us—— [*She laughs gaily.*

MR WADHURST. Do you go to the theatre much?

MR BURNHAM. No.

[*There is silence which is broken by the telephone ringing. Everybody jumps.*

MRS WADHURST. Oh, dear—do you think we ought to answer it?

MR WADHURST. I don't know.

[*The telephone continues to ring. Clare Wedderburn comes in. She is middle-aged, well-dressed and rather gruff. She is followed by 'Bogey' Gosling, a major in the Marines, a good-looking man in the thirties.*

CLARE. Hallo—where's the old girl?

MRS WADHURST. [*Nervously.*] I—er, I'm afraid I——

CLARE. [*Going to the telephone.*] Mix a cocktail, Bogey—I'm a stretcher case—— [*At telephone.*] Hallo—no, it's me—Clare—— God knows, dear—shall I tell her to call you back? —all right—no, it was bloody, darling—a gloomy dinner at the Embassy, then the worst play I've ever sat through and then the Café de Paris and that awful man who does things with a duck—I've already seen him six times, darling—oh, you know, he pinches its behind and it quacks *Land of Hope and Glory*—I don't know whether it hurts it or not—I minded at first but I'm past caring now, after all, it's not like performing dogs, I mind about performing dogs terribly—all right—good-bye—— [*She hangs up and turns to Mrs Wadhurst.*] Ducks are pretty bloody anyway, don't you think?

MRS WADHURST. I don't know very much about them.

CLARE. The man swears it's genuine talent, but I think it's the little nip that does it.

MRS WADHURST. It sounds rather cruel.

CLARE. It's a gloomy form of entertainment anyhow, particularly as I've always hated *Land of Hope and Glory*.

BOGEY. Cocktail?

CLARE. [*Taking off her hat.*] Thank God!

[*Bogey hands round cocktails, the Wadhursts and Mr Burnham accept them and sip them in silence.*

BOGEY. I suppose Piggie's in the bath.

CLARE. Go and rout her out.

BOGEY. Wait till I 've had a drink.

CLARE. [*To Mrs Wadhurst.*] Is Peter home or is he still darting about the Solent?

MRS WADHURST. I 'm afraid I couldn't say—you see——

BOGEY. I saw him last night with Janet——

CLARE. Hasn't she had her baby yet?

BOGEY. She hadn't last night.

CLARE. That damned baby's been hanging over us all for months—— [*The telephone rings — Clare answers it. At telephone.*] Hallo—yes—hallo, darling—no, it 's Clare—yes, he 's here—— No, I really couldn't face it—yes, if I were likely to go to India I 'd come, but I 'm not likely to go to India—— I think Rajahs bumble up a house-party so terribly —yes, I know *he* 's different, but the other one 's awful— Angela had an agonizing time with him—all the dining-room chairs had to be changed because they were leather and his religion prevented him sitting on them—all the dogs had to be kept out of the house because they were unclean, which God knows was true of the Bedlington, but the other ones were clean as whistles—and then to round everything off he took Laura Mersham in his car and made passes at her all the way to Newmarket—all right, darling—here he is—— [*To Bogey.*] It 's Nina, she wants to talk to you——

[*She hands the telephone to Bogey, who reaches for it and lifts the wire so that it just misses Mrs Wadhurst's hat. It isn't quite long enough so he has to bend down to speak with his face practically touching her.*

BOGEY. [*At telephone.*] Hallo, Nin—— I can't on Wednesday, I 've got a Guest Night—it 's a hell of a long way, it 'd take hours——

Piggie comes in with a rush.

PIGGIE. I am so sorry——

CLARE. Shhh!

BOGEY. Shut up, I can't hear——

PIGGIE. [*In a shrill whisper.*] Who is it?

CLARE. Nina.

BOGEY. [*At telephone.*] Well, you can tell George to leave it for me—and I can pick it up.

PIGGIE. How lovely to see you again!

BOGEY. [*At telephone.*] No, I shan't be leaving till about ten, so if he leaves it by nine-thirty I 'll get it all right——

PIGGIE. My husband will be here in a minute—he has to go to sea on Thursday, but he 's arranged for you to be taken over the dockyard at Portsmouth——

BOGEY. [*At telephone.*] Give the old boy a crack on the jaw.

PIGGIE. It 's the most thrilling thing in the world. You see how the torpedoes are made—millions of little wheels inside, all clicking away like mad—and they cost thousands of pounds each——

BOGEY. [*At telephone.*] No, I saw her last night—not yet, but at any moment now—I should think—— All right—— Call me at Chatham—if I can get away I shall have to bring Mickie, too——

PIGGIE. How much do torpedoes cost each, Clare?

CLARE. God knows, darling — something fantastic — ask Bogey——

PIGGIE. Bogey——

BOGEY. What?

PIGGIE. How much do torpedoes cost each?

BOGEY. What?—[*at telephone*]—wait a minute, Piggie 's yelling at me——

PIGGIE. Torpedoes—— [*She makes a descriptive gesture.*

BOGEY. Oh, thousands and thousands—terribly expensive things —ask Peter—— [*At telephone.*] If I do bring him you 'll have to be frightfully nice to him, he 's been on the verge of suicide for weeks——

PIGGIE. Don't let her go, I must talk to her——

BOGEY. [*At telephone.*] Hold on a minute, Piggie wants to talk to you—all right—I 'll let you know—here she is——

[*Piggie leans over the sofa and takes the telephone from Bogey, who steps over the wire and stumbles over Mrs Wadhurst.*

BOGEY. I 'm most awfully sorry——

MRS WADHURST. Not at all——

PIGGIE. [*To Mrs Wadhurst.*] It 's so lovely you being in England—— [*At telephone.*] Darling—what was the meaning of that sinister little invitation you sent me?

BOGEY. You know what Mickey is.

PIGGIE. [*At telephone.*] No, dear, I really can 't—I always get so agitated——

CLARE. Why does he go on like that? It 's so tiresome.

PIGGIE. [*At telephone.*] I 'll come if Clare will—— [*To Clare.*] Are you going to Nina's Indian ding-dong?

CLARE. Not without an anaesthetic.

PIGGIE. [*At telephone.*] She's moaning a bit, but I'll persuade her—what happens after dinner?—the man with the duck from the Café de Paris—— [*To the room in general.*] She's got that sweet duck from the Café de Paris——

CLARE. Give me another cocktail, Bogey, I want to get so drunk that I just can't hear any more——

PIGGIE. [*At telephone.*] But, darling, do you think it's quite *wise*—I mean Maharajahs are terribly touchy and there's probably something in their religion about ducks being mortal sin or something—you know how difficult they are about cows and pigs—just a minute—— [*To the Wadhursts.*] You can tell us, of course——

MR WADHURST. I beg your pardon?

PIGGIE. Do Indians mind ducks?

MR WADHURST. I—I don't think so——

BOGEY. Do you come from India?

MRS WADHURST. No, Malaya.

PIGGIE. It's the same sort of thing, though, isn't it?—if they don't mind them in Malaya it's unlikely that they'd mind them in India—— [*At telephone.*] It'll probably be all right, but you'd better get Douglas Byng as a standby.

CLARE. There might be something in their religion about Douglas Byng.

PIGGIE. Shh! [*At telephone.*] Every one's making such a noise! The room's full of the most frightful people. Darling, it definitely *is* Waterloo Station—— No, I'm almost sure he can't—he's going to sea on Thursday—don't be silly, dear, you can't be in the Navy without going to sea *sometimes*—— [*Peter enters, followed by Ally. At telephone.*] Here he is now, you can ask him yourself—— [*To Peter.*] Peter, it's Nina, she wants to talk to you—— [*To the Wadhursts.*] This is my husband and Commander Corbett—he's been longing to meet you and thank you for being so sweet to us—I told him all about your heavenly house and the plantation—

MRS WADHURST. [*Bridling—to Ally.*] It was most delightful, I assure you, to have Lady Maureen with us——

PIGGIE. Not him, him—that's the wrong one——

MRS WADHURST. Oh, I'm so sorry——

PETER. [*Shaking hands with Mrs Wadhurst.*] It was so kind of you—my wife has talked of nothing else——

PIGGIE. [*Grabbing him.*] Here—Nina's yelling like a banshee——

PETER. Excuse me. [*He takes the telephone.*] Hallo, Nin—what
for?——No, I can't, but Piggie probably can—— [*To Piggie.*]
Can you go to Nina's party for the Rajahs?

PIGGIE. We 've been through all that——

PETER. All right—I didn't know—— [*At telephone.*] No, I shall be
at sea for about three days—it isn't tiresome at all, I like it——

PIGGIE. [*To Mrs Wadhurst.*] How 's your daughter?

MRS WADHURST. [*Surprised.*] She 's a little better, thank you.

PIGGIE. Oh, has she been ill? I 'm so sorry.

MR WADHURST. [*Gently.*] She 's been ill for five years.

PIGGIE. [*Puzzled.*] How dreadful for you—are you happy with
that cocktail, or would you rather have tea?

MRS WADHURST. This is delicious, thank you.

PETER. [*At telephone.*] I honestly can't do anything about that,
Nina, you might be able to find out from the Admiral—well,
if his mother was mad too that is an extenuating circumstance
—he 'll probably be sent home—— [*To Clare.*] Did you know
that Freda Bathurst had once been in an asylum?

CLARE. No, but it explains a lot.

PIGGIE. Why?

PETER. Her son went mad in Hong Kong.

CLARE. What did he do?

PETER. I don't know, but Nina 's in a state about it.

PIGGIE. I don't see what it 's got to do with Nina——

PETER. He 's a relation of some sort—— [*At telephone.*] What
did he do, Nina?—— Oh—— Oh, I see—— Oh—well, he 'll
certainly be sent home and a good job too, we can't have that
sort of thing in the Service—— If I were you I 'd keep well
out of it—all right—— Good-bye.   [*He hangs up.*

PIGGIE. What was it?

PETER. I couldn't possibly tell you.

PIGGIE. Poor boy, I expect the climate had something to do
with it—the climate 's awful in Hong Kong—look at poor old
Wally Smythe——

ALLY. [*To the Wadhursts.*] Did you ever know Wally Smythe?

MRS WADHURST. No, I 'm afraid not.

CLARE. You didn't miss much.

PIGGIE. I adored Wally, he was a darling.

CLARE. He kept on having fights all the time—I do hate people
hitting people—— [*To Mrs Wadhurst.*] Don't you?

MRS WADHURST. Yes.

   [*There is suddenly complete silence—Piggie breaks it with
   an effort.*

PIGGIE. [*Vivaciously to the Wadhursts.*] Maud was so frightfully sorry that she couldn't come to-day—she's pining to see you again and she asked me to ask you if you'd lunch there to-morrow.

MRS WADHURST. How very kind of her.

PIGGIE. She's got a divine little house hidden away in a mews, it's frightfully difficult to find—— [*The telephone rings.*] I've got millions of questions I want to ask you, what happened to that darling old native who did a dance with a sword?—— [*At telephone.*] Hallo— [*Continuing to every one in general.*] It was the most exciting thing I've ever seen, all the villagers sat round in torchlight and they beat—— [*At telephone.*] Hallo—yes, speaking—— [*Continuing*] beat drums and the —— [*At telephone.*] Hallo—darling, I'd no idea you were back—— [*To everybody*] and the old man tore himself to shreds in the middle, it was marvellous—— [*At telephone.*] I can't believe it, where are you speaking from?—— My dear, you're *not!*—— [*To everybody.*] It's Boodie, she got back last night and she's staying with Norman——

CLARE. Is Phyllis there?

PIGGIE. [*At telephone.*] Is Phyllis there?—— She's away?—— [*To Clare.*] She's away.

PETER. [*To Mr. Wadhurst.*] That's the best joke I ever heard.

CLARE. It's made my entire season, that's all, it's just made it.

PIGGIE. [*At telephone.*] You'd better come and dine to-night— I'm on a diet, so there's only spinach, but we can talk—— Yes, she's here—absolutely worn out—we all are—— Oh yes, it was pretty grim, it started all right and everything was going beautifully when Vera arrived, unasked, my dear, and more determined than Hitler—of course there was the most awful scene—Alice flounced upstairs with tears cascading down her face and locked herself in the cook's bedroom—— Clare tried to save the situation be dragging Lady Borrowdale on to the terrace——

CLARE. [*Sibilantly.*] That was *afterwards!*——

PIGGIE. [*At telephone.*] Anyhow hell broke loose—you can imagine—Janet was there, of course, and we were all worried about her—no, it hasn't arrived yet, but the odds are mounting—— [*To everybody.*] She hasn't had it yet, has she, Peter?

PETER. If she has it was born in the gramophone department at Harrods—I left her there at four-thirty——

PIGGIE. [*At telephone.*] No, it's still what's known as on the way—I'll expect you about eight-thirty—I've got to do my

feet and than I 'm going to relax—all right—yes, she's
here—— [*To Clare.*] Here, Clare, she wants to talk to you——
[*Clare in order to reach the telephone comfortably has to kneel
on the sofa.*
CLARE. Excuse me.
MRS WADHURST. I 'm so sorry.
CLARE. [*At telephone.*] Darling—I 'm dead with surprise——
PIGGIE. [*To Mrs Wadhurst.*] Now you must tell me some more——
MRS. WADHURST. Well, really, I don't——
CLARE. Shhh!—I can't hear a word—— [*At telephone.*] He
what?—when?—— He must be raving——
PIGGIE. [*In a harsh whisper.*] Have you still got that sweet dog?
MRS WADHURST. [*Also whispering.*] Yes, we 've still got
Rudolph.
PIGGIE. [*To everybody.*] Rudolph's an angel, I can never tell
you how divine he was—he used to come in every morning
with my breakfast tray and jump on to the bed——
MRS WADHURST. [*Horrified.*] Oh, you never told me that, how
very naughty of him—he 's very seldom allowed in the house
at all——
PIGGIE. [*Puzzled.*] But—but——
MR WADHURST. Perhaps you 're thinking of some other dog,
Lady Maureen—Rudolph is a Great Dane—
PIGGIE. [*Bewildered.*] Oh, yes, of course, how idiotic of me——
CLARE. [*At telephone.*] Well, all I can say is she ought to be
deported—you can't go about making scenes like that, it 's
so lacking in everything—all right, darling—call me in the
morning—I 've got a hairdresser in the afternoon, why don't
you make an appointment at the same time?—lovely——
Good-bye.   [*She hangs up.*
PIGGIE. Do sit down, Clare, and stop climbing about over every-
body. [*To Mrs Wadhurst.*] You must forgive me—this is a
mad-house—it 's always like this—I can't think why——
CLARE. [*In a whisper to Peter, having noticed Mr Burnham.*]
Why 's that man got a roll of music, is he going to sing?
PETER. [*Also in a whisper.*] I don't know—he ought by rights
to be a lovely girl of sixteen——
MRS WADHURST. Have you been in London for the whole season?
PIGGIE. Yes, it 's been absolutely frightful, but my husband is
getting leave soon, so we shall be able to pop off somewhere——
ALLY. [*To Mr Wadhurst.*] I suppose you 've never run across a
chap in Burma called Beckwith?
MR WADHURST. No, I 've never been to Burma.

ALLY. He's in rubber too, I believe—or tea—he's very amusing.

MRS WADHURST. [*To Piggie.*] We did hope you'd come and lunch with us one day—but I expect you're terribly busy——

PIGGIE. My dear, I'd worship it—— [*The telephone rings.*] Oh really, this telephone never stops for one minute—— [*At telephone.*] Hallo—yes, speaking—— Who?—Mrs Rawlingson—— Oh, yes, yes, yes—— [*She hands the telephone to Mrs Wadhurst.*] Here—it's for you——

MRS WADHURST. [*Astonished.*] For me? How very curious——

PIGGIE. Give me a cocktail, Bogey—I haven't had one at all yet and I'm exhausted——

MRS WADHURST. [*At telephone.*] Hallo — what — who? — I'm afraid I don't quite understand——

BOGEY. [*Giving Piggie a cocktail.*] Here you are—it's a bit weak——

MRS WADHURST. [*Still floundering.*] I think there must be some mistake—just a moment—— [*To Piggie.*] It's for you, Lady Maureen—a Mrs Rawlingson——

PIGGIE. [*Laughing.*] Now isn't that the most extraordinary coincidence—— [*She takes the telephone.*] Hallo—yes—speaking—— [*She listens and her face changes.*]—Oh yes, of course, how stupid of me—— [*She looks hurriedly at the Wadhursts, then at Peter.*] I'm so awfully sorry, I only just came in—— Oh, what a shame—no, no, no, it doesn't matter a bit—— No—indeed you must call me up the first moment he gets over it—— Yes—I expect it was—yes—— Good-bye.

> [*She slowly hangs up the receiver, looking at the Wadhursts in complete bewilderment. She makes a sign to Peter over Mrs Wadhurst's shoulder, but he only shakes his head.*

PIGGIE. [*Brightly, but with intense meaning.*] That was Mrs Rawlingson.

PETER. Good God!

PIGGIE. [*With purpose, sitting next to Mrs Wadhurst.*] Did you ever meet the Rawlingsons out East?

MRS WADHURST. No—I don't know them.

PIGGIE. Maud and I stayed with them too, you know.

MRS WADHURST. Where?

PIGGIE. It was in Malaya somewhere, I think—I do get so muddled.

MRS WADHURST. I think we should have heard of them if they lived in Malaya.

> [*Peter meanwhile has gone to the piano and started to strum idly—he begins to hum lightly at the same time.*

PETER. [*Humming to a waltz refrain, slightly indistinctly but clearly enough for Piggie to hear.*] 'If these are not them who are they? Who are they? Who are they?'
[*Piggie rises and saunters over to the piano.*
PIGGIE. Play the other bit, dear, out of the second act——
[*She hums*]—you know—'I haven't the faintest idea—— Oh no—I haven't the faintest idea.'
PETER. [*Changing tempo.*] 'Under the light of the moon, dear— you'd better find out pretty soon, dear.'
CLARE. What on earth's that out of?
PIGGIE. Don't be *silly*, Clare—all I ask is that you shouldn't be *silly*!
CLARE. [*Understanding.*] Oh yes—I see.
[*There is silence except for Peter's playing—every one looks covertly at the Wadhursts. Piggie goes over to Mr Wadhurst.*
PIGGIE. [*With determination.*] What ship did you come home in?
MR WADHURST. The *Naldera*.
ALLY. P. & O.?
MRS WADHURST. Yes.
PIGGIE. I suppose you got on at Singapore?
MR WADHURST. No, Penang.
PIGGIE. [*The light breaking.*] Penang! Of course, Penang.
MRS WADHURST. Yes, we have some friends there, so we went by train from Singapore and stayed with them for a couple of days before catching the boat.
PIGGIE. [*Sunk again.*] Oh yes—yes, I see.
PETER. [*At piano, humming to march time.*] 'When you hear those drums rat-a-plan—rat-a-plan—find out the name of the place if you can—la la la la la la la la——'
PIGGIE. [*Persevering.*] How far is your house from the sea? Maud and I were arguing about it for hours the other day——
MR WADHURST. It's right on the sea.
PIGGIE. That's exactly what I said, but you know Maud's so vague—she never remembers a thing——
CLARE. I suppose it's hell hot all the year round where you are?
MRS WADHURST. Yes, the climate is a little trying, but one gets used to it.
BOGEY. Are you far from Kuala Lumpur?
MRS WADHURST. Yes, a long way.
BOGEY. Oh, I knew some people in Kuala Lumpur once.
MR WADHURST. What were their names?

BOGEY. Damn it, I 've forgotten—something like Harrison——

PIGGIE. [*Helpfully.*] Morrison?

ALLY. Williamson?

PETER. Lightfoot?

BOGEY. No, it 's gone——

PIGGIE. [*Irritably.*] Never mind—it couldn't matter less really, could it?

MRS WADHURST. [*Rising.*] I 'm afraid we must really go now, Lady Maureen——

PIGGIE. Oh, no—please——

MRS WADHURST. We have to dress because we 're dining and going to the theatre—that 's the one thing we do miss dreadfully in Pendarla—the theatre——

CLARE. We miss it a good deal here, too.

PIGGIE. [*Remembering everything.*] Pendarla—oh dear, what a long way away it seems—dear Mrs Wadhurst—— [*She shoots a triumphant glance at Peter.*] It 's been so lovely having this little peep at you—you and Mr Wadhurst must come and dine quietly one night and we 'll go to another theatre——

MRS WADHURST. That would be delightful—Fred——

MR WADHURST. Good-bye.

PIGGIE. Peter—come and say good-bye to Mr and Mrs Wadhurst.

PETER. [*Coming over and shaking hands.*] Good-bye—I can never tell you how grateful I am to you for having been so kind and hospitable to my wife——

MRS WADHURST. Next time, I hope you 'll come and call on us too.

PETER. I should love to.

MRS WADHURST. Good-bye.

CLARE. Good-bye——

> [*Everybody says good-bye and shakes hands, Peter opens the door for the Wadhursts and they go out on a wave of popularity. He goes out into the hall with them closing the door after him. Piggie collapses on to the sofa.*

PIGGIE. [*Hysterically.*] Oh, my God, that was the most awful half-hour I 've ever spent——

CLARE. I thought it all went down like a dinner.

PIGGIE. I remember it all now, we stayed one night with them on our way from Siam—a man in Bangkok had wired to them or something——

ALLY. That was a nice bit you did about the old native dancing with a sword——

PIGGIE. Oh, dear, they must have thought I was drunk.

[Peter re-enters.

PETER. Next time you travel, my darling, I suggest you keep a diary.

PIGGIE. Wasn't it frightful — poor angels — I must ring up Maud—— *[She dials a number.]* I think they had a heavenly time though, don't you—I mean they couldn't have noticed a thing——

PETER. Oh no, the whole affair was managed with the utmost subtlety—I congratulate you——

PIGGIE. Don't be sour, Peter—— *[At telephone.]* Hallo—Maud? —darling, it's not the Rawlingsons at all, it's the Wadhursts—— *[To everybody.]* Good heavens, I never gave them Maud's address. *[At telephone.]* I forgot to give them your address—how can you be so unkind, Maud, you ought to be ashamed of yourself—they're absolute pets, both of them——

PETER. Come on, Ally, I've got to dress——

ALLY. All right——

CLARE. Shall I see you on Sunday?

ALLY. Yes—I'll be over——

PIGGIE. *[At telephone.]* They had a lovely time and everybody was divine to them——

CLARE. Come on, Bogey, we must go, too——

PIGGIE. Wait a minute, don't leave me—I've got to do my feet—— *[At telephone.]*—No, I was talking to Clare—— My dear, I know, she rang me up too—she's staying with Norman—Phyllis will be as sour as a quince——

[Peter and Ally go off talking.

CLARE. Darling, I really *must* go——

PIGGIE. *[At telephone.]*—All right—I'll try to get hold of them in the morning and put them off—I do think it's horrid of you though, after all, they were frightfully sweet to us—I've done all I can—well, there's no need to get into a rage, I'm the one to get into a rage—yes, you are, I can hear you—your teeth are chattering like dice in a box—— Oh, all right! *[She hangs up.]* Maud's impossible——

CLARE. Listen, Piggie——

PIGGIE. Wait just one minute, I've got to get the things to do my feet—— *[She rushes out of the room.*

CLARE. I really don't see why we should all wait about—— *[She suddenly sees Mr Burnham.]* Oh—hallo.

MR BURNHAM. *[Nervously.]* Hallo.

CLARE. I thought you'd left with your mother and father.

MR BURNHAM. They weren't my mother and father—I 'm from Freeman's. I 've brought the designs for the commander's speed boat—Mr Driscoll couldn't come——

CLARE. Well, you 'd better wait—he 'll be back soon——

MR BURNHAM. I 'm afraid I can't wait much longer—I have to get back to the shop——

CLARE. You should have piped up before——

BOGEY. Listen, Clare, we must push off——

CLARE. All right.

[*Mr Burnham retires again into the shadows as Piggie returns with several bottles, a towel, and a pair of scissors. She sits on the sofa and takes her shoes and stockings off.*

PIGGIE. —The trouble with Maud is, she 's too insular——

CLARE. Are you driving down on Saturday?

PIGGIE. Yes—I promised to stop off at Godalming and have a cutlet with Freda on the way—do you want to come?

CLARE. You know perfectly well I hate Freda's guts.

PIGGIE. [*Beginning on her feet.*] All right, darling—I 'll expect you in the afternoon—— [*The telephone rings—Piggie reaches for it with one hand and goes on painting her toe-nails with the other—at telephone.*] Hallo—yes. Oh, David, I 'm so sorry—I completely forgot—— [*Clare and Bogey kiss good-bye at her, she waves to them, and they go out.*] I couldn't help it, I had to be sweet to some people that Maud and I stayed with in Malaya—— Oh! David darling, don't be so soured-up—yes, of course I do, don't be so silly—— No, I 'm quite alone doing my feet—well, I can't help that, I happen to *like* them red—well, after all they are my feet, I suppose I can paint them blue if I want to—— [*Mr Burnham begins to tiptoe out of the room, he leaves his roll of designs on the table. Piggie catches sight of him just as he is gingerly opening the door. To Mr Burnham.*] Oh, good-bye—it 's been absolutely lovely, you 're the sweetest family I 've ever met in my life——

CURTAIN

HEWERS OF COAL

Joe Corrie

PERSONS OF THE PLAY

DICK, *a miner of middle age*
BILLIE, *a boy of fifteen years*
PETER, *a pit handyman, fifty years of age*
JOE, *a miner of middle age*
BOB, *a gaffer, fifty years of age*

HEWERS OF COAL

NOTE.—As different districts have different underground names and expressions, the producer may have to alter the words to suit his particular audience.

SCENE. *A 'heading' underground. It is a narrowly confined place about five feet six inches high, hewn out of the solid rock. A narrow strip of coal can be seen along the whole length of the back wall. A couple of props are at the back, a jacket hanging to a nail in one.*
The only entrance is in the right (spectator's) wall. This is an opening about four feet high, and three and a half feet wide, with a prop at each side of it and one across the top. Over this opening there hangs a coarse and dirty canvas 'screen'—one of the underground precautions for a better air current. A few old hutch sleepers and pieces of prop lie here and there, on which the men sit when they are taking their meal.
When the curtain rises Dick sits in the centre eating bread and cheese from a 'piece-tin,' and drinking from a tea-flask. At his side there is a larger can which holds water. At right (spectator's) Billy sits, also at his meal. They have been in the pit for three hours and their faces are black. Both have donned their coats, as is the custom in the mine when men are having their meal. Their safety lamps are beside them, but there should be a dim blue light added for stage purposes.
Billie, with his mouth full, puts his 'piece-tin' together and closes it with a snap. He puts it in his pocket as much as to say, 'Well, that's that.' Dick still taking his meal, looks round at Billie.

DICK. Finished with your meal already, Billy?
BILLIE. [*Still chewing.*] M-m!
DICK. You shouldn't eat so quick, lad, it isn't good for the stomach.
BILLIE. I've got a stomach that can digest nails. . . . Peter's taking a long time to come in for his ham and egg.
DICK. There's a smash-up of hutches down the slope. Didn't you know that?

BILLIE. That's why the haulage was stopped before stopping time?

DICK. Yes. Some smash, too, Peter'll be cursing, for he doesn't care about losing sweat, the lazy . . .

[*The fact that Billy is a boy keeps him from expressing himself to the full.*

BILLIE. [*Who has been eyeing Dick's tin.*] Is that scone you have with you?

DICK. Yes. [*Smiling.*] Want a bit?

[*Billie needs no second bidding. He is at Dick's side immediately. Dick, still smiling, hands him a piece of the scone. Billie takes a large bite.*

BILLIE. Thanks, Dick—a million!

[*He returns to his former seat enjoying the scone to the full.*

DICK. You seem to be fond of scone, Billie?

BILLIE. I could eat it till it was coming out o' my ears. . . . It was a bad day for me when my mother died, Dick. [*Sighs.*] She used to bake scones every day.

DICK. Doesn't your sister do any baking?

BILLIE. [*Full of scorn.*] Her! She hasn't time to bake for powdering her face and waving her hair. Pictures and dancing, that's all *she* can think about. Mad to get a man, Dick, and when she does get one she'll poison him with tinned meat. I've got a new name for her now.

DICK. [*Amused.*] Oh, what have you christened her, Billy?

BILLIE. [*With great satisfaction.*] Tin-opener Trixie. By gum! she's an expert at it. The back of our house is like a munition work with empty tins.

DICK. [*Still amused.*] They tell me she's a champion dancer?

BILLIE. Dancer, yes, but it isn't round a baking-board. [*Pause.* This scone is just great, Dick. You must be proud of your wife?

DICK. [*Suddenly thoughtful.*] Not as proud as I should be, perhaps. . . . The miner is a thoughtless kind o' fellow, Bill. He goes home on pay day with about forty shillings, hands it over to the missus like a hero, forgetting that the Chancellor o' the Exchequer himself would have to throw in the sponge if he had to feed and clothe a man, a wife, and five kiddies on it. How the hell they manage to keep their head above water is a mystery to me. . . . And yet they have the heart to laugh and sing, too.

BILLIE. My mother was always singing, Dick—always. [*With downcast eyes.*] By gum! I *do* miss her

DICK. Is your father keeping better now?

BILLIE. [*Rather hopelessly.*] Some days he's all right, other days he's all wrong. I don't think he'll ever get right now.

DICK. You've had a rotten time, Billie, between one thing and another.

BILLIE. Father says that we're lucky with me working. It helps to keep us going. So I'll have to try and keep my job, Dick.

DICK. [*Thoughtfully.*] A job! . . . The whole world seems to go round on a job. . . . No job, no bread—no bread, no laughter. [*Sighs.*] It's a strange way of running a world, in my opinion.
> [*There is a slight pause. Then we hear a pony neighing outside. Billie looks at Dick quite tragically.*

BILLIE. That's Danny. . . . And I forgot to keep him a piece o' my bread.

DICK. [*Lightly.*] He has plenty of oats, Bill.

BILLIE. He looks forward now to getting a bit o' my bread and a drink o' my tea. [*Pony neighs again.*] He and I are great pals, Dick. If ever I win a big coupon I'm going to buy him from the company and take him up to the green fields. [*Pleadingly, in a way.*] It was greedy of me eating all my bread and not thinking o' Danny, wasn't it?
> [*Dick holds out the last piece of scone he has left.*

DICK. Take that out to him, Billie.
> [*Billie immediately rises to get it.*

BILLIE. [*Taking it.*] Dick, you're Public Hero Number One.
> [*He goes towards the exit.*

DICK. Lift that screen, Billie, and give us a breath of air. It's beginning to suffocate in here.
> [*While Billie is lifting the screen to hang it up the pony neighs again.*

BILLIE. I'm coming, Danny—I'm coming!
> [*Billie goes off. Dick wipes his brow with his fingers and throws the sweat off them. Then he takes a long breath or two of the air which seems to be coming in now. He closes his tin, and puts it and his tea-flask in his jacket pockets. Peter enters. He is in his shirt sleeves, rolled up and is wiping his brow with a red and white spotted handkerchief. Dick is conscious of his entrance but doesn't look at him. Peter speaks on entering and goes to his jacket, which is hanging on the prop. He rolls down his sleeves and speaks in Dick's direction.*

PETER. The things that happen down this pit would break the heart of a saint.

[*He takes his flask and tin from his pockets.*

DICK. [*Looking up at him unpleasantly.*] What's the matter with you?

PETER. Didn't you see that smash at the bottom o' the slope? Four hutches broke away from that last race and jammed themselves right up to the roof. . . . Where's that boy?

DICK. What d' ye want with him?

PETER. The gaffer's coming up to speak to him about it. He put a coupling on twisted—that caused the break-away. I wouldn't be surprised if he gets the sack—Robert's flaming about it.

DICK. And how did Robert know it was a twisted coupling that caused the smash?

PETER. I told him.

DICK. [*Getting angry.*] And how did you know?

PETER. Because it was the only way it *could* come off.

[*Peter sits at left to have his meal.*

DICK. [*Angry.*] You're damned ready at spotting things like that for the gaffer, aren't ye? D' you think he loves you for it?

PETER. Who are *you* barking at?

DICK. You! The lad wouldn't put a coupling on twisted intentionally, would he? Mistakes *will* happen. Have you never made one in your life?

PETER. If you saw the mess that I had to clear up you wouldn't be so damned kind.

DICK. Isn't it your job in this pit to clear up messes? And, if you want my opinion, you're well suited to the job. Get what I mean?

PETER. Look here, Dick! If there's going to be any more o' this talk at meals I'm going to talk to the gaffer about it. I'm not going to stand insults from you.

DICK. If Billie gets the sack because o' this you'll have to stand a damned sight more than insults—I'll break your blasted neck.

PETER. It's no business o' yours, anyhow.

DICK. I'm *making* it my business. That lad can't afford to lose his job—it's the only thing between his family and starvation. Why did you tell the gaffer he was to blame?

PETER. If I had kept the blame off him it might have fallen on me.

DICK. Yes, and that would have been a hell of a tragedy,

wouldn't it? You with your extra shifts and your ham and egg—you selfish swine!

PETER. If a man doesn't look after himself in this pit nobody else will.

DICK. [*Scornfully.*] Is that your outlook on life?

PETER. It is.

DICK. There might come a day, Peter, when *you* 'll be depending on the help of someone. What 'll you do then?

PETER. That day will *never* come—don't worry about that.

DICK. Better men than you have needed help, and have been damned glad to accept it when it *did* come.

PETER. Well, there 's one thing you can be sure of, Dick. It 'll be a bad day for me when I 'm looking for help from *you*.

DICK. Don't boast, Peter. This is a strange world, remember, and some strange things happen in it.

PETER. That 's *one* thing that 'll never happen.

[*Billie returns. He immediately sniffs and looks at Peter, who is now busy eating.*]

BILLIE. There 's a grand smell o' ham and egg in here.

DICK. Ten shifts a week and no kiddies to keep. Makes a difference, Billie.

[*Peter glances unkindly at Dick for a moment, then looks at Billie.*]

PETER. [*To Billie.*] Did you see the gaffer out there?

BILLIE. [*Puzzled.*] No. . . . What does he want with me?

DICK. You 're getting the blame o' that smash.

BILLIE. Me? How?

PETER. You put a coupling on twisted and it came off going over the brow.

[*Billie is troubled.*]

BILLIE. [*To Dick.*] Does that mean I 'll get the sack?

DICK. If you have to go up the pit to-day, Bill, you won't be the only one.

BILLIE. What d' you mean, Dick?

DICK. Never mind just now. . . . Doesn't Joe know it 's stopping-time?

BILLIE. He 's not taking his food in here to-day.

DICK. Why not?

BILLIE. I don't know. He took his food into the coal face this morning.

DICK. Go and give him a shout, anyhow, and make sure that he 's all right.

[*Billie goes off, giving Peter a nasty look as he goes.*]

DICK. Billie's father's ill—you know that?

PETER. Well?

DICK. They're just scraping through on Billie's wage.

PETER. What has that to do with me?

DICK. You can tell the gaffer that you found a broken link on the slope, and that *it* caused the smash?

PETER. Yes, and if it was found out that I was telling the gaffer a lie it would mean the sack for *me*.

DICK. If Billie gets the sack because of this I'll——

[*Bob enters. He is a tall man wearing short leggings. He hangs his lamp on his belt.*

BOB. [*To Peter.*] There's a loose strand in that haulage rope. Get your splicing tools and run it in before starting-time.

[*Peter immediately closes his tin, rises, and hurries off.*

PETER. I'll not be a minute, Robert ... no more than a minute.

[*Peter goes off. Bob takes a note-book and pencil from his pocket and writes something down.*

BOB. If it isn't one thing down here it's two That's half an hour lost this morning.

DICK. Of course, a coal pit isn't like a biscuit works, Bob, where everything goes like a song?

BOB. There's too much carelessness. And I'm going to make an example this morning. Where's that pony driver?

DICK. He's in telling Joe Marshall to come in here for his meal.

BOB. Well, you can tell him not to start work until I speak to him.

DICK. Thinking of sacking him, are ye?

BOB. That smash was his fault and he'll have to pay for it.

DICK. Mistakes can happen with all of us, Bob.

BOB. We can't afford them happening with us.

DICK. [*Amused.*] We! Us! When did you get a share in the Imperial Coal Company, Bob?

[*Bob looks at Dick quickly.*

BOB. What d' you mean?

DICK. You said 'we'—'us.' Only the directors speak in the plural.

BOB. Oh, being sarcastic, eh? Cut it out, Dick, or you might be getting more fresh air than is good for the health.

DICK. So you *do* know what fresh air is?

BOB. Eh?

DICK. We could be doing with a lot more of it down here.

BOB. [*After looking at the entrance with the screen up.*] Seems to me you're getting a damned sight more than your share.

[*He goes to the entrance and lets the screen drop angrily.*

DICK. [*With a smile.*] It would be fine if everything in this pit could be remedied as easily as that, Bob—eh?

BOB. What are ye driving at?

DICK. Have you got that fall cleared up in the main aircourse yet?

BOB. What the hell have you to do with the main aircourse?

DICK. I was just trying to get information.

BOB. Well, what 'll happen to me if it isn't cleared up?

DICK. It isn't what 'll happen to you—it 's what 'll happen to the lot of us. [*Significantly.*] There 's no shortage o' gas down here, remember.

BOB. [*With a sarcastic smile.*] Is that so?

DICK. There 's a shortage o' props, a shortage o' air, but no shortage o' gas.

BOB. [*Thoughtfully.*] I see! . . . Dick, come into my office at finishing-time. I want a serious talk with you.

[*Peter returns carrying his splicing tools in his hand.*

PETER. I 'm ready, Robert.

[*Bob goes to the exit, stops and looks back at Dick.*

BOB. Gas in the pit, is there? And a fall in the main aircourse. And you 'd like the Government inspector to know about it—eh? I have a way of dealing with your kind, Dick. Keep mind o' that.

[*Bob goes off. Peter follows like a dog at the heels of its master. Dick smiles, but it is a troubled smile. Billie enters.*

BILLIE. Am I to get the sack, Dick?

DICK. Leave that to me, Bill. . . . Is Joe coming in?

BILLIE. Yes. But he 's had his meal, Dick; he took it at the coal-face.

DICK. He has never done that before.

BILLIE. He said he was too hungry to wait till stopping-time. [*Billie sits.*] If I get the sack I 'll be afraid to go home, Dick.

DICK. If you get the sack to-day, Billie, I 'll bring this bloody pit out on strike. And the company would have something to say about *that*.

[*Joe enters. He doesn't look at all well, and has a racking cough.*

DICK. That cough o' yours is getting worse, Joe.

JOE. [*Struggling for breath.*] That air down there is killing me, Dick—killing me.

DICK. Why do you work in it?

JOE. I wouldn't if I could get out of it. . . . But he knows he has me there, and won't give me another job. . . . I wish to

L 947

God I had never married, Dick—it has been hell ever since
. . . being chained down here.

DICK. They know when they have a lever all right. [*Joe sits
where Peter was sitting.*] Why didn't you take your breakfast
with us?

JOE. [*Guiltily.*] I . . . took it early.

DICK. Why?

JOE. My place was on the move . . . and I had to come out to
see if it would settle. . . . And I can't get any wood to secure it.
[*Hysterically.*] Dick! . . . I 'm getting afraid to work in there.
. . . It 'll come down some day and crush me to pulp!

[*Dick is alarmed at this outburst. Billie just looks at Joe in a
puzzled way. Dick goes to Joe.*

DICK. Joe, you 've got to pull yourself together, lad—you 're
letting your nerves get the better of ye.

JOE. But I can't help it! . . . I know it 'll come down on me
and . . .

DICK. I know what 's the matter this morning, Joe. It 's
hunger. You didn't *bring* a meal with you this morning?

JOE. No, Dick, I . . . I . . .

DICK. It 's all right, Joe, you needn't be ashamed of it. It 's
no crime to come to the pit without bread when there 's a
wife and kiddies to come first. [*Dick looks at Billie.*] [*To
Billie.*] Peter left a bit of his bread for the pony, didn't he?

BILLIE. [*Astounded.*] What, *he* did?

DICK. [*Nodding his head to Billie on the quiet.*] You were out at
the time and didn't hear him. . . . Danny has plenty of oats.

[*Dick lifts Peter's bread tin, takes the bread from it, and
pushes it into Joe's hand. Joe shrinks from it.*

JOE. No! . . . Peter would tell it all through the pit!

DICK. [*Forcing it into his hand.*] Take it and don't be a bloody
fool! . . . I 'll explain to Peter, and it 'll be all right. [*Joe
takes it, but reluctantly and ashamed.*] If you don't want to
take it here go into the coal-face and eat it.

[*Joe looks at Dick in a hopeless manner.*

JOE. Dick, I 'm tired. . . . I 'm not fit enough now to be working
here, but—there 's nothing else for it. . . . If that roof *would*
come down and put an end to me Mary would get compensation, and her troubles would be all over.

DICK. Joe! Get that idea out of your head. That 's the
coward's way out. . . . Go and eat that bread—it 'll do you
a world of good. [*Joe rises and goes off slowly. We hear him
coughing when he has gone.*] Joe 's just about a goner, I think.

BILLIE. Peter 'll be mad when he finds his bread missing.

DICK. [*With a smile.*] We 'll blame it on the rats, Billie. He has enough ham and egg in him anyway to last him for the rest o' the shift. If he hasn't it 'll do him good to feel hungry for once.   [*Peter returns hurrying and still cross.*

PETER. [*Entering.*] It 's little wonder my meals never do *me* any good. I never get peace to sit down to them. Always something going wrong. [*He sits in his previous position. He lifts his tin, getting a shock at the lightness of it. He looks suspiciously at Dick. Then he opens the tin.*] Here! What has happened to my bread?

DICK. A couple of rats came in and took it away, Peter.

PETER. [*Sarcastically.*] Oh, did they? Opened the lid, then shut it after them, eh?

DICK. Yes. They 're getting more human down here every day.
                                        [*Peter rises threateningly.*

PETER. Where 's my bread?

DICK. [*To Billie.*] Doesn't believe a word I say nowadays, Billie.

PETER. I want that bread back—see!

DICK. Too late, Peter, it 's away ta-ta.

PETER. Where is it?

DICK. Well, Joe Marshall came in here and I discovered that he didn't bring a slice with him to the pit. So I thought you wouldn't mind him having what you had left.

PETER. What! You gave my bread away to him! . . . And what am I going to do now?

DICK. I think you had a good tightener.
                        [*Peter lifts his tin madly and raises it above Dick.*

PETER. I 'll bring this down on your blasted head, you . . .
                        [*Dick protects himself. Billie jumps. Robert enters.*

BOB. What 's the matter here?
                                        [*Peter looks at Bob piteously.*

PETER. [*Whining.*] Robert, he stole the bread from my tin when I was out and gave it away.

BOB. [*Puzzled.*] Stole your bread?

PETER. Stole it and gave it to Joe Marshall.

BOB. [*To Dick.*] Is this true?

DICK. Joe came in here dead beat with hunger. I thought that Peter would be only too pleased to do a good turn to a mate for once in his life.

PETER. [*Still whining.*] He didn't even ask my permission, Robert. . . . And here I am, left without a slice.

BOB. Dick, pack up your tools and get up the pit. [*To Billie.*]
And you do the same.

DICK. Right-o! But before I *do* go I'm going to knock the
head off this greedy swine.

[*Dick angrily divests himself of his jacket. Bob gets between
him and Peter. Peter slinks back to a corner.*

BOB. [*To Dick.*] You know what it means to strike a man down
a pit?

DICK. [*Making towards Peter, and trying to get past Bob.*] I don't
care! Joe was hungry, and . . .

[*There is heard a terrific roar, like thunder. Immediately the
quarrel is forgotten. Like trapped animals they instinctively herd together and rush to the left wall. Billie
rushes to the shelter of Dick. The noise gets louder and
more terrible. There is a pause, then Joe staggers in,
falls, then crawls towards his mates.*

JOE. We're trapped—trapped!

[*The noise is now horrible, and the falling of debris is heard.
A stone, accompanied by a cloud of dust, falls on the scene.
A loud crash is heard at the entrance.*

[*Gradually the noise begins to fade, like thunder among the
hills. Then quietness falls, save for the echo of falling
debris in the working around.*

[*Dick goes cautiously to the entrance. He lifts the screen.
They all give a start, for the way out is blocked by fallen
stone. Dick turns and looks at his stricken mates.*

DICK. God! . . . We're entombed!

A SLOW CURTAIN

SCENE TWO

*Immediately after the close of the curtain, through the darkness,
we hear the voice of a wireless announcer.*

ANNOUNCER. This is the National Programme. . . . The death-roll in the Glendinning pit disaster has now reached forty-two, two other bodies having been found this morning. For the past five days the rescue parties have worked in relays, day and night. They are endeavouring now to reach the Hard Coal Heading, which, it is thought, a few of the men may have reached through old workings. Little hope, however, is being held of finding the men alive. Messages of sympathy have been received from his Majesty the King, the Prime Minister, the Minister for Mines, and the Archbishop of Cravenbury. A relief fund has been opened for the bereaved relatives to relieve the destitution, and contributions will be gratefully received at the office of the Miners' Federation, or may be sent to the Provost of Glendinning. . . . In the South Wales coal-field another strike has broken out, the men claiming an increase of wages. The strike is entirely unofficial and . . .

[*The last few words fade out as the curtain gradually opens.*

The scene is the old Hard Coal Heading. It is on a slope, rising from right to left. This can be done by using a sloped platform, a sloped frontpiece from about one foot at right to over two feet at left, with an irregular top edging to resemble coal. A black curtain can be lowered from the top at a corresponding angle.

There is a small opening at right, but it is only a hole big enough for a man to crawl through. It is no outlet to the world, as the workings around are all closed. The first thing to strike the eye will be five chalked strokes on the back wall.

There is only one lamp alight, hanging near Dick, who sits in the centre rather like a Rodin sculpture. Bob is at right on his knees, putting up a silent prayer. Billie lies asleep between Bob and Dick. Joe lies to left of Dick, also asleep, and looking deathly pale. Peter is at extreme left, looking hopelessly at the wall at left. They all wear their jackets, and it is easily seen that they are nearly done. It is the courage of Dick that has saved them up till now, that and the water-can which is close to Dick.

BOB. [*Just a faint whisper.*] Amen!
  [*There is a dead pause for a moment or two. Bob looks at Dick pleadingly.*
BOB. Can I have a few drops o' water, Dick?
  [*Dick slowly lifts the can to his ear and shakes it.*
DICK. It can only *be* a drop or two, Bob.
BOB. I know.
DICK. To-day 'll finish it.
  [*Dick hands the can over to Bob. Peter looks on the scene with staring eyes. While Bob sips, Peter begins to crawl towards him. Dick watches him closely. Bob hands the can back to Dick.*
PETER. Can I wet my tongue, too, Dick? [*Dick looks at Joe.*
DICK. I 'm afraid we 'll have to keep the rest for Joe. . . . You 've had your share to-day, Peter. . . . I 'm worried about Joe, he looks done for.
PETER. [*Piteously.*] Oh! . . . Just two drops, Dick—for God's sake! [*Dick is sorry for him.*
DICK. All right, but it must be your last—absolutely.
PETER. I know.
  [*Dick gives Peter the water-can, but holds on to it. He pulls it away when he thinks Peter has taken enough. Peter returns to his former position. There is a pause. Then Bob crawls to Dick and takes hold of his hand.*
BOB. Dick—before it is too late. . . . Thanks for all you have done for us. . . . It was your pluck that got us here . . . your hope that has kept us alive . . . if it has failed . . . Oh!
DICK. It might have been better if we had stayed where we were—it would have been all over now. . . . But life is sweet. . . . Still, we know each other better now—and that 's something.
BOB. Yes, but it 's a pity we don't know more of the good things in life until it 's too late.
  [*Bob returns to his former position. There is a pause.*
BOB. [*Hopelessly.*] Not a sound—anywhere!
DICK. [*Quickly.*] Listen! [*Dick, Peter, and Bob are all attention to listen. After a pause, hopelessly.*] No!
BOB. No!
PETER. No!
BOB. Strange that the hunger has passed away.
DICK. [*With a faint smile.*] It was hellish while it lasted. . . . No craving for food now—just water.
PETER. [*A sudden outburst, wildly.*] I 'm burning inside like a fire—roasting! [*He makes a sudden attempt to get the water-can.*

Dick gets hold of it. Bob is prepared to defend Dick. Madly.]
Give me that water!... Give me that water—or I 'll kill ye!
[*Bob lifts a stone from the floor and raises it above his head.*
BOB. Touch that water, and it 'll be your last.
DICK. [*Who is really master of the situation.*] Bob! No temper.
[*Peter goes back to his place.*
PETER. Oh, this is unbearable—unbearable! [*Then in desperation he beats his hands against the wall.*] Help! Help! Help!
DICK. Cut that out! D' ye want to waken the kid?
[*Peter sinks exhausted. Bob and Dick both look at the sleeping boy.*
BOB. Hasn't he been plucky, Dick?
DICK. Plucky? By God, he has!
PETER. [*Very slowly.*] Oh! this waiting—waiting on something that can never happen now . . . waiting!
DICK. Listen! [*Again they are all attention. There is a slight pause.*] No!
BOB. [*Very tired.*] Imagination again. . . . I wonder what has been happening? . . . How many have lost their lives? . . . And they 'll be blaming me! [*Hysterically.*] They 'll be blaming me!
PETER. [*Also hysterical.*] And you *were* to blame! . . . The main aircourse was never kept clear.
DICK. We were all to blame for something. If it wasn't greed and selfishness, it was fear and cowardice.... Thinking only of ourselves, and the others could go to hell. [*To Bob.*] And what has it been worth to-day?
BOB. If I live to come through this I 'll be a different man, Dick.
DICK. We 'll all be different men, I think.
[*There is a silence. Then Joe begins to rave in his delirium.*
JOE. Three hundred quid! . . . She 'll get three hundred quid! . . . Mary, tell the kiddies that you 'll get three hundred quid.
[*Joe laughs very weakly. The others look at him in suspense and fear.*
BOB. [*In a whisper.*] He 's started again.
DICK. [*To Bob.*] Is he too weak now to go mad?
PETER. [*Hysterically.*] Mad! . . . Oh, my God, we 'd have to kill him!
DICK. Peter, haven't you got one single kind thought in that miserable heart o' yours? In a short time we 'll all be knocking at the door of Kingdom Come. Let 's go with clean hands and hearts. [*Peter is ashamed*
JOE. Three hundred quid of compensation—the price of a dead

3

miner! Three hundred quid, Mary, and—a corpse. . . . Ha, ha!

PETER. I can't stand this, I tell ye!—I can't!

[*Again he beats his hands against the stone wall of his prison. Then he gives it up in absolute despair. There is another silence. Billie begins to talk in his sleep. Dick and Joe look at him.*

BILLIE. Mother! . . . Mother! . . . Dick says that I 've been brave. . . . You always told me to play the man. . . . Dick says I 've been great. . . . Danny was killed . . . my pony . . . We were great pals, mother.

DICK. Plucky kid! [*Softly.*] Sleep, Billie . . . sleep.

[*A silence.*

JOE. And Peter grudged me his bit o' bread. . . . [*Peter rises as if his conscience had stricken him.*] And I was hungry. . . . Oh, I was hungry. . . .

PETER. [*Piteously.*] I didn't grudge him my bread, Dick, did I?

DICK. No, Peter, it was all a mistake. You were angry because I didn't ask your permission. Forget about it.

JOE. Three hundred quid! . . .

[*Joe tries to sing a word or two of* Love's Old Sweet Song, *but he only gets a few notes out when he stops exhausted. There is a pause.*

BOB. [*Quietly.*] The sun! . . . Just to look up again at the sky! To walk through the woods! . . . To climb the hills! . . . To lie down and drink the clear, cold water! [*The mention of water makes Peter rise again and cast an envious eye on the water-can. Dick holds it tightly to himself.*] Five days in hell! And every day an eternity.

DICK. Give me your book and pencil, Bob. I 'm going to write to Elsie again. [*Bob gives him the book and pencil. Dick begins to write, after counting the chalk marks on the wall. Slowly as he writes.*] Friday—the fifth day. . . . Water now finished—keeping a drop for Joe . . . Billie sleeps—Joe very weak. . . . Last lamp now burning. . . . Still—hoping. . . . Don't worry. . . . Good night, Elsie. . . . Kiss the kids for me. [*Overcome.*] Oh! merciful Christ!

[*This outburst brings both Bob and Peter to attention, for it is the first.*

BOB. [*Quickly.*] Dick, for God's sake don't let yourself go like that! Don't let us down now.

[*Dick raises his head, and smiles.*

DICK. I 'm sorry. . . . It was the thought of the kiddies.

[*He tears the leaf from the book, and puts it in his breast-pocket. He gives Bob the book and pencil. Bob begins writing his letter.*

[*Joe opens his eyes and stares blankly round the cavern. Gradually he realizes where he is.*

JOE. Dick . . . can I have a drop o' water—water?

DICK. Sure, Joe. [*Dick goes to him with the can.*] Have you had a good sleep?

JOE. Yes . . . I don't know. . . .

[*He tries to put his hand to his head but is too weak. Dick holds the water-can to Joe's lips. Peter keeps looking at Joe in an attitude of fear. Dick lets Joe have all the water save for a drop or two which he is keeping for Billie. He returns to his seat with the can. Joe looks at Peter.*

JOE. Peter—I didn't eat your bread. [*They are all surprised at this.*] I didn't eat it . . . I put it in my box for the kids . . . and it was buried . . . buried in the fall. [*Dick and Bob exchange glances. Joe tries to laugh, but only coughs.*] Dick, I 'm done for.

DICK. No fear, Joe. You 'll live to sing a song yet on the Saturday night—eh?

JOE. Saturday—pay-day—bread—and margarine. Ha, ha!

PETER. I didn't grudge you my bread, Joe, I . . . didn't.

JOE. I 'm cold . . . cold.

[*Peter, to the surprise of Dick and Bob, feels Joe's hand.*

PETER. [*Softly.*] Cold!

[*He takes off his jacket and puts it over Joe. Dick nods his head to Bob in a well-pleased manner. There is a short pause, then Peter returns to his corner. Dick looks at the lamp.*

DICK. That lamp can't burn much longer. . . . We should put it out and save it.

BOB. No! I couldn't face the dark!

PETER. You might not get it to light again!

DICK. Well, when it does go out, we 'll know that the end *has* come.

[*Billie raises his head, opening, and rubbing his eyes. He looks all round him, then sinks down again with a little cry of hopelessness.*

DICK. [*Comforting Billie.*] You told your mother that you had been a man, Billie. . . . That 's the spirit, my lad. You 're made of the right stuff. I kept the last of the water for you, Billie. Have it now?

*L 947

BILLIE. Yes. [*He sits up and Dick lets him drain the can. The others hopelessly watch it go down.*] Anybody been here, Dick?

DICK. Not yet, Bill, but they 'll be here soon now.

BOB. [*To Billie.*] How d' you feel, Billie?

BILLIE. Okay!

BOB. You 're a great little fellow.

BILLIE. You won't give me the sack now, Bob?
[*He smiles, having now no fear of the gaffer.*

BOB. I 'll never give any one the sack now, Billie—I 'm through with gaffering. [*Billie looks up at the lamp suddenly. All look.*

BILLIE. That lamp 's going down!
[*It is flickering slightly. All stare at it tragically. There is a profound silence.*

JOE. [*Very quietly.*] Three hundred quid. And I thought I was only worth a few shillings. Ha!

BILLIE. [*Looking at Joe half in fear.*] What 's wrong with Joe, Dick?

DICK. Just dreaming, Billie.

BILLIE. But his eyes are open—look!

DICK. [*To take Billie's attention off Joe.*] Shall we have another little sing-song—eh! . . . What 'll we sing this time? . . . Our favourite again. . . . One—two: [*Sings.*]
        'Speed, bonnie boat, like a bird on the wing,
            Onward, the sailors cry,
        Carry the lad that 's born to be king,
            Over the sea to Skye.'
[*Billie joins Joe, then Bob, then Peter. It is a terrible struggle for them to sing, and the tune is just recognizable but no more. They are all affected by it, as they feel that it is the last song that will ever come from their lips.*
[*They are near the end of the verse when Dick stops suddenly and listens. The others do the same.*

DICK. Listen [*Dick lifts a piece of stone from the floor and taps with it steadily for a few moments on the rock bottom.*] Listen!
[*They put their ears to the floor. Through the stillness we can hear a very faint tapping away somewhere in the distance. Dick rises first.*] It 's the rescue party—we 're saved! We 're saved! [*They just look at each other in dumb amazement.*

BILLIE. Mother! Mother!

DICK. Sing like hell! . . . They *must* hear us! . . . Sing! . . . Sing!
[*A superhuman strength possesses them now. They sing quite loudly, looking left. Dick stops and holds his hands for silence. They listen breathlessly. Far away we can hear the rescue party*

singing the same song.] They 've heard us! Shout!... Hooray!
. . . Hooray! [*They all shout with the exception of Joe who is
still motionless.*] Elsie!... Elsie!... We 're saved.... [*Over-
come with the excitement he shakes Joe to waken him.*] Joe!...
Joe! . . . They 're here at last. . . . They 're quite near!
. . . They 've heard us!... We 're . . . [*He stops suddenly.*]
My God!

    [*Bob, Dick, and Peter exchange glances. Billie is puzzled.*
DICK [*To keep the truth from Billie.*] We 'll just let him sleep,
  Bob.
BOB. All right.
    [*There is a pause, then Dick removes his cap. Bob follows
    suit, then Peter. Billie watches them and does likewise.
    The lamp flickers more now and will soon be out. In the
    distance we can hear the tapping of the rescuers, still
    singing the song.*

THE CURTAIN FALLS SLOWLY

WE GOT RHYTHM

A SOCIO-ILLOGICAL EXTRAVAGANZA

Nora Ratcliff

First performed in November 1936 *by the Old Crescenters'*
Dramatic Society, with the following cast :

BUFFER GIRLS [1] .   .   *Josephine Hill*
                                Margery Coldwell
MINERS   .   .   .   *Louis Franks*
                               Alec Blakemore
PATRIOTISM .   .   .   *Annie Aizlewood*
IDEALIST, who is also
THE AUTHOR   .   .   . *Hugh Cotton*

Political Figures :

CASSOCK   .   .   . *Kenneth Rawlings*
STRIPED-SHIRT   .   .   *Thomas Kelly*
MILI-CLUBMAN   .   .   *Howard Wild*
RED-SHIRT .   .   .   *Dora Ballance*

SCENE. *Our own environment*

TIME. *A General Election*

[1] Women who polish silver plate on revolving padded wheels.

WE GOT RHYTHM

The scene should be played to plain, dark curtains, with openings at the back and at the four corners. Centre, close to footlights, are four red-plush seats, close together in a row, as at the cinema. There are no other properties or furniture on the stage except four small, upturned tubs (to be described later), one at each corner. When the curtain goes up there are four people on the stage.

Centre, and sufficiently to right not to be masked by the seats, are two Buffer Girls. Similarly, to left are two Miners at work. All movements are mimed. The Buffer Girls wear dirty masks, red turban-like handkerchiefs on their heads, and white, dirty overalls. They sway very slightly backwards and forwards as they stand, as if pressing the spoon, fork, etc., against the spinning buffer wheel.

Of the Miners, who are also wearing blackened masks and are dressed in singlets and old trousers, one is crouching back on his heels, as if at work with a pick at the coal-face; the other, standing a little up-stage of him, is shovelling dirt.

The change of masks, etc., can lie at the feet of each player.

The 'incidental music' is important : Mossolov's Steel Foundry. *Prokofiev,* Loves of the Three Oranges, *Scherzo and March.* Creole Love Call, *recorded by The Comedy Harmonists.*

Steel Foundry *starts before the curtain rises and fades out as the Buffer Girls begin to speak.*

BUFFER GIRLS:
LIZZIE. It's Friday to-morrow.
ANNIE. It's Thursday to-day.
LIZZIE. It's three weeks to Easter.
ANNIE. And Whitsun's in May.
LIZZIE. It's Easter in three weeks.
ANNIE. And Thursday to-day.
LIZZIE. To-morrow 'll be Friday
ANNIE. And Whitsun's in May.
BOTH. [*Singing.*] 'The music goes 'round an' around. . . .'

317

MINERS:

BILL. Gosh, I 'm stiff wi' three months' laking![1]

CHARLIE. T' referee were scared to warn 'im.

BILL. Soon be time for setting taties.

CHARLIE. Didn't ought t' a' gi'en that penalty.

BILL. Time for setting taties nearly.

CHARLIE. T' referee were scared to warn 'im.

BILL. Gosh, I 'm stiff wi' three months' laking!

CHARLIE. Didn't ought t' a' gi'en that penalty.

BOTH. [*Sing.*] 'Little man, you 've had a busy day. . . .'

ANNIE. Down to her ankles, with frills at the waist——

LIZZIE. 'So that 's what you takes me for,' I says to 'im.

ANNIE. Real ones is locked up; what she 's wearing is paste.

LIZZIE. So I give 'im a look—an' that finished off Jim.

ANNIE. Real ones is locked up; what she 's wearing is paste.

LIZZIE. 'So that 's what you takes me for,' I says to 'im.

ANNIE. Down to her ankles, with frills at the waist——

LIZZIE. So I give 'im a look—an' that finished off Jim.

BOTH. [*Sing.*] '. . . music goes 'round an' around. . . .'

CHARLIE. Never get a smell at Wembley!

BILL. Pictures is all right i' winter.

CHARLIE. Cost ten thousand for 'is transfer.

BILL. Hiking with her every Sunday.

CHARLIE. Cool ten thousand for 'is transfer.

BILL. Winter we go off to t' pictures.

CHARLIE. Never get a smell at Wembley.

BILL. Hiking with her every Sunday.

BOTH. [*Sing.*] 'Little man, you 've had a busy day. . . .'

> [*Over this bring up* Steel Foundry. *Hooter blows. Everything stops. Buffer Girls pull off their red headgear, change their dirty masks for clean pink-and-white simpering ones. They pull on little berets; remove dirty pinafores and tie bright silk scarves round their necks. Miners change masks; put on coats, white scarves, and caps. During this change the following dialogue—first Girls, then Miners, then both together until they are ready.*

ANNIE. Is it Charlie to-night?

LIZZIE. Yes, it 's Charlie to-night.   Are you going with Bill?

ANNIE. Yes, I 'm going with Bill.   Is it Charlie to-night. . . .

> [*When they have finished changing they turn to audience and mime the use of lipstick and powder.*

BILL. Lizzie?

---

[1] Playing; not at work.

CHARLIE. Ay. Annie?
BILL. Ay.
CHARLIE. Be'ave yersen!
BILL. Be good!
[*Bring up* Scherzo *as couples move round and meet back-stage. Music faint during dialogue.*
BILL. Well, Annie.
CHARLIE. Well, Lizzie.
LIZZIE. Well, Charlie.
ANNIE. Well, Bill.
[*They move to the four red seats, centre, and sit with arms round each other, each girl's head on her man's shoulder; their eyes glued to the imaginary screen in the auditorium. Fade off* Scherzo *to* Creole Love Call *during next dialogue, and keep under.*
LIZZIE. Isn't she sweet!
ANNIE. I think *he* 's loverly!
BILL. [*Looking at Lizzie.*] Can't afford to buy her chocolates.
CHARLIE. [*Looking at Annie.*] Wonder if she 'd let me kiss her.
LIZZIE. Always cry at Greta Garbo.
ANNIE. Can't see why Mae West 's so famous.
BILL. Fall asleep if I don't watch it.
CHARLIE. Risk it when the lights go down.
LIZZIE. Always cry at Greta Garbo.
CHARLIE. Wonder if she 'd let me kiss her.
ANNIE. Can't see why Mae West 's so famous.
BILL. Can't afford to buy her chocolates.
CHARLIE. Risk it when the lights go down.
BILL. Fall asleep if I don't watch it.
ANNIE. Isn't he loverly!
LIZZIE. Isn't she sweet!
[*Their voices have grown slower and heavier. They now sit closely embraced, the girls with their eyes still on the screen, the men, eyes closed and heads on the girls' shoulders. Bring up to full* Creole Love Call *and fade out lights. Long whistle of hooter, followed by* Foundry. *Lights up. All are back in original places. They have changed masks, etc. When ready, fade out under.*
LIZZIE. It 's Friday to-morrow.
ANNIE. It 's Thursday to-day.
LIZZIE. It 's three weeks to Easter.
ANNIE. And Whitsun 's in May.
BOTH. [*Singing.*] 'An' the music goes 'round an' around. . . .'

BILL. Gosh, I 'm stiff wi' three months' laking!
CHARLIE. T' referee were scared to warn 'im.
BILL. Soop be time for setting taties.
CHARLIE. Didn't ought t' a' gi'en that penalty.
BOTH. [*Singing.*] 'Little man, you 've had a busy day. . . .'
LIZZIE. It 's Friday to-morrow.
BILL. Gosh, I 'm stiff wi' three months' laking!
ANNIE. Down to her ankles, with frills at the waist——
CHARLIE. Never get a smell at Wembley.
LIZZIE. 'So that 's what you takes me for,' I says to 'im.
BILL. T' pictures is all right i' winter.
ANNIE. Real ones is locked up; what she 's wearing is paste.
CHARLIE. Cost ten thousand for 'is transfer.
BILL. Hikin' with her every Sunday.
LIZZIE. So I give him a look, an' that finished off Jim.
GIRLS AND MEN. [*Together.*]
    'An' the music goes 'round . . .'
    'Little man. . . .'
  [Foundry *up. Hooter. Repeat business of changing with
  same dialogue.*
ANNIE. Is it Charlie to-night?
LIZZIE. Yes, it 's Charlie to-night. Are you going with Bill?
BILL. Lizzie? etc.
  [Scherzo *up. As they are moving across the stage to meet as
  before, the figure of a woman appears through the opening
  at the back. She is dressed in classical costume and wears
  a mask or heavy make-up which shows a hardened,
  cynical, and prematurely aged face. She strides forward
  and arrests them with a very stagy gesture, and then
  speaks her lines in a bored perfunctory voice.*
PATRIOTISM. Stop! I am Citizenship, Civic Duty, Patriotism!
You cannot go on like this from day to day, living your own
selfish little lives. You must realize that you are parts of a
mighty whole. Great issues are at stake. In this democracy
of ours, every free citizen has not only privileges but responsi-
bilities. You cannot always take; there are times when you
are called upon to give. The cares of the nation are your
cares; the problems of the government are your problems—
and never more than when that government has got into
difficulties. [*With a prodigious yawn.*] To-day there is a great
decision to be made. It is for you to choose——
  [*She makes the gesture of the old game played with closed fists
  placed alternately one above the other.*

Handy pandy,
Sugar and candy;
Left or Right,
Peace or Fight,
Work or Dole,
Part or Whole,
Church or No Church—
Which hand will you have?

[She smiles benignly upon them and begins to back out.
Left or Right! Left or Right! I 've only two hands, you know, only two hands; so it 's quite easy to choose. Quite, quite easy!

[But before Patriotism can get away, Idealist enters from down-stage right. He is wearing a very young 'boy-scoutish' sort of mask or make-up, and is dressed in light grey flannels and a white cricket shirt open at the neck. He calls across to the disappearing figure of Patriotism.

IDEALIST. Hi! You can't go like that! You 're supposed to make an appeal to all that 's best in these people. Your job is to make them realize——

PATRIOTISM. My dear young sir, do *you* realize that this country has had manhood suffrage since 1918, and universal suffrage since 1928? And do you know how many General Elections there have been in that time? And every single time I have had to come along and say my piece. Is it surprising that I 'm getting a bit bored? It was good enough fun at the beginning, but nobody takes any notice now. Look at the women. Would you believe that less than thirty years ago they were starving themselves to death in prison; destroying His Majesty's mail; assaulting Cabinet ministers; chaining themselves to the railings outside Westminster—all because they hadn't got a vote? How many women care a brass farthing to-day what they do with their vote now they 've got it?

IDEALIST. Then it 's up to us to teach them to care. If the leaders get cynical and lose their faith in democracy where are we going to be? Where should I be if I took your disillusioned point of view?

PATRIOTISM. In Parliament, my son, right away!

IDEALIST. You 're a horrid, mocking old woman, and you ought never to have been trusted with a job like this. What do you know about the lives and hopes of these men and women? What do you know——

322 WE GOT RHYTHM

PATRIOTISM. [*In a deliberate effort to shock him.*] Aw! come off'n
it, sonny boy! You can't give me the low-down on nothin' in
this politics racket——

IDEALIST. There, you see! You can't even speak decent English,
and you call yourself Patriotism, and loaf around ready to sell
yourself to the highest bidder. What sort of a woman are
you to try to inspire the workers?

PATRIOTISM. You take my tip, sonny, and run off home
to mammy, or I predict that there 's going to be a big
disappointment coming to you. Inspire 'em, did you say?
Look!

[*She points to the workers, who are walking round in pairs
examining four figures that have appeared on the little
tubs, one at each corner. Down-stage right, on a purple
tub, is a figure wearing a purple cassock and clerical
bands, with a black biretta. Up-stage right, on a red tub
with gilt bands, is a military-looking figure. He wears a
blazer with large crest on the pocket; his striped tie is
wound once round his neck, the broad ends left hanging
down; huge gilt-tasselled epaulettes stick out from his
shoulders, and he has rows of medals on his right breast.
Up-stage left, an orator in a shirt striped brown and black,
high to the neck; neat breeches and leggings and a sort of
glengarry cap. His tub, too, is striped brown and black.
Down-stage left, on a bright red tub, a hatless, heavily bearded
figure in a Russian worker's blouse, red trousers, and top
boots. Patriotism and Idealist watch the workers as they
gape their way round the stage.*

PATRIOTISM. Can you see anything there that 's ready for
inspiration?

IDEALIST. Yes, I can! And so could you, you miserable old
hag, if you would only try to see it.

PATRIOTISM. [*Sulkily.*] There you go again! That 's the second
time you 've called me names. Let me tell you, young fellow-
me-lad, some of the greatest figures in our island story have
courted my favours. Why, not so very long ago there was
that fine old Englishman—what d 'ye call him? ... h'm—ah,
yes! Disraeli his name was—I remember him saying to me,
'Patty,' he said—he always called me Patty in private;
showed such nice feeling, I think—'Patty,' he said, 'if it
hadn't been for you——'

IDEALIST. I don't care what he said to you, or what Gladstone,
Lloyd George, the Elder and Younger Pitts, Thomas Becket,

Warwick the Kingmaker, or anybody else ever said to you! You 're past your job now——

PATRIOTISM. You think so, because you 've got a wrong idea of what my job really is. It 's interfering young fools like you that cause all the trouble. But if you think you can do the job better than I can, you 're welcome to it! If you think that with your golden voice and your pink-and-white cheeks you 're going to manage things better than me, with all my years of experience and resource, get on with it! Get *on* with it, I say!

IDEALIST. By Jove, and I 'm going to, too! Look at them! Here they come, like hungry sheep! If you 're not going to help, you can clear out! Your sickly emotional appeal was done for the minute you stopped believing in it yourself. You don't believe a word of what you said just now; so how can you expect them to believe? But I, I do believe in something. I believe in common sense. I believe that if you appeal to that common sense instead of to herd emotions, you can stir these people. I believe that every man is a thinking man; that he loves his home and his country——

PATRIOTISM. Young man, my heart bleeds for you! What a shock you 'll get when you wake up!

IDEALIST. It 's nothing to the shock that you and your like will get when the country wakes up and sends the lot of you packing. And I 'm going to help to wake up the country. I 'm going to show these people——

PATRIOTISM. [*Yawning.*] Well, well, I guess I 'll be off and snatch a spot of sleep before I 'm wanted in the Victory Processions. It 's very trying—whichever party wins, I 'm always called in as figure-head. That 's why my election speeches have always to be so vague. Mustn't ever commit myself.

[*She is just disappearing when she remembers that her exit should be dignified.*

PATRIOTISM. [*Returning.*] Once more, men and women patriots, the fate of the nation is in your hands. Once more Democracy is called upon to speak.

> Handy, pandy,
> Sugar and candy,
> Left or Right,
> Peace or Fight,
> Work or Dole,

Part or Whole,
Church or No Church—
WHICH HAND WILL YOU HAVE?
[*She disappears through opening at the back. The four
workers, who have been standing centre and watching,
cheer her as she goes. Then they turn to one another.*
ANNIE. What 's she mean?
BILL. We 've got to vote.
LIZZIE. Who 's got to vote?
CHARLIE. We 've got to vote!
ANNIE. I 've got a vote!
BILL. You 've got a vote!
ALL. All God's chil'un got votes! Hurray!
[*They take hands and dance round to* Scherzo. *Fade this
quickly under.*
IDEALIST. Friends, comrades, and fellow-countrymen——
ANNIE. [*As they stop dancing, to Bill.*] Eh, what 's yon chap
hawking?
LIZZIE. [*Pulling at Charlie.*] Come on and listen. It 's free!
IDEALIST. [*As soon as he sees they are listening, he drops his voice
to a note of reason and gentle persuasion.*] Friends, you have all
of you heard that you are called upon to make a momentous
decision for the future of your country. Within the next few
weeks you will be listening to many speakers; each will suggest
a different solution to the problems with which this country is
faced. Now I am not speaking on behalf of any of these
parties. I stand here in the cause of humanity and common
sense——
ANNIE. [*To Lizzie.*] Hasn't he got kind eyes?
BILL. [*To Charlie.*] I reckon he does this when he gets tired of
kissing the babies!
IDEALIST. I have come here to help you to think it all out for
yourselves. I have come to impress upon you the full significance of the privilege that you enjoy——
CHARLIE. Who 've we got to vote for?
BILL. Tell us who to vote for!
LIZZIE. What have we got a vote for?
ANNIE. Can I vote for you?
IDEALIST. No, no! You mustn't run blindly after any one.
Neither me nor any one else. I cannot tell you whom to
vote for. I wouldn't if I could. All I can do is to urge you
not to let slip this chance of helping to build a new nation on
the ashes of the old. Oh, friends, if I could but fill you with

half my zeal, half my courage, half my determination to build
Jerusalem—a new Jerusalem——
    [*The workers have wandered off. They are gazing, like
    children into a shop window, at the doll-like figures on the
    tubs.*
IDEALIST. [*Calling after them appealingly.*] Oh, I beg of you,
before you listen to them; before their professional jargon and
clap-trap has dulled your ears to the truth; before their
trumpet-blowing and shouting has drowned the still small
voice of reason——
    [*But the election campaign has started. Each figure raises a
    trumpet to his lips and all four blow a deafening discor-
    dant blast. During the next scene Idealist moves round
    to each tub in turn and whispers into the ear of a worker
    who is listening. Cassock, down-stage right, speaks first.
    The workers rush over and form a group to listen. The
    politicians not immediately concerned keep perfectly still
    in stiff, appropriate attitudes.*
CASSOCK.   Our Platform's sure foundation
        Is do as you are told;
        Rejoice in tribulation,
            Disease, starvation, cold;
        Believe in all that 's beautiful,
            And sweet, and good, and kind;
        And never be undutiful—
            The blind should lead the blind.
                [*Idealist whispers into Annie's ear.*
        We are the chosen nation,
            Our Empire covers earth——
ANNIE. What I want to know——
CASSOCK. In this Vale of Tears we cannot know—we can only
believe. Ask then no foolish questions, you 'll get no foolish
lies——
    [*Striped-Shirt interrupts with a trumpet blast. Cassock stands
    still. Workers dash up-stage left to listen to Striped-
    Shirt.*
STRIPED-SHIRT. [*With barking gusto.*]
    We 'll save the Country!   We know how!
(Come and cheer your Leader till the cows come home!)
    You don't have to think, all you 're here for is to do——
(Cheer, cheer our leader till the cows come home!)
    The State is your Father and your Mother, too!
(Come and cheer like Hades till the cows come home!)

March and wave your little flags and make a grand to-do·
  Keep the race untainted; out with the bloody Jew! [1]
  Muscle in on Leadership! Join the bally-hoo!
  Shut both eye and ear—ready for the cheer!
  Cheer and crow like bantam cocks—your LEADER's coming
    home!!
BILL. [*After Idealist has whispered.*] That sounds all right,
  but——
STRIPED-SHIRT. [*Jumping up and down in a fury.*]
  How dare you question me, Sir?
  Do you know who I am, Sir?
  Didn't I tell you, you mustn't think, you shouldn't think,
  You shan't think—you CAN'T THINK!
    *He maintains suitable pose. Mili-Clubman blows his
    trumpet. Workers rush across.*
MILI-CLUBMAN. [*Up-stage right, with a jovial after-dinner accent.*]
  We 're the leaders of the Team, me boys,
    Who beam, me boys,
  On the boys marching home again, hurrah!

    As steadily, boulder by boulder,
    Steadily, shade by shade,
  We 've built up a wall that you can't see over—
  No rude wind shall blast Tradition's flower!

  We 've got guns—but not for fighting.
  We 've got gunpowder—but not for lighting!
  We want peace! We 've always wanted peace!
  We never want to fight—but, by Jingo! when we do——
      Why, gad, sir, ay, sir,
      We 'll stand by, sir!

  And you 'll find that Nature's Gentleman
  Will always wear the Right School Tie!

CHARLIE. [*Prompted by Idealist.*]
      How 'll that be
      For chaps like me?
MILI-CLUBMAN. [*Fussing with his papers.*]
      I 'd convince you in a moment
      If I hadn't lost my notes.
      There 's an 1880 comment
    [1] Alternative line: 'The country is for *you*.'

That makes certain of the votes!
[*He becomes motionless as Red-Shirt blows his trumpet.*
Workers rush down-stage left.

RED-SHIRT. Listen to the Great Chief Red-Shirt!
Hearken how he built his wigwam—
Working through the year of winter;
Working daytime, working night-time—
Autumn, winter, spring, and summer!
Never is he tired of working.
For he is no longer toiling
For a bourgeoisie exacting,
Slaves no longer are the Workers—
Solidarity triumphant!
Deviation crushed and conquered!
We the skilled ones, we the craft-wise,
Everything technique deciding.
From each man as he is able,
To each man as he has need!
Compromise is not permitted;
Revolution is the secret!
Marx and Lenin—tempo, tempo!
Workers of the World—UNITE!

LIZZIE. [*Pushing away Idealist when he tries to whisper.*] Here,
not so fast! I can't keep up with you.

RED-SHIRT. The same old cry! The same old why!
You can't keep up!
Concentration—tempo, tempo!
Listen to the Great Chief Red-Shirt——

LIZZIE. You said that before!

RED-SHIRT. Yes, and once again I'll say it,
Shout it over every nation!
Listen how the Great Chief Red-Shirt——

[*Each politician begins to chant his formula, gradually rising
to a climax.*

CASSOCK. The blind shall lead the blind!

MILI-CLUBMAN. The Right School Tie!

STRIPED-SHIRT. Your leader's coming home!

RED-SHIRT. Workers of the world, unite!

*Workers circle back-to-back in centre of stage, spinning off
one by one : Annie to Cassock ; Charlie to Mili-Clubman ;
Lizzie to Red-Shirt ; Bill to Striped-Shirt.*

*Each politician hands a large cardboard voting-paper to his
listener. Idealist has withdrawn to centre back and is*

watching anxiously. When they have their voting cards,
and the politicians have given their final shout, the
workers run together to stage centre, shouting.

ANNIE. I 've got a vote!

LIZZIE. You 've got a vote!

BILL. All true citizens has votes!

CHARLIE. Every one has promised us heaven, an' we 're going
there!

> [*Suddenly silent, they march to the back of the stage (Prokofiev:*
> *March) and stand in a line, ready to choose. Each one*
> *starts by pointing to the figure he has been listening to.*
> *Lizzie and Charlie work anti-clockwise. Annie and*
> *Bill work clockwise.*

ALL. [*Pointing to each figure in turn.*]

> Eena, meena, mina, mo!
> If you understand or no,
> Mark your paper, just like so!
> Eena—meena—mina—MO!

> [*They mark their cards and march importantly to hand them*
> *in. Their counting will have brought each to the opposite*
> *side from the man he listened to.*

ALL. [*As they dash back and prance round in a ring to* Scherzo.]
Hurray! ! ! !

> [*Idealist, after a gesture of hopeless despair, has gone out*
> *centre back. Figures step down from tubs and each dis-*
> *appears into his own corner. Hooter breaks in on the*
> *dance. Black out.* Steel Foundry *up. Workers return*
> *to places as at beginning.*

LIZZIE. It 's Friday to-morrow.

ANNIE. It 's Thursday to-day.

LIZZIE. It 's three weeks to Easter.

ANNIE. And Whitsun 's in May.

BOTH. [*Singing.*] ' . . . an' the music goes 'round an' around. . . .'

BILL. Gosh, I'm stiff wi' three months' laking.

CHARLIE. T' referee were scared to warn 'im.

BILL. Soon be time for setting taties.

CHARLIE. Didn't ought t' a' gi'en that penalty.

BOTH. [*Singing.*] 'Little man, you 've had a busy day. . . .'

ANNIE. Down to her ankles, with frills at——

> [*Author walks on. It is the Idealist, but he has taken off his*
> *mask or make-up and pulled a grey sweater over his*
> *cricket shirt. In contrast to his mask, his face looks thin*
> *and tired.*

AUTHOR. O.K.! That 'll do, everybody. That scene should go all right now. [*Flat white lighting comes up.*

CHARLIE. [*Removing mask and coming down.*] I don't feel that we 've got it at all, you know. But then, I never was much use in comedy. Especially hopelessly light stuff like this.

AUTHOR. Comedy?

CHARLIE. Yes, you know—all this daft umptyiddy, rumpty-doody sort of poetry—verse, I mean.

AUTHOR. Comedy!

CHARLIE. M-mm. Cheer up, old chap! We can't all be Shakespeares. The stuff 's good enough, I dare say—in its own line. But I 've always been trained to take politics seriously——

BILL. [*Also unmasked.*] Nobody expects an artist to understand politics. All he looks for is something to hang a sort of song and dance on to, eh?

LIZZIE. [*Unmasked.*] By the way, talking of dancing, couldn't we put in a bit of the real stuff, instead of bouncing about like a lot of kids at a Sunday School treat? I mean after we 've handed in the voting papers. Work it up, you know—something like this—

[*She hums music and starts to improvise some 'tap' work.*

BILL. I get you, kid! Great idea! Come on!

[*He joins her. They begin to enjoy themselves.*

ANNIE. That 's giving your show a spot of 'ginger,' Mr Author. Come on, Charlie, we 're only short of a crooner! Won't you oblige?

CHARLIE. Not for me, thank you. It isn't my line. I 'm only in this light stuff for a rest——

ANNIE. Oh, come off it! You say that piece six times a day—before and after meals. I don't blame anybody for getting a laugh out of politics. It 's all rot, anyhow. And as for the vote—I 'd sell mine any day for a first-class dinner or a fur coat.

CHARLIE. Women have no moral standards.

ANNIE. Sez you! When are you paying me back that ten quid you borrowed for the day a month ago?

CHARLIE. [*Slapping Author on the back.*] Why so pale and wan? Come and have lunch with me.

AUTHOR. No, thanks.

CHARLIE. Oh, come, don't get sore over what I said. Truth is, I don't like to see a man like you wasting himself. There 's something more than this stuff in you. One of these days we'll have a heart-to-heart talk, and I'll teach you to take politics seriously. Well, so long. [*Pausing on the way out.*] Art for art's sake cuts no ice in a world like ours. Cheery-bye, everybody!

[*Charlie is nearly out when author calls him back.*

AUTHOR. [*A queer, grim smile on his face.*] Come back. I've changed my mind. You can't go—I haven't finished. Get your masks on, all of you—and jump to it!

CHARLIE. Here, I say, what's got you, old man?

AUTHOR. Never mind what's got me. It's what's going to get you!

BILL. But look here, I'm due at——

AUTHOR. You're *here*—and *now*!

ANNIE. We needn't bother with masks, need we?

AUTHOR. You'll bother with everything. That's what you're here for—to learn to bother! Get those masks on! [*Shouting.*] Behind, there! Stand by, will you?

VOICE [*off*]. O.K., sir!

AUTHOR. Lights!

VOICE. O.K.!

AUTHOR. [*When the actors are masked and waiting.*] Now listen, you waps! You're a crew of damned galley-slaves, chained to your job, do you hear? Chained! Chained by your own stupidity—though it's not your own fault, poor devils! [*The stage is darker than it has ever been. A lurid light is concentrated on the ' actors.'*] The only reason you can stand right end up is because you've got empty celluloid heads and clay feet; so you couldn't stop any other way if you tried. What's your precious life made up of? There are twenty-four hours in a day. You're chained to your galley benches for eight of them. You're chained to your bellies for three or four more. You're let out for a run, and you crawl to a celluloid dram-shop and tie yourselves up there, chained to simpering shadows and canned emotionalism for another three hours. What there is left—you sleep, and then crawl back to your benches again! Toot-toot! go the hooters, and you trot like a dog to a kennel! Bang-flop! Bang-flop! Whir-whir! go your looms, your wheels, your dynamos, and your shafting belts; battering your brains to pulp and keeping every nerve in your body on the jerk! . . . Now have you got me? Now do you know what this damned show's all about? Come on, then, with the comic stuff! I'll count the laughs! Are you ready? The whole screaming farce to the bitter, peevish end! Fire away, then! CURTAIN—UP!

[*Steel Foundry starts again, very loud. Author sprawls along the cinema seats, his arms spread-eagled over the backs, his back to the audience, watching the actors. The play starts again, at a greater speed and with an exaggerated intensity.*

ANNIE. It's Friday to-morrow——

[*Etc., etc., as opening.*

[*When the men begin to speak Author starts to laugh. His laughter is echoed, in crescendo, by cynical, high-pitched cackle off-stage.*

Whilst the girls are shouting their second set of lines

THE CURTAIN SLOWLY FALLS

THE DREAMING OF THE BONES

W. B. YEATS

CHARACTERS

THREE MUSICIANS (*their faces made up to resemble masks*)
A YOUNG MAN
A STRANGER (*wearing a mask*)
A YOUNG GIRL (*wearing a mask*)

Time: 1916

NOTE ON THE UNFOLDING OF THE CLOTH

The First Musician carries with him a folded black cloth and goes to the centre of the stage towards the front and stands motionless, the folded cloth hanging from between his hands. The two other Musicians enter and, after standing a moment at either side of the stage, go towards him and slowly unfold the cloth, singing as they do so and going backward a little so that the stretched cloth and the wall make a triangle with the First Musician at the apex supporting the centre of the cloth. The Second and Third Musicians now slowly fold up the cloth again.

THE DREAMING OF THE BONES

The stage is any bare place in a room close to the wall.   A screen, with a pattern of mountain and sky, can stand against the wall, or a curtain with a like pattern hang upon it, but the pattern must only symbolize or suggest.   One Musician enters and then two others; the first stands singing, as in preceding note, while the others take their places.   Then all three sit down against the wall by their instruments, which are already there—a drum, a zither, and a flute.   Or they unfold a cloth as described opposite, while the instruments are carried in.

[*Song for the folding and unfolding of the cloth*]

FIRST MUSICIAN [*Or all three Musicians, singing.*]

> Why does my heart beat so?
> Did not a shadow pass?
> It passed but a moment ago.
> Who can have trod in the grass?
> What rogue is night-wandering?
> Have not old writers said
> That dizzy dreams can spring
> From the dry bones of the dead?
> And many a night it seems
> That all the valley fills
> With those fantastic dreams.
> They overflow the hills,
> So passionate is a shade,
> Like wine that fills to the top
> A grey-green cup of jade,
> Or maybe an agate cup.

[*The three Musicians are now seated by the drum, flute, and zither at the back of the stage.   The First Musician speaks.*

The hour before dawn and the moon covered up;
The little village of Abbey is covered up;
The little narrow trodden way that runs
From the white road to the Abbey of Corcomroe
Is covered up; and all about the hills
Are like a circle of agate or of jade.
Somewhere among great rocks on the scarce grass

Birds cry, they cry their loneliness.
Even the sunlight can be lonely here,
Even hot noon is lonely.   I hear a footfall—
A young man with a lantern comes this way.
He seems an Aran fisher, for he wears
The flannel bawneen and the cow-hide shoe.
He stumbles wearily, and stumbling prays.
                    [*A Young Man enters, praying in Irish.*
Once more the birds cry in their loneliness,
But now they wheel about our heads; and now
They have dropped on the grey stone to the north-east.
        [*A Stranger and a Young Girl, in the costume of a past time,
          come in.   They wear heroic masks.*
YOUNG MAN [*Raising his lantern.*] Who is there?   I cannot see
        what you are like.
    Come to the light.
STRANGER.   But what have you to fear?
YOUNG MAN. And why have you come creeping through the
        dark?   [*The Girl blows out lantern.*
    The wind has blown my lantern out.   Where are you?
    I saw a pair of heads against the sky
    And lost them after; but you are in the right,
    I should not be afraid in County Clare;
    And should be, or should not be, have no choice,
    I have to put myself into your hands,
    Now that my candle's out.
STRANGER.   You have fought in Dublin?
YOUNG MAN. I was in the Post Office, and if taken
    I shall be put against a wall and shot.
STRANGER. You know some place of refuge, have some plan
    Or friend who will come to meet you?
YOUNG MAN.   I am to lie
    At daybreak on the mountain and keep watch
    Until an Aran coracle puts in
    At Muckanish or at the rocky shore
    Under Finvara, but would break my neck
    If I went stumbling there alone in the dark.
STRANGER. We know the pathways that the sheep tread out,
    And all the hiding-places of the hills,
    And that they had better hiding-places once.
YOUNG MAN. You'd say they had better before English robbers
    Cut down the trees or set them upon fire

For fear their owners might find shelter there.
What is that sound?
STRANGER.   An old horse gone astray.
He has been wandering on the road all night.
YOUNG MAN. I took him for a man and horse. Police
Are out upon the roads.   In the late Rising
I think there was no man of us but hated
To fire at soldiers who but did their duty
And were not of our race, but when a man
Is born in Ireland and of Irish stock,
When he takes part against us——
STRANGER.   I will put you safe,
No living man shall set his eyes upon you;
I will not answer for the dead.
YOUNG MAN.   The dead?
STRANGER. For certain days the stones where you must lie
Have in the hour before the break of day
Been haunted.
YOUNG MAN.   But I was not born at midnight.
STRANGER. Many a man that was born in the full daylight
Can see them plain, will pass them on the high-road
Or in the crowded market-place of the town,
And never know that they have passed.
YOUNG MAN.   My Grandam
Would have it they did penance everywhere;
Some lived through their old lives again.
STRANGER.   In a dream;
And some for an old scruple must hang spitted
Upon the swaying tops of lofty trees;
Some are consumed in fire, some withered up
By hail and sleet out of the wintry North,
And some but live through their old lives again.
YOUNG MAN. Well, let them dream into what shape they please
And fill waste mountains with the invisible tumult
Of the fantastic conscience.   I have no dread;
They cannot put me into jail or shoot me;
And seeing that their blood has returned to fields
That have grown red from drinking blood like mine,
They would not if they could betray.
STRANGER.   This pathway
Runs to the ruined Abbey of Corcomroe;
The Abbey passed, we are soon among the stone
And shall be at the ridge before the cocks

Of Aughanish or Bailevelehan
Or grey Aughtmana shake their wings and cry.
                    [*They go round the stage once.*
FIRST MUSICIAN [*Speaking.*] They've passed the shallow well and
    the flat stone
Fouled by the drinking cattle, the narrow lane
Where mourners for five centuries have carried
Noble or peasant to his burial;
An owl is crying out above their heads.
                    [*Singing.*]
        Why should the heart take fright?
        What sets it beating so?
        The bitter sweetness of the night
        Has made it but a lonely thing.
        Red bird of March, begin to crow!
        Up with the neck and clap the wing,
        Red cock, and crow!
[*They go round the stage once.   The First Musician speaks.*
And now they have climbed through the long grassy field
And passed the ragged thorn-trees and the gap
In the ancient hedge; and the tomb-nested owl
At the foot's level beats with a vague wing.
                    [*Singing.*]
        My head is in a cloud;
        I'd let the whole world go;
        My rascal heart is proud
        Remembering and remembering.
        Red bird of March, begin to crow!
        Up with the neck and clap the wing,
        Red cock, and crow!
[*They go round the stage once.   The First Musician speaks.*
They are among the stones above the ash,
Above the briar and thorn and the scarce grass;
Hidden amid the shadow far below them
The cat-headed bird is crying out.
                    [*Singing.*]
        The dreaming bones cry out
        Because the night winds blow
        And heaven's a cloudy blot.
        Calamity can have its fling.
        Red bird of March, begin to crow!
        Up with the neck and clap the wing,
        Red cock, and crow!

STRANGER. We're almost at the summit and can rest
 The road is a faint shadow there; and there
 The Abbey lies amid its broken tombs.
 In the old days we should have heard a bell
 Calling the monks before day broke to pray;
 And when the day had broken on the ridge,
 The crowing of its cocks.
YOUNG MAN.   Is there no house
 Famous for sanctity or architectural beauty
 In Clare or Kerry, or in all wide Connacht,
 The enemy has not unroofed?
STRANGER.   Close to the altar
 Broken by wind and frost and worn by time
 Donough O'Brien has a tomb, a name in Latin.
 He wore fine clothes and knew the secrets of women,
 But he rebelled against the King of Thomond
 And died in his youth.
YOUNG MAN.   And why should he rebel?
 The King of Thomond was his rightful master.
 It was men like Donough who made Ireland weak—
 My curse on all that troop, and when I die
 I'll leave my body, if I have any choice,
 Far from his ivy-tod and his owl. Have those
 Who, if your tale is true, work out a penance
 Upon the mountain-top where I am to hide,
 Come from the Abbey graveyard?
YOUNG GIRL.   They have not that luck,
 But are more lonely; those that are buried there
 Warred in the heat of the blood; if they were rebels
 Some momentary impulse made them rebels,
 Or the commandment of some petty king
 Who hated Thomond.   Being but common sinners,
 No callers-in of the alien from oversea,
 They and their enemies of Thomond's party
 Mix in a brief dream-battle above their bones;
 Or make one drove; or drift in amity;
 Or in the hurry of the heavenly round
 Forget their earthly names.   These are alone,
 Being accursed.
YOUNG MAN.   But if what seems is true
 And there are more upon the other side
 Than on this side of death, many a ghost

Must meet them face to face and pass the word
Even upon this grey and desolate hill.

YOUNG GIRL. Until this hour no ghost or living man
Has spoken, though seven centuries have run
Since they, weary of life and of men's eyes,
Flung down their bones in some forgotten place,
Being accursed.

YOUNG MAN. I have heard that there are souls
Who, having sinned after a monstrous fashion,
Take on them, being dead, a monstrous image
To drive the living, should they meet its face,
Crazy, and be a terror to the dead.

YOUNG GIRL. But these
Were comely even in their middle life
And carry, now that they are dead, the image
Of their first youth, for it was in that youth
Their sin began.

YOUNG MAN. I have heard of angry ghosts
Who wander in a wilful solitude.

YOUNG GIRL. These have no thought but love; nor any joy
But that upon the instant when their penance
Draws to its height, and when two hearts are wrung
Nearest to breaking, if hearts of shadows break,
His eyes can mix with hers; nor any pang
That is so bitter as that double glance,
Being accursed.

YOUNG MAN. But what is this strange penance—
That when their eyes have met can wring them most?

YOUNG GIRL. Though eyes can meet, their lips can never meet.

YOUNG MAN. And yet it seems they wander side by side.
But doubtless you would say that when lips meet
And have no living nerves, it is no meeting.

YOUNG GIRL. Although they have no blood, or living nerves,
Who once lay warm and live the live-long night
In one another's arms, and know their part
In life, being now but of the people of dreams,
Is a dream's part; although they are but shadows,
Hovering between a thorn-tree and a stone,
Who have heaped up night on wingèd night; although
No shade however harried and consumed
Would change his own calamity for theirs,
Their manner of life were blessed could their lips
A moment meet; but when he has bent his head

Close to her head, or hand would slip in hand,
The memory of their crime flows up between
And drives them apart.
YOUNG MAN.   The memory of a crime—
He took her from a husband's house, it may be,
But does the penance for a passionate sin
Last for so many centuries?
YOUNG GIRL.   No, no;
The man she chose, the man she was chosen by,
Cared little and cares little from whose house
They fled towards dawn amid the flights of arrows,
Or that it was a husband's and a king's;
And how, if that were all, could she lack friends,
On crowded roads or on the unpeopled hill?
Helen herself had opened wide the door
Where night by night she dreams herself awake
And gathers to her breast a dreaming man.
YOUNG MAN. What crime can stay so in the memory?
What crime can keep apart the lips of lovers
Wandering and alone?
YOUNG GIRL.   Her king and lover
Was overthrown in battle by her husband,
And for her sake and for his own, being blind
And bitter and bitterly in love, he brought
A foreign army from across the sea.
YOUNG MAN. You speak of Diarmuid and Dervorgilla
Who brought the Norman in?
YOUNG GIRL.   Yes, yes, I spoke
Of that most miserable, most accursed pair
Who sold their country into slavery; and yet
They were not wholly miserable and accursed
If somebody of their race at last would say,
'I have forgiven them.'
YOUNG MAN.   O, never, never
Shall Diarmuid and Dervorgilla be forgiven.
YOUNG GIRL. If some one of their race forgave at last
Lip would be pressed on lip.
YOUNG MAN.   O, never, never
Shall Diarmuid and Dervorgilla be forgiven.
You have told your story well, so well indeed
I could not help but fall into the mood
And for a while believe that it was true,
Or half believe; but better push on now.

The horizon to the east is growing bright.

[They go round stage once. The Musicians play.

So here we're on the summit. I can see
The Aran Islands, Connemara Hills,
And Galway in the breaking light; there too
The enemy has toppled roof and gable,
And torn the panelling from ancient rooms;
What generations of old men had known
Like their own hands, and children wondered at,
Has boiled a trooper's porridge. That town had lain,
But for the pair that you would have me pardon,
Amid its gables and its battlements
Like any old admired Italian town;
For though we have neither coal, nor iron ore,
To make us wealthy and corrupt the air,
Our country, if that crime were uncommitted,
Had been most beautiful. Why do you dance?
Why do you gaze, and with so passionate eyes,
One on the other; and then turn away,
Covering your eyes, and weave it in a dance?
Who are you? what are you? you are not natural.

YOUNG GIRL. Seven hundred years our lips have never met.

YOUNG MAN. Why do you look so strangely at one another,
So strangely and so sweetly?

YOUNG GIRL.   Seven hundred years.

YOUNG MAN. So strangely and so sweetly. All the ruin,
All, all their handiwork is blown away
As though the mountain air had blown it away
Because their eyes have met. They cannot hear,
Being folded up and hidden in their dance.
The dance is changing now. They have dropped their eyes,
They have covered up their eyes as though their hearts
Had suddenly been broken—never, never
Shall Diarmuid and Dervorgilla be forgiven.
They have drifted in the dance from rock to rock.
They have raised their hands as though to snatch the sleep
That lingers always in the abyss of the sky
Though they can never reach it. A cloud floats up
And covers all the mountain-head in a moment;
And now it lifts and they are swept away.

[The Stranger and the Young Girl go out.

I had almost yielded and forgiven it all—
Terrible the temptation and the place!

[*The Musicians begin unfolding and folding a black cloth.
The First Musician comes forward to the front of the
stage, at the centre. He holds the cloth before him. The
other two come one on either side and unfold it. They
afterwards fold it up in the same way. While it is
unfolded, the Young Man leaves the stage.*]

[*Songs for the unfolding and folding of the cloth*]

THE MUSICIANS [*Singing.*]

I

At the grey round of the hill
Music of a lost kingdom
Runs, runs and is suddenly still.
The winds out of Clare-Galway
Carry it: suddenly it is still.

I have heard in the night air
A wandering airy music;
And moidered in that snare
A man is lost of a sudden,
In that sweet wandering snare.

What finger first began
Music of a lost kingdom?
They dream that laughed in the sun.
Dry bones that dream are bitter,
They dream and darken our sun.

Those crazy fingers play
A wandering airy music;
Our luck is withered away,
And wheat in the wheat-ear withered,
And the wind blows it away.

II

My heart ran wild when it heard
The curlew cry before dawn
And the eddying cat-headed bird;
But now the night is gone.
I have heard from far below
The strong March birds a-crow.
Stretch neck and clap the wing,
Red cocks, and crow!

THE END

SWEENEY AGONISTES

Fragments of an Aristophanic Melodrama

T. S. ELIOT

Orestes: You don't see them, you don't—but *I* see them: they are hunting me down, I must move on.

Choephoroi.

Hence the soul cannot be possessed of the divine union, until it has divested itself of the love of created beings.

St John of the Cross.

CHARACTERS

Dusty
Doris
Sam Wanchope
Horsfall
Klipstein
Krumpacker
Sweeney
Swarts
Snow

No performance of this play may be given without a licence from
The League of Dramatists, 84 Drayton Gardens, London, S.W.10,
from whom all information about fees can be obtained.

The author wishes to point out that *Sweeney Agonistes* is not a one-act play and was never designed as such. It consists of two fragments. But as the author has abandoned any intention of completing them, these two fragmentary scenes have frequently been produced as a one-act play.

SWEENEY AGONISTES

Fragment of a Prologue

Dusty. Doris.

DUSTY. How about Pereira?

DORIS.   What about Pereira?
I don't care.

DUSTY.   You don't care!
Who pays the rent?

DORIS.   Yes he pays the rent

DUSTY. Well some men don't and some men do
Some men don't and you know who

DORIS. You can have Pereira

DUSTY.   What about Pereira?

DORIS. He's no gentleman, Pereira:
You can't trust him!

DUSTY.   Well that's true.
He's no gentleman if you can't trust him
And *if* you can't trust him—
Then you never know what he's going to do.

DORIS. No it wouldn't do to be too nice to Pereira.

DUSTY. Now Sam's a gentleman through and through.

DORIS. I like Sam

DUSTY.   *I* like Sam
Yes and Sam's a nice boy too.
He's a funny fellow

DORIS.   He *is* a funny fellow
He's like a fellow once I knew.
He could make you laugh.

DUSTY.   Sam can make you laugh:
Sam's all right

DORIS.   But Pereira won't do.
We can't have Pereira

DUSTY.   Well what you going to do?

TELEPHONE. Ting a ling ling
Ting a ling ling

DUSTY.   That's Pereira

DORIS. Yes that's Pereira

DUSTY.   Well what you going to do?

TELEPHONE. Ting a ling ling
　　Ting a ling ling
DUSTY.　　　　　　That's Pereira
DORIS. Well can't you stop that horrible noise?
　　Pick up the receiver
DUSTY.　　　　　　What'll I say!
DORIS. Say what you like: say I'm ill,
　　Say I broke my leg on the stairs
　　Say we've had a fire
DUSTY.　　　　　　Hallo Hallo are you there?
　　Yes this is Miss Dorrance's *flat*—
　　Oh Mr Pereira is that you? how do you do!
　　Oh I'm *so* sorry. I *am* so sorry
　　But Doris came home with a terrible chill
　　No, just a chill
　　Oh I *think* it's only a chill
　　Yes indeed I hope so too—
　　Well I *hope* we shan't have to call a doctor
　　Doris just hates having a doctor
　　She says will you ring up on Monday
　　She hopes to be all right on Monday
　　I say do you mind if I ring off now
　　She's got her feet in mustard and water
　　I said I'm giving her mustard and water
　　All right, Monday you'll phone through.
　　Yes I'll tell her. Good-bye. Goooood-bye.
　　I'm sure, that's very kind of *you*.
　　　　　　　　Ah-h-h
DORIS. Now I'm going to cut the cards for to-night.
　　Oh guess what the first is.
DUSTY.　　　　　　First is. What is?
DORIS. The King of Clubs
DUSTY.　　　　　　That's Pereira
DORIS. It might be Sweeney
DUSTY.　　　　　　It's Pereira
DORIS. It might *just* as well be Sweeney
DUSTY. Well anyway it's very queer.
DORIS. Here's the four of diamonds, what's that mean?
DUSTY. [*Reading.*] 'A small sum of money, or a present
　　Of wearing apparel, or a party.'
　　That's queer too.

DORIS. Here's the three. What's that mean?
DUSTY. 'News of an absent friend.'—Pereira!
DORIS. The Queen of Hearts!—Mrs Porter!
DUSTY. Or it might be you
DORIS.   Or it might be you
We're all hearts. You can't be sure.
It just depends on what comes next.
You've got to *think* when you read the cards,
It's not a thing that any one can do.
DUSTY. Yes I know you've a touch with the cards
What comes next?
DORIS.   What comes next. It's the six.
DUSTY. 'A quarrel. An estrangement. Separation of friends.'
DORIS. Here's the two of spades.
DUSTY.   The *two* of *spades*!
THAT'S THE COFFIN!!
DORIS.   THAT'S THE COFFIN?
Oh good heavens what'll I do?
Just before a party too!
DUSTY. Well it needn't be yours, it may mean a friend.
DORIS. No it's mine. I'm sure it's mine.
I dreamt of weddings all last night.
Yes it's mine. I know it's mine.
Oh good heavens what'll I do.
Well I'm not going to draw any more,
You cut for luck. You cut for luck.
It might break the spell. You cut for luck.
DUSTY. The Knave of Spades.
DORIS.   That'll be Snow
DUSTY. Or it might be Swarts
DORIS.   Or it might be Snow
DUSTY. It's a funny thing how I draw court cards—
DORIS. There's a lot in the way you pick them up
DUSTY. There's an awful lot in the way you feel
DORIS. Sometimes they'll tell you nothing at all
DUSTY. You've got to know what you want to ask them
DORIS. You've got to know what you want to know
DUSTY. It's no use asking them too much
DORIS. It's no use asking more than once
DUSTY. Sometimes they're no use at all.
DORIS. I'd like to know about that coffin.

DUSTY. Well I never!   What did I tell you?
    Wasn't I saying I always draw court cards?
    The Knave of Hearts!   [*Whistle outside of the window.*
                      Well I *never*
    What a coincidence!   Cards are queer!   [*Whistle again.*
DORIS. Is that Sam?
DUSTY. Of course it's Sam!
DORIS. Of course, the Knave of Hearts *is* Sam!
DUSTY. [*Leaning out of the window.*] Hallo Sam!
WAUCHOPE.   Hallo dear
    How many's up there?
DUSTY.   Nobody's up here
    How many's down there?
WAUCHOPE.   Four of us here.
    Wait till I put the car round the corner
    We'll be right up
DUSTY. All right, come up.
DUSTY. [*To Doris.*] Cards are queer.
DORIS. I'd like to know about that coffin.
    KNOCK KNOCK KNOCK
    KNOCK KNOCK KNOCK
    KNOCK
    KNOCK
    KNOCK

Doris.   Dusty.   Wauchope.   Horsfall.   Klipstein.   Krumpacker.

WAUCHOPE. Hallo Doris!   Hallo Dusty!   How do you do!
    How come? how come? will you permit me—
    I think you girls both know Captain Horsfall—
    We want you to meet two friends of ours,
    American gentlemen here on business.
    Meet Mr Klipstein.   Meet Mr Krumpacker.
KLIPSTEIN. How do you do
KRUMPACKER.   How do you do
KLIPSTEIN. I'm very pleased to make your acquaintance
KRUMPACKER. Extremely pleased to become acquainted
KLIPSTEIN. Sam—I should say Loot Sam Wauchope
KRUMPACKER. Of the Canadian Expeditionary Force-——
KLIPSTEIN. The Loot has told us a lot about you.
KRUMPACKER. We were all in the war together
    Klip and me and the Cap and Sam.

KLIPSTEIN. Yes we did our bit, as you folks say,
I'll tell the world we got the Hun on the run
KRUMPACKER. What about that poker game? eh what Sam?
What about that poker game in Bordeaux?
Yes Miss Dorrance you get Sam
To tell about that poker game in Bordeaux.
DUSTY. Do you know London well, Mr Krumpacker?
KLIPSTEIN. No we never been here before
KRUMPACKER. We hit this town last night for the first time
KLIPSTEIN. And I certainly hope it won't be the last time.
DORIS. You like London, Mr Klipstein?
KRUMPACKER. Do we like London? do we like London!
Do we like London!! Eh what Klip?
KLIPSTEIN. Say, Miss—er—uh—London's swell.
We like London fine.
KRUMPACKER.   Perfectly slick.
DUSTY. Why don't you come and live here then?
KLIPSTEIN. Well, no, Miss—er—you haven't quite got it
(I'm afraid I didn't quite catch your name—
But I'm very pleased to meet you all the same)—
London's a little too gay for us
Yes I'll say a little too gay.
KRUMPACKER. Yes London's a little too gay for us
Don't think I mean anything *coarse*—
But I'm afraid we couldn't stand the pace.
What about it Klip!
KLIPSTEIN.   You said it, Krum.
London's a slick place, London's a swell place,
London's a fine place to come on a visit——
KRUMPACKER. Specially when you got a real live Britisher
A guy like Sam to show you around.
Sam of course is at *home* in London,
And he's promised to show us around.

FRAGMENT OF AN AGON

Sweeney. Wauchope. Horsfall. Klipstein.
Krumpacker. Swarts. Snow. Doris. Dusty.

SWEENEY.   I'll carry you off
To a cannibal isle.

Doris. You'll be the cannibal!
Sweeney. You'll be the missionary!
  You'll be my little seven-stone missionary!
  I'll gobble you up. I'll be the cannibal.
Doris. You'll carry me off? To a cannibal isle?
Sweeney. I'll be the cannibal.
Doris.   I'll be the missionary.
  I'll convert you!
Sweeney.   I'll convert *you*!
  Into a stew.
  A nice little, white little, missionary stew.
Doris. You wouldn't eat me!
Sweeney.   Yes I'd eat you!
  In a nice little, white little, soft little, tender little,
  Juicy little, right little, missionary stew.
  You see this egg
  You see this egg
  Well that's life on a crocodile isle.
  There's no telephones
  There's no gramophones
  There's no motor-cars
  No two-seaters, no six-seaters,
  No Citroën, no Rolls-Royce.
  Nothing to eat but the fruit as it grows.
  Nothing to see but the palm-trees one way
  And the sea the other way,
  Nothing to hear but the sound of the surf.
  Nothing at all but three things
Doris.   What things?
Sweeney. Birth, and copulation, and death.
  That's all, that's all, that's all, that's all,
  Birth, and copulation, and death.
Doris. I'd be bored.
Sweeney.   You'd be bored.
  Birth, and copulation, and death.
Doris. I'd be bored.
Sweeney.   You'd be bored.
  Birth, and copulation, and death.
  That's all the facts when you come to brass tacks:
  Birth, and copulation, and death.
  I've been born, and once is enough.
  You don't remember, but I remember,
  Once is enough

Song by Wauchope and Horsfall

Swarts as Tambo.   Snow as Bones

Under the bamboo
Bamboo bamboo
Under the bamboo tree
Two live as one
One live as two
Two live as three
Under the bam
Under the boo
Under the bamboo tree.

Where the breadfruit fall
And the penguin call
And the sound is the sound of the sea
Under the bam
Under the boo
Under the bamboo tree.

Where the Gauguin maids
In the banyan shades
Wear palmleaf drapery
Under the bam
Under the boo
Under the bamboo tree.

Tell me in what part of the wood
Do you want to flirt with me?
Under the breadfruit, banyan, palmleaf
Or under the bamboo tree?
Any old tree will do for me
Any old wood is just as good
Any old isle is just my style
Any fresh egg
Any fresh egg
And the sound of the coral sea.

DORIS. I don't like eggs; I never liked eggs;
And I don't like life on your crocodile isle.

Song by Klipstein and Krumpacker

Snow and Swarts as before

My little island girl
My little island girl
I'm going to stay with you
And we won't worry what to do
We won't have to catch any trains
And we won't go home when it rains
We'll gather hibiscus flowers
For it won't be minutes but hours
For it won't be hours but years

Diminuendo
⎰ *And the morning*
⎪ *And the evening*
⎪ *And the noontime*
⎪ *And night*
⎨ *Morning*
⎪ *Evening*
⎪ *Noontime*
⎱ *Night*

DORIS. That's not life, that's no life
Why I'd just as soon be dead.
SWEENEY. That's what life is.   Just is
DORIS.   What is?
What's that life is?
SWEENEY.   Life is death.
I knew a man once did a girl in——
DORIS. Oh Mr Sweeney, please don't talk,
I cut the cards before you came
And I drew the coffin
SWARTS.   *You* drew the coffin?
DORIS. I drew the COFFIN very last card.
I don't care for such conversation
A woman runs a terrible risk.
SNOW. Let Mr Sweeney continue his story.
I assure you, Sir, we are very interested.
SWEENEY. I knew a man once did a girl in
Any man might do a girl in
Any man has to, needs to, wants to
Once in a lifetime, do a girl in.
Well he kept her there in a bath
With a gallon of lysol in a bath

SWARTS. These fellows always get pinched in the end.
SNOW. Excuse me, they don't all get pinched in the end.
  What about them bones on Epsom Heath?
  I seen that in the papers
  You seen it in the papers
  They *don't* all get pinched in the end.
DORIS. A woman runs a terrible risk.
SNOW. Let Mr Sweeney continue his story.
SWEENEY. This one didn't get pinched in the end
  But that's another story too.
  This went on for a couple of months
  Nobody came
  And nobody went
  But he took in the milk and he paid the rent.
SWARTS. What did he do?
  All that time, what did he do?
SWEENEY. What did he do! what did he do?
  That don't apply.
  Talk to live men about what they do.
  He used to come and see me sometimes
  I'd give him a drink and cheer him up.
DORIS. Cheer him up?
DUSTY.   Cheer him up?
SWEENEY. Well here again that don't apply
  But I've gotta use words when I talk to you.
  But here's what I was going to say.
  He didn't know if he was alive
                and the girl was dead
  He didn't know if the girl was alive
                and he was dead
  He didn't know if they both were alive
                or both were dead
  If he was alive then the milkman wasn't
                and the rent-collector wasn't
  And if they were alive then he was dead.
  There wasn't any joint
  There wasn't any joint
  For when you're alone
  When you're alone like he was alone
  You're either or neither
  I tell you again it don't apply
  Death or life or life or death
  Death is life and life is death

I gotta use words when I talk to you
But if you understand or if you don't
That's nothing to me and nothing to you
We all gotta do what we gotta do
We're gona sit here and drink this booze
We're gona sit here and have a tune
We're gona stay and we're gona go
And somebody's gotta pay the rent
DORIS.   I know who
SWEENEY. But that's nothing to me and nothing to you.

Full Chorus: Wauchope, Horsfall, Klipstein, Krumpacker

When you're alone in the middle of the night and you wake
    in a sweat and a hell of a fright
When you're alone in the middle of the bed and you wake like
    someone hit you on the head
You've had a cream of a nightmare dream and you've got the
    hoo-ha's coming to you.
Hoo hoo hoo
You dreamt you waked up at seven o'clock and it's foggy and
    it's damp and it's dawn and it's dark
And you wait for a knock and the turning of a lock for you know
    the hangman's waiting for you.
And perhaps you're alive
And perhaps you're dead
Hoo ha ha
Hoo ha ha
Hoo
Hoo
Hoo
KNOCK KNOCK KNOCK
KNOCK KNOCK KNOCK
KNOCK
KNOCK
KNOCK

A POUND ON DEMAND

Sean O'Casey

CHARACTERS

A GIRL, *in charge of Pimblico Sub-Post Office*
JERRY, *a working man*
SAMMY, *another*
A WOMAN
A POLICEMAN

A POUND ON DEMAND

SCENE. *A Sub-Post Office on a late autumn evening*

A Post Office. There is a counter to the right which comes out for about four yards, turning at right angles, and running to the back. That part of the counter facing front is railed, and has in the centre a small, bracketed window for selling stamps. Above the window is a card on which is the word STAMPS. *There is a swing-door in the centre at the back. To the right of the door a window having the words* POST OFFICE *on it to face towards the street. To the left is a table-ledge for the convenience of those who want to write letters, telegrams, fill in forms, or make out postal orders. Blotting-paper, quill pens, inkwells are on the ledge. Above ledge at back a telephone booth. Notices, such as, Save Saving Certificates and Saving Certificates will Save you; Buy by Telephone; Post often and Post early; Cardinal Virtues: Temperance, Prudence, Fortitude, Payment of Income Tax.*

Behind the counter, sitting on a high stool beside a desk, is a Girl, sorting and examining documents, and doing the routine work of a Post Office. Behind counter, on the left, a door. It is six o'clock or so in the evening of an autumn day; the sun is low in the sky, and his red light is flooding in through the window.

The swing-door suddenly opens and Jerry, pressing his body against the door to keep it open, while he holds Sammy, who is drunk, steady with his right hand, appears to view with an anxious and hopeful look on his face. Jerry is dressed in cement-soiled working clothes, and his trousers are bound under the knees with cords. He is about forty years of age. His friend, Sammy, is a workman too, and is dressed in the same way. Jerry wears a large tweed cap, and Sammy wears a brown trilby much the worse for wear. Sammy is in a state of maudlin drunkenness, and his reddish face is one wide, silly grin.

JERRY. [*Holding on to Sammy and calling in to the Girl.*] Yous do Post Office Savin's Bank business here, don't you, miss?

359

[*Before the Girl has time to reply, Sammy lurches away from the door, pulling Jerry with him, and the door swings shut again. The Girl looks round, but sees only the swinging door. A pause. The door opens again, and Jerry, holding Sammy with a firmer grip, appears and speaks in to the Girl.*]

JERRY. [*To the Girl.*] Savin's Bank's business's's done here, miss, isn't it?

[*Sammy lurches again, pulling Jerry with him, so that the door again swings shut. Again the Girl looks round and sees only the swinging door. She keeps her eyes on it. A pause. The door opens again and the two men appear, this time with Jerry behind Sammy, pushing him, and looking round him as he speaks in to the Girl.*]

JERRY. [*Looking round Sammy as he speaks in to the Girl.*] Savin's Bank business's's done here, isn't it, miss?

GIRL. [*Suspiciously.*] Yes.

JERRY. [*Exultantly to Sammy.*] I told you, Sammy, this is a Post Office where Savin's Bank business's's done. In we go.

SAMMY. [*Looking round vacantly.*] Where?

JERRY. In there, in here, can't you see? We're in port, Sammy —Post Office where Savin's Bank business's's done.

SAMMY. [*Vacantly.*] Where?

JERRY. [*Appealingly.*] Aw, pull yourself together, Sammy. Remember the mission we're on; don't let a fella down now. Remember what we want.

SAMMY. [*Vacantly.*] Want nothin'.

JERRY. [*Irritably.*] Try to remember, man—pound on demand— remember?

SAMMY. [*Stiffening.*] Pound on demand, wanna pound on demand.

JERRY. Why're you sayin' you want nothin', then? Don't make a fool of me when it comes to the push. You've only to sign a form—the young lady'll give it to you.

SAMMY. Sign no form; don't wanna form.

JERRY. [*Irritably.*] You can't get your pound, man, till you sign a form. That's the way they do Savin's Bank business's, see? Sign a form askin' a pound on demand, 'n hand it over to the young lady, see?

SAMMY. Wanna drink.

JERRY. You've no money for a dhrink. Can't get a dhrink till you get your pound on demand. [*Guiding Sammy over to the counter.*] Thry to keep your composure while we're doing the business.   [*The pair come to the counter.*

JERRY. [*In a wheedling way to the Girl.*] He wants a pound on demand, missie; [*to Sammy*] don't you, Sammy—a pound on demand? [*To the Girl.*] Give's the form, missie, till he pops his name down on it.

GIRL. [*To Sammy—ignoring Jerry.*] What can I do for you, sir?

SAMMY. [*Vacantly.*] Wha'?

[*A stoutish Woman of about forty comes in by the door with a minor kind of a rush, and hurries over to the counter. She stares for a moment at the two men.*

WOMAN. [*To the Girl.*] If I wrote a letter 'n posted it to catch the seven fifty-nine p.m. collection, would it get to Tarraringa-patam on Friday before twelve fifty-four in the afternoon, please?

GIRL. [*Trying to collect her wits together.*] What collection, madam?

WOMAN. [*Stiffly.*] I said the seven fifty-nine p.m. collection, I think.

JERRY. [*Impatiently.*] Gie's the little form, missie.

SAMMY. [*Drunkenly breaking into song.*] Jush a song at twilight, when the lights 're slow——

JERRY. [*Remonstrating.*] Eh, eh, there, Sammy!

SAMMY. [*A little subdued.*] 'N the flickering shadowish softly——

JERRY. [*Emphatically.*] Eh, Sammy, eh!

SAMMY. [*Ending it softly.*] Come 'n go.

GIRL. [*To the Woman.*] The destination of the letter, madam, please?

WOMAN. Tarraringapatam.

GIRL. Where exactly is that place or locality, madam?

SAMMY. Nex' parish but one t' ourish.

WOMAN. [*Indignantly, to Sammy.*] Keep your funny remarks to yourself, please. [*To the Girl.*] Tarraringapatam's in the most southern part of Burma.

JERRY. [*To the Girl.*] Fork over the form for the pound on demand, will you, missie? Before me pal gets too tired to sign.

GIRL. [*To Jerry.*] One minute, please.

SAMMY. [*Hammering on counter with his hand.*] A pound en deman', wanna pound en deman'.

WOMAN. [*To the Girl.*] Will a letter posted to catch the seven fifty-nine get to Tarraringapatam on Friday before twelve fifty-four in the afternoon?

GIRL. I'm afraid I couldn't say, madam.

JERRY. [*Briskly, to the Woman.*] Young lady doesn't know. [*To the Girl.*] Pound on demand form, miss.

WOMAN. [*Indignantly, to Jerry.*] Be good enough, sir, to confine your attention to your own business, will you? [*To the Girl.*] Will you find out?

JERRY. [*To the Woman.*] You can't be let monopolize the time 'n attention of an office for the use of the public at large, can you?

SAMMY. [*Briskly.*] Ish she tryin' to shtir up trouble, or wha'?

WOMAN. [*To Sammy.*] I'm making an ordinary inquiry at a public office, and I will not tolerate interference.

GIRL. [*Who has been running her finger along a list of names of places hanging on a card behind the counter.*] What name, again, please?

WOMAN. [*With dignity.*] Tarraringapatam.

GIRL. [*Looking at the list.*] Not on the list, madam.

JERRY. [*Ironically.*] Bus stop in the jungle, miss.

WOMAN. It must be there.

GIRL. [*To the Woman.*] Not on the list. [*To Sammy.*] What can I do for you, sir?

JERRY. [*Confidentially.*] Just wants a pound on demand, miss.

GIRL. [*Sharply, to Jerry.*] Let the gentleman speak for himself. [*To Sammy.*] What is it, please?

SAMMY. Ish she tryin' to shtir up trouble, or wha'?

JERRY. [*Loudly, to Sammy.*] Young lady's askin' if you want a pound on demand.

SAMMY. [*Wakening up a little.*] Yeh, wha'? Wanna a pound on demand, yeh.

JERRY. [*Briskly.*] Give's the form, 'n I'll get him to sling his name down, missie.

GIRL. [*To Sammy.*] Can I have your bank-book, please?

JERRY. [*Briskly.*] Bank-book, bank-book, Sammy; young lady wants the bank-book.

[*Sammy looks vacantly at the Girl and at Jerry.*

JERRY. [*Briskly.*] Get a move on. [*He puts a hand in Sammy's breast-pocket.*] Bank-book, bank-book, Sammy, me son; young lady wants bank-book.

[*He takes the book from Sammy's pocket, and hands it to the Girl.*

GIRL. [*To Woman, who is standing beside the counter.*] Sorry, madam, but I can't tell you what you want to know—the name's not on the list. [*She looks at the bank-book Jerry has given to her.*] Which is Mr Adams?

JERRY. [*Gaily indicating his friend.*] This is him, miss, all alive 'n full of beans.

SAMMY. [*Delightedly.*] Jusht a song at twilight when the lights aresh slow——

JERRY. [*Interrupting.*] Shush—young lady doesn't like singing in her office, Sammy.

SAMMY. [*Drunkenly.*] Sammy doesn't care about any young ladyish; don't care 'bout offish or young ladyish.

WOMAN. [*Going over indignantly to ledge to write her letter.*] A finely appointed Post Office, I must say, that can't give you even a hint about the commonest postal regulation!

[*The Girl slowly gets a form and reluctantly hands it out towards Sammy, but Jerry takes it out of her hand, and hurries Sammy over to the writing-ledge opposite.*

GIRL. [*Warningly.*] The depositor must sign himself; and his signature must correspond with that in the book.

[*The woman is writing her letter, and is taking up a great deal of space. She is right in the middle of the ledge with writing materials spread round on each side of her. Jerry leads Sammy to the space on her right, looks at it, then leads Sammy round to the space on her left.*

JERRY. Now you've only just to gather the pen into your mit 'n slap down the old name on to the form.

[*Jerry spreads the form on the ledge, gets an old pen and puts it into Sammy's hand, who lets it fall to the floor.*

JERRY. [*With irritation, as he picks it up, and places it again in Sammy's hand.*] Try to keep a grip on it, man, 'n don't be spillin' it all over the place. [*Sammy grips it like a sword.*] Aw, not that way. Don't go to the opposite extreme. [*Arranging pen.*] Nice 'n lightly between the finger 'n thumb. That way, see? [*Speaking over to the Girl.*] He's not used to this kind of thing, miss, but he'll be all right in a minute.

SAMMY. [*Standing still and looking vacantly at the wall.*] Wanna poun' on demand.

JERRY. [*Encouragingly.*] Go on, bend your back 'n write your name [*To the Woman who is writing her letter.*] Mind movin' over as far as you can, ma'am, to give him room to write his name—he wants a pound on demand?

[*The Woman looks indignant, but moves a little away. Sammy*

*bends down, gets the pen to the paper, slips and slides
along the ledge, nearly knocking the Woman down.*

JERRY. [*In dismay.*] Aw, Sammy, eh, eh.   Look at the form,
man.   Can't you keep your balance for a second?

WOMAN. [*Indignantly.*] This is a nice way to be scattered about,
writing an important letter to Tarraringapatam! [*To the Girl.*]
Aren't you going to exercise a little control here, please?

JERRY. [*To the Woman.*] He's sawl right, he's sawl right,
ma'am.

WOMAN. [*Angrily.*] No, it's not all right; it's anything but all
right. [*Violently, to Sammy.*] Remember you're in a Post
Office, sir!

SAMMY. [*With drunken indignation.*] Posht Offish!   What's a
Posht Offish?   Haven't to take me shoes from off me feet in a
Posht Offish, have I?

JERRY. [*Soothingly.*] It's sawl right.   No one wants you to
take your shoes from off your feet.   Here, lean on the ledge
till I get a new form.

[*He puts Sammy leaning against the ledge and goes over to
get another form.*

SAMMY. [*Meandering over to the Woman.*] Shuh want me to take
me shoes from offish me feet?

JERRY. [*To the Girl.*] Slip us another form, missie.

SAMMY. [*Close to the Woman—emphatically.*] Shuh hear me
talkin' to you?   Shuh want me to take me shoish from off
me feet?

JERRY. [*Impatiently to the Girl.*] Give's the form, miss, before
he begins to get lively.

GIRL. [*Busy at work.*] Oh, just a minute.   I gave you one a
moment ago.

SAMMY. [*Close to the Woman.*] You push off, ma'am, please;
thish plaish is occupied.   Have to write me namish; need
spaish; wanna pound on demand. [*The Woman ignores him.*]
Push off when you're warned, can't you?   Thish plaish ish
occupied.

JERRY. [*Speaking over to Sammy from the counter.*] Eh, eh,
Sammy, there, control yourself, man. [*To the Girl.*] Hurry up,
miss.   Steady, Sam!

SAMMY. [*More emphatically, as the Woman ignores him.*] Shuh
hear me talkin' to you?   Told you I wanted spaish.   Push off,
now—this plaish is occupied.

JERRY. [*Over to Sammy, in a warning voice.*] Sammy!   Steady!

WOMAN. [*Indignantly to Sammy.*] How dare you tell me to push off? I'll have you know this is a public office, and I am engaged in important business.

SAMMY. [*Aggressively.*] Shuh don't want a pound on demanish, so push off before I call the polish.

JERRY. [*Facing towards the Girl.*] Calm, Sammy, calm.

> [*Sammy pushes the Woman as she is writing her letter, but she indignantly pushes back, and he finds it hard to keep his feet. He recovers and returns to the charge, pushes her again, but she pushes him more violently than before, sending him more than half-way towards the door; by a great effort he recovers and staggers back to the Woman with a look of determination on his face.*

JERRY. [*To the Girl, as Sammy is staggering about—which Jerry does not see.*] For God's sake. give's a form, missie.

SAMMY. [*Pushing the Woman.*] I have you taped, me lassie; wanta wash what're we doin': I have you taped, but I'll block you, me lassie!

> [*He pushes the Woman, who pushes him back; he tries to recover, but she follows him up, and pushes again so that Sammy staggers to the door, hits it, the door opens, Sammy staggers out into the street, and the door closes again. The Woman goes back to the writing of her letter.*

JERRY. [*Who is ignorant of Sammy's disappearance, rapping impatiently on the counter.*] Eh, miss, missie, the form, miss, eh, the form, missie.

GIRL. [*Impatiently slapping down a form on the counter.*] That's the last you'll get.

JERRY, [*Combatively.*] Oh, don't get too cocky, miss, for, after all, you're only a servant to the public. [*Tapping his chest.*] It's the like of me that pays your wages. You're just here to serve the interests of the public, so don't get too cocky.

GIRL. [*Tartly.*] I don't want any impertinence, please.

JERRY. [*Hotly.*] You'll do what's here to do accordin' to regulations. I wonder what'd happen if I sent in a chit of a complaint to the Postmaster-General?

> [*He turns round to go over to the writing-ledge and finds that Sammy has disappeared.*

JERRY. [*Staring round in bewilderment.*] Where's he gone? Eh, where did Sammy go? [*He runs over to the Woman.*] Why the hell didn't you keep an eye on him when you knew he had a few up?

> [*He rushes to the door, pushes it open, and runs out.*

WOMAN. [*To the Girl.*] Nice pair of drunken scoundrels. What are the police doing?

[*The door swings open and Jerry enters, dragging Sammy in after him.*

JERRY. [*Indignantly, to the Girl.*] Eh, will you speak to that lady over there, 'n keep her from interferin' with people transactin' public business?

[*He leads Sammy back to the writing-ledge, spreads the form on the ledge for him, and carefully places a pen in his hand.*

SAMMY. [*As he is being led over.*] Have that lasshie taped; thash lasshie over there, have her taped, so I have.

JERRY. [*Placing the pen in Sammy's hand.*] Get your mit goin', Sammy, get your mit goin'. [*Sammy does not stir.*] Aw, get down to it, man.

SAMMY. Can't bend.

JERRY. Why can't you bend?

SAMMY. Can't bend, can't stand; wanna chair.

JERRY. [*Impatiently.*] Hold on tight, then, while I get you one. Hold tight, now.

[*Sammy grips the writing-ledge grimly, as he stares over at the Woman who is writing at the other end. Jerry runs to the counter, acting and speaking so impetuously that the Girl does what is asked of her before she realizes what is happening.*

JERRY. [*Rapidly to the Girl.*] The stool, missie, a lend of the stool; he can write his name safer sittin'; quick, missie!

[*The Girl hands over a high stool, Jerry runs over to Sammy with the stool, helps Sammy to sit on it, settles the form, and again puts the pen in his hand. Sammy protrudes his tongue, and seems to find his coat in the way.*

JERRY. Oul' coat in the way, eh? Take it off, then, so's it won't clog your movements; young lady won't mind.

[*After a good deal of pulling, Sammy, with the help of Jerry, gets off his coat.*

WOMAN. [*Sarcastically, staring at the pair.*] Why don't you pull down the blinds and keep the light from hurting his eyes?

[*Sammy gives a violent movement of anger, sweeping pen, ink, and form to the ground. Holding precariously to the ledge, he tilts his seat, slides over towards the Woman, and brings his face as close to hers as possible.*

SAMMY. [*Angrily to the Woman.*] Thish ish a Post Offish, see? No one allowed interfere with men hash businish to do. Wasn't reared yesterday, 'n I have you taped, me lasshie!

JERRY. [*Indignantly, to the Woman.*] Whyja go 'n cause a commotion just as the man was doin' nicely? You've no right to interfere with men transactin' public business. [*Over to the Girl.*] See that, miss, see the way she interfered the minute the man was just doin' nicely?

GIRL. [*Calmly.*] I didn't see the lady interfering in any way.

JERRY. [*Indignantly.*] Well, if you hadda had your eyes open, you'd ha' seen it. There doesn't seem to be any proper conthrol in the place at all.

> [*While Jerry is speaking, the Girl goes to the telephone, dials a number and listens. Jerry helps Sammy back to his original position on the stool.*

GIRL. [*At the telephone.*] Hallo; Pimblico Post Office speaking; send down one of your little boys, will you? Yes, at once, please.

> [*She replaces the receiver and stands watching the two men, glancing, now and again, at the door.*

JERRY. [*When he has settled Sammy.*] Now don't fall asundher any more, for God's sake. [*To the Woman.*] 'N no more of your condescendin' remarks, please, see?

WOMAN. [*Vehemently.*] One word more from either of you, 'n I'll go straight out 'n bring in a policeman!

> [*There are a few moments dead silence.*

SAMMY. [*Breaking out excitedly.*] Ja hear what she said? Ja hear? Bring a policeman in. That's what we get for trustin' people. What do I care for the poleish? Speak up, Jerry, 'n be a man—do I or do I not care for the poleish?

JERRY. [*Soothingly.*] No, never; every one who knows Sammy, knows that.

SAMMY. Not if they were round me in dozens—do I or do I not?

JERRY. Not a word, Sammy, not a word; we rest silent about them things.

SAMMY. Not a word. We don't rush round tellin' things; but we know, don't we, Jerry?

JERRY. Not a word. Don't let your nerves get jangled now. Slip your name down.

SAMMY. Not another word. Poleeish! Do I or do I not care for the poleeish—you know, Jerry?

JERRY. Not a word—go on, get your name down.

SAMMY. [*Excitedly.*] Let her send for the poleeish! Wouldn't be long till they didn't know what was happenin'. Poleeish to the right of me, 'n to the left of me, 'n nothing left of them in the end but silver buttons for souvenirs!

N 947

JERRY. Rags, bones, 'n buttons, wha'? Go on—slip your name down.

[*The door opens and a huge Policeman enters. He walks slowly in, goes over to the counter, looks at the Girl, who points to the two men; the Policeman nods knowingly.*

SAMMY. [*Leaning over towards the Woman.*] We often plastered the roads with policemen, 'n left them thryin' out how they were going to get themselves together again!

WOMAN. [*Scornfully.*] Oh, you did, didja?

SAMMY. [*Mockingly, to the Woman.*] Yes, we did, didn' we; we did did did didja, didn' we!

POLICEMAN. [*Coming over and standing near the two men.*] Now then, do what you have to do, 'n go about your business.

[*The two men look round and see the Policeman. They stare at him for a few moments, and then turn their faces away, fixing their attention on the form. There is dead silence for a time, for the near presence of a Policeman is a great discomfort and very disconcerting.*

JERRY. [*Almost in a whisper.*] Just there on the line, Sammy. Samuel, first name, see? Lead off with a big ess. A big ess, man, a big ess. Shape it into a big ess—capital ess—don't you know what a capital ess is? Here, I'll show you—give us a hold of the pen for a minute.

[*Jerry takes the pen from Sammy and makes the necessary correction, and returns the pen to Sammy.*

JERRY. There y'are now. No, on ahead, cautious: a, m, u—I think—yes, u, double e, l—no, one e 'n two double ells—good God, what am I sayin'—only one double ell, only one double ell, man! You're not listenin' to me, Sammy. There's nothin' to prevent you doin' it right, if you'll only listen. You've nearly a dozen of ells down. Show it to me for a second.

[*He takes the pen and removes roughly the unnecessary letters.*

JERRY. [*Warningly.*] Now the next name, Adams; 'n make the letthers a little smaller, or you'll be a mile away from the form before the last one comes in sight.

SAMMY. [*In a weary voice.*] Aw, I've had enough.

JERRY. You're too far ahead to give up now, man. T'other name, now. A big A for a start. Not as big as an elephant, now—you know what an ordinary capital A is. Oh, why did you let your hand slip? It'll have to do now. [*Turning and winking at the Policeman.*] He's got a few up, but he's sawl right. [*To Sammy.*] Now a little d, 'n a little u, 'n a little—wait a minute—I'm gettin' a little confused—a little m, a little n, 'n a little ess—a little ess, man! Now, come on, 'n we'll give it to the young lady.

WOMAN. [*Mockingly, to Jerry.*] The poor man'll need a long rest, now.

[*Jerry helps Sammy off the stool, and links him over to the counter, both of them trying to appear as if they were indifferent to the presence of the Policeman. He hands over the form to the Girl, who examines it, and looks at the name in the bank-book.*

JERRY. [*Humming, and trying to look unconcerned.*] Rum tum tiddley um tum, parley voo; rum tum tiddley um tum, parley voo; rum tum——

GIRL. [*Interrupting Jerry's humming.*] Couldn't give you a pound on demand with this signature. The signature on the form doesn't correspond with the signature in the bank-book in any way.

JERRY. It's his writin', isn't it, miss? An' both of the names is Adamsususes, aren't they?

GIRL. They don't correspond. Sorry; but I can't let you have the money. I don't even know that the gentleman is really Mr Adams.

JERRY. [*Wild.*] Didja ever hear such consequential nonsense! [*To Sammy.*] She says you're not Mr Adams. [*To the Girl.*] Of course he's Mr Adams. Who else could he be, only Mr Adams? Isn't he known all over the district where he lives, woman?

GIRL. Why, then, didn't he go to the Post Office in his own district?

JERRY. [*Impatiently.*] Because it's too busy an office, 'n we decided to come to a place where he could do what he wanted to do in comfort, 'n fill in his name at his ease.

GIRL. [*With decision.*] I'm sorry; but I can't let the gentleman have the money.

JERRY. [*Horrified.*] 'N what's he goin' to do, then?

GIRL. Better call back again to-morrow, or the next day.

JERRY. He wants the money now, girl.

GIRL. I can't give it to him.

JERRY. [*To Sammy.*] She says she won't give you the pound on demand.

SAMMY. Wanna pound on demand.

JERRY. [*To the Girl.*] Hear what the depositor says? He's gotta get it.

SAMMY. I've gotta get it.

JERRY. [*To Sammy.*] Of course you have. After the agony of gettin' things ship-shape, we're not goin' to stand any denial of our rights.

POLICEMAN. [*Coming near.*] Hasn't the young lady said she can't give it to you? So go on home, now, like decent men, an' forget all about it.

JERRY. [*To the Policeman.*] The man has gotta get his money, hasn't he?

SAMMY. [*Dreamily.*] 'Course I've gotta get it.

POLICEMAN. [*Importantly.*] Since he hasn't complied with the necessary preliminaries, he isn't entitled to withdraw his pound.

JERRY. [*Indignantly.*] The only preliminary was the signin' of his name, wasn't it? 'N he signed his name, didn't he? Y'awl seen him signin' his name, didn't you? [*A pause.*] Are yous all afraid to speak—did yous, or didn't yous?

POLICEMAN. G'on now, g'on. [*To Jerry.*] Y'ought to see that your comrade's incapable of discretion in withdrawin' anything from a Government corporation. G'on, now, like decent men.

JERRY. [*Appealingly.*] He wants that pound special, I'm tellin' you. [*To Sammy.*] Don't you, Sammy?

SAMMY. [*Dreamily.*] I gotta get it.

JERRY. [*To the Policeman.*] Hear that? Mind you, it's a serious thing to keep a man from gettin' his private property.

POLICEMAN. [*A little angry.*] Here, g'on the pair of yous, before I lose me temper! You've been shown every leniency; so go home, now, like sensible, decent men, before I lose me temper.

JERRY. Give us back the bank-book, then.

GIRL. Mr Adams might lose it—I'll post it on to him to-morrow.

JERRY. [*Frightened.*] He doesn't want you to post it. He wants it now—don't you, Sammy?

SAMMY. [*Wearily.*] I've gotta get it.

POLICEMAN. [*Peremptorily.*] Now go on home, like decent men, before I have to resort to exthremes. Go on 'n sleep over it, 'n to-morrow, after a wash 'n brush up, you'll be able to apply for your pound in an ordherly 'n sensible manner.

JERRY. [*Wildly.*] 'N are we goin' to get nothin' out of all our efforts? Mind you, there'll be throuble about this.

POLICEMAN. [*Roughly.*] Ay, it'll start now if the two of yous don't bounce off 'n be well on your way home in a minute. [*He gently pushes them towards the door.*] G'on, now, you know your way.

JERRY. [*Sorrowfully.*] 'N we thravelled miles to find this quiet place, so that he could sign his name in peace.

WOMAN. [*Mockingly, as they go out.*] Isn't it a pity to disappoint the poor little children!

SAMMY. [*As they go out.*] I've gotta get it.

[*They go slowly and sorrowfully out. The Policeman holds the door open for them, and closes it when they have gone. The Woman goes over to the counter with her letter.*

WOMAN. Registered, please.

[*The Girl takes the letter, registers it, and hands receipt to the Woman, who puts it in her bag and goes out.*

GIRL. [*To the Policeman.*] Glad you hunted that pair of money philanderers out of the place.

POLICEMAN. [*Taking her hand into his as he reclines over the counter.*] You're lookin' fit 'n fair 'n sweet 'n rosy to-day, so you are.

GIRL. [*Coyly.*] Am I?

POLICEMAN. [*Shyly.*] Yes, y' are, so y' are.

[*The door opens a little way, then closes again. The Policeman lets go the Girl's hand and stands stiff, while the Girl pretends to be busy with a document.*

GIRL. Thought that was someone.

POLICEMAN. Same here. [*He takes her hand again.*] Y' are, really, lookin' fit 'n fair 'n sweet 'n rosy to-day, so y' are.

GIRL. [*Archly.*] Am I?

[*The door suddenly swings open again, and Sammy appears, with Jerry steadying him from behind. They stand in the doorway, keeping it from closing with their shoulders. The Policeman and the Girl move away from each other.*

JERRY. [*Encouragingly to Sammy.*] Go on, give them your ultimatum: tell them straight that you're goin' to write to the Postmaster-General before you settle down for the night. Go on, now—give them your ultimatum!

[*They both come in towards the centre of the office.*

SAMMY. [*Pointing a finger towards the Girl and the Policeman, which shakes and wanders from the floor to the ceiling as he points.*] I have yous taped, two of yous 'n Postmaster-zheneral! Taped, well taped I have, Postmaster-zheneral!

JERRY. [*Trying to cover up Sammy's vagueness.*] Mr Adams, the depositor, has made up his mind to send a bitther complaint to the Postmaster-General about the way he's been shunted about by public servants durin' his application for a pound on demand. [*To Sammy.*] Haven't you, Mr Adams?

SAMMY. I'm tellin them, once for all, I've gotta get it.

JERRY. There y' are, you see; can't say I didn't warn you. Somebody will be made to sit up for this.

POLICEMAN. [*Loudly and ominously.*] If the pair of yous aren't gone for good in two ticks of the clock, yous 'll spend the night in a place that 'll give the two of you plenty of time to complain to the Postmaster-General. [*He makes a move towards them.*] Be off, I'm tellin' yous, yourselves an' your pound on demand!

> [*The two men are frightened by his move towards them, and Jerry manœuvres Sammy swiftly to the door, and both of them leave as quick as Sammy can travel.*

JERRY. [*As they reach the door.*] Somebody'll be made to sit up for this, I'm tellin' you!

> [*As the doors swing shut, they open again partly to show Jerry's face glaring savagely into the office.*

JERRY. [*Shouting in from the partly opened door.*] That's the last penny of our money the Government 'll ever get from us!

> [*His face disappears, the door swings shut, and the curtain comes down.*

THE BESPOKE OVERCOAT

WOLF MANKOWITZ

AUTHOR'S NOTE

LOVE is a luxury which very poor people can afford, and *The Bespoke Overcoat* is a story of this love. It is not a love which conquers all. Fender does not get enough food or a tailor-made overcoat, in this life. In life he does not find satisfaction, except in so far as he is able to accept with humour and humility the deprivations forced upon him. It is because this humour and humility is shared with his friend that Fender, in spite of everything, would prefer to go on living. To prefer to go on living is to love in the context of this story, and because this is loving at its most deprived the story is a sad one.

In producing *The Bespoke Overcoat* that remarkable artist Alec Clunes concentrated entirely upon this feeling which, by its intensity, animates a piece which is not well constructed. The story was written without any directions for staging or the production of effects. The only stage, the only effects, the only theatre I had in mind were in the heart of a drunken tailor. There was no indication of time past or time present, because a twinge of conscience lasts a moment or a lifetime, and *The Bespoke Overcoat* is about the unreasonable conscience felt by the poor who love the poorer with a love which conquers nothing.

So Alec Clunes's production, which was, in effect, the writing of the play for the practical stage, dispensed with sets, used the barest properties, used darkness broken by three constantly moving areas of light, to tell a simple story with great simplicity. He realized that Fender was not a ghost and that this story was not a ghost-story; he understood that *The Bespoke Overcoat* was a sustained, typically over-long Jewish joke—than which there is no sadder and no funnier story. And I am deeply grateful to him for having understood so much, for having made it available to other people, and for having taught me in the process, as he has taught so many other artists, something of the meaning of theatre.

WOLF MANKOWITZ.

'The Bespoke Overcoat' was performed for the first time at the Arts Theatre Club, London, on 22nd July 1953. It was produced by Alec Clunes with the following cast:

MORRY, a tailor	*David Kossoff*
FENDER, a warehouse clerk . .	*Alfie Bass*
RANTING, his employer . . .	*Harold Kasket*
THE NEW CLERK	*Oscar Quitak*

THE BESPOKE OVERCOAT

SCENE ONE

*The action of the play is distributed among three separate areas per-
manently set and used in turn.*

*Area 'A,' midstage right, is Ranting's warehouse, which consists of
a sizable table, placed obliquely, with a chair or stool left and to the
up stage end of it. Up stage of the table, and rather behind it, a
large rack supports a selection of overcoats on hangers.*

Area 'B' is down stage centre and has no furnishing.

*Area 'C,' midstage left, is Morry's room, which consists of a mattress
lying obliquely on the floor, and beside it right, at the up stage end,
a chair.*

*These three areas are encompassed by a black surround with en-
trances down right, down left, and up centre. During the entire
play, these are in total darkness, as are any two of the acting areas
not being used. Throughout, the stage directions will be related
to the three areas described.*

*When the curtain rises Morry is standing in the area 'B,' with a
navy blue overcoat over his arm. A barrel organ is playing, off,
and fades out as the light at 'B' fades in.*

MORRY. Fender dead. That old man Fender dead. Funny
thing. You're a good tailor, he used to say. You're a good
tailor. No, you're a good tailor. Look around. I don't
care where you look, he says, you are a number one tailor.
Look at this coat, he says. What, that old coat? A coat
must be twenty years old. Mind you, I can tell straight away
by the cross-stitch it's my coat. It's your coat, he shouts.
You made it. Twenty-two years ago I come to you for a coat.
This is him. I still got him. You got a good point. I tell
him, I'm a good tailor. It's only the truth. I'm a good
tailor. Straight away, I see I made a mistake. I fell in.
How much, Fender says, will you take to mend a coat like this?
I ask you. It's falling to pieces on his back. I told him
straight, no nonsense. Look, Fender, I told him, I can run
you up a pair of trousers from lining canvas you can walk up
Saville Road nobody can tell you from the Prince of Wales.
But, Fender, do me a favour. Take the coat somewhere else.

A new coat I can make, but the Union says no miracles. A rag, that's all. I got my clients to think about. Good afternoon. A lovely piece of worsted. Mind you, I got a suit length here: in a hundred year you wouldn't see nothing better. Clients. Fender dead. An old man. [*Turns up stage, still speaking.*] He sits in that stone cold warehouse all day long. [*Turns head round to audience.*] Who could mend such a coat? [*Moves slowly up stage to centre exit.*] That's enough. [*Light starts to fade.*] Leave me alone. All this nagging, nagging. [*He has gone, and so has the light.*

SCENE TWO

As the light fades in on ' c,' sitting cross-legged and hunched on Morry's mattress is Fender. He rubs his hands.

FENDER. Oi. How that Morry can thread a needle in this cold I don't know. Such a cold.

MORRY. [*Entering up stage centre.*] I got trouble of my own. After all, I'm in Bond Street? I'm a merchant prince? I'm not even a limited company.

FENDER. I thought you was a limited company.

MORRY. [*Turning.*] Me? Never. What do I want with shares and directors? So—what can I do for you? It's late, but . . .

FENDER. To be managing director is not a nice thing? You got no ambition? Terrible cold in here. My old guvernor—managing director three companies. Chairman—six companies. But what a man! [*Rises.*] Look, Morry. I still got no overcoat. Put on the gas ring.

MORRY. Fender! You ain't dead?

FENDER. Sure I'm dead. Would I sit up half the night in the freezing cold if I wasn't dead? I can tell you, I won't be sorry to get back. They got central heating, constant hot water, room service. And the food—as much as you like. Kosher, of course.

MORRY. [*Holding his head.*] I won't touch the rotten brandy.

FENDER. Drinks? You can have what you like, any time, day or night, on the house.

MORRY. Go on. So tell me, Fender. Is it really you?

FENDER. [*Holding out his hand.*] Feel my hand. Feel.

MORRY. [*Taking his hand.*] Believe me, you are cold. That lousy brandy. It kills you. [*Sneezes.*

FENDER. [*Sitting on chair.*] Gesundheit.

MORRY. Thank you.

FENDER. All I want is to get back.   Listen, Morry.   You know the first person I met down there?

MORRY. Down there?

FENDER. I tell you, Morry, a secret: everybody goes down there. You know who I met?   Lennie.

MORRY. Lennie from Fournier Street?

FENDER. Who else?   He's doing the same job.   And *what* herrings!   I tell you, Morry, I won't be sorry to get back.

MORRY. [*Kneeling on mattress.*] Fender!   You don't hold that overcoat against me, do you, Fender?   Believe me, if I had known you would catched a cold and died I would give you my own coat.

FENDER. That blankety coat.   For that coat I'm here and not at the hotel.   Look, Morry.   I got nothing against you.

MORRY. [*Rising to one knee.*] You ain't going to haunt me, Fender?   You wouldn't haunt an old friend?

FENDER. Don't talk silly, Morry.   That haunting is a special job.   They don't give it to new residents.   For haunting you get a commission.

MORRY. [*Rising and moving behind Fender. Crossing arms.*] So listen, Fender.   It goes without saying I am pleased to see you.   I'm glad you enjoy being dead.   But you won't think I am rude, if I ask what you want of my life?

FENDER. I'll tell you.   But first light that gas-ring so at least I won't freeze—listen to me—to death, I nearly said.   You don't know, Morry, [*The light begins to fade.*] what sort of life it was at that Ranting clothing company.   No wonder I didn't lose any sleep about dying . . .   [*The light has gone.*

SCENE THREE

The light fades in on ' A.'   Fender is sitting on the stool with his note-book and pencil on the table in front of him.   The conversation continues from the previous Scene.

FENDER. After that warehouse for forty-three years, any change would be a pleasure.   Forty-three years a shipping clerk.

MORRY. [*Off.*] So long?

FENDER. Forty-three years next Purim, if I didn't die before.
      [*Ranting enters down right carrying a board with lists.*
RANTING. [*To behind desk.*] And sixty gross denim trousers.

FENDER. [*Writing.*] Sixty gross denim trousers.

RANTING. And forty gross cellaloid collars.

FENDER. Cellaloid collars. Forty gross cellaloid.

RANTING. [*Tapping with pencil, impatiently.*] Cellaloid makes with a C, no S.

FENDER. And what more?

RANTING. Eleven dozen raincoats, Prussian collar.

FENDER. Eleven dozen raincoats.

RANTING. Prussian collar.

FENDER. You know something, Mr Ranting? It's cold in this warehouse. I said it's cold, Mr Ranting. I feel the cold something terrible.

RANTING. Fender, I don't think you enjoy your work like in the olden days.

[*Sits on table, head turned half down stage towards Fender.*

FENDER. What an idea! I enjoy my work? Certainly I enjoy. I feel the cold, that's all.

RANTING. Naturally, you are getting on. The work is hard. Nobody is as young as he used to be.

FENDER. What are you talking, Mr Ranting? Nobody is as young as he used to be? And how could he?

RANTING. I am saying, Fender, an old man is an old man.

FENDER. [*Rises.*] Certainly. Of course. An old man is an old man. Mr Ranting, I tell you something: my father, when he was seventy—no, over seventy—he can bend a horseshoe straight with his bare hands. And even he felt the cold.

RANTING. [*Getting off table.*] All I am saying, Fender, is stop driving me mad with your crying 'it's so cold, it's so cold.' Get a new overcoat; you won't feel it.

FENDER. I make an arrangement with you, Mr Ranting. I'll take one of the overcoats, the big ones with the sheepskin lining, and every week from my wages take off a certain sum. [*Holds out his hands.*] A proposition, Mr Ranting?

RANTING. One of them coats, Fender? Leave me alone. [*Fender moves as if to speak.*] Hup! A coat like this is worth twenty pound anybody's money. What do you make? With all due respect, Fender, what do you make? You won't live so long to pay off such a coat.

FENDER. [*Sitting on stool again.*] That's true. So what can you do?

RANTING. [*Reading from list.*] Seventeen dozen pair shooting breeches.

FENDER. [*Writing.*] Seventeen dozen pair breeches.

RANTING. Shooting.

FENDER. Shooting, shooting.   [*Indicates the entry in his book.*

RANTING. [*In disgust.*] Ah! [*Exit down right.*
FENDER. [*Rising and taking off his coat.*] Maybe Morry can mend the old coat again. [*Cross fade lights from 'A' to 'C.'*] After all he's a good tailor. [*Turns up stage as the light goes.*

SCENE FOUR

As the light fades in on 'C' Fender is standing up stage of mattress. Morry enters down left.

MORRY. Look, Fender, look. The seams is all rotten. Look, the lining is like ribbons. Look, the material is threadbare.
FENDER. A tailor like you, Morry, to make such a fuss. You should be ashamed.
MORRY. [*Sitting on chair.*] The padding is like an old horse blanket.
FENDER. Who asks for new padding? Only make the coat good. Who cares about the padding, so long as the coat is warm?
MORRY. It can't be done.
FENDER. Don't make jokes, Morry.
MORRY. If I say it can't be done, it can't be done.
FENDER. So, all right, charge a little more.
MORRY. Charge! What does charge matter? It can't be done.
FENDER. Why are you so hard for, Morry? After all, you can patch with off cuts. [*Morry holds head in hands.*] I am not asking, after all, for West End style; I should look so smart. I don't care how smart. Only mend the coat, Morry.
MORRY. Fender, listen to me, Fender. A good coat like I make has got twenty years wear. I double stitch the seams with best thread, no rubbish. Every stitch I test, [*Bites imaginary thread.*] so it's good and strong. I use good material: crombie, tweed, what you like. The best. I use a lovely lining; someone else would make a wedding dress from it, such a lining I use.
FENDER. You use marvellous lining, Morry.
MORRY. I make the whole coat, the buttons holes, the pockets, everything.
FENDER. Don't I tell everybody? Morry—a needle like Paganini. I tell everybody.
MORRY. I would make you such a coat for cost, Fender.
FENDER. How much costs such a coat?
MORRY. Three yards, say.
FENDER. Say two and a half.

MORRY. And lining.

FENDER. Don't worry yourself with lining.

MORRY. I can make you a good coat for twelve pound.

FENDER. You can't mend the old coat?

MORRY. Please, Fender, do me a favour.

FENDER. I can ask?   Twelve pound is money.

MORRY. [*Rises.*] Listen, Fender.   I break my neck: ten pound for the coat.   You got ten pound?

FENDER. I look like a banker?   I can save ten pound.

MORRY. So.

FENDER. [*As he starts to put on his old coat.*] So.   So I'm going to have made a bespoke overcoat.

MORRY. Bespoke is good.

FENDER. Certainly bespoke.   You think I would wear Ranting's rubbish?   [*Sits on chair.*

MORRY. [*Moving down stage left and reaching off-stage for patterns.*] What material you like?

FENDER. I can choose material?

MORRY. [*To Fender with patterns.*] Here, patterns.

FENDER. The grey is not nice for me.   The blue is better?

MORRY. [*Fingering the blue material.*] Blue is nice.   You can wear blue for any occasion.

FENDER. Nigger brown is smart.

MORRY. For a young man.

FENDER. Black is always good.

MORRY. Black is good, but a nice, dark blue is nicer.

FENDER. [*Rising, and moving down stage of mattress.*] Believe me, Morry, I think you are right.   The blue is good—and thick. What a material!

MORRY. [*Down to Fender.*] I should say.   So you can save ten pounds?

FENDER. Save?   Sure I can save.   An old man like me, if I got an overcoat, what do I need? [*Moving down stage centre to* 'B.'] If I got a bespoke overcoat, what more can I need?

                                          [*Exit into darkness down right.*

SCENE FIVE

Morry takes out black bread, etc., from his pocket
and moves to his chair.

MORRY. With a piece of black bread and a herring you can't go wrong.   You got in black bread vitamins, nutriment *and* a good flavour from herrings.   In the old days, [*Sits.*] sometimes six clients a week, all wanting coats, suits, a spare pair of trousers, something. The trade is not good any more. Believe me, if I had a boy I wouldn't let him see a needle and thread. It's a thing of the past. Things are so bad now, you know what I'm doing? I'm making a ten-pound coat for Fender. For ten pounds, it's a wonderful coat. The material, the seams. No wind can blow through a coat like this. [*Rises and moves down stage a few paces.*] Let it blow as much as it likes. I read an interesting thing somewhere. When it's cold, it's not really cold. You are hot; that's why you feel the cold. Also you pull in your muscles. That's bad. Fender: his trouble is he's pulled his muscles so far in they won't pull any more. [*Moving down left to exit, as light fades.*] I was always interested in science things like this. [*Cross fade to* 'B.'

SCENE SIX

Ranting enters down right with a plate of chopped liver and a fork.

RANTING. The chopped liver is tukke good, Alf. You want some? Good boy. [*Stops down centre* 'B.'] Bring some more chopped liver, Maisie. So I was telling you, Alf: this exhibition they got such machines you wouldn't believe. They got a machine there (I'm not telling you a word of a lie, Alf), they got a machine can add up how much you made last year, take away your overheads, knock off your income tax, and show you if you got anything left. By my life. It has a dictation machine, a suspended filing system, a place special for telephone directories, and a permutator for working out football pools so they should win. And I worry myself to nothing, worrying, worrying the whole time over an old clerk's mistakes. What you say? Can a machine laugh like a man? Can it cry like a man? What difference? So long as a clerk clerks good, what difference he's laughing or crying?

[Exit down right in black-out as we hear Fender laugh off.

SCENE SEVEN

The light fades in on Fender, laughing quietly, as he enters down right and moves to 'A' *below table, with the baigel half eaten and wrapped in paper.*

FENDER. A marvellous story, I must tell it to Morry. I enjoy a good laugh. [*He sighs and looks at the baigel.*] A baigel is enough.

After all, bread and salt is food. It's the same dinner, only I leave out the soup. That woman, terrible, but what soup. I'm not saying it's not worth a sixpence. A bowl like that, where could you get it for sixpence? In a big restaurant they bring you half as much, and charge terrible prices. A woman cooks soup like that must make somebody a marvellous wife. Mind you, boss-eyed and what temper, a terrible woman. Still a baigel is plenty. Eat it slow, careful, every crumb does you good. Soup! who wants soup? [*Moves up stage.*] When I get the coat, I put it on. I walk up to a table, [*Sits.*] I sit down in the overcoat, blue, nice: a bowl of coup, missus, and a baigel. [*Rises and moves a few paces down stage.*] Be careful! You want the soup should drop on this new overcoat—a bespoke overcoat—ruined. [*He laughs as, lifting the flap of his torn coat, his hand slips through a hole.*] I don't think I got room for these bits. No, I'm full up. I couldn't eat another thing, not even a fresh lutka or a piece of cheesecake. [*Turns to his accounts.*] Sixteen dozen flying jackets. [*Up stage to sit.*] With such jackets you can fly?

RANTING. [*Enters down right, moves behind table from which he brushes crumbs.*] How many times, Fender? Don't eat in the warehouse. It brings the mice. The mice eat the clothing.

FENDER. How many clothing can a little mouse eat?

RANTING. [*Reading.*] Twenty-eight gross denim trousers.

[*Fade out.*

SCENE EIGHT

Area 'C.'   *Fade in on Fender entering breathlessly up centre.*

FENDER. [*Calls.*] Morry, I come to see how the coat is coming, Morry.

MORRY. [*Footsteps, off.*] The coat is all right.

FENDER. Which is the coat, Morry?

MORRY. [*Entering down left, with half-made coat.*] Here! Here!

FENDER. Should I try it on?

MORRY. [*Holding out coat.*] Try it on. Don't be shy. What's a matter with you? You're a film starlet, you got to have a changing room else you can't take off the old coat. [*Fender removes coat.*] So. That's right. Take it off.

[*Fender gives his coat to Morry, who puts it on chair, and puts on the new coat.*]

FENDER. If I knew, I would put my other shirt on. You seen it,

Morry? The drill shirt, with tabs on the shoulders, very smart.

MORRY. And why should you? To-day is a bank holiday? Look. My own shirt. Everybody wears his old shirt for a working day. Nu. Try it.

FENDER. [*As Morry fits the coat.*] In Clacton the sun is hot. This makes him the sun, you understand. What a hot! You got a nice deck-chair, Mrs Felderman. I can see. A comfortable deck-chair. Certainly a new overcoat—a bespoke overcoat. [*Lifts the left arm with sleeve in it.*] Suits me? Under the arms is a bit tight.

MORRY. [*Feeling armhole.*] It's fine. You got plenty room, look, look.

FENDER. A coat like this makes a difference.

MORRY. [*Kneeling in front to fit coat.*] Fender, you like the coat? What about a couple of pound on account? I got expenses. [*Rising.*] Can you manage a couple?

[*Fender takes out purse, sorts out notes and silver, and hands them over with great dignity.*]

FENDER. Certainly. You know, Morry, twenty shillings, if you saved money like I do, thirty shillings, and didn't throw it away on that rotten brandy, thirty-five shillings, you would be a rich man. Forty shillings.

MORRY. And what would I do with my money?

FENDER. A question. What can you do with it?

MORRY. I can take an off-licence.

FENDER. An off-licence is a good idea. [*Taking off new coat.*]

MORRY. I use my knowledge. A special line in brandy. Old stuff—Napoleon—something good.

[*Takes overcoat from Fender and hands him his old one.*]

FENDER. How can you know it's good?

MORRY. I try every bottle, personal. I put up a smart notice, Morry's Napoleon Brandy; every bottle personal tasted. Thanks for the two pound. You can spare?

FENDER. Sure I can spare. The coat won't be long now, Morry?

MORRY. This week I make an exception. I have a drink to-night; that way to-morrow I take less.

FENDER. Tukke?

MORRY. Listen, Fender, drinking is by me not by you; it's my hobby so I shouldn't know? [*Exeunt. Cross fade to 'B.'*]

SCENE NINE

When the lights go up on 'B,' *Ranting is strap-
hanging down stage centre.*

RANTING. [*In a new coat.*] On the Central Line is always hot.
You like the coat? Yesterday I picked it up. America style.
[*Lurches.*] Sorry, miss. Dear? I should say it's dear! You
want me to wear one of me own coats? Twenty-five nicker
—a pony, this coat—I beg your pardon. Knock off the booze
and you'll be able to afford. My advice to you friend, is—
knock off the demon drink.

[*He goes out down right. Cross fade to* 'C.'

SCENE TEN

*Fender is asleep on Morry's mattress, covered by the half-finished
overcoat. Morry enters drunkenly, up stage centre, singing and
carrying a bottle.*

MORRY. It says on the label extra special reserve, cognac Napoleon brandy, old special reserve. A brandy like this is a brandy
like this. This. [*Drinks.*] A brandy. [*Turns to mattress.*] I
got company? So late? [*Up stage to put bottle on chair.*] Hey,
wake up. I got company. You sit here a minute. Don't go
way. I'll come back. [*Kneeling up stage of mattress.*] Wake up,
Fender, it's you? What an unexpected pleasure.

FENDER. [*Sitting up.*] I was having a dream. A flying overcoat
and inside the pockets bowls of soup. And do you know, the
soup never upset in the coat.

MORRY. I got here a brandy; you never drunk such a brandy in
your life.

FENDER. [*Peering at the label.*] Special reserve. Must be good.

MORRY. Take a little drop. Go on. Take.

FENDER. [*Trying it.*] Ahh, like fire. [*Hands bottle back.*] A good
one all right. Morry—Moishele.

MORRY. [*Holding out bottle in front of him.*] It's good brandy.

FENDER. I got bad news, Morry.

MORRY. Where can you find a brandy like this?

FENDER. That Ranting. He give me the sack.

MORRY. [*As he sits back on his heels and puts bottle on floor with a
thud.*] He give you the sack?

FENDER. He give me the sack.

MORRY. After so long he give you the sack?

FENDER He give me.

MORRY. He give it to *you?*

FENDER. The sack.

MORRY. Oi.

FENDER. I have with great regrets, Morry I must tell you, to cancel the coat. I came to tell you. Cancel the coat.

MORRY. [*Trying to give him the bottle.*] Take another drop brandy. Good for your cough.

FENDER. I don't fancy.

MORRY. Take. Don't be shy. Take. [*Fender drinks from bottle, and as he lifts his arm we see that the old coat is torn under the arm.*] If I could mend that coat, Fender, I would mend it, I want you to know. I defy any master tailor to make that coat good.

FENDER. What can you do? It's just an old coat, that's all.

MORRY. [*Rises.*] You can't find the rest of the ten pounds? I'll finish the coat.

FENDER. How?

MORRY. [*Puts arm round Fender and pats him on shoulder.*] With a needle. How else?

[*The lights slowly fade.*

SCENE ELEVEN

FENDER. [*At 'B,' down stage centre.*] I told him, polite, but strong. Mr Ranting, I been with this firm with your father and your uncle so many years. All this time I done the same job; nobody complains. Suddenly business is so bad you have to turn me off? Let him answer me that. No good. Excuses, anybody can find excuses. What I ask you, Mr Ranting, is, is it right? Let him answer me that. That's what I should have said. I should have told him off, big as he is. The governor, [*Turns up stage and spits.*] I used to give him a handkerchief he should wipe his nose. A little boy crying round the warehouse with his stockings down gives me the sack. Why didn't I tell him? Fender, he says, you got something put by, an insurance policy, something? I got something put by, don't worry. You got no family? Don't worry, I got plenty of family, I got friends. He worries about me. I even got a niece with a boarding-house in Clacton, and can she cook? Lovely weather the whole time. [*Turns up stage centre and then back to audience.*] Mind you, Morry is a good friend. In the morning I put on my new coat. I go to Ranting. I tell him. Give me that coat with the sheepskin. [*Coughs.*] Funny thing, a cough

like this, comes right through you.   Like a bowl of soup.   It
flies up through you like a flying jacket.   There he goes. [*He
traces the path of the imaginary jacket round the theatre.   It
returns as the threatening celluloid collars.   Fender is dying.*]
Seventeen dozen cellaloid collars, cellaloid makes with a C, no
S—or S, no C. [*Weakly.*] Funny thing, I don't seem to know
nothing any more.   [*Sinks down as the lights slowly fade.*

SCENE TWELVE

*The lights fade in on area ' A ' as a Clerk, followed by Ranting, enters
down right.   Ranting goes up stage to behind table.   Clerk sits at
table with note-book and pencil.*

RANTING. Thirty dozen pair shooting breeches.
CLERK. Thirty dozen pair shooting breeches.
RANTING. And a hundred dozen Balaclava helmets.
    [*Morry enters up stage centre with finished overcoat over his
    arm.*
MORRY. [*Coming to up stage of table.*] Mr Ranting. Excuse me, Mr
    Ranting.
RANTING. And sixty various drill jackets.   Can I help you, sir?
MORRY. I come for Fender.   I finished him a coat.
RANTING. And two gross khaki drill shorts.   He don't work here
    no more.   I say work, but you should understand he was past it.
CLERK. Two gross shorts.
RANTING. Khaki drill.
CLERK. What?
MORRY. Khaki drill.
RANTING. Thank you.   Fender lives by the arches in Flower and
    Dean Street.   Or maybe with his niece at Clacton or some-
    where.   Pardon me.   And twenty-eight pith helmets. [*Exit
    down stage right.*] Ah!
CLERK. Twenty-eight pith helmets.
        [*Rests his arms and head on table.   Cross fade ' A ' to ' C.'*

SCENE THIRTEEN

*Area ' C,' continuing as from Scene Two; Morry is up stage of
mattress, level with Fender, who sits in chair.*

MORRY. So I go to your lodging.   I knock on the door.   No
    answer.   I knock again.   An old woman comes.   She's a bit
    deaf.

FENDER. She's stone deaf. A bit, he says.

MORRY. I shout in her ear, where is Fender? Fender—Fender! Where should he be? He's dead. He didn't have my age, but he's dead. You can knock me over with a feather bed.

FENDER. She got her head screwed on, the old girl. I was dead all right. Mind you, she makes out she's older than she is. I don't like that sort of thing.

MORRY. But so sudden.

FENDER. [*Rising and crossing in front of Morry.*] Listen, Morry. You die when you are ready? You die when you have to, that's all. Still, I haven't done so bad. I can't complain. If only I kept my mouth shut I would be all right.

MORRY. I made the coat as quick as I can, Fender. [*Sits in chair.*

FENDER. Look, Morry, I got nothing against you. You behave like a perfect gentleman. I told everybody at the hotel. Morry's a wonderful tailor. You think you look smart? Wait until Morry gets here. No. It was that Ranting. You see, Morry, I didn't take too long dying, but the whilst I am screaming and cursing, using terrible language, all against that Ranting. And when I get down there, it must have been on my mind. So the first couple of weeks, I am stopping the porter, the commissionaire, the chambermaids, even the guests, telling them about the overcoat. At last, they can't stand it any more. The manager sends for me. Fender, he says, you like the hotel? It's a wonderful hotel, I tell him. Everything of the best. I am very satisfied. Look, Fender, he says, I am very glad if you are comfortable, but I have to tell you every one has a headache with your overcoat. Do me a favour: go down to the cloakroom, pick yourself any coat. Thank you, I tell him. It's not the same. I can see he is upset. I can't have the place turned upside down, he says. [*Pointing upwards.*] You'll have to go back for a while. When you get it, [*Points downwards.*] come back. It's on my mind, I told him. Next thing I know, I'm here. And here I am.

MORRY. [*Half rises.*] And I got your overcoat all wrapped up ready, Fender. Take it and good luck to you.

FENDER. [*Moving down stage level with bottom of mattress.*] It's no good, Morry. It wouldn't make me happy. Somehow, I got to have that sheepskin coat from Ranting. I am not saying your coat isn't wonderful. It is. But I must have from Ranting a coat. I give him forty-three years nearly. He must give me a coat.

MORRY. [*Moving down to Fender with bottle.*] You know what?

FENDER. What?

MORRY. We go to Rantings and take the coat. That's what.
[*Drinks.*

FENDER. [*As Morry offers him the bottle.*] Not a bad idea.
[*Drinks and returns bottle. Exeunt down stage left, with
Morry's arm round Fender. Cross fade to 'A.'*

SCENE FOURTEEN

*As the light fades in on 'A,' Ranting enters from up stage centre,
singing. The Clerk is seated at the table, writing in his note-book.*

RANTING. That book you been making up for the past hour,
what's the matter, you can't read?

CLERK. The old clerk had his own way of doing things. It takes
a little while to work out. But I mastered it.

RANTING. [*Taking hat off.*] You got your head screwed on right.
You go to the dog tracks in the evening?

CLERK. Not for me, Mr Ranting.

RANTING. Horses?

CLERK. No horses, neither.

RANTING. You must spiel something. Poker, shemmy?

CLERK. [*Rising and moving behind his stool.*] I'm developing
myself, Mr Ranting.

RANTING. Something new?

CLERK. The human frame has nine hundred seventy-six individual muscles, each of whom can be developed up to peak
power, give proper exercises and consideration.

RANTING. Nearly a thousand? So many?

CLERK. It has been proved by the best efficiency authorities that
each of these muscular resources is vital to one. And what do
we do? You sit cramped—like this. The muscles get slack
and useless. You stand like this. The muscles suffer.

RANTING. Sit and stand you can't avoid.

CLERK. [*Taking off his overalls.*] Look at this, Mr Ranting.
[*Rolls up sleeve and demonstrates muscle.*

RANTING. Marvellous. Like Kid Berg. You should be a boxer.

CLERK. Worse thing you can do for the muscles, boxing. Fatal
to the muscle tone.

RANTING. So what can you do with all them muscles?

CLERK. So far, I still have four hundred and eighty-nine muscles
undeveloped.

RANTING. And then?

CLERK. I hope to stand as Mr Universe.

RANTING. A meshuggus. Put back the coat.

CLERK. [*Restoring coat and moving down stage right.*] When I get these pecs up I'll take my first competition.

RANTING. Local?   [*Picks up clerk's note-book.*

CLERK. Down at the Roxy.

RANTING. Maybe I'll come.

CLERK. You'll enjoy it, Mr Ranting. The body beautiful.

RANTING. So I'll enjoy it. The whilst Mr Universe, go shut the door.   [*Pushes Clerk out down right and follows him.*

SCENE FIFTEEN

Morry and Fender enter down left and move towards area 'B' where the light now is. They come in arm in arm, singing and stumbling. Morry carries an empty beer crate.

MORRY. In your position, Fender, it's not professional to drink so much at once.

FENDER. You know I met Lennie?

MORRY. You were saying before. How is he doing?

FENDER. Very nice. They let him open a little stall outside the hotel, on the promenade. You can get any kind of herring from him.

MORRY. [*Puts crate down and stands on it.*] I get in the window and give you a lift up. Just a minute. [*Gets down.*] See if you can walk through the wall.

FENDER. [*Crossing to right of Morry, pauses.*] Don't talk silly, Morry.

MORRY. If you're a ghost you can walk through walls. And if you're not a ghost at least it's scientific experiment.

FENDER. It's true. I'll try. [*He tries.*] I feel silly. Get through the window, Morry. Just a minute. [*Takes key from pocket.*] A solution. I'll go round and open the door. [*Exit down right.*

MORRY. [*Gets on crate and tries to open window.*] I can give myself a stricture with this. Shift, you—it don't budge. Get up.

FENDER. [*Off.*] I done it. Come round. It's cold in here.

MORRY. [*Getting off crate and picking it up.*] It would be nice if he walked through the wall, like I told him. [*Moving right.*] I even got to tell him how to be a ghost proper.

                    [*Exit down right. Black-out.*

SCENE SIXTEEN

Area 'A.' Fender enters up stage centre with a torch and crosses right to switch on imaginary light.

FENDER. It's easy. You should try. I'll just switch on the light.

MORRY. [*Follows him in as the lights come on.*] Right. Now, let's see. You remember where the coat is?

FENDER. [*Moving up stage of stool.*] Wait a minute. Trousers over there. Jackets here. [*Turns to audience.*] Would you believe it? I haven't been away five minutes and they shift the jackets.

MORRY. [*Moving to up stage of coat rack.*] Here are the coats. What about this? What a terrible cut. This one?

FENDER. [*Taking his old coat off and examining coat rack.*] Not for me.

MORRY. The blue is nice.

FENDER. No.

MORRY. It's a silk lining. A good lining.

FENDER. For what?

MORRY. This?

FENDER. Too short. [*Takes out coat with sheepskin lining.*] Ah! Ah! This is different. This I'll take.

MORRY. It's a nice weight, Fender. [*Helping him on with it.*] but the workmanship. Not nice.

FENDER. [*Moving down stage centre.*] How many times do I have to tell you, Morry? It's not personal. Only I must have one of Ranting's coats. That's all. He owes me.

[*On these lines Fender becomes, it seems to us and to Morry, less mobile, more like a dead man.*]

MORRY. [*Moving down stage to right of Fender.*] Terrible cold in here. So Can you go?

FENDER. I can go.

MORRY. My work is better.

FENDER. Certainly your work is better.

MORRY. So now you're all right, heh?

FENDER. I feel all right.

MORRY. Fender, you know something. [*Hesitates.*] This brandy is good.

FENDER. So—thank you, Morry.

MORRY. So, Fender, you're going now? You'll go back to the hotel?

FENDER. [*Turning up stage.*] Where else have I got to go to?
MORRY. Fenderler—you should give to Lennie my best regards.
FENDER. [*Turning back to Morry.*] He's selling herrings like hot
cakes, all day long. [*Moves up stage.*] He'll be pleased.   A long
life to you, Morry.   Pray for me.
　　　　　　　[*His voice fades on this line and he has gone.*
MORRY. [*Calls after him.*] May you come to your place in peace,
Fender. [*Putting his hat on to pray.*] Yiskadal, Veyiskad-
dish . . .
　　[*The Hebrew Prayer for the dead is broken by barrel-organ
　　　music, off, as Morry's head sinks upon his chest.   Slow
　　　curtain as light fades.*

Printed in the United Kingdom
by Lightning Source UK Ltd.
121057UK00001B/35